POPULAR ARTS
OF
SPANISH
NEW MEXICO

E. Boyd

Museum of New Mexico Press
Santa Fe, New Mexico MCMLXXIV

ACKNOWLEDGMENTS

First and foremost my thanks go to the International Folk Art Foundation of Santa Fe, New Mexico, for their encouragement and support of this book and its publication.

To Dr. Myra Ellen Jenkins and Professor John Otis Brew I am indebted for many helpful comments and for reading the manuscript at various stages.

To others who have been so generous with their knowledge and time I am most grateful: archivists, conservationists, dendrochronologists, historians, librarians, linguists, museum directors and curators, owners of private collections, photographers and other specialists.

This is the proper place to note my obligations to good friends now gone who first launched me into research and writing on New Mexico Spanish arts: Donald Bear, Ralph Linton, H. P. Mera and Francis Henry Taylor.

Last but by no means least I wish to thank two able and patient editors, Merle Clark and Carl E. Rosnek.

E.B.
14 July 1973.

Copyright © 1974 by E. Boyd. Printed by Walker Lithocraft, Tucson, Arizona.

An excerpt from the first section of this book appeared in *El Palacio,* Volume 79, No. 3. Copyright © 1973 by E. Boyd and the Museum of New Mexico.

This book was funded by a grant from the International Folk Art Foundation of Santa Fe, New Mexico, U.S.A.

Library of Congress Catalog Card Number: 74-76660
ISBN 0-89013-064-7

CONTENTS

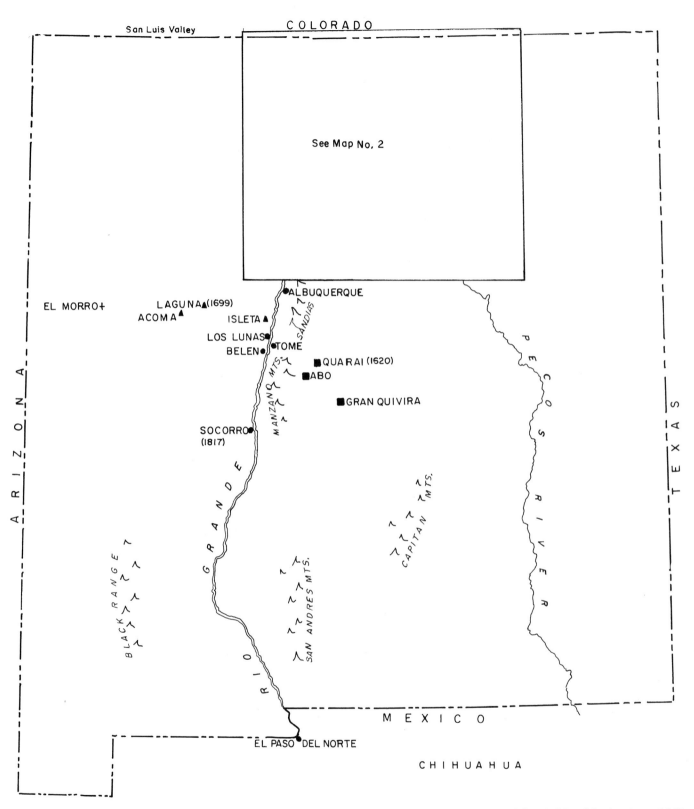

Map 1: New Mexico from 1540 to 1846.

vi

Map 2: North Central New
Mexico from 1540 to 1846.

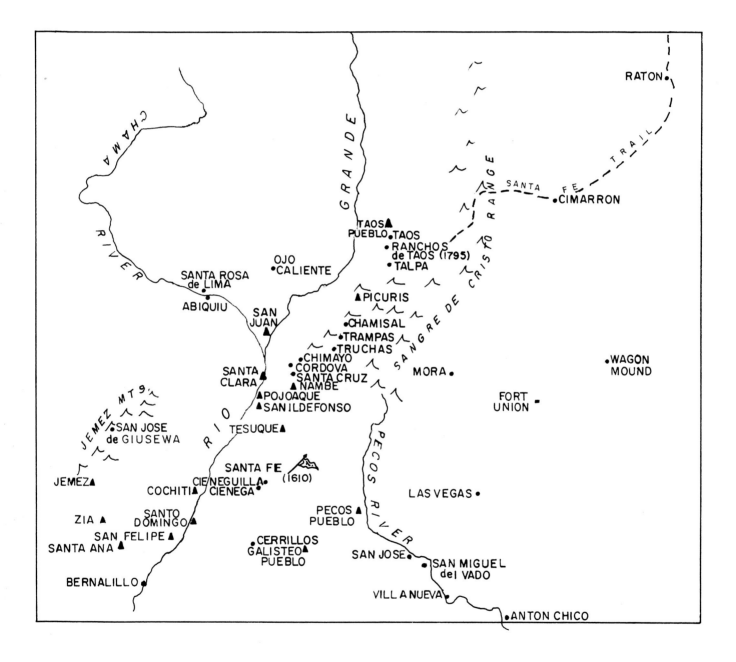

ABBREVIATIONS IN TEXT

A.A.S.F.	Archives of the Archdiocese of Santa Fe
A.S.F.	Archdiocese of Santa Fe
B.	Baptismal Books
Bur.	Burial Books
L.D.	Loose Documents
M.	Marriage Books
Pats.	Patentes
M.H.T.	Museum of History and Technology
M.N.M.	Museum of New Mexico
N.M.H.R.	New Mexico Historical Review
N.M.S.R.C.	New Mexico State Record Center
O.N.M.F.	Origins of New Mexico Families
S.I.	Smithsonian Institution
S.A.N.M.	Spanish Archives of New Mexico
T.M.	Taylor Museum
w.d.	Working Dates

DOMESTIC ARCHITECTURE

Seventeenth century homes in New Mexico were destroyed in the rebellion of 1680 together with other Spanish belongings. Reconstruction of early house plans at present can only be based on a few archaeological excavations. Continuous occupation and superposition of modern buildings have prevented effective investigation of 17th century structures in Santa Fe. In this period settlers lived with Indians at outlying pueblos, a practice which was later discontinued as both unsafe and undesirable. Ranch houses isolated from Santa Fe or Indian villages, and destroyed in 1680 have for the most part not been located, or their owners rebuilt them after the reconquest. In either case few have been excavated. A certain amount of information on the floor plans of convents of pre-1680 construction has been recovered, and, at least in regard to arrangements for storing and cooking of food, may be considered as probably applying to domestic dwellings as well.

Another factor in considering domestic architecture of 17th century New Mexico is the consistent conservatism of Spanish culture. If settlers continued to repeat construction techniques, house forms and decorative elements of the 16th century in Spain during the 18th in New Mexico, as they did, it is reasonable to infer that the same plans, furnishings and ornamental motifs were in use along the upper Rio Grande in the 17th century. The limitations of isolation, environment and available tools combined to preserve Hispanic modes like flies in amber until the end of Spanish rule when, coincidentally, new ideas were introduced by alien traders from our eastern states after 1821.

When Spaniards came to New Mexico they found sedentary Indians living in communal buildings several stories high with underground ceremonial rooms. These were sometimes of undressed ledge stone and pebbles, but where soil conditions were suitable they were made of mud laid up in courses, or of hand-shaped turtlebacks (mud patted into loaves). The Spanish therefore found natives already able to build with adobe and had only to introduce better methods. These were metal hoes to mix mud, wooden forms to make bricks, metal tools to shape timbers, and crowbars and pulleys to raise roof beams into place.

Making adobes is heavy work but requires little skill. While it is a labor for teams, it does not entail vast numbers of workers as did stone

Figure 1: Pouring mud and straw into adobe forms.

Figure 2: Mud is packed into forms.

Figure 3: Dried adobes are laid up with mud plaster.

monuments like the pre-Columbian temples to the south. Two or three men can turn out five or six hundred adobes in a summer day. Where the clay is good, a pit is dug out as close to the future house or room as possible. The loosened earth is mixed with water, sand and straw to form a heavy paste. The proportions of added sand and straw depend upon the qualities of the soil at a given spot. A dense clay dries and cracks, while one with a partly sandy content needs little added sand. Straw is chosen for its length, cleanness and freshness. It serves as a binder for bricks and plaster, and, where heavy red silts form the soil, is used in such quantities that it glitters on the walls. Well mixed mud was shoveled into molds, wooden frames without bottoms which allowed excess water to drain away quickly. When the mud held its shape the mold was removed leaving the brick on the ground. In a day it was turned, in another it was stood on edge; in three or four days bricks were stacked in rows, ready for use.

Old forms varied in size, making bricks up to 56 by 30 cm. Adobes found in the excavation of San Miguel, a Santa Fe chapel rebuilt in 1710, averaged 50 by 25 by 10 cm. Modern adobes are molded two at a time and are usually 36 by 25 by 10 cm. Two bricks of the old size laid end to end across a wall with mud mortar made a wall four feet thick. Spanish adobe walls found in early historic sites are easily distinguished from those built by the Indians, even when they are side by side, by the greater width of Spanish walls, the presence of molded bricks and, often, of river cobble foundations.

While dried mud is vulnerable to damage by water so that site drainage is necessary, as well as constant repair of roofing, mud walls have excellent qualities of insulation, far superior to those of stone, brick or modern pumice block. In addition, the mud was available at no cost except that of labor in preparation, it was familiar to Indian and Spanish, and, as a medium, it had the added advantage of being easily altered, added to or patched. Where no earth was suitable for making adobes in New Mexico, the Spanish used jacal construction (poles chinked with mud) as had Indians before them, but these were in constant need of plastering and more often used for animals, storage and in camps.

The Spanish introduced doors to Pueblo Indians, which replaced hatches in the roof reached by ladders. Since the latter were for defensive purposes, and the attacks of *gentiles* or non-Christianized nomadic Indians continued against both Spanish and Pueblos until mid-19th century, the door was a matter of prestige rather than of pure convenience. Certainly it diminished the security of massive blank walls. Windows, on the other hand, retained their indigenous, pre-Spanish form until the 19th century brought glass panes. They were set high in walls and were usually too small for a human being to crawl through. Some were unglazed and closed by heavy wooden shutters, while others had tiny panes of native selenite set between narrow strips of wood. These, like alabaster, were translucent but not transparent.

Contrary to some romantic writers on southwestern history, the Spanish do not appear to have built large, rambling haciendas in the early

Figure 4: Women traditionally did all plastering. (Four photographs by Margaret McKittrick)

Figure 5: A typical Colonial window. (Photograph by Karl Kernberger)

period as they did in the more prosperous era of republican Mexico. In fact, even after the founding of Santa Fe in a location deliberately chosen for its distance from an Indian village, Spanish families continued, in spite of official warnings, to live in or next to pueblos when not in the capital until the disastrous uprisings of 1680. The few land-owning families which did build on their outlying holdings, having neither warning of danger nor any nearby allies, were easier prey for the organized Indian rebels than those living in Santa Fe.

While few of the ruins of 17th century Spanish dwellings have been excavated, those that have been indicate a house of two or three rooms, ranging from six to nine meters in length by four and a half to five and a half meters in width. Room width was governed by the length of available roof beams, while length was optional, the timbers being laid across the short axis of the room and resting on rough beams or bed moldings laid on the adobe bricks in order to level the ceiling.

With the exception of perhaps the family of a governor, New Mexicans followed Spanish custom among the poorer classes, building fair sized, multipurpose rooms rather than many little cubicles, as did Indians. Even today Spanish farmhouses retain the characteristic use of a room for many domestic purposes in addition to those of food preparation, dining and entertainment. The poorer people in colder areas tended to sleep in the room where a fire had been burning. Until Spain very recently provided modern hotels in the smaller towns, travelers outside of the large cities still found Medieval inns in which men patrons slept together in one room and women in another, just as they did in the time of Cervantes. As recently as thirty years ago, in less well-to-do families of rural New Mexico the average house had three or four rooms, even when there were as many as a dozen members of all ages in the family.

If some Spanish settlers became rich in lands in New Mexico, most of them had come as adventurers or have-nots, and so had the habit of simple surroundings. For example, Alferez Diego Arias de Quiros was given several acres of land in Santa Fe by General de Vargas as a reward for his services in the reconquest of 1693. One side of his house was built next to the gate leading into the Santa Fe plaza from the north, which was set against the eastern tower of the Palace of the Governors. Yet Arias de Quiros, when he died, had only a two-room house with a zaguan (covered passage) on the property (SANM 1, 846).

The use of adobe walls in New Mexican architecture set a limit on the design of roofing. Only flat roofs could be built, unlike structures of brick, stone and even rubble which lent themselves to vaulted ceilings, arched openings or domes. Nor did New Mexicans make use of the peaked roof of wood like an inverted ship's keel so common in other forested countries. Roof beams, vigas, were generally of pine or spruce, unshaped after removal of the bark. Over these split lengths of wood, made with an ax and called *rajas* from the verb, *rajar,* to split or divide into sections, were laid diagonally. The other substitute for sawn boards was that of peeled small poles of juniper, or sometimes aspen, laid in

Figure 6: A ceiling of *latias,* peeled poles, in herringbone pattern. (Photograph by John Waggaman)

Figure 7: A traditional dirt roof. (Photograph by Margaret McKittrick)

diagonal or herringbone patterns over the vigas. These were called *savinos* (the name of native juniper) or, sometimes, *latías*. Over all a layer of earth, grass, twigs and other vegetal material was laid and packed down. *Pretiles* (fire walls) were raised to the level of two or three bricks above the roofing, sometimes with a false battlement of adobes in the period of defensive colonial life, a provincial continuation of fortified parapets in medieval stone buildings.

The roof was laid on a slight angle from one side to the other for drainage, and the low side faced preferably to the south, east or west, to avoid freezing of water in winter from the northern exposure. Canales or rainspouts of hollowed logs were placed in the firewalls but were usually inadequate since they were often clogged by trash, or, in high winds, directed runoff water from the roof against the wall below instead of to the ground. As storms removed earth from the roof and caused leaks which channeled walls and ran inside of the house, more earth was added to the roof. After years of piling fresh dirt on a roof, the weight became excessive, amounting to tons over relatively small areas. This burden on decaying ceiling timbers often resulted in the collapse of the roof. Except for portales, no overhang was provided on colonial houses, and the lack of adequate woodworking tools has been assumed to supply an explanation for the persistence of such inefficient roofing in the northern Rio Grande climate for well over two hundred years. During all of this time colonists were forced to constant labor on the repair and maintenance of roofs on their own homes as well as those of their churches, and suffered frequent damage to their possessions from interior leakages.

What has not been explained, however, is the apparent lack of initiative among the Spanish in setting up kilns in which to fire bricks, roof tiles, drains and paving as they did in Texas and California. Spanish architectural tradition had made extensive use of these ceramic conveniences for centuries, even in farmhouses. Spanish explorers in New Mexico made comments on the existence of suitable ceramic clays, and on the proficiency of Pueblo Indians in making pottery. However, Indian ceramics were uniformly low-fired and porous, making them useless for architectural purposes. While the Spanish imposed new shapes on native potters, such as the "soup plate," handle mug, and footed bases on dishes for table use, they seem to have left technical matters such as firing methods to their wards who continued to use their ancient methods. Thus fired bricks and terra cotta were never introduced into New Mexico. These would have provided both water- and fireproof roofing as well as arched and vaulted ceilings. Spanish indifference to the ceramic industry in New Mexico thus determined the flat roofed architectural style which is now associated with our southwest, variously called "Pueblo," "Spanish Colonial," "Franciscan," and, with added neo-Grecian trim, "Territorial Pueblo." At the same time the Spanish population committed itself to the discomforts of defective roofing for generations.

Normal erosion of adobe buildings by wind and water and the effects of storms cause a building to deteriorate in a few years unless it is constantly maintained. When time and labor were literally of no value it was easier to abandon old rooms and build new ones nearby than to repair them. As a result of this custom, 17th century buildings would have been replaced in a normal cycle under peaceful circumstances even without the destruction of the Indian rebellion, as most of the 18th century structures were. For these reasons any adobe house, or part of one, in New Mexico which has been kept in good condition for more than a century is worthy of attention.

The true fireplace and chimney were Spanish gifts to the Indians; prior to 1598 they had used firepits in the floor with a hole in the roof for ventilation. The Spanish kitchen had a large, hooded fireplace, made with upright posts, a cross beam, peeled poles and mud plaster. The construction resembled Spanish cooking hearths of the 15th through the 19th centuries but those were built of stone or fired brick, hard plaster and, often, glazed tiles. New Mexican versions had smooth mud plaster on the exterior of the hood while all of the interior wood and poles were exposed to the heat of the fire on the underside. In spite of this and the heavy soot created by burning pitch pine and piñon wood on the chimney interior, the wooden elements did not catch fire. The hood, of whatever size, hung over the small fire box, a built-in adobe and slab stone charcoal stove and the hearth. According to the location of the chimney, the fire was in a room corner or against the wall, just as these kitchen fireplaces had been made in both ways in Spain. The remains of such fireplaces are described in the report on Awatovi mission (Montgomery, Smith, Brew, 1949) and its convent and kitchen. They are also noted at Abo mission convent which was abandoned in 1672 (Toulouse, 1949).

Postholes in floors and smoked walls, the only clues to the previous existence of a hooded fireplace, are easier for the archaeologist to miss than remains of a solid adobe corner fireplace. The hooded fireplace may well have been overlooked in earlier excavations of historic ruins, but in recent years they have been identified in several historic sites.

Although Indians rejected the European's imposed religion and social regulations, they adopted material innovations such as metal implements, domestic animals and the fireplace and chimney. When de Vargas returned to reoccupy New Mexico in 1693, several Pueblo groups ran away in an attempt to escape Spanish rule and punishment. They went into what was then Navajo country in the Gobernador region south of the San Juan river in present-day New Mexico. These refugees stayed there for twenty and possibly many more years, living on high canyon and mesa ledges. The ruins of their houses, clearly Pueblo in style, contained crude but recognizable hooded fireplaces made of poles and mud plaster. Traces of whitewash were still visible on these as recently as 1940.

Provincial requirements changed the vertically sloping chimney hood into one that rose upwards only above the firebox while the rest of the length was reinforced by stronger upright posts and converted into a flat, plastered shelf. While this form has been called a "shepherd's bed,"

Figure 8: A traditional hooded fireplace. (Photograph by Arthur D. Taylor Jr.)

it was sometimes used to sleep on by anyone because of its warmth. The mild heat of the chimney shelf was also used for drying of gourds, squashes, jerky and other edibles. Such fireplaces were still in use in older Hopi houses on First and Second Mesas a few decades ago when their flat areas were observed to be used for both culinary and sleeping purposes.

Unlike southern Spain or the warmer parts of Mexico, New Mexican winters were too long and cold to make cooking with charcoal in otherwise unheated rooms practical all year around. Only one or two sherds of portable terra cotta braziers have been reported in southwestern historic sites, so it may be assumed that the built-in charcoal stove was more common. It could be used in winter in conjunction with the hearth fire, and in summer by itself.

At Nambe mission Dominguez noted ". . . the next room is the kitchen, a small room, but adequate for the purpose. There is a brazier on the floor with a wooden hood plastered with mud." The Indians, he went on, ". . . take turns in bringing the firewood necessary for the kitchen, the bread oven, and the hearths in the cells in which the father lives in winter." At Jemez mission firewood was used in winter only ". . . which the community carts, because in summer (this father says), to save carting, charcoal is brought, which two boys make every week in the forest." In summarizing the missionary's way of life in New Mexico at the time, Father Ruiz said that there were two kitchens, ". . . summer and winter. The cooking is done with charcoal winter and summer; this makes things much easier for the people, since the little loads of [char] coal that two boys . . . bring . ., would not be matched [in wood] by using the whole pueblo. The food is better, the cooks are not troubled, and filth does not fall into it. They have their little brick ovens with a grate, and if the father does not care for them himself he will eat poorly, the pueblo will work carting wood, and he will live in impatience. He should not permit the sacristans to remain in the kitchen . . . in the first place they do so for wanton dalliance, and in the second place, to eat up the dinner." (Dominguez, pp. 55, 56, 179 and 311.)

The custom of moving the kitchen seasonally persisted into this century in New Mexican country homes which by then had a number of rooms. The iron cookstove and all kitchen equipment were moved into a room with north exposure in the spring and back to a southern exposed room in the fall; often the other room was left empty and used for storage in the interim. When women left home only to work in their fields, to walk to church, the local store or the neighbors, this biannual moving was an exciting change which they greatly relished. It was the occasion for laying a new earth floor, or new linoleum in latter days, and fresh *jaspe* (homemade whitewash), on the walls. The smoky vigas were washed by hand, and other drastic cleaning accompanied the move to a different view.

There is a delightful story about the first cast iron cookstove to be brought overland by wagon to Taos in the 1860s. The family which had ordered it from St. Louis nearly went bankrupt as a result; everyone for

Figure 9: Plan of an 18th century Spanish house. Post holes of hooded fireplace and charcoal stove shown in Room Two.

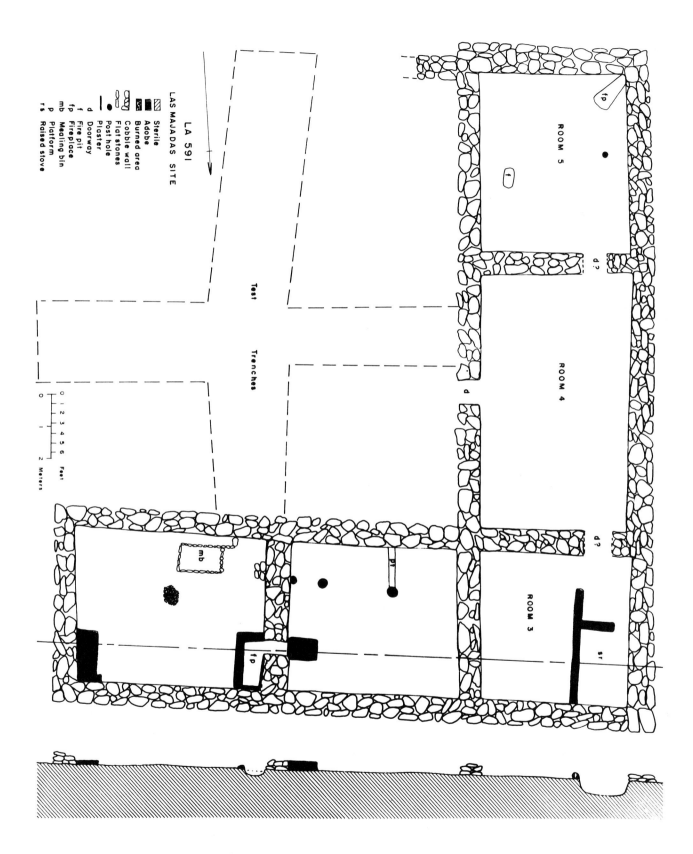

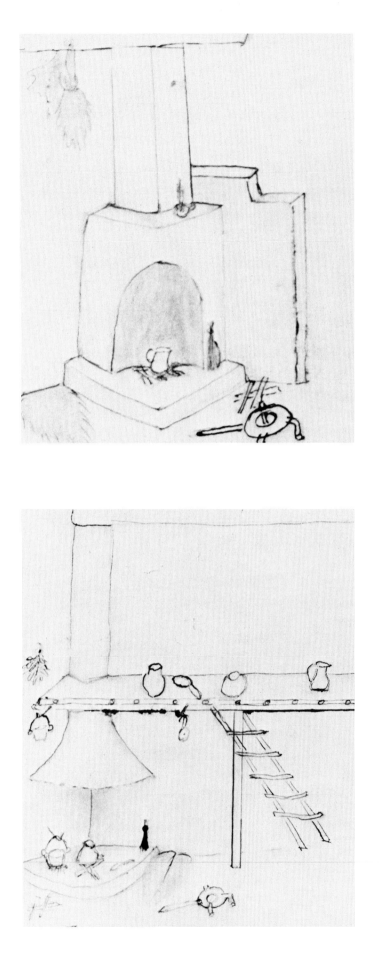

Figure 10: Corner fireplace for heating.

Figure 11: Bell-shaped fireplace and hood for cooking. (Sketches, by Cleofas Jaramillo, now at Museum of New Mexico. Hereafter, unless otherwise stated, all objects shown are in the collections at the Museum of New Mexico)

miles around came to see the marvel and how it worked, and many of them stayed for days as guests. In order to receive the visitors properly the hosts had replastered their large house, laid new *jergas* on floors, bought new windowglass and chinaware, new blankets for the guests' bedding, new clothing for themselves, and entertained the visitors with food and dancing, as well as caring for their horses.[1]

The relatively late arrival of factory-made iron stoves in New Mexico and the San Luis valley was mentioned in the reminiscences of an old-timer in 1933: "Up to forty years ago cookstoves were almost unknown among the Mexicans. Meals were prepared over fires outside or, during bad weather, at fireplaces in the house. Walter Carroll, who had a hardware store at Antonito, drove through the country one day with a cookstove in the back end of his spring wagon and developed a great trade in that article."[2] Thus for nearly 300 years domestic cooking in New Mexico continued to be done in fireplaces, charcoal stoves, outdoor barbecue pits and ovens. In small rooms the corner fireplace was used for heating. Originally of small proportions, the openings were from 35 to 50 cm. wide across the hearth and varied in shape from arched to horseshoe forms. The adobe bricks were laid up to form a slightly raised hearth, the firebox and a small mantel shelf were shaped with an ax, and the chimney was laid up with bricks set on edge to form the flue against the room corner. The interior of the fireplace was plastered, like all other mud plastering, by women who wrought a continuous interior halfdome from the back of the firebox with their hands. In northern New Mexico the best location of a fireplace was thought to be in the southeast corner of a room where prevailing southwest winds did not blow down the chimney. A fireplace which does not smoke and gives maximum heat usually has a small throat set forward rather than straight against the back wall; the firebox is fairly shallow. This combination throws heat into the room instead of up the chimney. The same principles were used by Benjamin Franklin when he designed his first iron "Franklin" stoves. Three sticks of wood standing on end in an adobe *fogón,* without grate or andirons, throw off a surprising amount of heat, and as the adobe itself also gives heat they are very economical. In the period of colonial life a large sala had two fireplaces at diagonal corners for better direction of heat.

The small space taken up by these corner fireplaces, their efficiency and picturesque look have all led to their continued construction in the southwest today. Unfortunately, changing of original proportions, the addition of arty or perhaps unrelated modern materials and ornamentation have produced some rather ugly results.

The Spanish also brought with them the *horno,* or outdoor beehive-shaped adobe oven, another Arabic trait. They were built near the house,

---

[1] Unpub. mss., by courtesy of Mrs. Eusebio Vasquez.
[2] Colorado Historical Society, Dec. (349/22), "Early Days of the Posthoff-Meyers Stores," C.W.A. project, 1933–34.

alone or in clusters of two or three, on a cobblestone or adobe plastered foundation with a narrow opening on the front and small hole in the back of the top for air. They served for extra cooking, principally in summer to keep the house cool, to bake bread, parch corn, and roast or dry many other staple foods. A wood fire was laid in the oven, the door sealed until the coals had passed their maximum heat, when they were raked out, the food put in and the door sealed again. The heat-retaining quality of adobe cooks slowly and evenly; no bread is better than that cooked in these ovens. Today they have been abandoned in towns, but rural villages still use them. More ovens of this type are found in Indian pueblos where they have been in use ever since the Spanish taught their construction, even though tanked gas and electricity are now available. In fact, they are so much a feature of pueblo villages that visitors assume that they have been an Indian tradition from time immemorial.

Doors, like windows, were kept small, as much to keep out cold and weather as for the oft quoted defensive purposes. A door into a house set at ground level, without steps, allows water to run underneath. Colonial doors had a raised wooden sill, often 30 cm. above ground. Most doors were shorter than ours of today, so that in passing through one of these one stepped up and bent down at the same time. For want of tools the single leaf doors in dwellings were narrow as well as short, and for want of bolts, nails or other metal fittings they were made without metal hinges, like European puncheon doors which were set in stone sills and lintels.

The origin of the puncheon door has been traced back to 4,000 B.C. in the near east, from whence it spread to northern Europe, Africa via Arab traders as far south as the northern Transvaal, into Spain and thence to the Americas. *

The puncheon door had extended ends at the top and bottom of the back of the doorframe which turned in sockets in the sill and lintel. Charred remains of sills and lintels found in the excavations of Abó and Awatovi missions contained door post sockets similar in size to others made in the 18th century.

Most of the 18th century doors in New Mexico have disappeared, decayed from exposure to weather or replaced by newer models such as the battened door of the mid-19th century made after hand tools and iron nails and hinges had been brought into the country (Ref. Sec. 2-B). Of those still known there were two styles, both simple. The first was a traditional European design with a grooved frame into which six or more small, beveled panels were fitted and secured by wooden pegs. The second was a colonial extravagance in its use of wood, a single slab of pine or red spruce with the same plain frame and carved with a central panel of elementary linenfold pattern.

There is reason to suspect that a third style was also made in 18th century New Mexico, that of the colonial baroque period, 1630–1730,

Figure 12: *Hornos,* outside ovens, and remains of torreon at Talpa. (Sketch by Robert Plettenburg)

Figure 13: Left, A battened door, late 19th century. Right, Colonial puncheon door. (Sketches by Kenneth M. Chapman, 1915)

---

* (Walton, James "Carved Wooden Doors of the Bavenda"; *Man,* V. LIV/46–75, March 1954.)

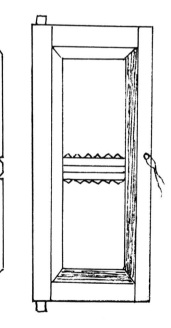

I-A

17

but as usual more crude in appearance than those made in New Spain. Remains of doors carved of live oak in the same pattern were found during restoration of San José mission, one of the missions below San Antonio, Texas, which were established after 1720. The design of interlocking, or keyed, small panels and moldings was reproduced in the mission repairs of the 1930s and also used in stabilizing the San Antonio Palace of the Colonial Texas Governors (Newcomb, Rexford, 1937. Pl. 15).

One pair of doors like these still exists in New Mexico, the inner doors to the Santuario de Esquipulas at Chimayó (Appendix, Sec. I-B). The chapel is well documented as having been licensed in 1814 and completed before 1818, when it was described as more elaborately furnished than most larger New Mexican churches at the time. The quaint inscription on the doors reads: "Esta puerta Hiso Pedro/Dominguez Por de/bocion del R.P.F./José Corea El a/ño de mil ocho/cientos diciseis/Por Solicitud del/esclavo del Señor." (Pedro Dominguez made this door as the offering of the Reverend Father Fray José Corea in the year 1816 by request of the servant of the Lord.)[3]

The Esquipulas chapel has a peculiar feature of two storerooms on the facade with a covered passage into the nave between them. Today the passage is called a narthex by architects, but in 1818 it was described as a zaguan (Appendix, Sec. 1-B, 1818–26). This entrance, paved with adobe sloped toward the exterior, gave shelter to those waiting to enter the chapel. The 1816 doors are thus protected from the weather and have remained in excellent condition while the plain outer doors have nearly disintegrated. It is probable that the design of small panels at right angles to one another was to be seen in other doors still in place elsewhere in New Mexico in 1816 which served as models for the Santuario. The lag in time between the 17th-18th century baroque period in New Spain and in New Mexico was consistent with other archaic style survivals on the frontier.

Lighting devices were few and simple, principally the light of the fire in winter. People arose and retired with the daylight. Documentary references to candles indicate their scarcity and that they were reserved for religious occasions. Outdoor lighting consisted of bonfires before the church and at public buildings on feast days, or burning brands carried by servants.

The imminence of Indian attack in New Mexico continued until the military establishment of Fort Union and its subsidiary chain of forts in the west, after 1851. New Mexicans, therefore, had had no desire for indefensible glass windows in their homes, either for lighting or for prestige, until after they became commercially available. In 1846 the

---

[3] "El Santuario de Chimayo, The Miraculous Shrines of Our Lord of Esquipulas in Guatemala and Chimayo, New Mexico," Stephen F. de Borhegyi, in *El Palacio,* V. 60/3, March, 1953, and "El Cristo de Esquipulas de Chimayó, Nuevo Mexico," S. F. de Borhegyi, in *Antropología e Historia de Guatemala,* V. 5/1, 1953.

Figure 14: A door to admit wagons, late 19th century.

Figure 15: A Colonial door with recent ironwork. (Figures 14 and 15, Photographs by John Waggaman)

Figure 16: Door of *alacena,* wall cupboard, of the Colonial period. (Photograph by John Waggaman)

Figure 17: Reconstruction of an 18th century room, New Mexico. (Courtesy of Museum of History and Technology, Smithsonian Institution)

only building with glass window panes was said to have been the Palace of the Governors, possibly another extravagance of Manuel Armijo. Taos houses in 1847 had either selenite glazed windows or open holes in the wall.

Portable furniture was minimal, again apparently because of the inability to work wood. Space limitations also discouraged bulky pieces in homes. Built-in features could be made of adobe like the house itself. These were adobe benches against the wall, recessed niches in the walls, and a more refined form of the same, a shelved recess with or without doors, called *alacena*. (Arabic, *aljizena,* a small basket, a hole in the wall for storage, a cupboard.) The alteration over centuries in the usage of words is reflected in the fact that in New Mexico today freehanging wooden shelves, called *repisa* in Mexico and Spain, have been given the name of *alacena,* while the freestanding cupboard, called *trastero* (cupboard for dishes) in New Mexico is now called *alacena* in Spain.

Since most of the colonists slept on the floors in beds of sheep pelts, wool sacks, buffalo hides and blankets, these were stored by day, together with extra clothing, on poles hung horizontally under the ceiling. Dominguez described the interiors of Tesuque Pueblo homes in 1776 thus: "The interior decoration of these houses varies according to the owner, but they usually have two or three prints, a wooden cross, some kind of chest . . . The arms of the men and the harnesses of the horses are hung from stakes, and there are some *metlacahuitl* (poles), on which, like the secondhand dealers of Mexico, they hang their skins of buffalo, lion, wolf, sheep and other animals, and also their cloaks if they have any, and the rest of the clothing belonging to both men and women" (Dominguez, p. 50).

Until recent years many older Indian families still had poles in their homes on which hung blankets, shawls and other garments, ropes, and bridles. In the colonial period when every family had to be self-sufficient, even horse gear was valuable enough to be kept in the house. Adobe floors and earth covered ceilings with their constant dust-making were strong reasons for keeping belongings above floor levels and for the hanging poles, wall cupboards and chests on stands.

Auxiliary storerooms were for farm implements and animal fodder. Storage of grains was in small *dispensas,* windowless, locked cells, or for better security, in immense grain chests indoors, while ground meal, flour and cooked breads were kept in smaller chests, all provisions against mice. The stone metates of footed, Mexican form that settlers brought from New Spain were usually kept in a milling room, each in a slab-lined bin. These hand grinding stones were in daily use by Indian or other servants. The process is slow and makes little flour at a time, but not until 1756 was a gristmill driven by waterpower built on the Santa Fe river (SANM, 1, 858 & 859). By 1776 there were three gristmills at Santa Fe and two small ones at Chimayó (Dominguez, pp. 31, 40 & 83). At the time Indians were forbidden to have mills, among other restrictions imposed by the military governor, but were required annually to give a specified amount of meal and flour to their missionary as the

Figure 18: The primitive grist mill ran on water power that turned a horizontal wheel causing the vertical shaft to rotate the millstones.

Figure 19: Grain falling from a hopper is ground by two stones. (Figures 18 and 19, Photographs by Margaret McKittrick)

first fruits or tithes for his support, and also had to grind as well as raise their own corn, the staple diet (Dominguez, p. 315).

It should be recalled that tithes required by the Franciscans were not entirely intended for themselves. Each convent had its own fields for which missionaries had to provide seeds and, when Indians were recalcitrant, even the labor. Tithes were stored in the convents for winter supplies as much for the clergy as for their Indians in case of crop failures or enemy raids. The overworking of Indians by Spanish landowners and the military left the natives with little time for their own crop raising, and, as a result, they made token offerings of a quarter of a bushel of corn, or less, to their missions. This situation was one of several which caused conflicts between religious and civil authorities while the victims of both factions adopted an attitude of "a plague on both your houses" which the Spanish called laziness.

Well-to-do Spanish families built *torreones* (towers) next to or near their houses for defensive purposes. These, of adobe, ledgestone or lava rocks according to their locations, were frontier extensions of medieval European fortified castles, at least in the minds of their owners. They had blank walls with crenellated adobe parapets above the upper room and a few peepholes in the upper walls to shoot through at hostile raiders. Either round or square in shape, the lower room was used to drive livestock inside when an alarm of approaching Indians was given. The upper room was for women, children and neighbors who had had time to reach the tower, and what food and water had been collected for the besieged. Fighting men behind the parapets endeavored to shoot down the enemy with their often inadequate old firearms. Nomadic Indians soon learned to hold the Spanish prisoners by staying out of gun range while others of their party drove off whatever human captives and livestock they could find in the neighborhood, seized corn and other loot and made good their escape. At best a torreon might save the lives of its occupants but more often this method of defense turned out to be the funeral pyre of those who had taken refuge in it.

In the upper corner of Miera y Pacheco's map of New Mexico, made for Governor de Anza in 1779 and now in the British Museum, there is a notation on the subject of torreones. De Anza, like some of his predecessors, advised that the settlers should give up their scattered homes and live in fortified plazas from which they could go out to their field by day. The governor pointed out that the custom of each family living on its own lands had made them vulnerable to the enemy many times and cited previous disasters such as that of twelve families living in the Taos valley. Warned of an approaching Comanche party they took refuge in ". . . a great house with large towers belonging to Pablo Villalpando — fourteen men with firearms and much ammunition. The enemy attacked . . . sneaked below the embrasures of the parapet and towers and . . . proceeded to open breaches at various points and set fires in them. To stop this maneuver, the besieged showed themselves upon the parapet, and then the said enemies took advantage of the opportunity to wound them with bullets and arrows. They all perished

and sixty-four persons, large and small of both sexes, were carried off." De Anza went on to cite the Pueblos still living in the same manner as when the Spanish first came ". . . with their two and three story houses joined together, forming plazas, and all the houses with portable ladders which they pull up in time of invasion, and the roofs and upper and lower terraces with embrasures in the parapets for their defense and for offense against the enemy." (Dominguez, p. 4.)

In his will of 1818, Juan Antonio Suaso, oldest son of Luis Suaso y Durante, an immigrant from New Spain, and Josefa Martín, itemized among his other property the following buildings: a house of three rooms at Truchas, the house of his residence at Embudo (now Dixon) ". . . which consists of three rooms, the sala, the bedroom and the kitchen," a torreon of two living rooms, one above and one below, another house within the plaza of two rooms, another torreon of two rooms, one above and one below, and another house consisting of two living rooms, one above and another below with a portal in the same house (Suaso Family Papers, N.M. State Record Center).

These torreones, long vanished, had been a part of the compact fortified plaza of San Antonio del Embudo, situated in the narrow canyon of Embudo creek. Like the Pueblo and Santa Barbara rivers of the Peñasco valley, the Embudo has its source on the Truchas Peaks. Through a pass, Apaches and Comanches periodically came down these valleys to raid the villages; the Embudo was a favorite trail to the Rio Grande, and the Spanish, boxed together above the bottomlands, had reason to defend themselves with fortifications. Whether the torreones left "in equal shares" to Juan Antonio Suaso's eight children had been built after de Anza's prescribed instructions is doubtful. Suaso's mother, Josefa, was a daughter of Francisco Martín Serrano, one of the descendants of the original Martín Serrano family which came to New Mexico with Oñate in 1598. Francisco's father, Pedro, and his family returned to the colony with de Vargas. With other members of their family they became powerful landowners in Rio Arriba. It is quite possible that Josefa's father Francisco and his neighbors may have built the Embudo towers. How long they served for defense is uncertain but the lower rooms of two of them were still visible, as storage rooms, and in poor repair, until 1965.

With extensive holdings of irrigated farmlands at La Bolsa on the Rio Grande, around Embudo, at Chimayó and Truchas, and with eight children, it is worth remarking that Suaso owned no house of more than three rooms, a typical domestic housing unit. In a land deed of 1801 a house of forty varas was described as having four doors and four windows, an approximate length of thirty-two varas divided into four rooms; older houses had an outer door for each room (Deed of sale to Miguel Quintana, son-in-law of Josefa Martín, of lands at Embudo and La Bolsa. Suaso Family Papers, N.M. State Records Center).

The same document of 1801 mentions *árboles* (trees) with their cedar-post fence. Juan Antonio Suaso's will of 1818 clarifies the matter by stating that he owns sixteen bearing apple trees. Of these he left one to

Figure 20: Remains of a torreon at Dixon, 1939.

Figure 21: Interior of the Dixon torreon, 1939. (Figures 20 and 21, Photographs by J. Robert Jones)

St. Anthony (patron of the Embudo chapel), and a second to "The Most Holy." The rest were to be equally divided among his eight children whom he admonished ". . . to keep up the fence around the trees, as it then stood, for the protection of the said trees, forever more, to the benefit of all concerned." Except for general references to orchards, fruit trees are seldom noted in colonial documents. This mention suggests their value at the time and the efforts involved in keeping destructive livestock away from the trees.

Until recent "progress" in demolition, two of the Embudo torreones were still to be seen, as high as the tops of doorways, at corners of the walled plaza. A few torreones elsewhere had been used as granaries but with the abandonment of many farming areas even these have mostly crumbled. Traces of the walled town plan are still to be seen in the old Chimayó plaza and at Villanueva on the Pecos river, a late 18th century frontier outpost.

The portal or porch was an amenity in many house plans. During the colonial period it was usually inside of the court or patio formed by the house and walls. Sometimes a portal was roofed with the same beams that covered a room but more often, as an afterthought, it had its own vigas, one end of these being set into the adobe house wall and the other resting on a long, or composite, beam across the front of the porch which was supported by posts. These posts were topped by corbels which distributed the weight of the roof. The portal might run across the front of a straight-line house, or follow the L or U plan of the house. These porches not only offered shade in hot sunshine but protected walls and doorways from rain and snow. Decoration of corbels in the portal apparently was the only place where ornamental woodcarving was applied to domestic buildings except for paneled doors and shutters. Otherwise ornamentation was reserved for religious structures.

The house of Bernardo Abeitia, builder of the Santuario chapel at Chimayó in 1813–16, was remodeled only a few years ago, but before had retained portales on its north and south faces which had solid walls at both ends. The portal floors were so high above ground level that they could not be reached except by a ladder and their steeply sloped foundations were faced with river boulders. They also had hand carved *barandales* (railings) across them as further deterrent to exterior approach. Meaningless today, these were visible witnesses of the precarious existence of earlier New Mexicans.

When it became safe to build as one pleased, adobe houses rambled in all directions; as rooms were added on they grew L or T or U shaped or ran in a line like a train of cars, topography sometimes deciding a plan, or the desire to face the road, or the south.

Except for torreones the two-story adobe house was introduced by Anglo Trail traders at about the same time they began to appear in California, where the type is now called the Monterrey style, during the 1840s. W. W. H. Davis noted in 1853 in his sketch of Santa Fe: "The houses are built of adobes or mud bricks dried in the sun, and are but one story in height; and there are only two two-story houses in the place, neither of which was erected by the Mexicans."[4] Los Luceros, a two-storied adobe some forty miles north of Santa Fe, is said to have been built by the family of that name in the early 1840s, and is still in excellent condition with upper and lower portales running on three sides, and with a large sala or ballroom on the upper floor in typically genteel, if archaic, European style. By this time glass window panes and handsaws had arrived from the east, and tall, narrow windows with small panes were faced with elementary forms of Greek revival style trim. Old paneled doors had been set with the puncheon post on the inner line of the house wall but after iron hinges were obtainable doors swung from the outer side of the door sill. Windows, however, continued to be set in line with the exterior of the walls so that their deep sills gave extra space for keeping an oil lamp and potted plants.

The zaguan, a covered passage which in our southern states is called a breezeway or dogtrot, connected separately built rooms and, if large, served as a wagon entrance into the patio. If only human passage was required the zaguan sometimes had a rear wall of adobe with doors in it which could be opened in summer to let breeze in. In warm weather the zaguan was often a family work area, and piles of drying corn, wheat, chile, melons, onions and tobacco were strewn in it for cleaning or tying in strings; farm tools and drying hides hung from the vigas.

Adobe plaster constantly scatters dust and darkens the interior by many degrees. New Mexicans kept their rooms covered with whitewash or jaspe, made of native gypsum baked and pulverized, to which flour and water were added. Lumps of gypsum were one of several materials, in addition to foodstuffs, that were hand ground on stone metates, one stone being reserved for this purpose. The making of jaspe was not quite the same as the preparation of gesso used in making santos since the latter contained a proportion of animal glue and was brewed to a consistency which allowed it to set in relief if desired. Jaspe was laid on with a scrap of sheep pelt, or a brush if there was one, like liquid paint. Having nothing in it to serve as a binder, jaspe always brushed off the walls on clothing of those who touched it. It is easy to understand why New Mexicans began to buy yards of cheap calicos from Trail traders as soon as they could do so, to cover walls from the floor up, as far as one would touch the wall when reclining on a woolsack on the floor.

Jaspe was not always white in color; earth deposits from selected locations mixed with the gypsum powder provided a range of cafe-au-lait to pinkish shades for wall coloring. The glitter of *tierra amarilla,* or yellow stained mica, available in many parts of New Mexico, was added to walls by pulverizing the laminated mica and blowing the particles on the still-wet wall paint. A more concentrated quantity of the same tierra amarilla mixture was often painted as a dado along walls above the floor and around fireplace openings. These points of wear were longer lasting if not painted white, and also supplied decorative interest.

---

[4] W. W. H. Davis, *El Gringo or New Mexico and Her People,* Santa Fe, 1938, p. 40.

Figure 22: A 19th century portale. (Photograph by Ansel Adams)

Figure 23: Threshing grain at Santa Cruz, 1943.

Figure 24: Drying the harvest for winter. (Figures 23 and 24, Photographs by Margaret McKittrick)

While house exteriors in colonial times were extreme examples of unrelieved plasticity, of almost nothing but the adobe's function as shelter, interiors were both functional and colorful. The hearth supplied heat, evening light and a center of culinary and social activities, and was, in addition, an adornment to the room. Necessities were at hand but did not take up floor space wanted for such purposes as cooking, eating, sleeping or working at the loom. White or pastel walls reflected light and served as foils for gaily colored blankets, floor carpets, painted chests, santos of all kinds, copper pans and strings of red chile and colored corn. The quality of harmonious color schemes that happened almost automatically when only natural dyes and pigments were available to folk craftsmen was unfortunately lost after synthetic colors were developed. In New Mexico the popular tradition was forgotten as cast iron cookstoves replaced fireplaces, hideous colors of calcimine as well as exterior paints came on the market, and the cheapest designs of linoleum, draperies and drab, factory-made furniture were assembled to create interiors of indescribable dinginess. It was still another instance of novelty held as a yardstick of quality, or the destruction of innate good taste by keeping up with the Joneses.

There were always some exceptions to the rule of adobe architecture, such as regions where ledgestone or river cobbles were used for all or part of a structure. In high valleys and forest margins, where most of the year was wet, log buildings were favored, laid up in crib style with the log ends notched to fit closely, and with steeply pitched roofs made of hand hewn, overlapping boards. These were built as homes and *moradas* as well as barns, corn cribs, animal pens and gristmills. It has been said in the past that pitched roofs appeared in New Mexico only after American sawmills had been built, or after Presbyterian missionaries arrived, but there is evidence of a longer tradition. ". . . there was given to her the room with the plank roof, and the little room with a plank roof" (*techo de tablita*) . . .[5] Yankee traders had then been in New Mexico only five years and neither sawmills nor two-man saws had as yet made their appearance. The hafted froe was known in Spain and New Mexico and was used to make barrel staves and shingles. Neither wood nor time was lacking to handshape planks with ax, froe and adz if anyone had the inclination. Only 35 years ago, in high forest valleys, Spanish-built log houses with steeply pitched roofs were covered with hand-split boards, overlapping vertically, or hand-made shingles.

Because religion was the core of colonial New Mexican life the private oratory was a feature of many homes. In Europe not only royalty but anyone with a title and land had a family chapel in the castle, mansion or house, even though he might be close to a church or cathedral. In New Mexico long distances over poor roads and the frequent absence of the priest from the nearest church increased the number of domestic oratories. These were not only for a visiting priest to say Mass in on rare

---

[5] "The Last Will and Testament of Don Severino Martinez, 1827," tr. by W. A. Minge in *New Mexico Quarterly,* V. 33/1, 1963.

Figure 25: A stenciled portale wall taken from a house in Penasco. In an exhibition at the Museum of International Folk Art, 1959. (Photograph by Laura Gilpin)

Figure 26: The oratorio de San
Buenaventura Plaza del Cerro.

Figure 27: Interior of the oratorio, 1955.

occasions, but for daily devotions of the family, friends and servants. When the priest did pass that way he stayed as a guest while Masses and novenas were said, and married and baptized any candidates in the neighborhood.

Sebastian Martín Serrano, another descendant of the settler who came with Oñate in 1598, while obtaining large land grants north of Santa Fe, built his home, La Soledad de Rio Arriba, ". . . a league north of San Juan Pueblo and on the same plain." His family chapel was mentioned as La Hermita de N.S. de la Soledad in 1729, and was described by Dominguez in his usual vein in 1776:

> This little chapel is adobe and resembles a small *bodega*. It faces west and is 14 to 16 varas long, five wide and six high. There is no choir loft. There is a poor window on the Epistle side facing south, and the door is squared with one leaf and a key. The roof is of wrought beams; there is a small belfry with its brass bell, and a little cemetery.
>
> The altar screen is nothing more than a middle-sized niche like a cupboard in the wall and in this there is a middle-sized image in the round whose title is Our Lady of Solitude, although her dress is a mother-of-pearl tunic and blue mantle, all of smooth ribbed silk, silver radiance, and linen apron. On the whole wall where the high altar is there are some large paintings of saints on buffalo skins in the local style. The altar table is adobe, with its altar stone, cross, candlesticks and a little bell. It has old vestments of flowered cloth with all accessories, including linen. Chalice, paten and spoon, all of silver, and glass cruets on a Puebla plate, and an old missal. The only functions here are two novenas and a Mass annually (Dominguez, p. 90).

Sebastian Martín had been dead for some years in 1776 but apparently the family still maintained altar furnishings and vestments for the use of the visiting priest in the custom of wealthy Spaniards of the time, so that the traveler did not have to carry anything but the holy oils and altar breads with his breviary.

After the visitation of Bishop Tamaron to New Mexico in 1760 the licensing of family chapels, or license renewals, were recorded as bishops or their delegates returned, and the distribution of these is more specific. They suggest by their location where the well-to-do landowners lived at a given date: Santa Fe, the Tomé area of Rio Abajo, and then Taos. A sister of the Martín clan married Luis Suazo and lived at Embudo, where they had an oratorio as well as torreones. The Santa Fe alcalde, Don Antonio José Ortiz, not content to repair and improve the Parroquia in 1804, the chapel of San Miguel in 1798, and to sponsor the new Rosario chapel in 1807–09, also had his private oratorio on west San Francisco Street in Santa Fe. So too did Domingo Fernandez and Juan Bautista Vigil. "On the west side there is a clean and beautiful oratory dedicated to the Holy Trinity."[6] There were also the private chapels of

---

[6] Barreiro, *Ojeada,* 1832, Quivira ed. 1942, p. 85.

the Bacas at Tomé, others at Las Padillas, and those of the Durans and Medinas at Peñasco, Talpa and Arroyo Hondo (Taos County), in the mid-1850s. Nearly all have vanished; their contents have been scattered and even their walls have disappeared, or they stand as crumbling ruins.

The practice of devoting a room in the house to devotional purposes however had spread among more modest families of Spanish New Mexicans; such oratories still exist in some Santa Fe homes as well as outlying villages. A charming example of these is the Oratorio de San Buenaventura at Chimayó, in the old plaza. It has simple woodwork within, a classic santero altar screen of pre-1850 style, an earth floor and a single-step rise forming a platform for the altar behind a low railing. Although the former owners, the Ortega family of Chimayó, no longer live in the old plaza, the chapel was originally one of the rooms forming the west side of the plaza. The present ceiling has written on its boards several names and the repeated date of 1873, which has sometimes been assumed to mean that the oratorio was built then. The year, on the contrary, was the last time that a new roof had been put on it before 1954.[7] The late Merejildo Jaramillo, who did the remodeling of the roof then, said that he had known some of the men whose names appear on the old ceiling boards when he was a boy. In point of fact, the Chimayó plaza is a good surviving example of the plan of a fortified plaza of the 18th century, although only the west side has been left in semiruins and other sides have been renovated by their owners. The presently fenced-off center of the plaza now planted with fruit trees and corn originally was community property, the open space for meetings, processions and festive occasions as well as for sheltering livestock during Indian raids. The narrow entrances and exits originally had heavy gates, now discarded and forgotten.

There has been confusion as to the difference between public and private chapels in some minds, but the ecclesiastical officials were quite clear about this when issuing licenses for the Mass to be said in a family oratory, or in a public chapel. The private chapel, or domestic oratory, was for the use of the owners and their servants and those whom they chose to invite into it. In homes where the priest was hardly expected to appear and the *capilla* was for the daily prayers of the women, children and servants, the formality of a license was omitted. The chapels of Esquipulas at Santuario, San José de Chama at Hernandez, Rosario and the Ortíz oratory at Santa Fe and many others, although built and furnished by private individuals, received licenses as public chapels auxiliary to their parish churches, Santa Cruz de la Cañada, San Juan and the Santa Fe parroquia in the cases cited. Such chapels were built to relieve the necessity of long trips from a new village to the old church (except for the annual function for which the Rosario chapel of Santa Fe was constructed), so that a priest might journey to the congregation instead of vice versa; they were intended to be open to all persons at all times.

Figure 28: A 20th century family oratory.

Figure 29: The interior. (Figures 28 and 29, Photographs by J. Robert Jones)

---

[7] "Repair of the Oratorio of San Buenaventura at Chimayo," E. Boyd, in *El Palacio*, V. 62/4, 1955.

Because of the essentially domestic character of the family oratory in New Mexico, it is discussed with domestic, rather than ecclesiastical, architecture. Not every owner provided a raised platform at one end of the room for the altar, and the 19th century furnishings were according to the family fancy, often quaint but what is today referred to as "liturgically unacceptable," with flowered wallpaper or other novelties around the walls, tinsel and toys adorning the images and so on. A few family chapels were open-air structures, but whatever they might be they were an important part of New Mexican life.

The Palace of the Governors at Santa Fe, at first called *las Casas Reales,* or the Royal Houses, is known to have been commenced in 1610 or 1611. It is the oldest public building in the United States and was constructed entirely of adobes. While the building served as official seat of New Mexican government for Spanish and Mexican administrators and as the military defensive core of the colony, and contained a chapel, it was also the residence of the governors and may therefore be considered as an example of domestic architecture. Descriptions of the Palace before 1800 were either negative or deprecatory; at various periods visitors from New Spain described it as made of mud and more or less in disrepair.

To envision the Casas Reales in the Spanish period it is necessary to imagine a very different aspect than that of the present time. We must picture the block-long facade shorn of its portal and with large torreones at east and west ends, standing forward on what is now public street. The buildings and grounds extended north to present Federal Place, two blocks away. In the lands behind the present building were servants' quarters, kitchens, storerooms, stables, garden plots of various kinds and fruit trees. This, together with the plaza, parish church and houses around the plaza, was surrounded by an adobe wall making Santa Fe, at least in theory, a walled city. Water ran by a ditch from a spring near the foot of present Fort Marcy hill under the wall and into the Palace and its grounds. The complacency of the Spaniards in regard to a natural water supply was their undoing in 1680 when they were besieged within the Palace and the rebellious Indians cut off the ditch and thus forced them to abandon the Palace and all of New Mexico for twelve years.

As has so often been the case throughout history, the victorious Pueblo Indians did not profit by experience. Instead they repaired the town wall, built a warren of cubicles inside the Palace by robbing the parroquia for adobes, and repaired the ditch for their water supply. When de Vargas returned in 1693 and the Indians refused to surrender the Palace to him, he in turn cut off the water. A spirited assault by the Spanish and the lack of water induced the Indians to surrender the Palace and Santa Fe to the general.

From de Vargas' account of the Reconquest we know that there was a chapel in the east torreon of the building. A temporary chapel was required for all of the Spaniards as well as Palace staff, but the priests were reluctant to use the old tower since the Indians had profaned it by

Figure 30: "View of Santa Fe,"
painted by Anthony Kellner,
5th Infantry, 1866.

making it into an estufa (kiva, ceremonial room). Pagan profanation of the chamber was expunged with purification by the Franciscan chaplain; the chapel must have been in use for some years by the townspeople as the parroquia was only completed in 1713–14. It is reasonable to assume that the chapel was close to the governor's apartments as well as accessible to the plaza, which implies that the private quarters were at the eastern end of the Palace. This chapel was torn down in 1714 to straighten the Plaza plan (*The Santa Fe Cathedral,* Fr. A. Chavez, 1947).

It was also noted in more than one document that the west end was devoted to the military branch, containing guardroom, armory, barracks, stables and horse gear as well as the jail. Drills took place on the plaza and as married enlisted men lived with their families in the town and total military strength ran around 80 to 100 men for most of the Spanish period, there were in fact not too many soldiers quartered in the Palace at one time. Although referred to as a presidio, military inspectors from New Spain dismissed the notion because, they said, the Palace was strategically indefensible and too many of the garrison lived outside of it in case of emergencies.

The early Palace would have had a few very small windows on the exterior and, like other private houses, a long portal on the inner patio where the private life of the occupants took place. There were, undoubtedly, walls dividing the inner patio so that the governor's family and friends were screened from the business of soldiers, stables and kitchens. The private apartments were as plain in interior design as the rooms existing today; so much repair and remodeling has taken place in the past century and a quarter that there is no clue left as to what area was used for any specific purpose.

Remodeling of 1912–14, when the Palace was converted into the Museum of New Mexico, has left a discrete collection of late 19th century windows and doors, and even worse, early 20th century specimens, with a fictional portal in pre-Spanish or pueblo style on the facade. At the time that this was done the American territorial portal of rather simple, Neo-Classic revival style posts and balustrades, which had been a natural accretion of the territorial annexation period and which was logically related to the window and door additions of the same time, was demolished. It had replaced a plain pine portal of the mid-19th century.

Governors sent from Spanish New Spain, with few exceptions, lived to return there. In the custom of their epoch they would have brought personal furnishings with them such as Flemish verdure tapestries, used to hang on walls as well as in field tents while on the march, traveling desks and boxes, folding chairs, stands and camp beds as well as personal domestic silverware. While these would have furnished the official rooms of the Palace for their term of office, they would have returned to Mexico with their owners. The general practice of moving from rooms in poor condition to others of better-maintained state was, from stray comments over years, also observed in the Palace.

Figure 31: The Palace of the Governors during the territorial period. (Museum of New Mexico photograph)

Curiously, no handsome carved corbels or beams, which might have been expected in the royal houses, were ever mentioned. One corbel was said to have been found. Roof beams of course had to be replaced from time to time and they are now plain, undressed tree trunks. After annexation in 1846, no floor plans are known to have been made of the building, perhaps because the military government considered itself so temporary that there was no reason to record the building. Plans made in 1867 and 1869 show a symmetrically disposed series of windows, doors and cross halls with many small rooms on the interior which suggest that a good deal of remodeling had already taken place since the Spanish and Mexican periods.[8]

By this time the military activities had been removed by the United States forces to barracks and parade grounds to the north and west of the Palace. Old New Mexican procedure had been to require male citizens to serve a revolving term in the militia, which was virtually the only military protection of the territory in late Spanish and Mexican years. Although on call in emergencies, members of the militia returned to their homes while not on active duty. In times of peace only sentries and a skeleton company had been attached to the Palace for some time prior to 1846.

The high ceilinged, bare rooms of the Palace, except for the personal belongings of transient governors, were undoubtedly like those of landed New Mexicans, filled with pelts of lion, buffalo, and deer, Spanish blankets, arms and leather armor stacked or hanging in convenient corners. Interior furnishings were probably very little different in earlier centuries than when Pike had an undesired opportunity to inspect the Palace in 1807. ". . . a crowd followed us to the government house. When we dismounted we were ushered in through various rooms, the floors of which were covered with skins of buffalo, bear or some other animal." Pike also gave a clear picture of the plan of the Santa Fe plaza:

> In the centre is the public square, one side of which forms the flank of the soldier's square, which is closed and in some degree defended by the round towers in the angles which flank the four curtains; another side of the square is formed by the Palace of the governor, his guard houses, etc.; the third is occupied by the priests and their suite, and the fourth by the *Chapetones* [for *Gachupín,* Spanish born people] who reside in the city. The houses are generally only one story high, with flat roofs, and have a very mean appearance on the outside; but some of them are richly furnished, especially with plate.[9]

At some time between 1807 and 1831 the country style pine portal had been added to the Palace front, and, apparently, the ruinous torreones torn down. Perhaps this was the work of the enterprising Governor

---

[8] "The Adobe Palace," Clinton P. Anderson, in *New Mexico Historical Review,* V. 19/2, 1944.

[9] *The Expeditions of Zebulon Montgomery Pike.* A New Edition, Elliott Coues, editor. II V., F. P. Harper, New York, 1895.

Narbona (1825–27), who provided a rock sundial in the plaza of nearly three yards in height, inscribed, "Vita fugit sicut umbra" (Life fleeth like a shadow, Job, 14:2). This was then the only timepiece in Santa Fe for public use.[10] Barreiro's remarks on the Palace itself were confined to these:

> The north side [of the plaza] is taken up by a building known as El Palacio, and by a small portion of the wall. This building, although substantial, is partly in ruins and in a general state of neglect. The political chief of the territory lives in it, here is the chamber where the delegation holds sessions. The various rooms used as administrative offices of the company, commissary, barracks and jail are all in the worst condition imaginable.

Whether or not Governor Armijo actually had gold and silver beds and bathtubs in his period of residence in the Palace, they had vanished when Lt. Gibson was given a tour of the building by General Kearny in the summer of 1846. He was shown the ballroom and private chamber of the governor's lady (presumably the departed Señora Armijo).

> The ballroom is a large, long room, with a dirt floor, and the panels of the interior doors made of bull or buffalo hide, tanned and painted to resemble wood. There are various other rooms besides the antechamber, which has the lady's private apartment at one end and the ballroom immediately back of it and parallel to it. The office of Secretary of State is on the east side, and the guard room and prison on the west end of the block.
>
> The rear contains kitchens, bake ovens, and ground for a garden, the whole being roomy, convenient, and suitable to the dignity of a governor in New Mexico. Some parts of the building appear to be made bomb proof or so to be intended, but it would hardly be a defense against American arms. Many parts of the building are in a state of decay and have been neglected for some time, especially the apartments near the calabozo. The walls are thick and it contains as few doors and windows as possible.[11]

The features of thick walls, buffalo hide interior doors and a ballroom were as typical of the 18th century as of 1846, and without doubt had been the same in the 17th century.

Within seven years, Yankee improvements had made drastic changes in the Palace, as well as elsewhere in New Mexico, according to the comments of W. W. H. Davis, assigned to New Mexico as a United States attorney in 1853. Although Davis shared the common puritanical attitudes of other non-Latin and non-Catholic tourists then arriving in New Mexico he took pains to mention a good many details of the manners and customs of this strange, nonconformist addition to the United States in his account of his stay there, published in 1856. While the

---

[10] Barreiro, *Ojeada sobre Nuevo-Mexico,* 1832.

[11] George Rutledge Gibson, *Journal of a Soldier Under Kearny and Doniphan,* quoted in Anderson, *Adobe Palace.*

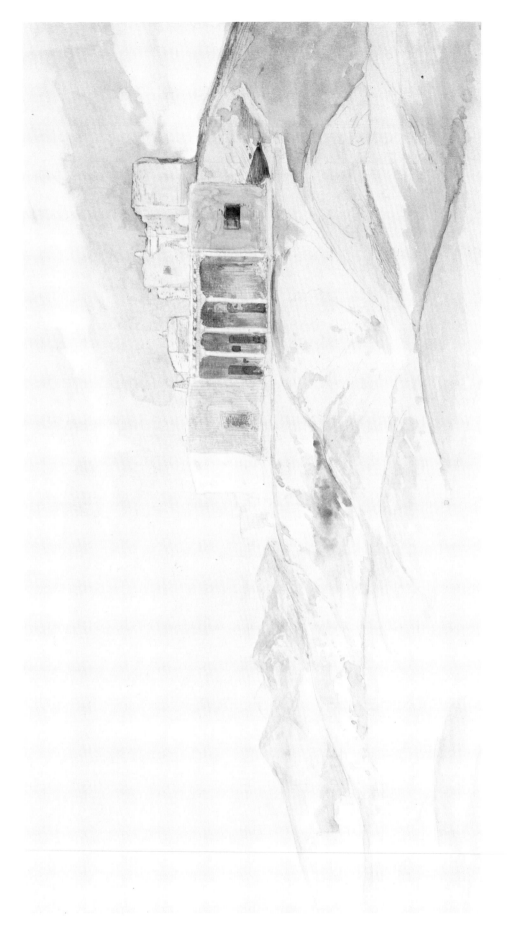

Figure 32: The Roque Lobato house and ruins of La Garita, watercolor by Peter Moran. (Courtesy of the Amon Carter Museum, Fort Worth)

I-A

secretary of the Territory used two rooms then, at the east end "behind the post-office," they were still "primitive" in appearance: ". . . the roof supported by a layer of great pine beams, blackened and stained by age; the floors are earthen, and the woodwork is heavy and rough, and in the style of two centuries ago." The Legislative Council room, however, had a "good hard floor"; the president occupied a raised platform at one end, which was ornamented with "a little red muslin drapery." Figured calico was tacked to the walls to prevent members from carrying away the whitewash on their coats. In the executive chamber opposite were chairs, an old sofa and bureau with a pine center table. "Within the last year the luxury of an American-made carpet has been indulged in, but before the advent of which the floor was covered by a domestic article called gerga, worth thirty cents per yard. This change is an evidence of pride in the executive. Bleached muslin is tacked to the beams overhead for a ceiling, and a strip of flashy calico, about four feet wide, is nailed to the four walls." The territorial library, not more than fifteen feet square, was filled with some two thousand volumes of legal nature and installed since civil government replaced the military. There was an office for the Indian agent and a room for Indians to wait in, where they were fed while they visited.[12]

The young Pennsylvania lawyer left an excellent picture of New Mexico in general and of the methods and appearance of architecture as he saw it. His emphasis on the archaic styles and behavior of the people, such as the lack of windows in houses, and the New Mexican woman's preference for sitting on the floor even if she had "American" furniture, and his repeated reference to "the style of two centuries ago" testifies to the survival of traditional manners. The spirit of 16th century Spain very obviously persisted in New Mexico, without any need of historical or patriotic propaganda, but simply by reason of having had no alternative example, into the 19th century.

While the roof that sifts dust or streams of water below suggests a distasteful nuisance to comfortable existence (and it was), the adobe house offered many solid virtues. No other material rises so naturally above the ground from which it was made; a line of adobes along a rolling hillside seems to grow out of the earth, sometimes forming patterns of geometric interest and at others vanishing into the landscape, according to the sunlight or shadow of the moment. The building corner buttresses and in-tapering walls below the roof line, the subtle tones of light on handsmoothed mud plaster, the patterns of viga ends casting long shadows over the walls at sundown, are all esthetic experiences conspicuously lacking in other houses made of other types of building materials.

To live in adobe is something like realization of the old saying: "An Englishman's home is his castle." The silent walls give the occupant a sense of security and refuge from the rest of the world, as if one had

---

[12] W. W. H. Davis, *El Gringo, or New Mexico and Her People,* Santa Fe, 1938.

found the inner chambers of a cavern deep down below the earth's surface. Anyone who has grown accustomed to waking up and looking at the richness of repetition-with-variety patterns of beamed ceilings is spoiled when he returns to the insipid monotony of plaster, papered or synthetic board ceilings. The adobe interior lends itself to practically any style of furnishing that the owner may prefer and as a setting in which to advantageously display pieces, or objects, of quality, the whitened adobe wall is more sympathetic and less obtrusive than any other background. Basically, it is a timeless style of architecture with thousands of years of human association in its past. An adobe building is one of function; the material itself determines its appearance and there is no surface veneer of a passing fashion to first distract and then detract from its unpretentious honesty.

The same flexibility of adobe as a material, which allowed changes in windows or doors and the making of convenient niches in which to keep smoking apparatus and other little things, has sometimes led to romantic legends of buried treasure and the literal destruction of old houses. No doubt valuables were from time to time hidden in a plastered-over wall recess or under a floor and forgotten as they also were in old houses in Europe and our eastern states. On the other hand neither coins nor jewels in any amounts were to be found in colonial New Mexico. Folklore, even today, is constantly circulating tales of buried treasure found, invariably, by a friend of a friend who promptly left the country. Neither the treasure itself nor the alleged finder can ever be tracked down. Instances of finding a cache of a pottery jar containing corn have actually been known; such burials would have been to keep the grain from mice over the winter. Nevertheless more than one serviceable adobe has been torn down by the burrowings of an owner in search of rumored hidden treasure left by an earlier owner.

RELIGIOUS ARCHITECTURE

In 1940 George Kubler wrote:

> The religious architecture of New Mexico has hitherto received attention chiefly from historians, whose admirable studies discuss the organization and influence of the Church throughout the province. . . . The churches themselves have never been considered pertinent to the history of building . . . Coherent, organized architectural form characterizes these churches. The material is the soil itself piled high and thick, pierced by few windows, with a roof line that recalls the deck levels of ships at sea upon the desert. The scale of these buildings dominates the urban profile; where the town buildings hug the landscape in low files, the churches stand forth in a scale that is neither human nor canonical, but military and hieratic. Inside, the treatment of light is theatrical: the nave is cool and dark, but at the sanctuary there prevails an intense daylight, focussed and concentrated by vertical skylights installed at the difference between the nave and the sanctuary . . . A closer examination of the older monuments reveals their construction as an unusual feat of European adaptation to limited materials and aboriginal techniques . . . Since its formulation in the early 17th century, the architectural type has persisted, unchanged but for the progressive coarsening of its early refinement. [1]

Kubler's work has not been improved upon nor displaced by other authors in the course of a generation; since it is still the basic reference on religious architecture of New Mexico I shall neither quote from it at length nor duplicate its text, but recommend that it be read intact. The European sources, Mauresque and Romanesque, which determined church architectural style in New Mexico into the 19th century, are extensively cited by him, as are the Renaissance roots of surface ornaments such as frescoes and facades of 16th century Mexican structures which, in time, came north to be translated into the media of mud, wood and painted hides.

---

[1] Kubler, George, *The Religious Architecture of New Mexico in the Colonial Period and Since the American Occupation.* The Taylor Museum, Colorado Springs, 1940. (Reprinted in facsimile, Rio Grande Press, 1964.)

Figure 33: Foundations of the
pre - 1680 rectangular sanctuary, San Miguel chapel, 1955.
(Photograph by David Weber)

Figure 34: The adobe parish
church, Santa Fe, with *almenas*
or crenellated parapets.

From the viewpoint of ground plan the earlier structures seem to have had small, rectangular sanctuaries instead of those with outward angled walls characteristic of most 18th century churches which gave better visibility from the nave. A clear example of this is the chapel of San Miguel at Santa Fe where excavations in 1955 exposed the pre-1680, square sanctuary below the level of the present, angle-sided one. Foundations of the older adobe altar, two side altars, steps and platforms were intact. The present sanctuary walls stand on different foundations from those of the square structure, indicating that San Miguel chapel was completely rebuilt in 1710, the date carved on the choir loft beam at the back of the church.[2] Although a small chapel, the proportions of San Miguel reflect those of the 17th century, ceiling height being greater in proportion to length and width than most of those of the 18th century.

New Mexico missions and churches that still exist have been so extensively remodeled in the past 100 years that, without reference to earlier descriptions and photographs, it is now difficult to visualize most of them as they looked originally. Barnlike roofs of sheet metal have spoiled the proportions of the buildings and also blocked the clerestory windows which had so efficiently lighted altar and sanctuary. These low, horizontal openings were set into the wall across the nave where the roof level is raised to a higher level above the sanctuary. In a cruciform church like Las Trampas the clerestory was on the nave side of the transept as the roof level rises there. In more usual, straightsided churches the clerestory was placed above the sanctuary steps. In an interior with only one or two other small windows set high in the nave walls this was not only effective lighting; it provided a beautiful light which fell upon the desired location, the altar and tabernacle, with a minimum of fenestration.

As window glass was unobtainable, the wooden grills were sealed with hand-shaped squares of native selenite, perhaps 10 by 10 centimeters, laid up like shingles between the dividing wooden grills. Like the alabaster window panes of Ravenna's Byzantine churches, selenite is not transparent but is translucent, giving a subdued bath of light to the interior. Electric bulbs dangling by a cord, fluorescent tubes and plastic shades that have been installed in several chapels to replace the obstructed clerestory windows give, in comparison, sorry lighting.

While most of the existing missions and chapels of New Mexico are of adobe, the fortified Romanesque church plan was continued into the later 19th century. In the 1870s the *parroquia* and San Miguel at Santa Fe still had *almenas* or adobe crenellations around their roofs. Earlier descriptions of other missions and their convents also mention such crenellated parapets, reminders that the Church was then responsible not only for the salvation of souls but for human lives and emergency food supplies in case of enemy attack. When the territory had been paci-

Figure 35: San Miguel chapel
before 1872 when the tower
collapsed. (Courtesy of George
Eastman House Collections)

[2]Kubler, George. *The Rebuilding of San Miguel Chapel at Santa Fe in 1710,* Colorado Springs, 1939. Stubbs, Stanley A., and Bruce T. Ellis, *Archaeological Investigations at the Chapel of San Miguel and the Site of La Castrense, Santa Fe, New Mexico,* Santa Fe, 1955.

fied by the United States, the foreign clergy began to install inexpensive imitations of Neo-Gothic window frames and, when possible, colored glass whose mediocrity is only matched by its unsuitability to the architecture.

Today it is difficult to realize what discomforts, by our standards, were endured and taken for granted by those hearing Mass in New Mexico churches. The majority of the congregation walked to church; horses were reserved for the *ricos*. The churches were not heated; 18th century Franciscans spoke of the holy oils congealing and the holy water fonts being frozen in severe winter cold. No traces of fireplaces are recorded from the excavation of 17th century churches nor in later ones. Only after the Civil War were pot-bellied iron stoves introduced, and these, lighted just before the Mass, had little effect in winter upon the frigid walls.

Floors were of packed earth, swept weekly and laid each year by women of the community with new mud mixed with straw. They may yet be seen in the missions of Acoma, Laguna, Santa Ana and Zia. In addition to the priest's chairs in the sanctuary there were only one or two other chairs for officials such as the governor. If they chose to do so, members of the congregation brought blankets on which to kneel or sit, and stood up for the rest of the Mass and the sometimes lengthy sermons. Uncluttered, massive yet subtly plastic wall surfaces led mind as well as eye toward the sanctuary which was bathed in the light of the unseen clerestory window.

Out of ingenuity and the few materials at hand — undressed ledge stone, sun-dried adobes, hand-hewn timbers and a few native minerals — the Franciscans devised an architectural style which, beginning at old El Paso, now Juarez, and extending over Spanish New Mexico, persisted for some 250 years. This hybrid of Romanesque and Mauresque features, combined with the aboriginal adobe and rubble construction methods, is quite unlike Spanish colonial religious architecture in New Spain, California, Florida, or Texas.

Interior furnishings were few; altars were usually of adobe although a few were boxes of stone slabs filled with adobes. One to three adobe shelves or steps, which held candles, ornaments and a tabernacle, ran above and behind the altar. Above this were usually two niches or wall recesses containing a crucifix and an image of the mission's patron saint. Sometimes one or two oil paintings or a few little engravings had been sent by the King's mission fund from Mexico. A wooden pulpit, like a goblet in shape, with its sounding board and ladderlike steps, rose on a pillar from the earthern floor. Most of these have been replaced by public address systems. Although dogmatic discussion as to the location of early pulpits in colonial missions is divided, those still in place toward the end of the 19th century were on the right hand side of the nave as one faces the altar.

If we were to judge only by the description just given, and the fact that interior walls were supposedly covered by mud-colored or white plaster, we might assume that the flat-roofed temples were austerely bare

Figure 36: The adobe mission of San Agustin, Isleta Pueblo, remodeled in late 19th century. This view shows visit of King Albert and Queen Elizabeth of Belgium after World War I. (Photograph by Odd S. Halseth)

Figure 37: The church of San Francisco de Asis, Ranchos de Taos, before it was hard-plastered. (New Mexico State Tourist Bureau photograph)

and cold to the eye as well as the thermometer. In fact this was not the case as Franciscans, since their early arrival in Mexico, had made a point of painting directly on church walls.* At first this was for the instruction of neophytes while language barriers and lack of professionally painted visual images made communications difficult. Where lack of skilled artists, money or materials made it necessary, amateur painting on church walls was continued well into the 18th century in New Mexico. In many respects a more conservative order than some others of the Roman church, the Franciscans were merely continuing a tradition of fresco painting which had been in practice in the 13th century during the life-time of their founder, Francis of Assisi. The extent of their efforts in New Mexico in painting church walls is little realized now because they used water soluble pigments on mud and plaster. Unlike true fresco these are easily damaged by water, cracking, or abrasion; they are as ephemeral as paper flowers, and have nearly all been lost to view.

The first chapel at "Cuarac," now called Quarai Pueblo, is thought to have been built between 1615–1620. It was apparently razed when the great stone church at Quarai was completed and forgotten until the foundations were excavated in 1959. The little chapel's interior walls were found to have been painted with red iron oxide. The rear of the sanctuary wall was still five feet high when uncovered, and the adobe-filled stone altar was found to have been painted white.[3] Five or six layers of paint were counted. Whether scrolls taken from textiles, or tile patterns, or figural images, were painted above the red wall areas is of course unknown. Even the simple red and white color scheme would have made the Quarai chapel interior attractive to its congregation.

During the 1921 excavations at the stone mission of San José at Giu-sewa, an early historic pueblo of Jemez Indians and Franciscans, fragments of painting on the adobe plastered interior were exposed to view. These were simplified renderings of Renaissance borders, or dados, and of an all-over majolica tile pattern.[4]

The 17th century church of San Bernardo de Aguatubi (Awatovi), which was excavated by the Peabody Museum of Harvard and called Church No. 2 in their exhaustive report on the work, had four to five layers of painted wall decorations on the interior walls and sacristy.[5] In addition to dados or panels of solid colors there was a variety of designs imitating glazed tiles and Renaissance textile patterns. Comparison of designs on the adobe altar front at Awatovi (supra, Fig. 59), and at

---

*Toussaint, Manuel, "La Pintura Mural en Nueva España" in Artes de Mexico, No. 4, May-June 1954, pp. 8–29.

[3] " 'New' Old Churches Found at Quarai and Tabira (Pueblo Blanco)," Stanley A. Stubbs, El Palacio, V. 66/5, 1959.

[4] Reproduced in: Arnold, Charlotte, 1930, Fig. 1 & 7, and Kubler, G., 1940, Fig. 141, and Smith, W., 1949, Fig. 61-d.

[5] "Franciscan Awatovi," Montgomery, Ross Gordon, Watson Smith and John Otis Brew, Papers of the Peabody Museum, Harvard University, V. XXXVI, Cambridge, Mass., 1949.

Giusewa, suggest a common source for both, perhaps a Franciscan priest who was assigned at one time or another to both missions. It has been assumed that the limited color schemes, crude brush work and simplified renderings of these murals were the work of Moqui converts who were unfamiliar with, and therefore inept at, painting European motifs. However, even a well trained painter would have trouble in brushing flowing curves or subtle shadings on roughly surfaced adobe walls with improvised local pigments.

It has also been suggested that the painted wall designs of San Bernardo, Church 2, had been taken from actual altar cloths and glazed tiles sent from New Spain with mission supplies. This possibility was cited on the basis of an order regarding mission supplies issued in 1631 which stated that, among other goods, one box of *loza de Puebla* was to be shipped to each mission every three years.[6] This, however, did not mean glazed tiles (*azulejos*), but an assortment of plates, bowls, and other dishes for the domestic use of the missionary convents: *loza,* an assortment of household crockery. No record of wall or roofing tiles shipped to New Mexico has been found, nor have any fragments of glazed tiles been reported from excavated historic sites, but numerous sherds of Puebla ware glazed dishes have been collected from Spanish sites over the southwest.

When Dominguez inspected New Mexico in 1776, mission supplies from New Spain had evidently dwindled. Before he left Nambe mission, Dominguez made a writ of visitation in which he noted the absence of basic articles in the convent and ordered that each departing priest should leave his successor a minimum of said necessities, including "6 plates, 6 cups, 2 jars, and 4 candlesticks, all of clay and manufactured in the pueblo" (Dominguez, p. 57). While describing other missions Dominguez repeatedly said: ". . . and it is the same as what I have said about Nambe." We may infer that there were the same scanty furnishings elsewhere, and that the Visitor ordered that basic dishes were to be supplied by the Indians of each pueblo, except at Abiquiu where, he noted, they did not know how to make pottery (Dominguez, p. 123).

The principle of overall patterns taken from tiled walls was quite foreign to Indian decorative traditions, but was more amenable to the painting materials and surfaces in early missions than were flowering arabesques. The trompe l'oeil or illusion of three dimensional form seen in the narrow stairs painted against a wall at Awatovi was certainly the work of a man with European background rather than of Moquis who had then no notion of the theory of perspective.[7] The general organization and sources of the Giusewa and Awatovi frescoes may be assumed to have been laid out by Franciscans, who drew upon their memories of Spain or New Spain, rather than by Indians who copied samples of textiles or tiles.

---

[6] Smith, W., 1949, p. 304.
[7] Smith, W., 1949, Fig. 55/11, Church 2, & Fig. 60.

Persistence of the Renaissance style in New Mexico is noted elsewhere (Sec. I-E, Paintings on Hides) long after it had been discarded by European artists and architects. Many churches in 16th century New Spain were built on the plan of a Romanesque fortified temple since defensible buildings were needed at the time, but they often had facades and interior decorations of Renaissance style. Of these, San Miguel de Huejotzingo, near Puebla and on the old road from Vera Cruz to Mexico City, was quite probably a direct source of ideas for many New Mexico structures. Begun in the 1520s by some of the first Franciscans to land in New Spain, in use by 1541 and said to have been completed in 1570, this stone church had a high, vaulted ceiling. The roof proportions and *almenas* may well have been models for the more modest chapel of San Miguel in Santa Fe. The Huejotzingo church received elaborate altars in Renaissance, Baroque and Neo-Classical styles over the years, but the convent was decorated with true frescoes in nearly pure early Renaissance traditions. Large walls were painted with scenes of the Annunciation and Crucifixion, with archangels, apostles, Franciscan saints, portraits of the first twelve Franciscan missionaries to New Spain, and even processions of Penitentes. These were bordered by painted scrolls, acanthus, fruits, flowers, ribbons, cherubs, and griffins.

Many Franciscans who came to New Mexico had been stationed at Huejotzingo whose frescoed convent walls they may well have memorized. A minor detail, such as painted columns and scalloped shells in Huejotzingo murals, could have been the source of a more naive rendering of these in the sanctuary of San Miguel chapel at Santa Fe. During the investigation of San Miguel in 1955, fallen bits of plaster from the rear sanctuary wall exposed areas of color beneath the outer layer of adobe plaster. The rear wall contained a recess, about one meter twenty centimeters high, originally divided into two niches one above the other and both located above the altar.[8] These contained the crucifix and the gilded statue of St. Michael, already owned by the confraternity of San Miguel by 1709 before the rebuilding of the chapel.

Scraping away plaster layers from the outside to the painted one revealed this sequence: (1) thick, dark adobe plaster, (2) adobe plaster, (3) plain or white *yeso,* or gypsum plaster, (4) adobe plaster, (5) painted decoration on gypsum plaster, (6) adobe plaster on adobe brick walls. All six layers were present on the left or north side of the central niches but only layers one through four were found on the south side. Apparently water from the roof had damaged the first two layers so severely that the plaster was scraped off down to the bricks and replaced. The center and north side containing the painted layer were merely replastered, but no further decorative painting was done.

The painting included an arch formed by crudely "marbleized" columns with a fluted shell at the top and urns of flowers at each side. There were also single columns painted on each of the angled side walls. All

Figure 38: Removal of five layers of house paints from retable of San Miguel chapel, Santa Fe, 1955.

Figure 39: The adobe niche of 1710 behind the wooden screen. (Figures 38 and 39, photographs by David Weber)

[8]Stubbs & Ellis, 1955, Figs. 1, 2 & 3.

Figure 40: Reconstruction of painted decorations on sanctuary wall. Scale: 2.5 cm. to 15 cm.

Figure 41: Fragments of painted elements on side walls.

of these had been laid out with a sharp implement with which the design had been scratched into the plaster. The arch was only eight centimenters off center. Pigments were water soluble and limited to shades of indigo blue, black, and mineral or earth yellow except in the urns of flowers where small amounts of dull red were used. While there were large losses, the design could be reconstructed from existing sections. There is a space of only 62 centimeters between the present wooden altar screen made in 1798 and the rear wall which is 275 centimeters high by 266 centimeters wide. It was impossible to take photographs of the painting in this limited space, so color renderings were made instead. After being covered with lime-bearing plaster, this kind of pigment usually fades upon being again exposed to air. As an experiment in 1955, each six-inch square of color was sprayed with commercial, clear plastic to try to fix the colors. However, in view of the crumbling and battered condition of the whole plastered surface it is doubtful if it will last much longer.

Since the painted layer was on the first coat of adobe plaster, it was presumably done soon after 1710 when San Miguel was rebuilt, and when the chapel had no more ornaments than the statue of the patron and perhaps paintings on buffalo hides. Another version of this traditional Franciscan motif of the painted columns and fluted shell flanked by urns was to be seen until recently in the ruined mission at Cocóspera, Sonora. Built by Padre Kino in 1703 and abandoned after Apache raids in 1746, it was rebuilt by Franciscans when they replaced the Jesuits in 1768. Like other missions of Sonora it was of fired brick, stone, rubble, and hard plaster instead of adobe. These materials permitted sculptural elements, so the fluted shell and columns at Cocóspera were in low relief, but the forms and colors were hardly more sophisticated than at San Miguel. Blue, yellow, orange, green, and small areas of red were used, but having been painted over wet stucco they had more resistance to time, earthquakes and weathering than the colors at Santa Fe's San Miguel.

Among items listed in the expenses of rebuilding San Miguel in 1710 were *morillos* or wooden timbers for scaffolding. These were laid across the adobe walls at suitable intervals with ends projecting on the outside to support scaffolding and left in place for future repairs. They are still laid through the sanctuary wall, visible from the street outside, and in the wall niche within. Neither these timbers nor the exposed adobe bricks shows any traces of burning which is additional confirmation that the chapel was entirely rebuilt in 1710 and not merely reroofed.

When Dominguez saw San Miguel in 1776 the military congregation had moved to La Castrense on the Plaza, built in 1760–61, and the older chapel had been neglected. He said it looked like a granary inside, but noted the statue of San Miguel and eight paintings on canvas which are still in place.* Four of these were half-length images of saints in oval

---

*The statue and four oval canvases were stolen from the chapel in the summer of 1972.

Figure 42: The sanctuary of Mission Santiago de Cocospera, Sonora.

Figure 43: Detail of painted urns, Cocospera mission. (Figure 43, Photograph by Tad Nichols. Figures 42 and 43, courtesy of George B. Eckhart Collections)

frames and seem to be part of a larger set that included two more oval-framed pictures now at Santa Ana mission. The latter were not mentioned in inventories at Santa Ana in the 1740s; no early inventory of San Miguel has been found. However, the paintings, although of workshop quality, reflect the painting style admired in New Spain around 1750, and probably came to New Mexico after that date. It may have been the arrival of these pictures, with three others and the canvas of St. Michael by Miera y Pacheco (Sec. I-D), that decided the guardians of the chapel not to paint decorations on the sanctuary wall again.

San Miguel's nave had been covered with hard plaster in late years; removal of this in 1955 exposed traces of painting in black and red at eye level, but so damaged that no design was recognizable. On the south wall, however, a brick chimney had been laid up against the adobe wall when a pot-bellied stove was installed in the late 19th century. When the bricks were torn out, mud plastering remained behind them. Under this was a painted plaster area on which was a scroll form in black outlines. This may have been half of a painted frame around one of the stations of the Cross which, in some form, would have been present along the nave walls and, quite possibly, all in similar painted scrolls. Along the lower part of the walls was the traditional dado of tierra amarilla.

San José mission at Laguna Pueblo is thought to have been built in 1699; the present wooden altar screen was done between 1800–1809 (Sec. I-G). In the century or so between these dates the sanctuary walls were repainted several times, but what the designs may have been we do not know. However, small chunks of plaster taken from the rear wall and examined by Dr. Rutherford Gettens were reported by him to have nine alternating layers of plain plaster and painted white layers. One of these included azurite in the pigments, the only other report of use of this native, mineral blue color in Spanish times in addition to its appearance in Awatovi's Church 2.[9] Another painted layer at Laguna contained particles of mica, a popular colonial material used to produce a pearly effect. The painting on the sanctuary walls between the wooden retable and rail was well planned and strongly brushed in subtle shades of gray, black, greenish gray and ochre yellow. The pomegranate flower and leaf pattern was probably after a textile. While the lower parts of these painted "hangings" were retouched with modern paints, the upper parts were in the original, water soluble pigments. They gave an excellent idea of how handsomely adobe walls could be "painted like a tapestry" at little expense by someone with the taste and skill to do so. Except where a lightning bolt struck the north side of the roof a few years ago, these wall paintings were in good condition until 1968, when they were whitewashed. The flower forms and bold brushwork, although of a different color scheme, resembled those on the wooden retable. It is quite probable that the painted walls were done by the Laguna santero when he carved and painted the altar screen, between 1800–1809.

_____

[9] Gettens and Turner, *El Palacio,* V 58/1 Jan. 1951.

Something like Laguna's painted walls may have been in Nambe mission when Dominguez saw it. He said that above the high altar ". . . the whole wall is painted like a tapestry, but it is ugly" (Dominguez, p. 53). At San Ildefonso he wrote: "The whole wall around the sanctuary is painted blue and yellow from top to bottom like a tapestry, and not too badly. This was done at Father Tagle's expense" (Dominguez, p. 65). Tagle served in New Mexico from 1701 to 1727; the frescoes had been there for at least fifty years when Dominguez grudgingly allowed that they were not too bad. At Acoma, he said: "The whole area that I have been describing, up to the top, has arches painted with colored earth, executed by the Indians" (Dominguez, p. 191).

Of las Trampas, barely completed in 1776, Dominguez said that above the one and only altar there was: ". . . a board niche painted and spattered with what they call talco here (it is like tinsel, but very flexible)" (Dominguez, p. 100). The niche contained a statue of San José and was disposed of when the present hand hewn wooden retables were installed. Behind the main altar screen at las Trampas there are still fragments of painting on adobe plaster. In the middle there is an unpainted space where the board niche was. Around it are bands of diagonal blocks, some encrusted over the pigments with large flakes of mica. Above are painted flowers and birds, the whole framed by a painted arch which spanned the entire sanctuary rear wall.

Scattered as they are, the existence of these vanished, or now fragmentary, painted walls has been summarized in order to point out that they were common to most, if not all, of the 17th and 18th century northern missions. Some church walls of the colonial period may, even today, bear underlying layers of Franciscan paintings.

By 1776 when Dominguez made his minute inspection, the more prosperous churches of New Mexico already had wooden altar screens put up after the completion of the stone retable in the Santa Fe *castrense* in 1761. If wooden cornices, pilasters, and panels were not as grand as their stone prototypes, they were certainly more imposing and more substantial than perishable paintings on adobe plaster. Dominguez described the wooden retables that he saw as being "in the manner of this kingdom, very ugly" or as "all in perspective." They were in the Santa Fe *parroquia,* which was "jasperized" with niches for statues; at Santa Cruz, San Juan, San Geronimo de Taos, and Santo Domingo. Each altar screen was planned to display statues or canvasses already belonging to the church. It was only in newer churches at recently founded villages that had no images from New Spain that santeros painted figures on the altar screens.

Although Albuquerque had only twenty-four houses around the plaza, the owners had rich ranches and could afford to adorn the church of San Felipe de Neri in what was then a high fashion in the outer world, painted architectural masonry: "High altar: Father Fray Rafael Benavides installed an altar screen in perspective on canvas. It is very seemly. It consists (as it is painted) of two sections, and beginning at the gradin it rises about six varas across the width of the wall. The first section contains three pictures. . . . Near the middle of the second section (it is understood that all is painted), a crucifix, and on either side of it Lord St. Joseph and St. Augustine. At the top, the Eternal Father with an angel at each side" (Dominguez, p. 146). With the substitution of other images here was a pattern evidently followed by the makers of many later New Mexican altar screens who did not, however, devote any attention to the intellectual refinement of imitation architectural perspective.

To the west Miera y Pacheco had recently completed an altar screen at Zuñi which was of wood with statuary and "half gilding" of which Dominguez grudgingly approved in spite of his oft repeated gibes at that "citizen of this kingdom" (Sec. I-D). Fragments of this are now in the collections of the Smithsonian Institution of Washington, D.C., notably an archangel.

Of the "new" painted altar screens seen by Dominguez only one is left, at Santa Cruz, but all that is of his period are the hand-hewn boards. They were repainted in shiny enamels in 1947, in the already antiquated Neo-Gothic style of Viollet-le-Duc.

Between 1780 and 1830 wooden altar screens had been put up in San Miguel and Rosario chapels in Santa Fe, at Santa Clara, Nambe, el Santuario, at las Truchas, las Trampas, Picurís, Ranchos de Taos, and the church of Guadalupe on Taos plaza; in the Rio Abajo at Zia, Santa Ana, Cochiti, and at Laguna and Acoma. Of these some of the original work is still to be seen (1971) at Laguna, San Miguel in Santa Fe, el Santuario at Chimayó, the old church of Rosario at las Truchas, and San Francisco de Ranchos de Taos. Whitewash, wallpaper covering, or amateur improvements have accounted for others. The work of José Gonzales in las Trampas, done soon after our Civil War, is the one happy exception in the decline of folk art in New Mexico, since he was still a part of the traditional itinerant santero school (Sec. III-A, José Gonzales). Other existing retables were painted after 1830, or were in private chapels.

The elegance and dignity which a painted wooden altar screen added to an adobe church is best seen at San Miguel in Santa Fe as an example of late colonial sophistication, and at San José at Laguna Pueblo for the finest flowering of the New Mexican santero style. Aside from the perennial claim of being the oldest church in the United States, San Miguel's history is closely interwoven with that of Santa Fe. While the earlier chapel, destroyed in 1680 at the outbreak of the rebellion, had been designed for Indians, the one rebuilt in 1710 was the home of the military confraternity for fifty years, until la Castrense, or chapel of Our Lady of Light, with its stone altar screen replaced San Miguel in fashionable Santa Fe circles in 1761. Married soldiers, Spanish laborers, and assorted Pueblo and genízaro Indians lived along the south bank of the river around San Miguel but it seems to have been allowed to deteriorate physically for several decades, and was used only for two Masses yearly, on May eighth and September twenty-ninth, in honor of St. Michael.

In 1798 the citizen Antonio José Ortiz repaired the walls, roof and, quite possibly, added the pyramidal three-storied tower. Certainly he commissioned the wooden retable whose inscriptions, once again exposed from an overlay of five coats of house paint, declare that he had had it made and painted at his own expense in 1798. It is the oldest dated wooden altarpiece left in New Mexico and, apparently, the first one made in the province using salomonic, or spiraled, columns. Extensively employed in Spain and New Spain in the 17th century the salomonic form was no longer popular with architects by 1798 but, of course, could then be seen in many places. Although the stone altar screen at La Castrense unquestionably was the model for later wooden examples in New Mexico the designers of these did not attempt to reproduce the flat pilasters decorated all over with carving. Instead they made the full rounded, salomonic pillars of an earlier period. It had for some years been supposed that the well proportioned, heavy columns on the Laguna altar screen were the first to have been seen in New Mexico, mainly due to the reading of the fragmentary date on the back of the Laguna retable as "780," interpreted as a year in the 1780s. However, in my opinion, the figures in Spanish style read "180–," allowing the decade 1800–1809 for the work. It had also been believed, until 1955, that Antonio José Ortiz had San Miguel chapel repaired in 1805, but the uncovering of the San Miguel dated cartouches fixed the repairs and new retable as of 1798, thus proving that the San Miguel project was finished before the Laguna retable was started. No images were painted at San Miguel, but only floral elements framing canvasses and the patron's statue; the color scheme is sophisticated, of soft coral pink and sage green. The personal mannerisms of flower forms and brushwork resemble those of the anonymous Laguna santero who may well have been the designer and painter of San Miguel's retable. The introduction of a new architectural form in New Mexico was more likely to have happened in the capital, Santa Fe, than in a distant pueblo, just as the innovation of carved stone as a material had been installed at Santa Fe a quarter century earlier. Thus the Laguna santero may have introduced the even-then archaic salomonic columns to New Mexico in 1798. These, in dwindling sizes and angular versions, were repeated by later santeros well into the 19th century. It is unfortunate that the original tabernacle front in the lower tier of the San Miguel retable was long ago destroyed as it might well have contained some element which would have given a more positive clue to the personal painting mannerisms of the santero.

New Mexico missions were not always planned by Franciscans; sometimes a contract was made between them and a well-to-do citizen who undertook to build a church and convento in return for certain commodities that were at the disposal of the missionaries. For example, Don Salvador Garcia de Noriega of Santa Cruz bound himself to build a new church at San Lorenzo de Picurís on April 18, 1777. At the time no church existed but a missionary lived in a room at the pueblo. The new mission was to be:

... of the size of the old church, with transept, walls, guide lines one

Figure 44: "This altar was made through the devotion of señor the royal Alfarez Don Jose Antonio Ortis, 1798."

Figure 45: "This was painted through the devotion of the royal Alferez Don Jose Antonio Ortis, 1798." Two inscriptions on the retable of San Miguel chapel, Santa Fe. (Figures 44 and 45, photographs by Laura Gilpin)

I-B

Figure 46: Silver helmet, 18th century New Mexico.

Figure 47: Polychromed statue of San Miguel brought from New Spain by 1709. (Photograph by Duncan MacInnes)

Figure 48: The sanctuary of San Miguel chapel, 1865–1955.

Figure 49: The central niche for the statue of the patron, San Miguel, 1798. (Photograph by David Weber)

meter apart (for the thickness of the walls), door and two windows to the east, choir loft with board (floor), corbels, and round beams. And because some beginning has already been made on the site where this church is to be built, I obligate myself, in addition . . . to build three covered rooms for a dwelling for the missionary . . . so that the outside walls of said rooms may join the church with the pueblo, but I do not obligate myself to put doors or windows on the said three rooms.

The work was to be completed in a year and a half in return for:

12 cows, 12 yearling calves, 25 ewes with a stud ram, a fine she-mule, 100 fanegas of maize and wheat, 100 pounds of chocolate (Dominguez, p. 323).

Garcia said he was satisfied with the payment which he had already received. This kind of architectural enterprise in some ways resembled those of today's jerry-built subdivisions whose designer-contractors are not bound by standards or guarantees that could trim profits, and who can work with a minimum of time-consuming details. It was undoubtedly responsible for some of the less well proportioned, or poorly built, churches of the 18th century in New Mexico which did not hold up against the erosion of wind and water. Whether because of Garcia's skimping on the mission construction or the workmanship of the Picurís Indians as laborers, and their indifference or open hostility to the missionaries for the previous 175 years, the Picurís church has been crumbling or in the process of being repaired ever since. Recently it was torn down nearly to ground level and rebuilt by the pueblo over a two year period. The mission bell, of the long-waisted shape that was sent from Zacatecas to New Mexico both in the 17th century and after the reconquest, was suspended from a frame of poles set into the ground by the church entrance where it would be struck with a stone by the bell ringer when wanted. There it stood in 1776 and there it has stood for the years since elapsed. The weight of bronze bells on adobe roofs or in belfries was a constant problem in colonial New Mexico, first to hoist them up, then to reach them for tolling, since most of them had no clappers and were struck with a stone until their lips wore thin. Many bells crashed to the ground as their rawhide lacings dried and broke, or the tower in which they were hanging crumbled. Experience decided that the bell was better placed near ground level, unorthodox as it seemed to strangers. In New Mexico no attempt was made to build a separate bell tower like those in many other Spanish areas, but merely a plain wooden framework.

A religious or layman with personal taste and enthusiasm, however, could and did plan a church, using the same materials, with monumental character, dignity and good proportions. The missions of Santa Ana, Zia, Acoma and Laguna Pueblos, Bernardo Abeyta's Santuario del Señor de Esquipulas at el Potrero de Chimayó and the mid-19th century chapel of San José de Chama are good examples of this architectural flair although the last-named was, unfortunately, ruined by 1950 by cheap and injudicious improvements. In making repairs it is a human trait to add to or change what was there before. Only recently has it been considered desirable to return an old structure to its original aspect. This opinion is presently held by a limited number of persons, or members of organizations, with strong historical as well as architectural convictions who believe that accretions of synthetic materials in pseudotraditional designs have no place on an older building of a given style.

In colonial records all repairs were described as new construction or building, thus shedding luster upon those in charge at the time but confusing historians today as to the exact year when a certain building was actually begun or completed. More than one adobe church suffered a collapsed wall, apse or tower. When these were replaced they were recorded as "newly built" or "the new church of —" and, undoubtedly, were not quite like the earlier feature. The pyramidal tower of San Miguel in Santa Fe was a case in point; it was not in existence in the 18th century. To support it two cubes of adobe were laid against the former facade with a space between them which formed an ill-proportioned porch for the chapel door. Across this empty space and the adobe pedestals the tower was then built entirely outside of but against the original facade. The greatest weight of the three storied adobe and wooden belfry, although tapered, was directly above the open porch below; settling of the supporting adobe blocks may well have caused the collapse of the upper sections of the tower in 1872. In 1887 the tower was rebuilt with stone buttresses to prop it up and in 1955 the wooden louvers in this were removed. The only extension feature of the facade which apparently survives from the pyramidal tower phase is the small window over the door, a hand-carved, small-paned New Mexico rendering of the Neo-Gothic style of *ca.* 1840. It is worth noting that the 19th century church of Guadalupe in Santa Fe had a similar, but not identical, tower and a window much like that of San Miguel's over its main door. These towers reflected a desire for more imposing, if less structurally sound, church facades while the windows record the advent of Yankee hand tools and glass panes in the second quarter of the 19th century.

In rural villages where small chapels sprang up from about 1815 to 1830, several were built with a rounded apse, a functional and pleasing plan which did not, however, lend itself to solid wooden altar screens. New Mexico rural churches, still built by community labor and without architects, tended to be smaller, more cramped in width and with low ceilings, although a few of them retained traditional massiveness. Later, alien influences introduced red brick, dressed stone, barn roofs, even the notion of using shingles or galvanized iron sheeting to curtain adobe walls. In the 1930s the pendulum swung full circle when not only Catholic but Protestant churches, service club houses and even gas stations were built in colonial Spanish style. With few exceptions, such as the church of Cristo Rey at Santa Fe, these are not constructed of adobe. The pueblos of Cochiti, Isleta and San Ildefonso have hired architects to restore or rebuild their missions from 19th century, makeshift incrustations to the colonial facades of the Spanish period.

Figure 50: The Eldodt store and old mission, San Juan Pueblo. (Courtesy of Jane Howe)

I-B

Figure 51: San Miguel chapel and college dormitory before the mansard roof was burned.

Figure 52: San Juan Pueblo mission, signed "Chain, 1881." (Courtesy of the Fred Harvey Foundation Collections)

APPENDIX
Religious Architecture

The de Guevara inventory of el Santuario de Esquipulas* of 1818 explains the purpose of the two rooms built against the facade of the chapel between which the so-called narthex passes into the church. This feature does not appear in existing New Mexico churches and chapels, except at el Santuario, and it has been the subject of some discussion in the past. Having already listed the wooden door of the chapel proper (the doors carved with the date of 1816 and the names of Pedro Dominguez and Father Correa), the inventory goes on:

"Un saguan agregado a la capilla con su puerta de madera, con dos piezas, con puertas y ventanas."

After this follows:

"Bienes perteneciente al capilla.

"Dos bestias, mula y macho

1 docena de medias

20 varas de sallal

6 sarapes

1 sabana de sabanilla labrada de cinco varas

---

*A chapel at el Potrero de Chimayó built 1813–16 over an ancient curative hot spring.

1 colcha nuebo
　　　1 casa de tres piezas con puertos y bentanas
　　　　　dies libras de cera
　　23 p(esos) 2 reales en dinero
　　　2 botijas de vino."
Further:
"Efectos que se entraron a bender con Dⁿ Juan Vigil.
　　14 sarapes
　　24 varas de jerga
　　17 varas de sallal
　　　1 fresada atildada azul
　　　1 Sobremesa
　　　6 pares de medias
　　　1 conchelle　　　　　　　　　7　Maio, 1818."

*A zaguan (or breezeway), built against the chapel with its wooden door,
with two rooms, with doors and windows.*
Goods belonging to the chapel:
　　Two beasts, she-mule and mule
　　　1 dozen stockings
　　20 varas of sayal[11]
　　　6 sarapes
　　　1 length of embroidered woolen homespun of five varas
　　　1 new colcha
　　　1 house of three rooms with doors and windows
　　10 lbs. of wax
　　23 pesos and two reales in money ($23.25)
　　　2 jugs of wine
Things which have been brought to sell with Don Juan Vigil:
　　14 sarapes
　　24 varas of jerga (floor carpet)
　　17 varas of sallal (coarse cloth)
　　　1 patched blue frieze cloth
　　　1 tablecover
　　　6 pairs of stockings
　　　1 conch shell　　　　　　　　7 of May 1818

While it was normal for a church to own livestock for its necessities
and a small house, wax, wine, occasionally a bit of money and carpets or
cloth for the church furnishings, the other items are unusual and suggest by their kind and quantity that this was in part a supply of assets to
bring in funds for the maintenance of el Santuario. The next list which
plainly specifies "Things which have been brought to sell with Don Juan

---

[10] (AASF, Accounts, Book LXII, Book 2, 1818)

[11] *Sayal,* a coarse, thick cloth, from *sayo,* and Latin *sagum,* long piece of cloth with
hole to go over head as outer garment.

Vigil" leaves no doubt whatsoever that pilgrims and visitors to the chapel were then able to purchase goods, by barter or with cash, with which income the buildings were to be kept in repair and such necessities as wax and wine could be procured. Vigil, apparently, was Abeitia's storekeeper.

It is probable that the donor-builder of the chapel, Don Bernardo Abeitia, had devised this plan to provide for his chapel of Our Lord of Esquipulas. He must have designed the two rooms which stand today, although recently modernized, in front of the belltowers of the chapel and flanking the zaguan leading into it to serve as storerooms for the goods which he would have for sale to devotees. It is permissible to speculate on the possible exchange of goods or monies for the privilege of taking away a bit of the miraculous earth from the oratorio. This provision for the support of the chapel bears the stamp of a businesslike mind which seems to have been one of Don Bernardo's characteristics.

The inventory of 1818 referred to the chapel as *El Santuario del Potrero, Capilla Publica que corre con el nombre de Potrero, tres leguas distante de la Villa de la Cañada.* The manuscript goes on to state that there is a parochial school whose masters are paid by a pious fund. The 1826 inventory repeats nearly word for word the 1818 description of the chapel and its contents, of the altar screen with gilding, choir loft, oratorio which is "the original" with its painted *colateral,* the Crucifix of Esquipulas and the thirty-eight bultos "without counting the small ones," the Christ Child of ivory, the doors and windows, and the doors and windows in a zaguan, etc. One almost suspects that it was simply copied from the earlier list, but the last part adds considerably to our knowledge of the mercantile and maintenance business.

"Alajas a fabor de la Capilla

    3 varas de puesta de plata
    1 fistol de oro
    1 par de ojos de plata
    1 medalla de plata
    2 limetas
    4 violines
    4 alfombras
  34 varas de zallal
    1 colcha
  10 santos de bulto
  30 zarapes
    6 varas de encaje ancho
    6 relicarios de oro y plata
    2 anillos de oro
    2 platas de metal
 119 rosas
    1 guitarra
    6 zarapes
    1 fresada
  12 libras de cera

Figure 53: The zaguan, el Santuario de Chimayó. View before walled-up doorway, left, to a salesroom was reopened. (New Mexico State Tourist Bureau photograph)

Figure 54: The last and largest adobe church; Cristo Rey under construction, 1939–41. (Photograph by Margaret McKittrick)

3 botijas de vino
1 caballo
1 macho
7 alfombras
1 burro
1 becerro
2 fanegas de sal
42 velas de cera
2 paños polvos
1 panuela polvos
1 zarape
1 par de medios
8 manojos de punche
4 imagenes de bulto
18 gergas
1 corateral que hiso un deboto
1 novillo
1 relicario
1 reboso negro
1 alfombra chica
11 imagenes de retablo
6 cortinas labrada, algunas de musolina o indianilla
8 espejos
1 imagen de Ma Sma. de Dolores"

Ornaments in favor of the Chapel (or which are assets to it)

3 varas of silver brocade
1 gold scarf pin
1 pair of silver eyes (ex votos)
1 silver medal
2 flasks
4 violins
4 carpets
34 varas of coarse cloth
1 colcha
10 images of saints in the round
30 sarapes
6 varas of wide lace
6 reliquaries of gold and silver
2 gold rings
2 metal plates
119 roses (REF. Sec. II-D).)
1 guitar
6 sarapes
1 frieze saddle blanket
12 lbs. of wax
3 jugs of wine
1 horse
1 mule

Figure 55: Detail of stone altar screen from la Castrense, now in church of Cristo Rey. (Photograph by Edith Eustis)

Figure 56: 17th century stone carving, prototype of Castrense style, 1761. (Courtesy of Archivo de Monumentos Coloniales, Mexico)

Figure 57: Remains of stone altar frontal from la Castrense lettered: "This building was made at the cost of 8,000 pesos ..." The date of 1761 was mis-carved as 1791.

Figure 58: When la Castrense was closed the altar frontal was removed and carved with Mexican eagles and serpents on the reverse. Lettered "Correos de Santa Fe," it served as window and letter drop for the Santa Fe post office. (Figures 57 and 58, Photographs Arthur D. Taylor Jr.)

```
  7 carpets
  1 burro
  1 bull calf
  2 bushels of salt
 42 wax candles
  2 dust cloths
  1 little dust cloth
  1 sarape
  1 pair of stockings
  8 handfuls of (native grown) tobacco
  4 images of Saints in the round
 18 floor carpets
  1 altar screen made by a devotee
  1 young bull
  1 reliquary
  1 black reboso (head scarf)
  1 small carpet
 11 images on retablos
  6 embroidered curtains, some of cotton muslin or of printed cotton
    (imported)
  8 mirrors
  1 image of Most Holy Mary of Sorrows.[12]
```

Wax, candles, wine, rings for arras, embroideries and even little dust cloths might be construed as property of the chapel, but such quantities of blankets, yardage of cloth and carpeting, pairs of hose, and miscellaneous reliquaries and ex-votos point only to a stock in trade. In the almost total absence of cash, an intricate process of goods changing hands can be assumed. Abeitia may well have had weavers and needleworkers in his employ who made shop goods for him. Goods might also have been given by devotees to the chapel, or left there on consignment as was noted in the 1818 inventory, or traded for other goods. When it is recalled that the chapel itself then possessed, besides the large crucifix, thirty-eight large bultos "not counting small ones," and seven under glass, the Nacimiento group with the Christ Child of ivory, eight bultos in the oratorio, the additional fifteen bultos and eleven retablos in the "assets" list must undoubtedly have been for sale. What could have been a more desirable thing to bring home from El Santuario, besides the miraculous earth, than a santo? The altar screen "made by a devotee" also is notable. Was it one of those eventually placed in the chapel by a donor? This could hardly have been in the storerooms which formerly had small doors and windows, but a half-sized, or portable, painted retable, more easily carried by wagon, could have been put into them.

The "assets" of the chapel, as apart from the ornaments of the chapel proper, present a fascinating glimpse of the textile industry in and about Chimayo in the first quarter of the 19th century. The few items such as

---

[12] AASF, Accounts, LXIV, Book 1, 1826.

the lace, brocade, rebozo and cotton yardages were the only fabrics that would have been imported. The majority, embroideries, blankets, carpeting by the yard, woolen cloth and stockings, were all products of home industry. After about 1822 cotton yard goods mentioned on inventories may have arrived from the Chihuahua Fairs or over the Santa Fe Trail. Before then they are increasingly scarce in the 18th century when cotton is hardly spoken of except in the form of cords, or kerchiefs.

The mystery of the original purpose of these little rooms, built onto the chapel from its beginning, and the entrance into it between the rooms, is clearly explained by these inventories. Goods, and particularly local weaving, were to provide for the maintenance of el Santuario. By the 20th century all this was forgotten, and the little rooms were dark and leaky with only bits of lumber and candle ends in them. In 1957 a new roof was put on the *tiendas,* modern, plain floors, doors and windows were installed, and they are used as a religious shop by church officials. Thus, after more than a century, Abeitia's original provision for the support of his chapel is once more active. One cannot refrain from wishing, however, that the wares on sale were hand-embroidered hangings, homespun blankets and hand-carved santos rather than the stereotyped, pinchbeck religious goods found everywhere today.

Figure 59: Architect John Gaw Meem designed Cristo Rey church and its clerestory window for the stone retable from la Castrense. (Photograph by Tyler Dingee)

GRAPHIC ARTS
An Influence on New Mexico Imagemakers

The first printed books in New Spain were brought from Spain or Flanders. Even after printing plants had been set up in the New World, title pages and other illustrated sheets were sent from Spain to be bound into Mexican printed books.

At first Spanish policy encouraged the teaching of useful arts and trades among the skilled Indian populations as part of their program of conversion and civilization. But as shiploads of European artists and craftsmen, attracted by the new Golconda, landed in "the Indies" it was found that competition with the Indians was far too active. Complaints to authority brought new laws forbidding Indians to make holy images, to work with precious metals, or in other arts which would compete with Europeans. Natives were accepted as apprentices and assistants to what were in effect guild members, with degrees of restrictions depending on their status as pure or mixed breeds. In this way many of them learned their masters' trade perfectly.

Another matter of concern to Spanish authorities was the Indian passion for gambling. The Spanish were no less fond of playing for recklessly high stakes. With the dual objectives of protecting Indian morals and the economic stability of New Spain it was decreed that no playing cards might be imported into the colony. Bootleg cards were promptly made; by 1553 over 9,000 dozens of packs of cards had been stamped from woodblocks cut by several colonial printers. The first graphic efforts in colonial Mexico were for games of chance rather than religious or scholarly purposes.

In the second half of the 16th century Mexican printing presses turned out religious works, Greek and Latin classics, Spanish and Indian grammars, accounts of exploration and native peoples, narrative poems, and so on. These had ornamental title pages of coats of arms, views of towns and buildings, or portraits, and were garnished with Renaissance motifs such as caryatids, pediments, fauns, and cornucopias. Much of the printing and engraving as well as painting and sculpture done in Spain was by Flemish artists; after the Spanish had seized Mexico many of them sailed to the New World. It is natural that their style is still to be seen in the earlier colonial schools of Mexico and Peru.

One of the Flemish emigrants was Samuel Stradanus, an engraver from Antwerp, who landed in New Spain in 1600. At some time between 1613 and 1622 he was commissioned by the Archbishop of Mexico to make a large copperplate of the Virgin of Guadalupe. The prints were indulgences to those who bought them, and the proceeds were to help pay for the new and larger church of the Guadalupe then under construction and dedicated in 1622. The Flemish treatment of the Guadalupe suggests a buxom Antwerp housewife more than the slender figure of the original painting. While this is by no means the earliest copperplate made in Mexico it is the oldest engraving of the Virgin of Guadalupe that is known at present.

When Peter Paul Rubens opened his studio in Flanders in 1605, after a prolonged visit to Italy, he employed a swarm of apprentices to execute the many portraits, murals, ceilings, and out-of-door theatrical sets required for royal processions for which he was constantly commissioned. Working from his sketches and under his supervision the workshop completed these often massive paintings. Rubens had studied the Renaissance masters and also the newly fashionable baroque, and was to be a culminator of the style. He was flooded with commissions from crowned heads of Europe, cardinals, princes, dukes, abbots and churches. At the same time he managed to turn out small paintings intended for the engraver. One of these is the *Allegory in Honor of the Franciscan Order* which was also entitled *Headpiece to a Thesis* in 19th century catalogs of prints after Rubens.* The painting is of the Virgin of the Immaculate Conception, and in addition to angels, chariots drawn by eagles, lions and other symbolic figures, shows the late Philip II, presumably at his heavenly rest, King Philip III, and a cardinal and armed nobleman, probably the royal cardinal and the Duke of Lerma, with groups of Franciscans. Painted in more finicky details for the engraver's purpose than was usual for Rubens, the plate was engraved by Pontius. The only difference in the print is the usual one: the figures are reversed from left to right.

With the exception of the absence of the Holy Child of Prague in the Rubens original, the central figures of the Virgin and St. Francis in the miraculous image of Our Lady of Pueblito, patroness of the city of Queretaro in Mexico, were obviously carved after Ruben's painting of the *Allegory in Honor of the Franciscan Order,* but most probably after the Pontius print rather than the original canvas. The Pueblito figure was made by Fray Sebastian Gallegos in 1632; it was fifty-five centimeters high and painted and gilded. It was then entitled Our Lady of the Immaculate Conception. She stood upon clouds supported by the kneeling St. Francis who held up three globes, symbols of the three orders founded by him. At the side was a small Santo Niño de Praga. The statue group was placed in a little chapel at El Pueblito, two leagues

---

* Illustrated in "Rubens' Sketching in Paint," Michael Jaffe, in *Art News,* V. 52/3, 1953.

from Queretaro. Soon the Lady's influence won many heathen conversions and intercessions on behalf of the faithful. In a few decades a large church and convent were built there in her honor to accommodate the pilgrim crowds. Numerous *estampas* or prints were struck in the form of indulgences or souvenirs for pilgrims to carry home; everyone could afford a print.

Four such plates of the Virgin of Pueblito are listed as made in the 18th century: José Mariano Navarro, 1769 (retouched and issued again, 1798); Manuel de Villavicencio, 1771 (another, n.d); and two more dated 1809 and 1814.* In the collections of the Museum of New Mexico is a print from a copperplate of El Pueblito dated 1776 and not listed in Romero de Terreros. It is unsigned, but the delicacy of line, hachure, and details of crenellated fortresses and cherubs suggest the work of one of the more accomplished 18th century printmakers of New Spain. In this print the Virgin wears a wide court gown studded with pearls and rosettes, and floats above St. Francis with his three globes. A small Santo Niño de Praga is at one side and a well-drawn cartouche containing the title and inscription is at the other.

Prints, inexpensive and easily carried, came to New Mexico in numbers, but for lack of glazing many were pasted on boards, overpainted, varnished, and otherwise defaced so that relatively few have survived. However, they have supplied the identity, source, and relative date for many New Mexican santos which, peculiarly aberrant or lacking inscriptions, had previously been puzzling as to subject matter. The prints of the Virgin of Pueblito, for example, clarify the panels by the "A.J." santero of the same subject, one of which is dated 1822 (Sec. III-C). Clearly the New Mexican santero had one of the prints for his model, possibly the one now in the Museum of New Mexico. The Virgin seems to be draped in a sarape, the heavenly castles have vanished with the cartouche, but the artist used some of the inscription from the print in a meandering streamer around the top of the panel.

Another retablo, by Pedro Fresquís, the "Calligraphic Santero" (Sec. III-a), had been a puzzle as to its subject for some years when a copperplate by Montes de Oca was presented to the collections. Prints struck from this plate plainly identified Fresquís' retablo as an image of Santa Coleta, a somewhat obscure 15th century saint who had helped to organize the Third Order of St. Francis in France, but whose canonization had only taken place in 1807 — precisely at a time when the engraver Montes de Oca and Pedro Fresquís were both active. Another print from Mexico used as a model by the same santero was one of the Flight Into Egypt.

A source of material for frontier santeros which was printed in Antwerp at the Plantin Press was the missal sent to colonial missions and churches. The Plantin Press enjoyed a virtual monopoly, or franchise, for the printing of missals, Bibles and breviaries to be used in all Hispanic

---

* Romero de Terreros, Manuel, 1948.

countries during some three hundred years. This franchise was periodically renewed by the ruling Pope and King of Spain, the complete wording of both current and previous licenses being published at the front of such missals. In a bound volume containing the Roman Missal, the Hispanic Missal and the Missal for the Three Orders of the Friars Minor of St. Francis, dated 1724 and 1725, which was formerly in a New Mexican church, the illustrations scattered among its pages were quite evidently consulted by local santeros as points of departure for their own works.[1]

While no printing was done in colonial New Mexico, the influence of imported graphic work was great and should not be overlooked. In the 19th century, illustrated books, novenas, and broadsides came from republican Mexico and had a rejuvenating effect on the work of the later santeros. The flood of commercial prints and mission cards which was loosed on New Mexicans after Bishop Lamy's arrival unfortunately had the opposite effect and hastened the decline of the santero school, as much by meretricious example as by replacing creative work altogether.

---

[1] Kelemen, Pál, *Baroque and Rococo in Latin America,* New York, 1951. pp. 114 & 213. Pls. 58-d, 190-g, 139-e, 191-i. Also E. Boyd, "A Roman Missal," *El Palacio,* V. 64, No. 7, July 1957, p. 233.

Figure 60: "Allegory in Honor of the Franciscan Order," by Peter Paul Rubens. (Courtesy of the John G. Johnson Collection, Philadelphia)

Figure 61: "True Portrait of the Miraculous Image of Our Lady of the Pueblito who is venerated in her sanctuary outside of the walls of the City of Queretaro, the Year of 1776." Copperplate engraving. (Photograph by Ernest Knee)

V R. de la Mila
rosa. Imagen de
Nuestra Seño
ra, de el PUEB
LITO, que se
Venera en su Santu
ario extramuros de la
Ciudad de Queretaro.
Año de 1776.

Figure 62: Statue of Our Lady of el Pueblito as it appears today, the patroness of Queretaro. (Courtesy of Ross Parmenter)

Figure 63: Our Lady of el Pueblito, retablo by the anonymous santero A.J., dated works 1822, New Mexico.

Figure 64: Folk painting of Our Lady of el Pueblito signed and dated "Cervantes, March 1874," oil on canvas. Courtesy of the First National Bank of Santa Fe.

I-C

Nra. Sra. del Pueblito de Querétaro.

Figure 65: Brussels tapestry, 16th century; the Trinity shown as three identical persons appears seven times. Colonial American Catholics repeated this iconography into the 20th century. (M. H. De Young Memorial Museum. Gift of William Randolph Hearst Foundation)

Figure 66: The Most Holy Trinity by Pedro Antonio Fresquís, New Mexico, 1749–1831. (Courtesy of the Taylor Museum)

Figure 67: St. Anthony of Padua, Mexican print.

Figure 68: San Antonio de Padua, anonymous santero "A. J." 1822.

87

MISSÆ PROPRIÆ
SANCTORUM
HISPANORUM,
QUI GENERALITER
IN HISPANIA CELEBRANTUR,
Ex Apostolica Concessione , & Auctoritate
PII V. GREGORII XIII. SIXTI V.
CLEMENTIS VIII. & URBANI VIII.
Summorum Pontificum.

ANTVERPIÆ,
EX TYPOGRAPHIA PLANTINIANA.
M. D. C C. XXV.

Figure 69: Missal title page for Masses celebrated in Spanish empire, Plantin Press, Antwerp, 1725. Santiago, patron of Spain.

Figure 70: Santiago, by Pedro Antonio Fresquís, New Mexico.

MISSÆ PROPRIÆ
SANCTORUM
TRIUM ORDINUM
FRATRUM MINORUM
S. P. N.
FRANCISCI,

Ad formam MISSALIS ROMANI redactæ, & exactius examinatæ conformiter Breviario, à SS. D. N. INNOCENTIO PAPA XII. approbatæ, novoque Kalendario, & Rubricis locupletatæ.

ANTVERPIÆ,
EX TYPOGRAPHIA PLANTINIANA
M. DCCXXIV.

Figure 71: Missal title page for Masses of three orders of St. Francis, Plantin Press, Antwerp, 1724. St. Francis receiving the stigmata.

Figure 72: St. Francis receiving the stigmata, Pedro Antonio Fresquís. (Museum of New Mexico photograph)

I-C

Figure 73: The Archangel Michael, Cristobal de Villalpando, 1645–1719. (Courtesy of the Wadsworth Atheneum)

I-C

Figure 74: The Archangel Michael, Bernardo Miera y Pacheco, San Miguel chapel, Santa Fe. (Photograph courtesy of F. duPont Cornelius)

Figure 75: Woodcut, Archangel Michael, Mexico.

Figure 76: The Archangel Michael by an amateur, over the painting by Miera y Pacheco (Fig. 74), *ca.* 1869. Both Figures 75 and 76 were after a painting by Raphael Sanzio. (Photograph courtesy of F. duPont Cornelius)

Figure 77: Woodcut by Zuñiga, Santa Barbara.

Figure 78: Santa Barbara, Bernardo Miera y Pacheco.

Figure 79: Crucifix with urns, woodcut, Mexico.

Figure 80: Crucifix with urns, Pedro Antonio Fresquís, New Mexico. (Fred Harvey Foundation Collections)

Figure 81: Crucifix with mourning figures, woodcut, Mexico.

Figure 82: Crucifix with mourning figures, Jose Aragon, w.d. 1820–35, New Mexico.

18th CENTURY PAINTING AND SCULPTURE IN NEW MEXICO

A few panels painted in oils over gesso on wood identified as Rio Grande pine reflect late 18th century Mexican rococo by intention if not always in performance. Some have rather muddy color and vigorous treatment, others are more conventionally insipid with rosy pink coloring. Formerly classed as "mission supply" pictures from Mexico they are now recognized as the earliest works of artistically inclined colonists that we know of, with the exceptions of the Castrense stone carvings and fragments painted on adobe walls that have survived into the present. The panels of northern New Mexico pine, the lack of professional skill, and clues provided by contemporary documents have confirmed the regional origins and also the names of most of this group beyond a doubt.

It was formerly assumed that only the Franciscans of the 18th century could have painted or carved ornaments for their missions, but they were not alone in their creative efforts. Even the missionaries had little time, talent, or inclination for the arts. A friar who did was remarked upon, not always favorably, in the reports of Visitors from Provincial Headquarters. The man most cited in this connection was Fray Andres Garcia, born in La Puebla de los Angeles, Mexico. He was stationed in New Mexican missions, including Santa Fe, Santa Cruz and Albuquerque as well as the pueblos, for thirty-two years after his arrival in 1747. At some he spent a few weeks and at others several years. Fray Garcia is recorded as having built new adobe structures and additions, and to have carved pulpits, altar rails and screens, and religious images.

One of his statues of Our Lady of the Rosary was described by Father Dominguez as having very red cheeks. Fondness for rosy color is still visible in the painted gesso of the nearly life-sized figure of Christ in the Sepulchre (a wooden chasse without glass panels) which Fray Garcia made for his church of Santa Cruz. As yet unretouched it still occupies the wall alcove in the nave where it was originally installed. The equally large and similarly constructed figures of Christ in the Sepulchre and Our Lady of Sorrows, which he made for the now-ruined mission of San Geronimo at Taos Pueblo, somehow survived its burning, probably because they had been removed to safety prior to the rebellion of 1847.

Figure 83: The Holy Family, miniature group by Fray Andrés Garcia.

Figure 84: The Nativity by Fray Andrés Garcia, in painted shrine.

These are now in the new pueblo church of the same name, but over-painted with modern oils. An image of hollow-frame construction of Our Lady of Solitude, formerly in the Santa Fe *parroquia,* may also be said to be the work of Fray Garcia. It combines professional Mexican techniques such as jointed arms, the hollow frame, and concentration of attention on face and hands, all common to the *imagen a vestir,* or statue to be clothed with fabric garments. It also strives for the highly enamelled *encarnación* facial tints of Mexican statues which Fray Garcia seems to have been unable to achieve with his rather matte surfaced pigments.

Fray Garcia was probably responsible for a series of small bultos of somewhat rococo feeling, with gesso-dipped cloth draperies and hectic red cheeks. All of the series are painted in tempera.

Apparently Fray Garcia painted suitable pictures on wood panels at the request of his well-to-do parishioners, either as devotional gifts to his churches or for their private family chapels in which he celebrated Mass from time to time as a normal part of his duties. While the panels assumed to be his are undated, the tree-ring analysis of a group of these at the Taylor Museum (none of which gave a bark date) indicates that he either reused old wood or wood cut within the period 1747–77, according to the estimated loss of outer rings (Appendix I-G). On the basis of coincidence of his years of New Mexico service with the dating of panels, as well as his rather sweetly conservative style, these pictures are assigned to his hand. One lettered "Sr. SAN JOSEPH, A Dⁿ DE D. DIEGO PENA" looks as if the neat block letters had been laid out with tracing paper, or at least with a ruler.

Franciscans however were not the only possible authors of semi-academic art in 18th century New Mexico. A few wooden figures and pictures, now widely scattered, have in common ambitious compositions, theatrical poses, a quality of human naturalism, athletic muscularity and realistic details which suggest that they were the work of a layman rather than of a priest. This layman is easily identified in the archives of New Mexico as Captain Bernardo de Miera y Pacheco. Born near Burgos, Spain, he spent twelve years in El Paso before moving with his family to Santa Fe about 1754. A professional soldier, the captain's claim to historical recognition heretofore has been his ability to make maps, including a knowledge of latitude and longitude. While these appear quaintly inaccurate today they are invaluable for their crowded local landmarks and place names, many of which have since been forgotten or shifted to other locations. Other and earlier maps of our Southwest were made in Europe by persons using second- or third-hand information on the topography, but Miera y Pacheco covered the ground himself. As a cartographer he was employed by Governor de Anza to map the attempted overland route to California with Father Velez de Escalante, as well as the overall area of colonial New Mexico. The historian, Father Chavez, has called him "a Jack of all trades." Miera y Pacheco served as war captain and alcalde at several pueblos, had a ranch from which he sold livestock and grain, and made carved statues which he sold to Indians for their churches. One of San Felipe still remains in the church

Figure 85: *El Santo Entierro;* Corpus and sepulchre by Fray Andrés Garcia, in church of Santa Cruz.

I-D

Figure 86: The Archangel Michael by Bernardo Miera y Pacheco.

Figure 87: The Archangel Gabriel by Bernardo Miera y Pacheco. (Figures 86 and 87 from the old Zuni mission, courtesy of the Museum of History and Technology, Smithsonian Institution)

I-D

and pueblo of that name, now overlaid with new oil paints; according to Dominguez it was "ugly."

A polychromed figure of St. Joseph has survived in remarkably good condition. It is carved from one log of pine, including the triangular base. The robes are painted in simulated brocade pattern with gold and silver. The medium is oil over gesso and more expertly planned than the carving which, in order to fit into the dimensions of the wood, some-what flattened the uptilted heads of St. Joseph and the Christ Child. Stylistically however there is more of Spanish monumentality in this piece than of Mexican rococo feeling; the captain must have recalled the merging of Renaissance with Baroque which belatedly occurred in Spain and which he had ample occasion to see in his youth.

A nearly identical statue of San José, but about 90 centimeters in height, including its carved base, is still beside the high altar in San José de Gracia at las Trampas, New Mexico. The animated motion of the figure and the peculiarly flattened heads of St. Joseph and the Child are as like the larger bulto as possible. Surface painting of drapery is less elaborate but largely original. This image is at present swathed in fabric garments. It was most probably the original image of San José the patron mentioned by Dominguez as placed in the wooden niche covered with talco above the main altar at las Trampas in 1776.

Two carvings of archangels collected from the ruined Zuñi mission by Stevenson and Cushing in 1880 are now among the Smithsonian collections.[1] In spite of the loss of much paint and gesso from exposure to weather these are closely related to other works of Miera y Pacheco by their rugged physical characteristics, broad earthy faces, and attention to costume detail. While the figures and bases of these were also cut from one block, the forearms, wings and attributes were added separately and as a result have been partly lost. The remaining wings of St. Gabriel resemble others carved by Philadelphia's William Rush a few decades later in their attention to ornithological structure and the limitations of working in the medium of wood. St. Gabriel here resembles a robust village boy rather than a supernatural spirit, while St. Michael, the patron saint of the military, suggests that a contemporary of Miera y Pacheco's actually posed for the shrewd, somewhat cocky face — perhaps a young *alférez,* or lieutenant, in the Captain's company of militia. The unclut-tered rendering of the ubiquitous Baroque tunic and cuirass, greaves and plumed helmet show that Miera y Pacheco was familiar with these artistic conventions and not, like the later 19th century santeros, confused by their strangeness of shape and materials.

Carved pilasters with cherub heads and a small relief plaque of the Sacred Heart beneath a crown are survivals of the Zuñi mission orna-ments now owned by the Brooklyn Museum and the Smithsonian. They were undoubtedly also carved by Miera y Pacheco at the same time he made the two angels. Father Velez de Escalante redecorated the Zuñi

---

[1] One was unfortunately damaged by fire in 1965.

mission during his service there and from acquaintance with Miera y Pacheco's skills, as cartographer and saintmaker, may have had him do a set of altar figures and ornaments. One wonders what became of the others. The lettered shield of the Zuñi St. Michael is one of the clues which connects the existing works of the captain by its motto: "QVIS VT DEVS." This is a nonscholarly rendering of the Latin phrase often associated with images of St. Michael: "Quae est ut deus," literally "Who is as God," in reference to his role as the heavenly messenger to earth. Aside from the poor Latin the shield also indicates acquaintance with a classical but non-Spanish form of shield. It is oval, neither the *rodela,* or round shield, nor the *adarga,* a nearly heart-shaped form, both used by Spanish soldiers over centuries, including Miera y Pacheco's period.

Paintings attributed to the captain have several features in common, including oddly lettered inscriptions, usually muddy coloring, and robust subjects. One which he must have done soon after he came to Santa Fe is the large picture of St. Michael which now hangs on the altar screen in the chapel of San Miguel in Santa Fe. It is remarkable in that it is painted in oils on good quality linen canvas instead of on a wooden panel or on the loosely woven burlap of *ixtle* (maguey fibre cloth), on which many of the mission supply canvases from Mexico were painted. The archangel stands, with one brawny leg foreshortened, upon a sinister though amorphous-looking dragon, flourishing a sword and bearing an oval shield, this time lettered "QVIEN COMO DIOS" — a somewhat colloquial Spanish form of the Latin motto. The angel wears a well-drawn cuirass, jeweled tunic, cloak and plumed cap. The wings are impractically small to waft such a stalwart figure aloft, but are painted with the structure of live bird wings and plumage. Amateurish as the painting is, it is easily traced to its Mexican prototype, a picture of St. Michael by Cristobal Villalpando (1648–1714), now in the Wadsworth Atheneum, Hartford, Connecticut ("Art in Colonial Mexico," a catalogue, John Herron Art Institute, 1951, No. 21).

The Miera y Pacheco canvas has this inscription on a lower corner:

ADEBOCIOИ
DEL TEИIEИTE Ð EL
PRESIDIO Ð SAИTAFEE
Dⁿ MAИVEL SAИZ Ð GAR
VISO

("By the Devotion of the Commandant of the Presidio of Santa Fe, Don Manuel Saenz De Garvisu")

Reversal of the letter N was common in 18th century block letters, as was the placing of a horizontal line across the letter D when DE was meant, but the general spacing of letters and aberrant spelling are those of a man with little clerkly practice, even though he could read and write, or carve and paint.

The picture has had a checkered history. It was probably done on commission from the donor who was commander of the Palace garrison or presidio in the 1740s, officially and socially prominent. A native of Spain, Saenz de Garvisu had married the granddaughter of a pre-1680 settler of Santa Fe in 1743. The land on which his house stood, east of the Palace of the Governors, is now occupied by four homes of 19th century families, the former county courthouse (now a medical office building), a gas station, various shops, patios, and orchards. The two Spaniards, both military men and members of the Confraternity of San Miguel, must have made this gift to the chapel of San Miguel prior to 1760 when the Governor, Marín del Valle, built the new military chapel, or Castrense, on the Plaza and dedicated it to a new patron, Our Lady of Light. In view of Miera y Pacheco's arrival in 1754, it is reasonable to limit the date of the painting between that year and 1759 when San Miguel chapel was no longer fashionable and was let stand in neglect, according to the description by Dominguez in 1776.

Dominguez in his meticulous but disapproving way listed eight paintings in San Miguel chapel. During extensive restorations of the 18th century interior of the chapel in 1955, six paintings on canvas were accounted for in spite of the fact that three of them had been overpainted by a later amateur. There was a large rectangular canvas, apparently an attempt to copy a well known picture of the Archangel St. Michael by Raphael Sanzio, but through the medium of a lithograph, by an amateur using household enamel paints, and in the color scheme of a Neapolitan wine garden. In the annals of the Christian Brothers, whose order has had the custody of the chapel for over a century, it is noted that one of their number had painted the overlayer in 1869 in thanksgiving for his improved health, and had then left the order. Whether he took to sign painting later is not known.

When this picture was taken down in 1955 it was seen that it was done on good handwoven linen canvas of 18th century type. It was promptly shipped to F. DuPont Cornelius, an experienced fine arts conservator, formerly with the Metropolitan Museum's conservation laboratory and now with the Cincinnati, Ohio, Art Museum. After making several small tests on different parts of the canvas he reported that there was another painting beneath. It seems that good quality painting canvas was as scarce and precious in New Mexico in 1869 as it was a century earlier.

After long and patient labor Mr. Cornelius succeeded in removing all the overpainting, thereby revealing Miera y Pacheco's St. Michael and its inscription. The canvas had been cut down, probably at the time of its reframing in 1869, and the superfluous weigh scales had been added prior to that date. A silent witness to human vanity was exposed by Mr. Cornelius, who found that an opaque layer of resinous substance covering the inscription at the bottom of the canvas was laid on before it had been completely repainted. All the pictures had hung on the adobe walls of the sanctuary until 1798 when a new hand-hewn and painted altar screen was presented by Don Antonio José Ortiz, whose name as donor was painted in the two cartouches on the screen (p. 61 & Fig. 44-45).

Figure 88: St. Joseph and the
Christ Child, Bernardo Miera y
Pacheco.

I-D

Although this was designed as a setting for the pictures on canvas one suspects that the name of the earlier donor was discreetly painted out at this time. This would account for the fact that the inscription is in better condition than other parts of the canvas, since it was sealed away from dust and light for 158 years before being cleaned — and only 40 years after being painted — while the rest of the canvas was exposed to damage from dust, light and water for 111 years before it was repainted in 1869.

At Nambe mission in 1776 Dominguez listed ornaments as follows: the high altar, two paintings on canvas of San Francisco and Our Lady of Guadalupe, hanging on the painted wall. Two crucifixes, three prints on little boards and two dozen "ugly old candleholders of rough wood which Father Toledo provided" made up the remainder of the ornaments (Dominguez, p. 53). A later inventory made by Fray Diego Martinez de Arellano,[2] January 1, 1805, shows additions.

"On the high altar there is a retable of wood with the images painted directly on the boards. In the middle tier hangs a picture of our father San Francisco as patron of this pueblo. In the same is a niche which was made for the tabernacle in which is placed Our Lady in Her advocation of la Purisma. At the sides of said altar are two others of boards, one with the image of Our Lady of Carmen and the other with the image of San Antonio." Lacking the Boswellian passion for detailed minutiae that makes Dominguez such interesting reading today, Fray Martinez failed to name the images painted on the wooden retables. The canvas of San Francisco was probably the same "King's gift" from New Spain as that noted by Dominguez with its painted wooden frame. From the item of clothing and little jewels of Our Lady of the Conception, following, we learn that this image was in the round. Her adornments included "a new crown of silver renovated by my solicitude, earrings of fine pearls, a necklace of fine pearls and little, twisted papers . . ."

Another *Ynbentario Formal de la Yglesia de San Francisco de Nambe* (Formal inventory of the church of St. Francis of Nambe) was made September 6, 1850, by the parish priest, Juan de Jesus Trujillo.[3]

Father Trujillo listed a wooden altar screen as tall as the sanctuary behind the altar table with six painted images and three bultos. On each side of the chancel were small retables, each with two painted images.[4]

Of the many adobe churches that have stood in Nambe Pueblo the one referred to by Dominguez and in the two later quoted inventories was built by Governor Juan Domingo Bustamante in, or by, 1725. Due as much to age as to the stresses of a modern gabled roof that had been put on it, the walls caved in early in this century. About 1915 the historical interests and enterprise of the late painter Gerald Cassidy and his wife

---

[2] Martinez, a Franciscan, served in New Mexico from 1791–1827 and was at Nambe in 1799–1802, 1804, 1805, 1808.

[3] Secular serving in New Mexico 1837–69.

[4] Book of Nambe Mission Inventory, New Mexico State Records Center.

Figure 89: Virgin of the Immaculate Conception, panel from lost altar screen, Nambe mission, by Bernardo Miera y Pacheco.

I-D

Ina Sizer Cassidy led them to salvage part of the mission ornaments with the permission of the Pueblo Indians. Together with carved corbels, beams and the choirloft beam dated 1725, they rescued four altar screen panels in various states of preservation. These were installed in their home in Santa Fe, cut down to fit the interior measurements of a hallway and door. One of these panels represents La Purisima and although unsigned as usual, is unmistakably in the manner of Miera y Pacheco, although coarser in brushwork than are his other extant paintings. The rough strokes were partly due to the uneven surface of the boards on which he painted, prepared as they were with only ax and adz. The cloth strips laid over chinks between the boards and the uneven gesso over-layer provided a far more textured ground than a sized canvas or well primed small wood panel. Miera's age may also have hampered his brush, as he died in 1785. The panel had to have been done between 1776 and 1785, which gives an inkling as to the probable date of installation of the whole high altar screen and its other panels.

If Miera y Pacheco was past his artistic prime his fondness for broad, pasty faces, heavy draperies and bravura accents is easily identifiable.

Other panels attributed to Miera y Pacheco were painted in oils over gessoed wood. All share his personal style and characteristics. One of Santa Barbara, a patroness of the military then and now, is identifiable as a reversed and colored enlargement of a wood block by Andrés de Zuñiga y Silva of Puebla, Mexico, dated 1725. Zuñiga managed in nearly all his prints to introduce some masonry structure; the tower in Miera y Pacheco's painting echoes Zuñiga's interest in masonry per se.

Three retablos are inscribed and dated, respectively:

(1) "A Debo
zion de Se
ñora Rosa
lia Baldez.
Año de
1754"

(2) "A Debozion de
el Capitan Don
Salbador Gar
cia de Noriega
Año
de 1783"

(3) "Sⁿ Raphael
Medezina de Dios
Ruego por nosotros
amen.
A devocion de Do
ña Polonia de Sando
bal.
Ano de 1780"

All three are written in script, and in spite of more than ample space the placement of the words is crowded together and obviously unplanned.

The first two, of St. Anthony and St. Joseph, are in the collections of the Taylor Museum. That of St. Joseph has the inscription on a painted pedestal (Reproduced in *Magazine of Art,* Vol. 33, No. 3, 1940). The retablo of St. Raphael bears its inscription on a shield in the lower left corner (Reproduced in *The Concise Encyclopedia of American Antiques,* Hawthorn Books, New York, 1958, V. II, Pl. 343-B). The archangel, like the Zuñi statues and the St. Michael painted on canvas, suggests that a live and not particularly ascetic-appearing youth posed for the anatomical details of the central figure, while the wings, although bent to fit into the picture, show knowledge of the feathers of real birds. The jagged, barren mountains in the background, and an unmistakable catfish held by St. Raphael, seem to be naturalistic reminiscences of the years when Miera y Pacheco lived in El Paso del Norte. Two of the donors named in these panels were prominent in their time. Salvador Garcia de Noriega lived north of Santa Fe and was a captain of the militia, alcalde, rancher, and contractor of church building, in which latter role Father Dominguez made certain caustic comments of him. He took Apolonia Sandoval, a widow, as his second wife in 1767. Perhaps when she commissioned the painting of St. Raphael the Physician of God in 1780, one or both of them were invalids.

If the vigorous and sketchy brushwork and solidly three-dimensional carvings of Miera y Pacheco are easily isolated from other contemporary artistic efforts of New Mexicans, it is the semiliterate script of these panels which actually ties together the work and the name. A comparison of his handwriting on the map of New Mexico which he made in 1779 and facsimiles of his signature with these inscriptions leaves no doubt that the same hand executed maps, carvings and paintings. Through the handwriting the earlier attribution is confirmed on the basis of stylistic factors, while the group of type carvings and paintings with common characteristics of reference to visual experience, robust expression and typical religious imagery is explained as the work of an uninhibited layman.

Some years ago I noticed that there was no evidence of the making of oil pigments in New Mexico (E. Boyd, 1946, p. 30) nor has any such reference appeared to my notice as yet. However, since at least three men seem to have employed oil paints in northern New Mexico — Miera y Pacheco, Fray Andrés Garcia, and another, anonymous, of the same period — it must be inferred that they received shipments of oil colors from time to time from the south. Garcia spent thirty years in the colony, Miera y Pacheco at least thirty-one; they would hardly have brought along enough art supplies upon their arrival to last for such a long time. Fray Garcia used tempera over gesso in some of his figures, such as the Christ in the Sepulchre at Santa Cruz, possibly for lack of oil paints at the moment. It is therefore apparent that oil painting was no more a part of New Mexico's artistic tradition than was the stone carving of la Castrense. On the other hand, the after-effect of the Castrense altarpiece and the images of Spanish-born Miera y Pacheco and Puebla-born Fray Garcia may be said to have stimulated the indigenous santero school of New

Mexico, which in the next two generations turned out the finest altar screens, panels and figures of its production cycle.

The only possible follower, perhaps an apprentice or relative of Miera y Pacheco, is nameless for lack of any sort of lettered inscription on his panels, or documentary notice. The title "18th Century Novice Painter" was chosen by W. S. Stallings, Jr., some years ago and is appropriately descriptive. This santero's work is totally devoid of any knowledge of painting, of the techniques of applying pigments, or of the use of brushes or paint thinners; certainly the novice knew nothing of drawing and composition and was furthermore unable to pick up any understanding of it. Basically his method was that of the academic artists of New Spain in the late 18th century; a bolus ground, or all-over layer of thick, dark reddish-brown paint was placed over the entire picture surface, over which lighter areas of color were built up. Where shadows or dark masses were wanted the priming coat was left exposed. The workshops of Mexico turned out sets of such pictures speedily and easily for little money, some of which found their way to New Mexico missions, but the novice seems not to have been exposed to such training. While he evidently used Miera y Pacheco's work as his model, when his efforts are placed beside the captain's paintings they make the latter's seem the work of an Old Master. Some of the same subjects, destitute of anatomy or life, are blobbed in with even muddier pigments. A few of the novice's panels are gayer, with some definition of form. His inclusion of drapery folds running in impossible directions and floral borders on some panels indicate at least a recognition of outer world conventions.

Although none of his thirteen panels tested for tree-ring dating gave an outside or bark date, the mean average based on heartwood-sapwood relation was given as 1776 plus 10 (W. S. Stallings). Out of twenty-four panels of this style examined by me, five were of St. Anthony of Padua, five of Our Lady, two of Christ, two of Santiago and one each of Sts. Acacius, Ann, Barbara, Joseph, Raphael, Rita and the Holy Family. The subjects of the other three were not identified. Stallings has summed up the novice series very well:

"Its stylistic influence on succeeding styles was not appreciable."[5]

After the novice other santeros, with the exception of the much later José de Gracia Gonzales, used tempera entirely until the arrival of wagon and house paints in general stores after 1880.

---

[5] Stallings, W. S., unpublished manuscript on santos in possession of the Taylor Museum, Colorado Springs. See Appendix I-G.

Figure 91: Our Lady of St. John of the Lakes, Eighteenth Century Novice Painter.

Figure 90: Santa Rosa de Lima by the Eighteenth Century Novice Painter. (Courtesy of the Taylor Museum)

APPENDIX
Miera y Pacheco

Whatever may have been the basis of Father Dominguez' dislike for Miera y Pacheco, he has at least left a trail of clues throughout his 1776 report which helps us to know what the Spanish captain made and where his images were placed. Even when he is not named, the rumbles of scorn and disapproval which emanate from Dominguez are unmistakably directed toward effigies made by the "Citizen." Dominguez spoke of him by name, at San Felipe, as follows:

> The Gossipy vulgar herd have always considered St. Philip the Apostle as the titular patron of this mission and have celebrated his feast as such on this day. A European citizen of this kingdom, called Don Bernardo Miera y Pacheco, supported this opinion by selling to the Indians of this pueblo (at a high price in proportion to those of this land) an image of the said Holy Apostle, a large carved statue in the round, which he made himself. And although it is not at all prepossessing, it serves the purpose and stands on the high altar at this mission (Dominguez, p. 160).

At Santo Domingo Pueblo Dominguez says that in the nave, over an altar was:

> . . . a large oil painting on canvas in a wooden frame of Our Lady of the Conception. This was painted at the said father's expense by an incompetent craftsman, but it serves for devotional purposes. . . There is an image of Our Father St. Dominic on the left-hand altar, all carved in wood and a vara high. The natives of the pueblo bought it. It is a product of this kingdom and by the same hand that painted the above-mentioned Immaculate Conception. And my statement about the said painting will indicate that this work is not very fine. (Dominguez, p. 133).

At Acoma there was, over the high altar:

> . . . an ordinary painted wooden niche to hold a completely carved St. Stephen of rather medium size. The Indians bought this statue, or image, along with the niche (Dominguez, p. 191).

Fray Dominguez would note that other images, even when unfavorably described, were King's gifts or those of a Father or private citizen; that this citizen sold them seemed intolerable to him. He was less critical of the Zuñi altar piece in the mission at Halona, which included four carved objects collected by Stevenson and Cushing in 1880 from the ruins of the mission and now in the collections of the Smithsonian Institution. The principal carvings are of two archangels described by Dominguez as Gabriel and Michael, and similarly described in the Smithsonian catalog. It is a matter of record that the image of St. Gabriel seldom

Figure 93: *San Rafael Arcangel,* by Bernardo Miera y Pacheco, dated 1780.

appeared in New Mexico except in a canvas of the Annunciation, and was still less depicted by the popular saintmakers of the 19th century. Instead the popular archangels were Michael and Raphael. In the case of the Zuñi figures it is problematic since the questionable statue has lost whatever it held in its left hand. My own guess is that it depicts St. Raphael, of whom Miera y Pacheco painted at least two other images. Dominguez' observation at Halona was:

> High altar: It has a small new altar screen, as seemly as this poor land has to offer, which was paid for by Father Velez (de Escalante) and the Indians of the pueblo. It consists of two sections, as follows: in the center of the whole thing, almost from top to bottom, there is a framework lined with coarse brown linen and very well painted, in which a large oil painting on canvas with an old frame, newly half gilded, of Our Lady of Guadalupe, which the King had given before, hangs. Below this painting is a very old lacquer Child Jesus vested as a priest, the clothing (is) also old.
>
> The lower niches contain St. Michael on the right and St. Gabriel at the left, new middle-sized images in the round. In the two in the second section above those (mentioned) are — St. Dominic and St. Francis — painted half life size. Above at the top a bust of the Eternal Father in half relief.

We may follow Dominguez' derogatory paper-chase in such statements as an object being paid for at least in part "by the Indians" and "newly half" gilded, as well as in the preliminary wording. Another clue is the mention of coarse brown linen, with which Miera y Pacheco seems to have been well supplied.

It is worth remarking that this early New Mexican artist left descendants who continued to be prominent through the Mexican republican period and whose later generations have held various offices in both territorial and recent years. The family, however, has been known as Miera, dropping y Pacheco by the third generation.

Figure 96: Seventeenth century fresco, "Christ Washing the Feet of the Apostles," Franciscan convent, Huejotzingo.

Figure 97: Early 18th century painting on two hides, "Christ Washing the Feet of the Apostles" by "Franciscan F," New Mexico.

Figure 94: Seventeenth century fresco in Renaissance style, Franciscan convent, Huejotzingo, Mexico.

Figure 95: Eighteenth century painting on hide, Our Lady of the Angels, New Mexico. (Fred Harvey Foundation Collections)

I-D

PAINTING ON TANNED
ANIMAL HIDES

Soon after the reconquest, and probably before there was much permanent rebuilding of missions, a few resourceful Franciscans painted religious subjects on buffalo, elk and deer hides. These, tanned soft, were a common material in New Mexico, and when spoken of by the Spanish were generally called *anta blanca,* no matter which animal had supplied the skin. Since neither professional paintings, nor oils, canvases nor other art supplies were likely to come to New Mexico in sufficient amounts, the Franciscans rolled up their sleeves and made their own pictures, apparently as much to help in the instruction of the Indians as to adorn the walls of new chapels and churches.

These paintings were of the Crucifixion, of persons associated with the life of Christ, and a few Franciscan saints. If the supports and pigments were crude — indigo from New Spain and vegetal dyes used by Indians — the missionaries knew the rudiments of composition, perspective and anatomy, and had had previous practice in drawing. At first glance the provincial Renaissance style of the major group of these paintings seems to be an impossible anachronism. Renaissance principles of design had been out of fashion in Europe for two centuries before the reconquest. However, the Franciscans who then came to New Mexico had been stationed at one or more of the 16th century churches built in New Spain, such as those at Acolman, Actopan, Cholula, and Huejotzingo. These had extensive frescoes in their convents and churches in the Renaissance manner and must have been the sources used from memory by New Mexican missionaries.

The most ably composed and drawn series of these pictures has several striking characteristics. One is the consistent use of plain, linear borders painted dark brown, tan, or yellow, where the hides have not been cropped. A number of the backgrounds contain a mannered zigzag cloud formation against dark skies, which is easily traced back to a favorite mannerism of El Greco. Architectural details and utensils shown are typically of Spanish rather than of colonial forms. Where lettering is used it is proficient and literate. Iconographic details are consistent with the conventions of the Renaissance period, as is the classically uncluttered treatment of the subjects. These are as unmistakably the

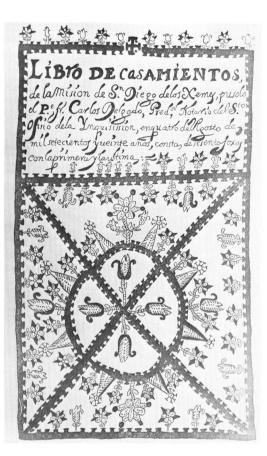

Figure 99: Title page of Book of Marriages, Jemez Pueblo, 1720, by Fray Carlos Joseph Delgado. (A.A.S.F.)

Figure 98: Shrine of wood, gesso and buffalo hide painted by Molleno, w.d. 1804–45.

Figure 100: St. Joseph, painting on hide by "Franciscan B" possibly Fray Carlos Delgado. (Fred Harvey Foundation Collections)

I-E

work of one person as specimens of any pronounced style of handwriting.

The most important and successful of this group depicts in its larger area Christ washing the feet of the disciples. At the left He stands with the four evangelists while a distant view of the Last Supper is seen through a window in the upper left corner. A large chimneypiece, steps, three kinds of lighting devices and a water ewer show experience in drawing as does the assured treatment of figures and drapery. On a table at the left is impressed the block letter "F." This has been guessed to stand for "Franciscan," "Fe," (Faith) or "fecit." With no more to offer than simple speculation as evidence, it is irresistible to consider the fact that only one Franciscan who came with the reconquest had a last name beginning with the letter F. He was Fray Francisco Farfán, a native of Cádiz, Spain, who arrived in Santa Fe with a train of new colonists in 1694. In 1698 he went to Acoma to pacify the recalcitrant dwellers of that mesa, and during his seventeen years in New Mexico he served at Galisteo, San Ildefonso, Pecos, Tesuque and Santa Ana, as well as being military chaplain and ecclesiastical judge for intervals at Santa Fe. There is a saying that only the busy find time for extra work, so it is not impossible that Fray Farfán found the spare time to paint between his other duties.

On the other hand several Franciscans then had the first name of Francis. It is also possible that the letter F in the painting had some quite different meaning than the name of the painter. Examination of the handsome lettering and script done by another friar who came only a few years later, Fray Lucas de Arébalo, as found in the Book of Baptisms that he made in 1711 at Galisteo, provokes the thought that here was a man who had artistic leanings and skill in handling the pen (AASF, B-16, Galisteo, Box 17, 1711-29), and who also may have been the author of the paintings on tanned hides.

The third possible suspect is even more markedly associated with inclinations toward artistic expression, Fray Carlos Joseph Delgado, who had forty years of service in New Mexico, beginning in 1710. He is known to have decorated church record books with boldly inked, freehand ornamental title-pages at several missions (AASF. Patentes, Book II, Box 2, Pecos, 1716; Baptisms-17, Jemez, 1720; Marriages-12, Jemez, 1720). In addition Father Delgado drew floral borders and tail-pieces on his pages of entries for further decorative effect. It has been remarked that "Father Delgado's entries are always in bold, thick, clear script, often decorated with flowers, but the contents imperfect" (Chavez, Fray A., AASF, 1957, p. 202). It is easy enough after seeing his designs to imagine him able and willing to paint large pictures on hides, if they were required. While all three of the above hypothetical artists are named solely on the basis of deduction, and have not been proven responsible for the paintings on animal skins, they are reasonable candidates for the honor. Fray Delgado has also been suggested as having had a part in the building, or rebuilding, of Pecos mission (Dominguez, p. 209), which in its heyday was as much ornamented as any of the northern missions.

In his usual, if disapproving, itemized descriptions of the New Mexico missions of 1776, Father Dominguez repeatedly noted that images painted on animal skins were old, new, or quite new. This fact indicates that he could have seen painted hides made during an approximate time spread of eighty years, or that friars continued to paint pictures on hides for their mission long after the reconquest.

The group next to that of Franciscan "F" in stylistic consistency I have called, for convenience, Franciscan "B." Where uncropped, these have borders painted like carved and gilded picture frames. In style they reflect the late 17th century rather than an earlier period, and also in variation of iconographic details. Red pigment seems to have become more available than it was for the first, or "F" painter, in New Mexico. The slightly over-ornate style of these paintings has a relationship to the title pages done by Fray Carlos Delgado, and is at least contemporary with his years in New Mexico.

Other known paintings on hides made in New Mexico are listed in the Appendix. Most, but not all, of these were the work of 19th century santeros or folk painters of the lay world. As is always the case, although this record has been in preparation for a period of thirty years, and during this time the known number of these scarce works has increased from twenty-five to fifty-seven, there are undoubtedly more examples still hidden away (E. Boyd, 1946, pp 9–26). It is hoped that as these are found they will be reported and published. The ones included here are only those which I have seen, and with a known location. It is worth noting that a medium-sized painting of Our Lady of Guadalupe, which was stolen from the walls of the Museum of New Mexico in 1944, has not yet been retrieved or returned. Another large painting on tanned bison skin was published in 1921.[1] It depicts the Crucifixion with mourning figures, the cup-bearing angel and distant architectural features. The measurements were given as 6 feet 6 inches by 5 feet 5 inches, and it was said to have been owned by Captain Sebastian Martín of La Villita, near San Juan Pueblo. When Martín's daughter married Don Carlos Fernandez she took the painting to Taos, where like others of its class it eventually ended in a morada. It was stated in the article of 1921 that the painting "disappeared from the morada some years ago." No documentary source was given for these statements. In the autumn of 1969 this painting turned up in storage among the Fred Harvey Foundation Collections. It is now on loan to the Museum of New Mexico.

Tanned hides with painted decorations had many other uses in colonial New Mexico than serving as supports for pictures. The inventory of Santa Ana mission, begun in 1712, listed "Two painted skins that serve as *el cielo* [the sky] for the altar." Twenty-odd years later they were again mentioned as "two old hides that serve as *guarda-polva* [dust-guard] for the main altar" (AASF, L.D. 1712, No. 1). This was evidently a prac-

---

[1]*El Palacio,* Vol. 8/1, Jan. 31, 1921, p. 64.

Figure 102: Our Lady of Guadalupe, painting on hide stolen
from Museum of New Mexico
in 1944, never recovered.

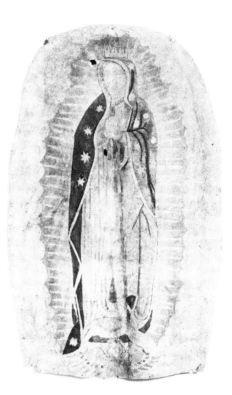

Figure 101: Our Lady of Guadalupe by "Franciscan F."

Figure 103: Santiago, by New Mexico santero Molleno. (Courtesy of Joslyn Museum, Omaha)

Figure 104: St. Anthony of Padua by "Franciscan F" with cloud forms after El Greco. (Courtesy of Museum of History and Technology, Smithsonian Institution)

I-E

tical local expedient for protecting the altar from constantly filtering dirt from the church roof. Such canopies may still be seen in the missions of Laguna and Acoma Pueblos.

At Laguna the canopy is handsomely painted, combining the Indian symbols of sun, moon, rainbow, etc., with motifs taken from the wooden altar screen beneath, which was painted by the "Laguna santero" (Sec. I-G). The 1840 inventory of San José mission at Laguna noted that over the main altar was "a canopy of bison, well painted and very nicely attached to the ceiling." (AASF, L.D. 1840, No. 9.) About 1895 Charles Lummis took photographs of the interiors of both these missions; the negatives are now in the Southwest Museum. The interior view of Laguna shows that the canopy, altar screen, frontal, and wall paintings were in as good condition as they are today. At Acoma the painting on the wooden retable was already much damaged, and the canopy above was in tatters. Enough, however, is visible in the Acoma view to prove that the two altar screens, in the design of the wooden construction as well as the painted panels, were both originally the work of the "Laguna santero" and that the altar canopies or dust-guards were also similar. Unfortunately, when restoration of the retable and canopy at Acoma was done, in the 1920s, one or more amateurs completely overpainted all the historic interior ornaments of the mission, so that nothing of the original painting remains.

In San José mission at Laguna there is still a delightfully painted bison skin altar frontal with urns of flowers that remind us of early Christian frescoes (retouched with synthetic colors in 1964).

Painted, tanned hides were also used in doorways as curtains, or substitutes for doors, and as small carpets in the sanctuary of various missions. At San Ildefonso, Dominguez noted that before the high altar in the church "the carpet is a painted buffalo skin, now old but large and serviceable." In the sacristy he described a "plank table with legs — the front is painted to look as if it had drawers with locks and handles. Stretched tight above is a white buffalo skin painted with flowers and very pretty. This provides a place for the priest to vest" (Dominguez, pp. 65-67). There are in fact too many citations of painted hides scattered through 18th century records of New Mexico to list more.

What is important is the period of their destruction, disappearance and cutting up for utilitarian purposes, which seems to have begun with the visitation of de Guevara during 1817-20. Wherever his inspections took him he left thunderous instructions about the removal of images painted on animal skins, beginning with the *parroquia* at Santa Fe. There he dictated that "the painting of Santa Barbara on elkskin must be removed and done away with completely as it is improper as an object of veneration and devotion of the altars." In fact Don de Guevara began the crusade to do away with "indecent" images in churches of New Mexico, since he objected as much to those "of the country" as to those painted on hides, and to others that were damaged. He required that the large crucifix above the main altar at the *parroquia* be kept in the sacristy until it was repaired, or a new one provided, as it was no longer

Figure 106: St. Dominic of Guzman, companion to Figure 105. (Courtesy of Taylor Museum)

Figure 105: St. Francis of Assisi by "Franciscan F."

in perfect condition. At Santa Cruz he ordered that the six paintings on tanned hides be removed from the church, and further: "In accord with the edicts of the Holy Office the Reverend Father Cura has been instructed not to make another crown of tanned hide for the statue of Our Father Jesus the Nazarene. For lack of a better one he is to make a crown of wood and take away the one of HIDE." This was the life-sized bulto of the Nazareno which is still in the Santa Cruz church, but a smaller figure of the same subject, also crowned with hide, was commanded to be "dedicated to the fire" (AASF. Book of Accounts, LXII, Box 5, de Guevara Visitation, Santa Fe, Book 2, 1817).

Clearly it was Visitor de Guevara from Durango who inaugurated the reform of New Mexico church ornaments, and not the French Bishop Lamy who followed him thirty years later. Succeeding visitations of the Bishops of Durango or their representatives before 1851 continued to stress the "indecency" of religious images painted on skins. However, there is no reason to suppose that, although most of these were obligingly removed from the churches at the time, they were destroyed altogether. As we have seen, many were hidden away in homes or in moradas. Others, however, were cut up for sacks, saddlebags and book bindings. Dozens of the ancient volumes now preserved in the chancery vault of the Archdiocese of Santa Fe were bound with fragments of large paintings on hides. Floral borders, bits of church towers or walls, decorative space fillers and other details were cut from bigger compositions and not painted primarily to fit these record books.

The custom of painting religious images on tanned hides in New Mexico may definitely be said to have existed for at least 125 years. It was another example of ingenuity and self-help in the face of a deficiency of what might have been more desirable, but was not available in the kingdom. Nothing as yet has been found to prove that any of the surviving examples were, as has been suggested more than once, made before 1680 and saved by pious Pueblo Indians. On the other hand, tanned skins, if kept away from damage by water and rodents, remain amazingly fresh and soft. Tanned buckskin buried in dry caves, whose associated artifacts suggest an age of more than 1,000 years, has been found in equally fresh condition.

As to the end of the making of these paintings, the 19th century santero Molleno, at least, did make some paintings on hides. It is uncertain whether he did these before or after Visitor de Guevara's anathemas upon such pictures, although the general style of Molleno's two larger paintings (Nos. 47 and 48) is certainly that of his maturity and not of his earlier, copyist paintings (Sec. III-B). Like other New Mexican customs, the making of paintings on hides may well have persisted in the face of official disfavor.

As for the crowns of plaited buckskin, despite the edicts of the Holy Office and Visitors from the Diocese of Durango, they continued to be made, neatly finished and painted by various hands, if no longer by the Reverend Cura. Bultos of Christ in several aspects as well as that of the Nazarene, and of other saints, were supplied with these as needed, until recently when braided, colored plastic telephone wire, tinsel and similar materials have been adopted. Many, but by no means all, of these crowns were for figures in Penitente moradas.

Like other customs so often described as peculiar to New Mexico, the use of tanned hides instead of canvas for painting supports was common in any part of New Spain where conventional artist supplies were not obtainable, just as adobe walls were frescoed for the same reason (Kelemen, 1951, p. 210, and Pl. 137-f).

There is no basis for the theory that tanned skins were hauled from New Mexico to be painted by professional artists in New Spain and returned to the northern colony (Espinosa, 1960, p. 21). The more academic groups here classed as works by Franciscans "F" and "B" are not professional work, in fact, although more proficient than the santeros of 100 years later. Professional artists of New Spain would have scorned to use hides when they had plenty of flax or *ixtle* (agave fiber) canvas as well as hardwood panels and copper plates. What is certain is that the cost of such artistic work and round-trip freighting would have been prohibitive for New Mexicans, who had to pay with their pesos *de la tierra,* or four times the silver peso, for imported luxuries. Any New Mexican who could afford it would have required pictures painted on canvas with oils, and in gilded frames if he were to spend his pesos in the south.

Inventories later than those of 1776 or 1796 continued to note paintings on hides as well as other minor uses of painted hides in churches. It was during the visitations of de Guevara, Fernandez de San Vicente, and Zubiría (1817-20, 1826, 1833) from the Diocese of Durango that these rustic improvisations were discarded from most of the churches.

Figure 107: Painting on hide by "Franciscan F" of the Crucifixion with mourning figures. (Fred Harvey Foundation Collections)

Figure 108: Painting on hide by "Franciscan F" of the Crucifixion with mourning figures.

SUBJECT	STYLE	SIZE	DESCRIPTION	CONDITION	REMARKS	LOCATION
1. Christ Washing the Feet of the Disciples	Franciscan "F"	170 cm x 253 cm	On two skins sewn together painted with indigo, brown & yellow transparent dyes. Plain linear border.	Good. Skins supple. No retouching.	Block letter *F* at left. Collected from morada at Dixon (old Embudo) in 1920.	Museum of New Mexico A.14.53.1
2. Crucifix with Mourning Figures & Cup-Bearing Angel	"F"	182 cm x 134 cm	On single skin, indigo, brown, yellow dyes; red paint. Plain, linear border.	Fair, some fading, no retouching. Lower part eaten away by mice.	Zigzag cloud pattern, background, after El Greco. European architectural features.	Museum of New Mexico L.5.58-34
3. Crucifix with Mourning Figures & Cup-bearing Angel	"F"	200 cm x 165 cm	Single hide, indigo, brown, red ocher, yellow. Plain, linear border.	Fair, paint worn, no retouching.	Cloud pattern after Greco. Buildings differ from those of (-) 2.	Museum of New Mexico L.69.23-31 Fred Harvey Collection.
4. Crucifix with the Instruments of the Passion	"F"	170 cm x 120 cm	On single skin, indigo, brown, yellow & green dyes. Plain, linear border.	Good, no retouching.	Cloud & sky pattern after El Greco.	A.S.F. Church at Galisteo, New Mexico
5. Crucifix with the Instruments of the Passion	"F"	139 cm x 120 cm	On single skin, indigo, brown, yellow & green dyes. Plain, linear border.	Cut off at bottom. Some retouching, about 1920.	Cloud & sky pattern after El Greco, from Santa Cruz Church, 1902.	Denver Art Museum A.173
6. Crucifix with the Instruments of the Passion	"F"	173 cm x 118 cm	On single hide, indigo, brown, yellow dyes. Plain, linear border.	Top cut off, waterstained & patched. No retouching.	Cloud patterns after El Greco. Small Virgin with heart below Cross.	A.S.F. San Miguel Chapel

SUBJECT	STYLE	SIZE	DESCRIPTION	CONDITION	REMARKS	LOCATION
7. Crucifix with the Instruments of the Passion	"F"	157 cm x 134 cm	On single hide, dark brown outlines, yellow dye. Linear border.	Torn, waterstained, brittle. No retouching.	No solid paint areas, much detail. Probably after engraving.	Museum of New Mexico L.5.59-39
8. St. Francis of Assisi	"F"	176 cm x 102 cm	On single hide, indigo, brown, yellow & green dyes. Plain, linear border.	Skin supple. Red & solid black areas retouched. Borders partly cut.	Architectural style retouched to show New Mexico mission of 19th C style, with 17th C Spanish bell.	Museum of New Mexico A.62.15-1
9. St. Dominic (Santo Domingo de Guzman)	"F"	164 cm x 138 cm	On single hide, indigo, brown, yellow, green & black dyes. Plain, linear border.	Large part of skin lost — center to bottom. Black areas may be retouched.	Originally a companion to #8 which had same type of background. #9 shows two Spanish-shaped bells.	Taylor Museum #1636
10. St. Anthony of Padua	"F"	118 cm x 67 cm	On single skin, indigo, brown, yellow, green dyes. Plain, linear border.	Skin supple. No retouching.	Collected at Santo Domingo Pueblo, 1897. Clouds after El Greco.	Smithsonian Institution #176.402
11. St. Joseph with the Christ Child	"F"	174 cm x 143 cm	On single hide, brown black, yellow & green dyes. Plain, linear border.	Skin supple except for waterstains at bottom. No retouching.	This was on the mission inventory in mid-18th C.	Diocese of Gallup, Mission of San José, Laguna, N.M.
12. St. John Baptist	"F"	157 cm x 144 cm	On single hide, indigo, brown, yellow & green dyes. Plain, linear border.	Bottom cut off, waterstained. Face, hair, tree foliage & cloak- retouched.	Lettered: "Ecce Agnus Dei/ ece qui" (illeg.) Cloud patterns after El Greco.	Taylor Museum #1635

SUBJECT	STYLE	SIZE	DESCRIPTION	CONDITION	REMARKS	LOCATION
13. St. John Baptist	"F"	110 cm x 91 cm	On single hide, indigo, brown, yellow, green dyes. Plain, linear border, mostly lost.	Cut down, water-stained, background retouched.	Lettering on banner similar to #12.	Museum of New Mexico A.5.52-19
14. Nuestra Señora de la Begoña	"F"	146 cm x 108 cm	On single hide, indigo, brown, yellow, green & red dyes. Plain linear border.	Hide supple, good condition, no retouching.	Architectural niche and details indicate this was of a statue in its shrine, probably taken from an engraving. The inscribed date would refer to the original statue and shrine, or to the making of the plate which was the model for the skin painting. Lettered, top: "Assumptea est Maria Regina Coelum." Lettered, bottom: "La Milagrosa Imagen de N^a /S^a De Begoña 1608."	A.S.F. Church at Galisteo, N.M.
15 St. Francis of Assisi	"F"	63.5 cm x 33 cm	On two hides sewn down center. Indigo, brown, yellow dyes. Saint wears blue habit, is smooth-shaven, holds footed cross. Foliage in background.	Original, no retouching. Cut down from much larger composition.	Features are outlined as if drawn from a live model, or anatomically delineated portrait. Said to have been collected near Socorro, N.M.	Private owner
16. St. Barbara V.M.	"F"	125 cm x 96 cm	On single hide, brown, black, yellow dyes. Plain, linear border.	Brittle, cut down, damaged by water. Face and Holy Spirit retouched.	Lettered: ". . . B . . rbara," damaged.	Museum of New Mexico A.5.57-13

SUBJECT	STYLE	SIZE	DESCRIPTION	CONDITION	REMARKS	LOCATION
17. St. Anthony of Padua	"F"	60 cm x 70 cm	On single hide, indigo, brown, yellow dyes. Plain linear border.	Hide supple, condition good, No retouching, lower half lost.		Museum of New Mexico L.5.54-1
18. The Creation (fragment)	"F"	1 m x 25 cm	On single hide, indigo, brown, yellow & green dyes, plain, linear border.	Hide supple, water stains, no retouching. Lower part cut off and lost.	Details of light and rain shafts, etc. strongly reminiscent of Renaissance prints.	Museum of New Mexico L.5.59-38
19. San Cayetano (fragment)	"F"	87 cm x 67 cm	On single hide, brown, yellow, red & green dyes, plain, linear borders.	Hide supple, no retouching, lower half cut off and lost.	Ornate costume details after an engraving.	Private owner.
20. Franciscan Saint Bearing Cross	"F"	1 m x 58 cm	Grisaille & brown, on patched scraps of hide.	Cut down & put on stretchers, water-stained, cloth scraps pasted over surface. Face retouched.		Museum of New Mexico A.5.54-46
21. St. Anthony of Padua	"F"	180 cm x 111 cm	On single hide, indigo, brown, yellow & green dyes. Plain linear border.	Original painting still partly visible at top, mostly washed away & overpainted by 19th C santero in opaque pigments. See # XX (betw. 49–50.)	Head, cowl & lilies by "F", still visible. Cf. #10 for similar, intact, composition.	Museum of New Mexico A.5.52-12
22. Our Lady of Guadalupe (fragment)	"F"	108 cm x 54 cm	On single skin, indigo, brown, yellow & red dyes.	No retouching, hide cut down, borders lost.		Private owner

133

SUBJECT	STYLE	SIZE	DESCRIPTION	CONDITION	REMARKS	LOCATION
23. Our Lady of Guadalupe	"F"	177 cm x 141 cm	On single hide, brown, yellow & green dyes, very little indigo. Dark brown linear borders. Well planned composition, fine drawing.	Hide supple, intact, some old water stains. No retouching.	Ornate costume details after original painting, elaborate treatment of clouds & nimbus. Red pigment virtually lacking.	Museum of New Mexico FA.66.56-1
24. St. Joseph with the Christ Child	Franciscan "B"	152 cm x 109 cm	On single hide, indigo, brown & yellow dyes. Borders painted like carved & gilded picture frame, 18th C style.	Skin supple, overpainted with opaque red, yellow & white paints which obscure parts of original.		Fred Harvey Collection #1653, on loan to Museum of New Mexico
25. St. Anthony of Padua (fragment)	"B"		On single hide, indigo, brown & yellow dyes. Borders painted like carved & gilded picture frame.	Hide cut down, no retouching.	Collected at Tesuque Pueblo, 1897.	Smithsonian Institution #A.31785, 176-401
26. St. Anthony of Padua (fragment)	"B"	65 cm x 38 cm	On single hide, indigo, brown & yellow dyes. Borders painted like architectural niche.	Cut down, no retouching.		Fred Harvey Collection #1645
27. St. Anthony of Padua	"B"	71 cm x 46 cm	On single skin, indigo, brown & yellow dyes. Borders painted like architectural niche.	Original size, skin supple, no retouching except right arm.		Fred Harvey collection #1649

SUBJECT	STYLE	SIZE	DESCRIPTION	CONDITION	REMARKS	LOCATION
28. St. Anthony of Padua	"B"	77 cm x 52 cm	Transparent dyes, architectural painted frame, desk, book and inkwell at side.	Original painting, very little cropped.		Museum of New Mexico FA.68.20-1
29. St. Michael, Archangel	"B"	76 cm x 46 cm	On single hide, indigo, brown & yellow dyes. Borders painted like architectural niche.	Original size, water stains, opaque white painted dots added.		Fred Harvey Collection #1651, on loan to Museum of New Mexico
30. Our Lady of Guadalupe	"B"	177 cm x 44.7 cm	On single skin, no retouching. Indigo, brown and yellow dyes. Borders painted like architectural niche.	Hide supple.	Probably once a part of series with Nos. 26, 27, and 29.	Taylor Museum #515.
31. Our Lady of Guadalupe	"B"	75 cm x 50 cm	On single hide, she faces right. Architectural frame.	Opaque red spots on her cheeks & cherub's. Hide supple.	Ex collection of Dr. H. J. Spinden, from Taos ca. 1910.	Museum of New Mexico L.5.71-14
32. Our Lady of Begoña (?) or Remedios (?) (fragment)	"B"	87 cm x 93 cm	On single skin, indigo, brown, yellow and green dyes. Stands in architectural frame.	Cut top and bottom, opaque pink pigment on hands & face, thong mending & buckskin patches, ochre smears over patching.	Said to have come from Taos, Church of Guadalupe torn down ca. 1910. If originally N.S. de Begoña, may have been cut down to remove lettering (cf. #14) when different advocation was wanted.	Museum of New Mexico, A.71.31-2
33. Our Lady of Solitude	"B"	88 cm x 64 cm	On single hide, indigo. brown & yellow dyes.	Hide supple, no retouching. Cut down on all sides.		A.S.F. on loan to Museum of New Mexico #L.1.56-1

SUBJECT	STYLE	SIZE	DESCRIPTION	CONDITION	REMARKS	LOCATION
34. Our Lady of Guadalupe	"B"		On single hide, indigo, brown & yellow dyes. Borders painted like carved frame.	Skin supple, no retouching. Cropped. Damaged by fire, 1965.	Collected at Peñasco, 1897.	Smithsonian Institution #200-826
35. Our Lady of Guadalupe	"B"	75 cm x 50 cm	On single hide, indigo, brown & yellow dyes. Borders painted like gilded picture frame.	Margins partly cropped. Skin supple. Some opaque red pigment added.	Ochre smears over thong repairs, removed by E. B. 1949. Probably Taos Indian repairs.	Museum of New Mexico, A.71.31-1
36. Our Lady of Guadalupe	"B"	125 cm x 66 cm	On single hide, brown & yellow dye outlines.	Margins all cut down, no retouching. Skin supple.	Ex L. B. Prince collection. Stylistically able, unidentifiable, outline of "original" image. Might be "F" or "B" work.	Fred Harvey Collection #1652
37. Crucifix with Instruments of the Passion	"B"	90 cm x 58-68 cm	On single hide, indigo, brown & yellow dyes.	Hide supple, overpainted in opaque red, white & mauve pigments.	Done after No. 6. Has image of Virgin & heart, zigzag cloud forms.	Museum of New Mexico #A.5.52-15
38. San Luis Rey de Francia	"B"	91 cm x 67 cm	On single hide, indigo, brown & yellow dyes. Borders painted like gilded picture frame.	Top & bottom cropped, water-stained. Face overpainted with opaque pigments.	Ex L.B. Prince collection.	Fred Harvey Collection #1648

Plate 2: San José by Fray Andrés García.

I-E

137

SUBJECT	STYLE	SIZE	DESCRIPTION	CONDITION	REMARKS	LOCATION
Unidentified Examples, later 18th Century.						
39. Friars in Cloister	X	122 cm x 152 cm	Pieced sections of tanned hide, indigo, brown & yellow dyes.	Waterstained, torn, patched, large sections cropped. All-over retouching with opaque pigments.	Original style overlaid as well as subject.	Museum of New Mexico #B 87/290
40. Crucifix with pair of urns and flowers	X	104 cm x 72 cm	On single hide, indigo, brown & yellow dyes.	Cropped, water-stained. Aniline red dye stains from former calico print pasted over surface (now removed).		Museum of New Mexico #A.5.57-12
41. Our Lady of Sorrows	X	102 cm x 51 cm	On single hide, indigo & brown dyes.	Cropped, water-stained. Features overpainted with opaque pigments.	Ex L.B. Prince collection.	Fred Harvey Collection, #1646
42. Our Lady of the Immaculate Conception	X	76 cm x 58 cm	On single hide, indigo, brown, yellow & red dyes; opaque white, after a statue painting.	Cropped, skin supple, no retouching.	Provincial rendering of rococo costume, altar, swags & urns.	Fred Harvey Collection, #1650
43. Our Lady of Sorrows	X	124-130 cm x 66-72 cm	On single hide, brown & yellow dyes. Scoring of skin in atypical method.	Cropped, over-painted in opaque, chalky white, blue, red, yellow & black.	Amateur overpainting obscures original.	Private owner

SUBJECT	STYLE	SIZE	DESCRIPTION	CONDITION	REMARKS	LOCATION
44. Fragment	X	73.5 cm x 48 cm	Two skins sewn together down center. Left, kneeling Virgin; right, man with banner and ox; trees in foreground.	Cut down from larger composition. Paint losses.		Taylor Museum #1637

SANTERO, or 19th Century Paintings on Hides, or Overpainted Examples.

SUBJECT	STYLE	SIZE	DESCRIPTION	CONDITION	REMARKS	LOCATION
45. Our Lady of Guadalupe	18th C Novice Painter	94 cm x 51 cm	On single hide, indigo & brown dyes; opaque red & green pigments, original.	Cropped, water-damaged.		Museum of New Mexico #L.5.57-42
46. Santiago	Molleno, in his earlier style, ca. 1805	84 cm x 76 cm	On single hide, red, yellow & opaque white pigments, with indigo & brown dyes. After popular prints.	Good, not cropped, now on wooden stretchers. Has had oil on it, removed 1962.	Stick figures under horse, lying dead, or holding guns, bows, swords; pair of mortars. Unlike other recorded N.M. images of Santiago.	Joslyn Art Museum—C36. Collected by Capt. John Bourke, 1881. Pojoaque, N.M. (Pub. in Joslyn Bull. #4, 1962.)
47. Santiago	Molleno, in his mature style.	150 cm x 76 cm	On single hide, gesso ground, indigo brown, yellow, green, red, opaque white.	Excellent, is now on stretchers.		Museum of New Mexico #A.5.52-13 (Pub. in R. E. Twitchell, "Leading Facts of New Mexican History," 1911, V.I., p. 128)

Plate 4: San José, painting on tanned hide, Laguna Mission. (Photograph by Ernest Knee)

Plate 3: The Virgin of Sorrows by Bernardo Miera y Pacheco. (Photograph by Eliot Porter)

I-E

SUBJECT	STYLE	SIZE	DESCRIPTION	CONDITION	REMARKS	LOCATION
48. St. Francis of Assisi	Molleno, later style.	150 cm x 90 cm	Single hide, gesso ground; indigo, brown, yellow, red, opaque white tempera pigments.	Excellent.	Probably was companion to #47. Souls in Purgatory reflect confusion with the heads of Moors in #47.	Brooklyn Museum (Pub. in PARNASSUS, V. VIII 7, 1935, p. 9)
49. God the Father	Molleno, early style.	77.5 cm x 54.3 cm Arched at top.	Hide gessoed, tempera paints, God has flowered robes, papal tiara and sceptre.	Sides cut down, was once on stretchers, gesso and paint losses.	Said to have come from Santa Ana Pueblo.	Taylor Museum #514
XX St. John Nepomuk (See #21 supra)	Santero anon.	180 cm x 111 cm	Opaque black, red, orange, yellow, green & white pigments over image of St. Anthony in style of Franciscan, "F."	Good.	Iconographically, Christ Child has no place in image of this saint, but was overlaid on drawing of original Christ held by original St. Anthony, cf. #10 & #17, supra.	Museum of New Mexico #A.5.52-12
50. St. John the Baptist	Santero anon.	118 cm x 87 cm	On single hide, indigo, brown & yellow dyes.	Fair.	Not overpainted, but naive rendering after #12 & #13.	A.S.F. in San Miguel Chapel, Santa Fe
51. Our Lady of the Angels	Santero anon.	84 cm x 68 cm	On single hide, indigo, brown, yellow dyes. Naive architectural details.	Cut in two across center, cropped at 3 sides; also large hole cut above head. No retouching.	Arch framing figure is good drawing of multiple corbels used to substitute for arch in N.M. colonial missions.	Fred Harvey Collection #1647, on loan to Museum of New Mexico

SUBJECT	STYLE	SIZE	DESCRIPTION	CONDITION	REMARKS	LOCATION
52. St. Rosalia of Palermo (?)	Amateur	110 cm x 76 cm	Original brown dye, outlines visible of framing arch like #51 above, later over-smeared painting.	On stretcher. Present figure of saint possibly over original of same subject.		Museum of New Mexico H.S. 87/40
53. Santiago	Santero, very naive	84 cm x 84 cm	Opaque indigo, brown, red & yellow pigments; bright blue horse.	Present figure overpainted on Franciscan "B" image of tonsured saint. The hide was cut down when overpainted. Scroll and cruciform space fillers on this are also on a record book bound with painted hide in AASF, possibly cut from this painting.		Museum of New Mexico #A.5.52-17
54. Our Lady . . .	?	Small scrap	Smeared all over with resinous substance. Small crude metal head, clawlike hands & arms, attached to hide.	Probably fetish; ex votos attached. Collected at Tesuque Pueblo in 1897.		Smithsonian Institution #176.402
55. Santiago	Santero	118 cm x 70 cm	Opaque pigments.	Good.		A.S.F. in Mission at Santo Domingo Pueblo
56. St. Anthony	Amateur	50 cm x 41 cm	Opaque pigments.	Overpainting.		Southwest Museum
57. St. Stephen	Amateur	Large, not measured	Opaque overpainting by Indians in 1920's.	Original painting of 18th century now completely invisible.		Diocese of Gallup, in Mission at Acoma Pueblo

144

PANELS IN GESSO RELIEF

Wood panels built up in more or less relief with layers of wet gesso
were common in Medieval art beginning with the period of gold grounds
in Italy. In Spain, especially in Catalonia, the technique persisted into
the 16th century. Hardly one hundred years later the Mannerist school
revived the use of gesso but on a more robust scale, covering armatures
with stucco to make almost freestanding figures in the round which
were incorporated into facades, ceilings, staircases and other architectural features.

In New Mexico there had been some wooden statues or bultos
made with wet gesso and cloth as substitutes for the carving in wood
where drapery and decorative ornaments were wanted. Perhaps some
individual decided to experiment with the gesso on wood panels,
although none of these appears to have had any cloth in its construction. To achieve relief surfaces by carving resinous pine which splits
easily with the grain was obviously difficult and the maker of these
panels must have found that he could give his retablos the same interesting depth by using gesso. There is no mention of wooden panels
in relief in Dominguez' report of 1776. In view of the few tree-ring
dates for these they may not have existed at that time, but there is no
mention of them in later inventories either.

Of the thirty-five panels recorded with a common style of modeling
and coloring, there are two main sizes: one of 80 to 85 centimeters by
45 centimeters with a pediment at the top, and a smaller series approximately 22 by 16 centimeters. The still intact panels have similar framing moldings dowelled on the board and the same decorative shells in
relief in the pediments. These may have been made as sets for private
chapels which could explain their absence from church inventories
(Appendix I-F).

The panels are of yellow pine and the framing moldings were
covered with gesso, making them part of the panel. Drapery and attributes were built up with gesso without much sharpness of definition.
The saintly heads, treated as the most important element, were carved
in wood in the half-round and set into the wet gesso. In time both wood
and gesso dried and shrank, so these delicately carved heads have sometimes been lost. When the gesso work was completed and dried it was
polished and painted with the same palette of water-soluble tempera
colors used by New Mexico folk artists of the 19th century: indigo,
iron oxides and vegetal yellows.

Figure 109: Late 18th century, St. Joseph. (Private owner)

Figure 110: Our Lady of Sorrows.

A few of these panels are of intermediate sizes and less successful in composition. They also duplicate the subjects of those made in sets, mostly those of St. Anthony and the Virgin. It is possible that these were made by other santeros or else were repainted by them. A few others were given new coats of oil base house paints after 1880 when the latter became available in stores. Even in this condition the mannerisms of the original artist, the curving, boneless hands, the small, sweet faces, the uniformity of pediments and drapery treatment are recognizably the work of the same anonymous maker.

Seven of these panels were tested for possible tree-ring dating by Stallings. One panel gave a bark date of 1796, indicating that the tree from which the panel was shaped had been cut in that year. The other six panels had missing outside rings; and estimated mean average for these suggested that their wood had been cut between 1780-1800 (Appendix I-F).

The iconographic conventionalism of these sets, their planned compositions and delicacy of coloring have been interpreted as the work of one of the Franciscan missionaries. The indefatigable Father Garcia, known to have made santos, had left New Mexico in 1779, too early to have been the author of these. Most of these panels have passed through various hands so that their original locations are unknown. The exceptions, a panel collected by J. Walter Fewkes at Jemez Pueblo in 1897 (S. I. No. 176, 405), and another from Punta de Agua, a tiny village east of the Rio Grande (MNM No. A.9.54-139-R), only suggest that they had already been moved away from their primary situations.

The santero Molleno has also been considered as the possible author of this series on the basis of certain characteristics found on retablos by him and also on some of the gesso relief panels. Among these are the large clawlike hands, opaque white decorative elements painted over dark backgrounds, free brush strokes and fondness for red pigments (Sec. III-B). Molleno executed large retables, bultos and paintings on hides, and made some use of built-up gesso on his figures in the round. Perhaps he had been commissioned to repair and repaint one or more of the 18th century panels and decided to try his hand at this medium also. Of the panels by Molleno that were examined for dating, the earliest found was a bark date of 1804-05. The painting is in his younger manner, a somewhat painstaking and timid rendering of a canvas or print from New Spain and with a dark colored background, instead of the white gesso ground which he used in later years. Time may bring forth conclusive proof that some of the gesso relief panels were the work of Molleno, but for the present it is only possible to state that they were made toward the end of the 18th century and, apparently, by one man.

Fifteen other panels are the work of several 19th century folk artists of various degrees of skill. Three are unmistakably by the santero Pedro Fresquís (Sec. III-A), most of whose religious works seem to have been done in the last decades of his long life. They are trans-

Figure 111: St. Cajetan.

Figure 112: St. Teresa of Avila.

lated into the half round from prints, that of St. Francis receiving the stigmata being adapted from a title page in one of the missals made for the three Franciscan orders by the Plantin Press at Antwerp (Sec. I-C Fig.71). Fresquís made little use of gesso relief in these panels in comparison to those just discussed, and in one he laid narrow sticks of wood into the wet gesso as a shortcut with the result of angular instead of curving forms.

A small panel of the Veronica image has painted decoration in the manner of José Aragon (Sec. III-D). Still others range from the semicompetent to a rather childish panel which resembles gingerbread figures. The surface painting of these is in the 19th century folk style. Either the later santeros did not understand the method of making built-up relief with gesso, or it was not popular among their patrons, for none of the santeros after the mid-19th century seems to have made use of the medium.

Figure 114: St. Joseph and the Christ Child.

Figure 115: The Holy Child of Atocha; anonymous 19th century New Mexican.

Figure 116: Our Lady of Carmel, 18th century. (Private owner; photograph by Lansing Brown)

Eighteenth Century Gesso Relief Panels in the Collections of:

SUBJECT	Museum of New Mexico	Taylor Museum	W. R. Nelson Gallery	Private Owners	Santa Barbara Museum of Art	Archdiocese of Santa Fe
St. Anthony of Padua			1, medium size, original paint.	2, small, original paint.		1, medium size, recently overpainted in oils.
St. Barbara					1, large, original paint.	
St. Cajetan (San Calletano)	1, medium size, original paint.					
St. Flora of Cordoba		1, tree-ring dated, estim. cutting date between 1774-1780.				
St. Francis of Assisi		1, tree-ring dated, estim. cutting date between 1771-1783.				
St. Gertrude	1, large, original paint.					
St. John Nepomuk	1, large, head lost, original paint.			1, small, original paint.		
St. Joseph	1, large, two layers of santero gesso and paint.			1 small, original paint		
St. Michael Archangel		1, small, tree-ring dated, estim. cutting date after 1780.		1, original paint.	1, medium size, original paint.	
Our Lady of Carmel	1, small, much repaired.			4, original paint.		

SUBJECT	Museum of New Mexico	Taylor Museum	Dallas Museum of Fine Arts	Detroit Art Institute	Private Owners
Crucifixion		1, anonymous			1, by Pedro Fresquís
St. Francis of Assisi Receiving the Stigmata					
The Holy Child	1, miniature, anonymous				
The Holy Child of Atocha	1, anonymous				
St. Ignatius Loyola	1, by Pedro Fresquís				
St. Joseph	1, anonymous				
Our Lady of Guadalupe	1, by Pedro Fresquís	1, anonymous			
Our Lady of the Immaculate Conception	1, anonymous				
Our Lady of Refuge	1, by José Aragon				
Our Lady of Sorrows		1, anonymous			
Our Lady of Talpa	1, anonymous				
St. Rita of Cascia			1, anonymous		
St. Veronica's Veil Image	1, by José Aragon			1, anonymous	1, anonymous

SUBJECT	Museum of New Mexico	Taylor Museum	Archdiocese of Santa Fe	Denver Art Museum	Smithsonian Institution	Stanford University
Our Lady of San Juan de los Lagos.			1, large, original paint.			
Our Lady of Light		1, large, overpainted in oils. Estim. cutting date, 1784.				
Our Lady of Sorrows	1, large, original paints, part of panel missing.			1, large, original paint. Bark date 1796.	1, large, original paint, some losses.	1, large, original paint; 1 medium size, santero repainting.
St. Raphael Archangel	2, medium size, original paint, 1 has lost head.	1, large, original paint.				
St. Raymond Nonnatus		1, small				
St. Rosalie of Palermo		1, medium size, original paint; 1, large, overpainted in oils.				

SUBJECT	Museum of New Mexico					School of Am. Research
Veronica's Veil, Image.	1, small, nearly solidly carved of wood, original paint, straw decoration on frame.					
St. Teresa of Avila						1, small, original paint.

THE SANTERO OF
LAGUNA MISSION

By far the most beautiful and best preserved altar screen in New Mexico is that in the mission of San José at Laguna Pueblo, forty-five miles west of Albuquerque. Unknown by name, the santero must have had some experience in painting before he received this commission and, at about the same time, another to make a taller but similar altar screen at Acoma's mission of St. Stephen. The people of Laguna have taken pains to keep their retable in original condition, but at Acoma, where the leaking roof had extensively damaged the tempera painting, the old altar screen was completely overpainted along the "original" themes by well-intentioned amateurs of the pueblo over forty years ago. In fact, a photograph made at Acoma by Monsen in 1905, and now at the Southwest Museum, shows that the upper lunette on the altar piece already had been heavily repainted before 1905, although the lower tiers and salomonic pillars appear to be original painting. The condition of the sagging vigas, water-channeled sanctuary walls and tattered buffalo hide canopy above the altar in the picture indicate the cause of damage to the altar screen. In spite of overpainting at Acoma, the two wooden altar screens are visibly alike, and, from the old photograph, so were the style of painting and two of the subjects, Sts. Joseph and John Nepomuk.

At Laguna the only serious loss of paint was on the two cartouches on the lower tier of panels where the name of the donor and date of making would have been. Long ago washed off in cleaning, these now contain recent renderings of the Franciscan emblem. When Lt. Abert visited Laguna in 1846 he admired the retable. While measured scale drawings of important landmarks were being made by the Historic

American Buildings Survey in the early 1930s, Laguna Mission was included in the series. In order to verify measurements, survey workers gained access to the plastered-off area behind the wooden retable and found, high up on the back, this inscription: "Se pintó este coral y se yso a costa del alcalde mallor D^n José Manuel Aragon este año de 780."[1]

In the brief text on the mission's history the HABS editor made no attempt to interpret the above date but stated that the church had been renovated in 1818, and further noted that tree-ring tests on roof beams over the sanctuary at Laguna and Acoma agreed or cross-dated, but at Acoma, it was stated, read 1810.[2] However, replacement of roof beams and installation of a new retable did not necessarily happen at the same time. Aragon was alcalde and war captain for Laguna, Acoma, Cubero and outlying villages from 1792 to 1813; he was a Spaniard and while at his post lived with his family at Laguna.

Father José Benito Pereyro[3] was missionary at Laguna and Acoma between 1798 and 1803. While at Taos, 1808 to 1818, he busied himself with alterations and improvements in his chapels (Sec. III-B and Appendix), and may well have done so at Laguna, at least to the extent of inducing Alcalde Aragon to sponsor a new altar screen. However, personal inspection of the inscription on the altarpiece has led me to consider that it may be read as any year between 1800 and 1808 (Appendix, I-G 1950). W. S. Stallings, Jr., a dendrochronologist, has suggested that Pereyro himself was the Laguna santero, but he had left Laguna by 1803 and supervised ornamentation of Ranchos de Taos chapel of St. Francis. It is apparent that the existing santero paintings there are not by the same hand as those at Laguna. They are part of the large body of work by the santero Molleno (Sec. III-B). Stallings also theorized that Molleno was an apprentice or helper of the Laguna santero. The early works of Molleno certainly do reflect the influence of the Laguna santero, but lack the organization of composition, color and confidence of brushwork of the latter. Molleno's iconography was far more aberrant, or original, but his decorative inventiveness in space-filling was less fluid and coherent; Molleno tended to assemble small panels in mosaic form on an altar screen rather than to relate painted elements with architectural form. The main retable at el Santuario del Potrero is an excellent example of his composition.

Architecturally the proportions of the Laguna and Acoma retables are superior to any others existent in New Mexico, except that of San Miguel chapel in Santa Fe (Sec. I-B). While others made use of twisted

---

[1] "This coral was painted and made at the expense of the chief magistrate Don Jose Manuel Aragon, this year of 780." "Coral" was an abbreviation of the Mexican corruption: "corateral" for "colateral," an object against the wall, as the altar screen, which is not freestanding.

[2] Historic American Buildings Survey, N.M. 31 — Laguna, 1, Sheet 1, and N.M. 31 — Acoma, 2, Sheet 3.

[3] Peyrero, J. B. SANM, Vol. 1, No. 1191, SRC.

Plate 6: The altar screen, San José de la Laguna Mission.

pillars they were notched from narrow poles and lack the fine, massive bulge and handsome capitals of the Laguna santero's devising. It is possible that he was one of many arrivals from New Spain after the administration of Governor de Anza, and brought with him the notion of salomonic pillars that he had seen in some 17th century church to the south.

The old assumption that the Laguna santero appeared from nowhere to make the retables of Acoma and Laguna and then vanished was never plausible. He had had working experience and would have made altar screens in some Spanish center before he received a commission from the alcalde to come to the more westerly pueblos. That the retable of San Miguel in Santa Fe was the work of the Laguna santero is fairly self evident if we compare architectural details and ornaments. The major difference is that at San Miguel there were canvases from New Spain and no images were needed in the panels. The santero did not bother to gesso or paint on areas behind the canvases. The San Miguel retable was dated 1798 in two cartouches.

Since about 1930 the altar screen in the church of the Assumption at Zia Pueblo has been overpainted. The work was done by a member of the pueblo, Andrés Galvan, in shades of red, brown and yellow. The composition is curiously unlike that of other twentieth century folk artists or of contemporary pueblo artists. A cornice runs between the solid salomonic pillar and divides the lower part of the retable into three panels. To the viewer's left is San Juan Nepomuceno, in the center the Virgin of the Assumption and at the right is San Lorenzo. Above the cornice a sprawling inverted V form is painted, its outer ends with bottle-shaped finials, framing an oval in which is an image said to be of Christ. In spite of the limited color scheme the floral panels on the lower tier and pendant scallops below the cornice are notably well designed.

L. Bradford Prince in *Spanish Mission Churches of New Mexico* described the altar screen at Zia, prior to 1915 when this book was published:

> The altarpiece, which occupies the entire west end of the church, is of carved wood with a large canvas painting of the Assumption in the center, under which is another picture of the Virgin and Child being crowned by angels.

The remains of these two 18th century canvases, badly water damaged, are in the sacristy. Galvan used the major painting as his model for the existing central panel. The other painting is a stereotype rendering of Our Lady of Light, probably one of those from New Spain that followed the building of the Castrense in Santa Fe in 1761.

Prince went on to say:

> Above these is an oval frame, and between oddly formed wooden scrolls is a representation of the Saviour, with outstretched hands as if bestowing a benediction, and on the sides are four other oval pictures of saints with the quaint surroundings which characterize the Mexican work of a century ago. The whole was the pious offer-

ing of Don Victor Sandoval and his wife, whose memory is kept fresh in the minds of the grateful people by the following inscription: "Hizo este altar a devosion de Don Vitor Sandoval Y de su esposa Dna. Ma. Manuela Ortiz en el año de 1798."

No illustration of this retable is included in Prince's book.

In 1923 repairs to the roof of Zia mission were undertaken by concerned citizens of Santa Fe in cooperation with the Museum of New Mexico. A staff member of the Museum, Odd Halseth, was in charge of the work (El Palacio, V. 16/1, 1924 and V. 77/3, 1971). In his brief report on the project Halseth noted that a part of the neo-Gothic woodwork in front of the retable was removed, exposing older painting behind the banal superstructure. Although Halseth's report was about the Zia mission, an interior view of San José at Laguna was used to illustrate the 1924 report. It was only recently, in going through photographs made by Halseth during his years with the Museum of New Mexico, that his photograph of the Zia sanctuary and retable came to light and was recognized. The clerestory window, still functioning in 1971, clearly lighted the altar screen or that much of it visible behind rustic Viollet Le Duc trumpery. The salomonic columns and painted scrolls, finials and cornice ornamentation are quite comparable to those of San Miguel in Santa Fe and to San José at Laguna. Here the Laguna santero had three canvases from New Spain already made to coordinate with his design. Frustratingly, the four ovals of saints with quaint surroundings and whole lower part of the retable are invisible, but from what is to be seen there can be no doubt of the identity of the santero. Both the San Miguel and Zia retables were dated 1798; Victor Sandoval and his Ortiz wife were most probably moved to make the donation to Zia after having seen the completed altar screen of San Miguel, commissioned by Antonio José Ortiz.

A hard look at Santa Ana mission leads to the conclusion that the Laguna santero originally made the altar screen there, although for fifty years or more it has been covered with flimsy boards painted white, so that only the twisted pillars are visible. However, the well defined panels formed by cornices and columns are there to suggest the hand of the Laguna santero. Santa Ana Pueblo is just downstream from Zia; why would not the donors have retables made for both pueblos? Evidently Santa Ana's altar screen had been painted over before Prince saw it; he merely noted that over the altar is "a large painting of John the Baptist and the Saviour, the latter much smaller than the Baptist, and with a dove over his head." This identification is amusing, for the canvas is still in place and represents the patroness, Saint Ann, with the little Virgin; the painting was sent from New Spain soon after the rebuilding of Santa Ana mission in the early 18th century.

As no record was made of altar screens in the Santa Fe parish church after the Spanish period (and rather sketchy descriptions then) we may wonder if the Laguna santero had worked there. But from existing evidence such as old photographs and the stylistic trademarks of the santero himself, it now appears that he did work in the capital and,

Following Page:
Plate 7: Detail, San Juan Nepomuceno, Laguna Mission.

within a few years, executed commissions in at least three and possibly more pueblos to the south.

Nine single panels by the same santero are all that I have succeeded in isolating as his; most of them are larger than those made in New Mexico except for an altar screen. Three represent St. Joseph, four are of St. John Nepomuk and one each depicts the Virgin of Sorrows and Our Lady of Guadalupe (Ref. Appendix I-G for tree-ring dating). The first two subjects repeat those of the altar screen of San José at Laguna. While all of these retablos reflect contemporary Mexican canvases in their poses, dress and details, they are presented in a truly popular style and not to be confused with the semiamateur attempts at Baroque sophistication of Franciscan Father Garcia and the military Miera y Pacheco. The Laguna santero, working just at the end of the 18th century, was a true folk artist in his use of tempera pigments and abandonment of perspective and realism for two-dimensional treatment of his subjects. His example may well have shaped the New Mexican santero school as much as the 1760 stone altarpiece influenced the plan of all the succeeding wood altar screens made after that date.

In view of many deprecatory comments on the popular painting of New Mexico by newcomers from Mexico, from Dominguez in 1776 through the first part of the 19th century, the comment of Cura José Tomás Abeyta in 1840 is somewhat surprising:

> On the main altar screen is the image of San José in retablo painted in tempera of various colors, fine and very firm. Adorning this altar screen are four columns, turned and well made. Three shells of medium size, prettily placed, and finials at the tops. Above is the image of the most holy Trinity, at the right that of San Juan Nepomuceno and at the left Santa Clara. [The panel at the viewer's left, in facing the altar, is of San Juan Nepomuceno and that on the right side is of Santa Barbara, not Clara.] There is a very pretty crucifix . . . four very old carpets, two more of old, red jerga . . . a tanned buffalo hide, well painted and attached to the ceiling with much nicety.[4]

Here called *un curtido,* or tanned hide, the buffalo skin canopy had been a feature of New Mexican churches to prevent adobe particles, dust and other things from falling upon the altar. An inventory of Santa Ana mission in 1743 notes, ". . . two painted buffalo hides that serve as a 'heaven' over the altar" (dos antas pintadas que sirve por cielo en el altar). Following the item is the familiar note in a later hand: *no parese* (not visible).[5]

The fire-eating Visitor de Guevara, in a general report on New Mexico upon his return to Durango, October 23, 1820, wrote his summarized comment thus:

---

[4]AASF, L. D. 1840 No. 9, July 3, 1840.
[5]AASF, L. D. 1712, 1, Fgmt. Inventory, Santa Ana, 1712–1753.

Of 35,500 and more souls, one thousand Spanish and mixed know the Christian doctrine. Thirty of these read and write with some orthography. But the Indians of all missions except Senecu barely know any more of God than do the Gentiles . . . From so much irreligion comes the indecent decayed state of the churches, lack of ornaments, the fatal desolation of the House of God . . . The most attended mission in all of the Province, that of El Paso del Norte, is worse than a grog shop of pulque in Mexico City . . . So many birds perch on cornices over the altars of these churches, and bathe in the holy water and baptismal fonts that they are filthy. When I have played the organ I have been accompanied by the swallows.[6]

LAGUNA SANTERO

A method of dating wood specimens by their annual growth rings was devised by the late Dr. Andrew Ellicott Douglass.[7] Properly known as dendrochronology, it is more often called tree-ring dating. Its accuracy attracted the interest of archaeologists, who have used it for some decades in dating prehistoric sites, although Dr. Douglass' original object was to study long-term weather cycles from annular records of tree growth. Only trees that make a single growth ring a year lend themselves to the study. Such trees include pine, fir and piñon in the southwestern United States, all of which were used in construction at most archaeological ruins there.[8]

When tree bark is found on one edge or surface of a wood specimen, the outside ring is said to give a bark date, telling the exact year that the tree was cut; obviously none of the outer growth rings has been lost. However, a bark date does not give the year when the wood was used by builders or by a santero. Its value is in the fact that we know that the wood specimen could not have been put to use *before* the year of the bark date. While many roof beam specimens give bark dates, or those close to bark, hand-hewn logs shaped into approximately rectangular panels do so less often. In such cases the outside dated ring (hereafter called ODR), is given with the symbol $+ X$. Thus, 1800 $+ X$ is read, "1800 plus X number of years." While some examples might lack a hundred rings between ODR and bark, it is more often the case that plus X represents only a few missing rings, or years.

[6] AASF Accounts LXII, Box 5, Santa Fe, Book II, J, fo. 143 vo.

[7] *Climatic Cycles and Tree Growth.* Carnegie Institution of Washington, Pub. 289, Washington, 1919, 1928, 1936.

[8] *Dating Prehistoric Ruins by Tree-rings,* W. S. Stallings, Jr., Laboratory of Anthropology, Santa Fe, 1939.

If the tree-ring method of dating seems imprecise as well as tedious, which it is, it is far more accurate than the recently developed and much more costly technique known as Carbon 14 which provides dates for prehistoric and geological specimens in terms of thousands of years. Such broad dating is useless for historic materials where the researcher wants to know whether an object was made in one year or the next.

Tree-ring tests have given bark dates for a few New Mexican retablos and more + X dates which agree within reasonable limits with other available controls such as church inventories, vital statistics, information of descendants of santeros and a few boards dated by santeros.[9]

Due to the labor connected with fashioning logs into boards in colonial as well as territorial New Mexico, any serviceable piece of shaped lumber was reused after it had served its original purpose (Ref. Sec. II-B, Woodworking). Retablos were painted on boards that had first been parts of a chest, as is witnessed by traces of the dovetail joins on edges, or fragments of straw decoration. Others were simply painted over a new layer of gesso on an older, damaged panel. This is why tree-ring dating of a series of panels by one santero will turn up with one or more ODRs as much as 50 or 75 years earlier than the rest of the series. These are clear cases of reuse of salvaged boards and should be evaluated as such.

One of Dr. Douglass' first students of dendrochronology was W. S. Stallings, Jr. After working with tree-rings for archaeological dating purposes, he became interested in applying the method to New Mexican retablos; to my knowledge he is the only dendrochronologist who has done so. Hoping to arrive at precise dating of specimens in spite of missing rings, he experimented with a system of estimating the number of annual rings from the point of heartwood-sapwood contact to the absent outer bark. After testing several hundred retablos, Stallings came to the conclusion that his estimates made on this basis were not accurate, as is to be seen in the following table, but they came close enough to the actual ODRs to supply a general working date for a santero.

I am indebted to Mr. Stallings, and to Dr. George Mills, former Director of the Taylor Museum, for permission to read and to quote from the uncompleted manuscript.

Six panels by the Laguna santero tested for tree-ring dating by Stallings, using heartwood-sapwood contact to estimate bark date:[10]

1. Virgin of Sorrows, L. 5. 52–7 (MNM), ODR 1770, estimated tree cut between 1795–1801 (minimum-maximum estimate).
2. St. Joseph, L. 5. 52–6 (MNM), ODR 1771, estimated tree cut between 1786–1791.

---

[9] See dates given for other santeros, Sections I-D, -F, III-A, -B, -C, -D, -E, -G, -H

[10] Three other panels, of Our Lady of Guadalupe, W. R. Nelson Gallery No. A. 33-1343, of St. John Nepomuk, L. I. 56-3 (MNM), and of the same, F.A. 68, 20-4, have not been tested for tree-ring dates.

Plate 9:Detail, Santa Barbara, Laguna Mission.

3. St. Joseph, A. 5. 52–9 (MNM), ODR 1792, estimated tree cut between 1794–1803.
4. St. Joseph, T. M. 1615 (TM), ODR 1795, estimated tree cut between 1791–1803.
5. St. John Nepomuk, T. M. 875 (TM), ODR 1775, estimated tree cut between 1797–1799.
6. St. John Nepomuk, L. 5. 53–15 (MNM), ODR 1776, estimated tree cut between 1771–1817.

This table shows that estimates based on heartwood-sapwood contacts for cutting dates slightly overshot the actual ODR in the cases of Nos. 4 and 6. The estimated minimum-maximum cutting dates for panel 6 are earlier than those for the rest of his panels and for the Laguna altarpiece. The estimates for the other five panels are, if reduced to a mean average, close enough to the postulated dating of 1800–1808 for the altarpiece to establish a rough working date for the Laguna santero between 1790 and 1808, placing him as a turn-of-the-century folk painter.

CONSERVATION OF THE LAGUNA MISSION ALTAR SCREEN, 1950

While the well-prepared gesso ground and pigments of the San Jose altarpiece had withstood a century and a half of exposure to atmospheric changes, and had had better care than was the fate of some other mission ornaments, shrinkage of the heavy hand-hewn boards had allowed them to settle in their frames, thus starting flaking of gesso along the edges of each board. This condition is visible in several photographs taken before 1950, and had the added complication of some fifty nails which had been driven into the surface at random, even on the faces of the images, for the purpose of hanging up greens and harvest fruits at Christmas and other feast days. Cracks originating at the nail holes were radiating in all directions.

The missionary at the time was Father Agnellus Lammert, O.F.M., whose memory will be kept green by all of the Indians of Laguna, Acoma and their outlying villages. In the nearly twenty years that he ministered to them, his competence, enterprise, practical religious teachings, genial personality and devotion to pueblo welfare left a record of spiritual and material benefits to his charges only matched by their affection and respect for Father Lammert. Between the duties of the church he found time to successfully defend pueblo claims to land grants which had been extorted from them in the previous century and to restore and protect the physical structures of the two old missions, whose history he had made it his business to learn. The condition of the Laguna altarpiece, although a relatively minor detail in his far-flung program, was a matter of concern to him. As a result of this I was able to interest the late Dr. Frederick Webb Hodge, then director of the Southwest Museum, in sponsoring the project of conservation of the altar screen, which the Southwest Museum's Board of Trustees graciously approved (Ref. Masterkey, V.XXV/1, 1951, p. 8).

Equipped with materials and employing methods as advised by Dr. Rutherford Gettens, chief of technical research, Smithsonian Institution, I spent my vacation of 1950 at Laguna on scaffolding set up by Father Lammert and his assistant, Father Robertson. Cleaning off layers of dust exposed sound, hard gesso where there was no cracking, and the brilliant colors of the original tempera. Gesso losses were filled in where nails were removed and along the edges of the loose boards, and then colored to match the adjacent color areas with transparent water color paints (Bourgeois Aíné). The entire retable — panels, pediments, cornices, finials, shells and twisted pillars — was given two coats of hot liquid wax-rosin. The cooperation of the pueblo and the Franciscans who have succeeded Father Lammert has, thus far, kept the altar screen unchanged, and its protective treatment should enable it to last for many years.

While working on the lower tier of panels I asked permission to remove the small one on the Epistle side of the old tabernacle, and was then able to crawl behind the wooden framework. The space between it and the rear sanctuary wall is about fourteen inches; empty five-gallon oil drums could just be stacked in it as substitute for a ladder. With a flashlight, Father Robertson and I located the inscription on the back of the panel of the Trinity, about in the center, scribbled in blackish brown color. In entirety, it resembles the sketch:

Se pinto este
coral yse yso
á costa del Al^{de}
Mallor D^n José
Manuel Aragon
este año 180

The first numeral is the accepted Spanish script for one, and clearly is not a seven. The two doodles to the left suggest practice figures for the missing word *de*. The entire lack of spacing indicates a rough note, jotted on handy lumber while it was still on the floor, to refresh the santero's memory when he came to letter the cartouches on the front. No benefactor would consent to have his gift memorialized in sealed-away darkness in those days, but expected that his name would be visible to all like the inscriptions on the stone retable of la Castrense that commemorated Governor Marin del Valle and his wife in 1760. Since the loss of the Laguna inscriptions this casual note on the back is a fortunately preserved bit of evidence. The incomplete date may have been intentional, depending on the actual time of finishing the work. Such projects were often done in winter when men were in the village instead of the fields and indoor work was practical. Time was not important; for example the altar screen might have been begun in November and not completed until February or later. The santero would brush in the date when the time came.

My reason for reading the notation on the back of the screen as 180– rather than –780 is based on the report on the missions of New Mexico made by Father Joseph Pereyro in 1808, in which he said that the retable at Laguna was made by 1803. Pereyro seems to have given rose colored reports to judge by comments on them by the Visitor de Guevara in 1817–18 but it is justifiable to assume that the altar screen was certainly completed by 1808. The dating of beams in the sanctuary as of the 1780s did not necessarily have any relationship to the installation of the screen below. No such systematic method of replacement or foresighted repairs was the rule.

Plate 10: The old tabernacle, Laguna Mission.

(Plates 6 through 10, photographs by Ernest Knee.)

Since 1950 San José mission at Laguna suffered a lightning bolt which struck the roof on the north side just above the chancel rail. By some miracle the dry timbers did not burn; only a section of the plaster was lost in the painted textile design on the sanctuary wall.

By 1966 only minor overpainting of the sanctuary ornaments had taken place: that of the portable wooden tabernacle and of the buffalo hide altar front. An unfortunately large new altar table was added to the furniture of the sanctuary in order to comply with the recent ecumenical reforms, but the more important treasures of Laguna Pueblo's mission were preserved until 1967. In the autumn of 1969 I found the church in poor shape. The hard plaster on exterior walls had cracked, causing leaks on the interior in spite of several new patches at the roof level. A large channel in the inside wall came from a south window of the nave. A hailstorm the day before had caused the latter, I was told, but there were previous leaks in the roof elsewhere. The sacristan said that the year before the whole sanctuary roof had been replaced because the old vigas were rotted. They had been cut off flush with the inner walls, their hand hewn stumps still visible from the outside. The new vigas, plain and skimpy, were spaced as far apart as possible and stained dark brown. Instead of replacing the old herringbone latias above the vigas, white ceiling board sheets had been laid up.

The richly painted, tapestrylike frescoes of the angled side walls which had survived, with the exception of the small area struck by lightning, for some 160 years had been crudely whitewashed. Here was a major example of wallpainting on adobe walls from the Franciscan period, now lost. The sanctuary now contrasts painfully with the still intact colonial beams, corbels and latias of the nave. Lacking a clerestory window the altar screen is lost in darkness unless a dangling electric bulb is lighted, and now is isolated from the rest of the church by the loss of the painted wall surfaces so well devised by the Laguna santero.

Other work on San José mission at the time included the removal of plaster from the front of the beam supporting the choir loft, when a carved inscription came to light.

"Se acabo el 6 de Agosto en el año de 1811" (Completed on the 6th day of August in the year of 1811). In 1776 Dominguez had said that there was a choirloft in Laguna mission, reached by a stone stairway from the convent; this inscription suggests later repairs or rearrangement of the stairs as they now are, inside of the church.

TEXTILES AND COSTUME

Plate 11: *Jerga*, carpet, of diamond twill weave. (Plates 11 through 17, Photographs by Eliot Porter)

By the end of the Middle Ages in Europe weaving had become a professional trade, and the cities most distinguished for their products had powerful guilds regulated by various standards and often enjoying special privileges. At the same time the rural population continued to spin and weave at home, so that the spinning wheel and loom were fairly common items of domestic furniture for the making of what was required for family use rather than for commercial trade. Such goods, whether of wool or linen, were generally classed as homespuns, and did not compete in quality of fineness or design with Cloth Hall fabrics. Colonial settlers brought this tradition with them to New Mexico as well as flocks of sheep whose progeny, it was hoped, would furnish both meat and fleeces for the future.

The first Spanish explorers had been impressed by the skill of Pueblo Indian weavers who made their clothing of cotton raised for the purpose, and who used some other vegetable fibers as well. The Spanish called the Indians' rectangular kilts, shawls, and dresses by one name, manta, a general term for cotton cloth. After the conquest each pueblo was required to give so many mantas, along with foodstuffs and unpaid labor, as part of its tribute. However, the imprecise terminology of Spanish documents does not make it clear when Indian weavers took up weaving with wool and began to abandon cotton except for their own use in ceremonial garments. The manta is mentioned as a trade commodity in the 18th century, but whether these were all of wool is not stated (Appendix, Mantas).

Church inventories of the early part of the 18th century note that liturgical articles such as the alb, amice, and towels were of linen, from "Ruan" (Rouen), Cambrai, or Brittany.[1]

By 1776 the Rio Grande pueblos seem to have abandoned the growing of cotton altogether; Dominguez noted at Isleta that in the kitchen garden of the convent "cotton is also sown in it and a small amount is gathered for candles" (Dominguez, p. 205). Here he made it clear that

---

[1] AASF, L. D. 1712, No. 1 (Book LXXVIII) Fragment of Inventory of Santa Ana Mission.

it was used for candle wicks, but does not mention cotton elsewhere except among the Moqui.

Certainly Spanish sheep had adapted to the new environment and had multiplied enough to allow a changeover from cotton to wool weaving in the 17th century. The result was that cotton fabrics, like linens and silks, became exotics until after 1805 when the fair at Valle de San Bartolomé was officially established (See p.217 on cottons).

For the colonial period the basic fabric was plain-weave woolen homespun woven of natural yarn, 50 to 60 centimeters in width. Originally called bayeta (in English, *baize*), as it still is in Spain and in the Andean Highlands, the New Mexican name has become *sabanilla,* from Spanish *savana* ("sheet" or "plains"). Woven of natural yarns, it was then dyed if so desired, usually indigo, sometimes red. Homespun clothing was made of this, as well as wool sacks for mattresses. It was also the support for *colchas,* wool embroidered hangings. Nineteenth century New Mexican usage of the nouns bayeta, colcha, and sabanilla have resulted in present-day confusion of the definition of these materials. As late as 1812 Pedro Bautista Pino specifically wrote of *bayetones* and bayetas being woven in New Mexico, baize with nap, and plain baize.

Later on in the 19th century bayeta came to mean only the imported, factory-made English baize which was shipped to Mexico in many colors where it was in demand for clothing and interior decoration. As trade goods to Indians it was raveled and rewoven in some southwestern Indian blankets. A popular tradition of the early 20th century was that the raveled red yarns in these blankets had been obtained by despoiling dead Spanish or Mexican soldiers of their uniforms, presumably on battlefields. This was another of our great American myths, for there were not enough Spanish or Mexican soldiers in uniform — dead or alive — to provide such material for half a dozen blankets. The cloth, commonly called Manchester cloth from the English textile center of that name, was received by the bolt and valued for its bright red color which our Indians had not been able to obtain before. Manchester cloth was also made in dark blue, brown, green and yellow, but these colors were not scarce among Indian or Spanish weavers. Scraps of Manchester cloth in all of these colors as well as red are to be seen on old petacas or rawhide trunks made in Mexico which have squares of baize laced into place by rawhide thongs over their outer surfaces. When new the gay colors and white lacings stitched in geometric patterns presented a bright splash of decoration.

It is uncertain whether or not the European upright spinning wheel was brought to New Mexico in colonial times. If it was it was soon replaced by the Indian, pre-Spanish *malacate* or spindle, a slender, pointed stick with a small disc at one end. Wrapped with raw cotton or wool, the stick was twirled between the hand and thigh of the spinner. Indians had made spindle whorls of gourd rinds or ground potsherds since they became weavers. Whorls of historic pottery have been found in quantities in the excavation of historic mission ruins of our southwest where it is assumed that spinning was done by the Indians. However, they have also been found in quantities, with a few discs made from glazed majolica vessels, in ruins of Spanish homes where it may be argued that spinning was done either by colonists or by Indian servants.

A horizontal spinning wheel, made and used in New Mexico, may be described as a sloping sawhorse hewn roughly from logs with a medium sized wheel at one end and a small guide wheel at the middle of the sawhorse. This wheel used the spindle whorl as a bobbin, and turned out coarse thread or yarn. Parts of the same type were found during the excavation of La Purisima Concepción mission at Lompoc, California, which was abandoned about 1835. In the valley of Mexico, weavers at Santa Maria Chiconcoac use the same form of spinning wheel today, operating it by hand or foot power to spin heavy yarns for the thick wool rugs which are their specialty.[2] On the basis of this fact it is reasonable to infer that the sawhorse form of spinning wheel was used in New Mexico to spin yarns for the formerly common jerga or floor carpet, while finer spinning for blanket and cloth yarns was done by hand with the spindle whorl.

The New Mexican loom was massive, hewn from tree trunks with no more shaping than could be done with the ax and adz, but it was basically of European design — the same horizontal loom which had been used for centuries in Spain and in Arabic North Africa. The tall corner posts support a frame like a large fourposter bed and canopy, from which four or more harnesses are hung. Warps are strung horizontally; at each throw of the shuttle the weaver presses a foot pedal to pack down wefts. The shaft on which finished cloth rolls up is usually stowed below the level of the warps, and has a crudely carved, solid wooden wheel with notches on the rim which the weaver turns with a stick to roll up the cloth. Shuttles were carved of juniper or fruitwood and smoothly finished. Today, when local weaving is done on factory-made looms, older weavers still prefer the old country-made shuttles.

On these clumsy looking looms the bayeta or sabanilla (homespun) yardage was woven, as were the *fresada* or sarape (blanket) and the jerga (carpet). They were the three basic textiles of colonial New Mexico.

DYESTUFFS

Dyes used in coloring these textiles were partly local since Indians of the region had already made many experiments with them in pre-Spanish times, and had obtained shades of earth red, yellows, and purplish black from various shrubs and herbs. These had been used to

---

[2] Pemex, Vol. XVII, No. 290-a, Mar. 1957. Bulletin of Petroleos Mexicanos.

dye basketry as well as fabrics, and as paints on wooden objects, or for kiva wall paintings. When the Spanish arrived they found Indians of the warmer parts of Middle and South America using a variety of indigo plant native to the Western Hemisphere *(indigofera añil)*, but they also imported the original indigo *(indigofera tinctoria)* to their new colonies. This seems to have been a staple crop, and the dye was probably sent to New Mexico in the 17th century; we know it was commonly sent here in the 18th century from the evidence of documents, painted ornaments and textile fragments. When this blue dye was mixed with yellow or red the additional colors green and purple were then available for dyeing textiles. There is no indication that indigo was, or could be, raised in New Mexico.

The red dyes available to the Old World had been Tyrian "purple" — extracted from a shellfish known to the ancient Phoenicians and Greeks, but so rare and costly it was reserved for kings — and madder, for the commoners, which produced a rather dull red. Since pre-Cortesian times Indians in the warmer parts of Mexico had collected small red insects from the fleshy bracts of several varieties of what we call the prickly pear cactus and the Mexicans call nopal, which are named by the Linnaean system *coccus cacti.* The insect, *(dactylopius coccus)* is called cochineal in English, and *cochinilla* in Spanish — derived from the Latin *ceccinus,* or scarlet. With controlled solutions, the dyes made from these infinitesimal insects can be made to range from intense clear red through shades of pink, always on the cool side or with a bluish tone, but never muddy.

These useful, although nearly invisible, insects can only exist on the cactus of their preference, and will not live when transplanted to other flora; they are parasitic like aphis, but the latter are far less choosy as to their host plants. In order to profit from a monopoly of this exotic red dye the Spanish tried commercially to cultivate the prickly pear and its cochineal on a large scale for European markets as early as 1525. With his usual attention to every detail in the global Spanish empire, Philip II also took interest in cochineal production. Royal edicts, franchises for the landowners who would undertake cultivation of nopal and cochineal, regulations of dye-workers' guilds, subsidies and other devices figure in colonial documents. There were, however, limitations to the total success of the industry: limited areas where the cactus would grow, colonial concern with the more spectacular rewards of mining or ranching, or political advancement, and the lethargic indifference of serfs, peons, or encomenderos who were charged with the transplantation of cactus and the care and collection of the cochineal crop. In Oaxaca and parts of Guatemala natural conditions were ideal, as in pre-Cortesian times.

From these regions cochineal dye was carefully collected and shipped out, but it remained a costly dye compared to the more common indigo. As a result little cochineal reached New Mexico in the colonial period. Instead, what was called *brasil* was used for red and pink colors in textiles. In fact the red extracted from the sap of this tropical hardwood tree gave its name to the country of Brazil, and it was extensively used in Portuguese-Spanish colonial times, but little or none reached the northern frontier. Instead New Mexicans made similar dyes from the native mountain mahogany, a small hardwood tree found here at about 7,000 feet altitude. These colors were attractive, giving a range of deep, warm, red-golden color, or faded Venetian red through paler hues to café-au-lait. The dye, locally called brasil in Spanish or logwood in English, could not produce a true scarlet, crimson, or magenta red.

Protective measures were taken to prevent the nopal and live cochineal from being smuggled to Europe, but it is said that British pirates made an overland raid from Honduras and stole some plants and insects. Thus the secret of the source of the dye became known, but the theft and precautions against it seem absurd today because neither cochineal nor the host plant could exist in Europe. Even the Mediterranean shores experience long-cycle periods of freezing winters which damage imported tropical flora.

After their independence, serious effort by the governments of Guatemala and Mexico to improve their international credit balances led them to real expansion of cochineal raising and production of its dyestuff. By 1846 cochineal exports from Guatemala paid to the republican treasury $239,201 more than the total cost of all goods imported in the same year from England, France, Spain, the United States, Cuba and British Honduras. In 1856 prepared cochineal dyes, sent principally to the London market brought Guatemala revenue amounting to $1,381,245, in addition to profit from the internal consumption of the dye.

Unfortunately the same year, 1856, saw the success of experimental research in German chemical laboratories on synthetic dyes. As might be expected, large factory owners waited for a few years to observe the practical performance of the new aniline dyes, but cochineal sales began to dwindle. Credit balances in Guatemala shrank as sales of cochineal tumbled to $246,388 in 1876, and to $9,200 by 1883. By that time nopal plantations had been abandoned, and coffee was added to the list of export market crops of indigo, cocoa, sugar and tobacco.[3]

For the reasons given above, more cochineal seems to have reached New Mexico weavers in the second quarter of the 19th century than before, and to have been more or less discarded in the third quarter when packaged dyes became a common mercantile item. Presence of any amount of cochineal dye in New Mexico blankets or wool embroideries is a fairly justifiable criterion for assigning such examples to the period of, roughly 1830–70 — as it is also for fine sarapes made in Mexico. The aforesaid period of maximum use of the dye does not imply

---

[3]Rubio Sanchez, Manuel, "La Grana O Cochinilla." In *Antropologia e Historia de Guatemala,* V. XIII, No. 1, 1961. Bulletin of Instituto de Antropología e Historia de Guatemala.

that cochineal was not used in New Mexico before this time, but simply that a little more was used than previously.

BAYETA

The homespun woolen of the 18th century, such as was used in garments, could hardly be expected to survive the wear and tear of 200 years in a country where everything was patched and used over again until it disintegrated. Clothing of the period before 1800 can be reconstructed from various graphic sources in Mexico and in the costumes of some New Mexican santos, but the actual appearance and texture of colonial New Mexico homespun might never have been definitely known had it not been for a series of pious acts. In 1759 the Governor of New Mexico, Francisco Marín del Valle, had inquiries made among the Indian pueblos as to their legends of former Franciscans who had seemed to them exemplary models of goodness and devotion. Two such friars were named whose memory as holy men had been kept green in the minds of Indian generations, and their bones were duly exhumed from the missions where they had been buried and brought to Santa Fe. There they were reinterred together in a stone sarcophagus of two compartments which was sealed and laid up at eye level in the massive adobe wall of the sanctuary of the parish church as a constant reminder of piety to the sometimes less virtuous citizens of the capital.

Although the adobe parish church has been torn down for over eighty years its sanctuary was left as part of the new stone cathedral until 1966. Ten years earlier, in 1957, the stone sarcophagus was removed from the old sanctuary and inset into the west wall of the chapel of Our Lady of the Rosary whose statue, more generally known as *La Conquistadora,* it also contains. During the process of this transfer the stone lid of the casket was opened and the remnants of two blue woolen Franciscan habits were seen wrapped around the remaining bones of the venerable friars.[4] Through the kindness of the Franciscan fathers attached to the cathedral, samples of these woolen textiles were given to the Museum of New Mexico.

One habit was of a plain-weave wool homespun, or bayeta cloth, dyed a fairly deep indigo blue, wrapped with the bones of Fray Ascensión Zarate, who died and was buried at Picurís in 1632, according to the inscriptions on the stone sarcophagus. The material has twelve warps and fourteen wefts per centimeter. The habit of Fray de la Llana, also of medium indigo blue, was not of bayeta but a very finely woven

---

[4] "The Unique Tomb of Fathers Zarate and de la Llana in Santa Fe," Fray Angelico Chavez, N.M.H.R., V. XL/2, p. 101.

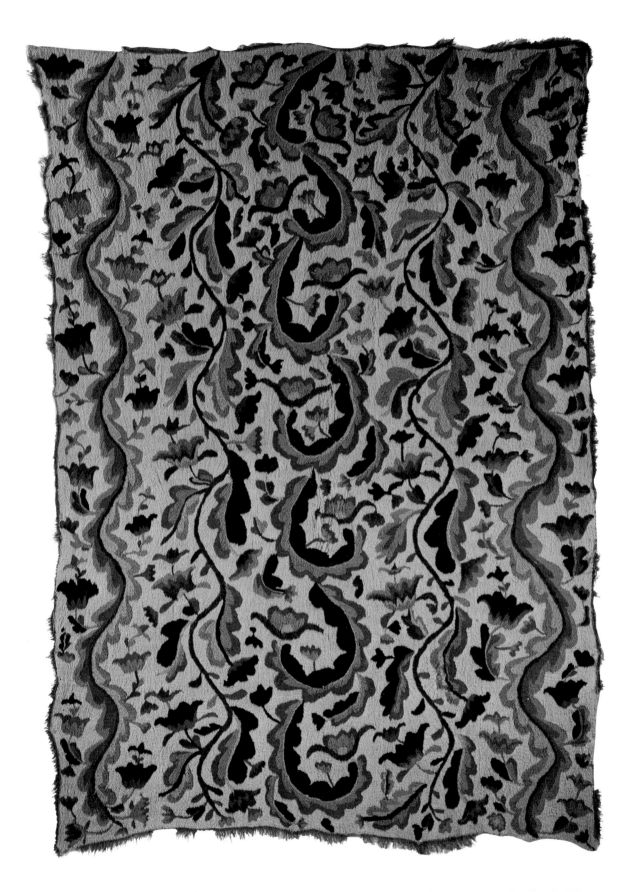

Plate 13: Embroidery in the
colcha stitch, natural dyes, on
homespun wool support.

178

Plate 14: Colcha stitch embroidery, natural dyes including cochineal.

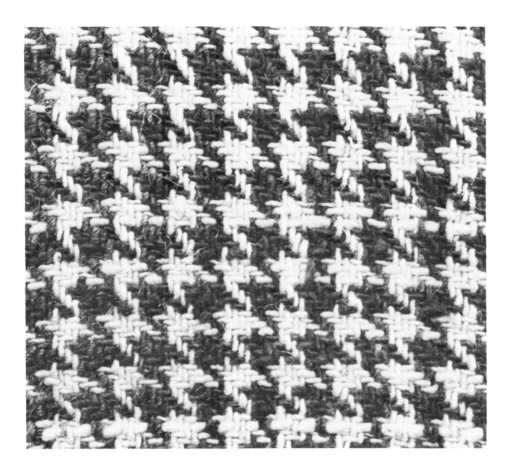

Figure 117: *Jerga* or floor carpet, diagonal twill weave.

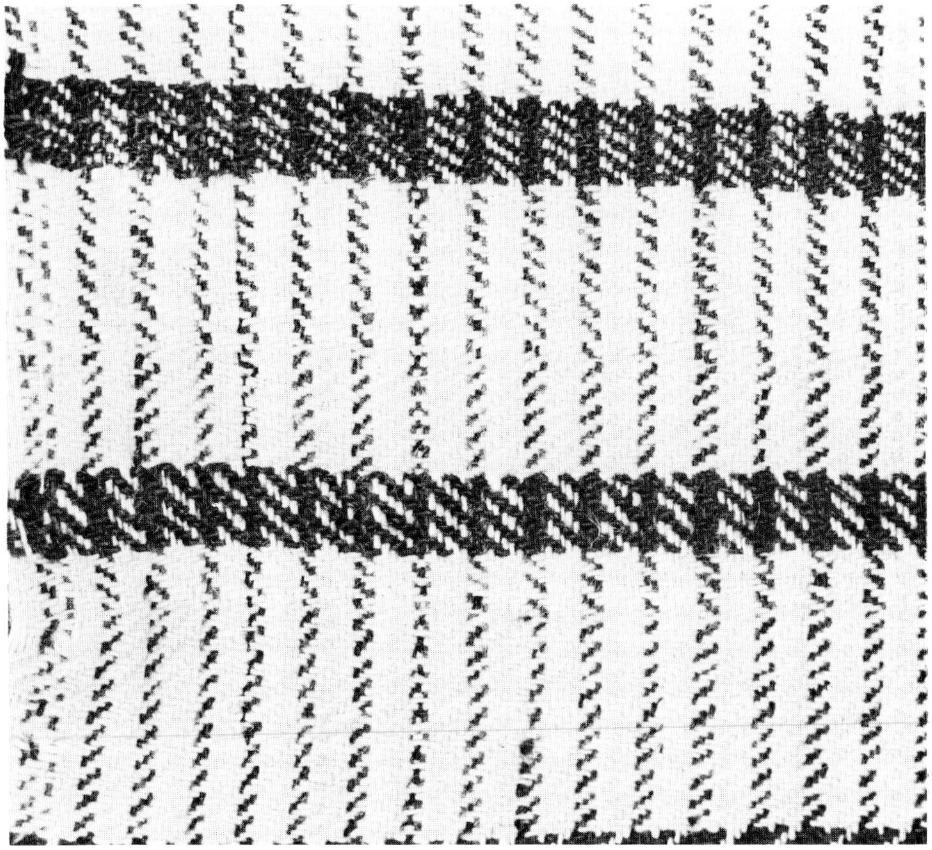

Figure 118: Checked jerga of natural yarns.

diagonal twill of silky texture like baby flannel. The hood of this habit was intact and was stiffened by rows of small stitches about one centimeter apart. Fray de la Llana had been buried in the floor of Quarai mission in 1659 and Fray Zarate had lain in the mission at Picurís for 127 years. Both churches were in ruins in 1759 and had been for eighty-seven and seventy-nine years, respectively. When the venerable bones were brought to Santa Fe in 1759 they were evidently wrapped in new habits before reburial. That the two habits were not alike suggests the scanty supply stocks of the colony at that time. The twilled weave habit was undoubtedly sent from New Spain as missionary equipment, while the bayeta one may very well have been woven in New Mexico. Both samples are unfaded since they were protected from sunlight, and are visible testimony of the kind, quality and color of the blue habits worn in colonial New Mexico by Franciscans.

THE JERGA

We tend to forget that only in the days of Tudor Queen Elizabeth did the fork begin to be used by the nobility whose personal fork and knife were carried in fancy leather cases with other baggage. Even then food bones and table scraps were tossed to the dogs on rush-strewn stone floors. For this reason carpets were reserved for audience chambers and church sanctuaries and were not used on the floors of domestic rooms until certain niceties were introduced into the habits of our ancestors. Colonial merchants of our Atlantic states, when prosperous, had one or more "turkey carpitts" in the best parlor but these were, as a rule, used as a table cover. The floor was more likely to be covered with a painted floor cloth or drugget, or to be of bare, polished wood.

In 1761 a wealthy young man of Mexico City listed a carpet of various colors and seven and one-third varas in length among his assets in a formal letter offering himself as a son-in-law, as proof of his eligibility. Twenty-three years later the same man, by then a widower and very wealthy, owned two carpets in his Mexico City home. One was in the reception room and the other in the family oratory.[5]

Floors in well-to-do homes were either of stone, tile or elaborate parquetry. Fine carpets from the Near or Far East were scarce and those who did own them were apt to hang them on bare walls like tapestries. While carpets were not then regarded as indispensable articles of furnishings, they were beginning to be more familiar through the Manila galleon imports. Thus it was not due to isolation nor barbarism that New Mexicans began to have some sort of carpets in their churches

---

[5] *Una Casa del Siglo XVIII En Mexico,* edited by Manuel Romero de Terreros, Mexico, 1957. The carpet in the chapel measured nine by three and one-quarter varas.

late in the 18th century at about the same time as in the vice-regal capitol. On the frontier, carpets were more modest but were certainly an improvement over bare adobe floors and animal pelts. There probably was some sort of homespun carpet in public rooms of the Palace of the Governors in Santa Fe by 1780 but no inventories of the furnishings of this building in colonial days have been found. As for the first use of the jerga in ordinary New Mexico homes, there is no record until near the end of the 18th century when it is mentioned in various inventories and wills.

Like many other Spanish words the term jerga was absorbed from the Arabic *xerca,* "searge or sack cloth," as it was defined in John Minsheu's Dictionary in Spanish and English of 1599. Regional uses of the word included a thick, coarse cloth, beggar's dress, misfitting clothing, a coarse blanket, saddle blanket, animal bed, poor speech as spoken by someone who has not learned his own language properly, the special jargon of students, gamblers, bullfighters, etc. In recent years rural Spanish New Mexicans have taken to calling all sorts of floor coverings *jerga,* including rag rugs, factory-made carpeting or linoleum. In 18th century documents the word appears as *jerga, gerga* and *xerga.* In contrast to the finely woven or embroidered carpets, *alfombras,* from the Orient, the name was appropriate for the homespun lengths of checks and plaids used in New Mexico.

No samples of jerga now in existence can be proven to be older than the 19th century, and most of these, other than pieces made with natural light and dark wool yarns, contain one or more commercial dyes. As the jergas were laid directly on packed earth floors they naturally wore out from the friction of rock particles and footsteps. Many miles of jerga must have been woven on family looms in New Mexico since it was used not only on floors but as covering for the loads on pack animals.

Yarns for jerga were spun much thicker than those for bayeta or sarapes, of the same general weight as those used in common Navajo rugs. The material was woven on the same harness looms used for blankets in widths of twenty-two to twenty-six centimeters and as long as the weaver chose to make it. These widths were sewn together to make as large a covering for the floor as was wanted. The most common jerga was made of undyed natural yarns worked into checks or, less often, plaids or stripes. The usual weave was diagonal twill, and some pieces were woven in herringbone twill weave. A few specimens were woven in diamond twill called *ojo de perdíz,* or partridge eye, which required more skill and attention to produce. Jerga that is colored with indigo, logwood and vegetal yellows may be supposed to have been woven prior to 1865, or before commercial dyes began to arrive in New Mexico. Later examples sometimes were woven of indigo, natural yellows and commercial red dyes. The warmth and gaiety of these wall-to-wall carpets must have added greatly to simple, whitewashed rooms.

The translators of the Dominguez report quote him as mentioning carpets of frieze, the English word for *frazada* (blanket). New World Spanish-speaking countries have corrupted this to *fresada,* meaning

Plate 15: *El Cibolero,* the New Mexico buffalo hunter. A rare record of the costume 1820–50.

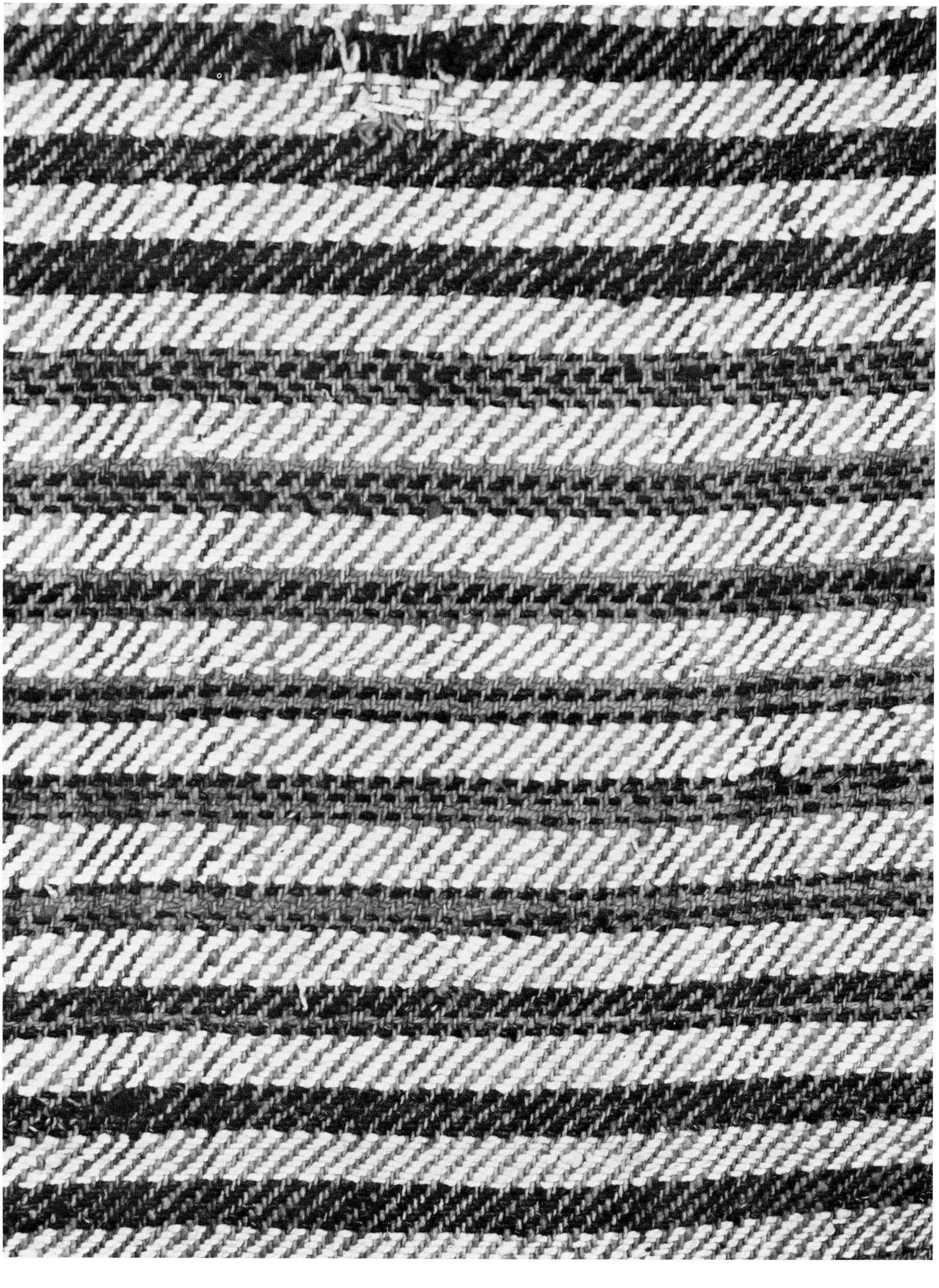

II-A

coarse wool cloth, a blanket or poncho, a hairy, woven coverlet. Goods exported from New Mexico in the colonial and Mexican periods included many bales of fresadas, but today we are quite uncertain about how the article was made and looked. In the inventory of assets of el Santuario de Chimayo in 1818 both fresadas and jergas appear in the same document, from which it may be inferred that two kinds of textiles were meant and that the two nouns were not synonymous (Appendix IB). Dominguez also noted, "a carpet dyed with cochineal which the Indians wove in Father Pino's time." Father Pino was stationed at Acoma at intervals between 1745 and 1767 (Dominguez, p. 191). Of those in available collections, no specimens of jerga have been recorded that contain cochineal dye.

In 1787 there were in the then new chapel of the Third Order of St. Francis, on the south side of the church of Santa Cruz de la Cañada, "two gergas that serve as carpets." After this entry, in another hand, is the notation: "These gergas are those that are now at Abiquiu." Also listed was "one new, colored gerga," which was again commented upon by a later visitor thus: "This belongs to Carmen." The new jerga seems to have been borrowed for the Third Order chapel from the older one of Our Lady of Carmel on the north side of the church.[6]

In the first half of the 19th century, jerga is frequently mentioned in both Spanish and Anglo documents. Surveyor George Champlin Sibley, who had been sent to lay out a feasible road for the newly thriving Santa Fe trade from Missouri, spent the winter of 1825–26 in Taos and Santa Fe. In his diary and accounts of personal purchases he had made to send home in advance of his own return he itemized, among other things:

"No. 1 Bale   6 yds. Herga for Wrapper, canvas and rope"
"No. 2 Bale   1 piece 52 and ¾ yds. Herga. 1 piece 18½ yds. Ditto. 4 yds. for Wrapper. 75 yds. in all, canvas and rope."
"No. 3-4 Bales 1 piece Herga 19 yds., 1 ditto 11½ yds., Wrapping Herga 9½ yds. (Total) 40 yds."

Farther on he again itemized his shipment with valuations; "120 yds. Woolen Herga @ .20 — $24.00." These having been prices paid by Sibley he added, from the viewpoint of his Missouri background: "The Whole Cost of What I have sent home when there delivered may be set down at $165. or very nearly. I think they are fairly worth as follows Vizt. — "120 yds. Herga @ .50¢ . . . 60.00 . . ."[7]

Susan Magoffin in her observant letters to her family, written from Santa Fe in 1846, described the sala of the house which her brother-in-law had rented for her and her husband, in part: "The floor too at the same end of the room is covered with a kind of Mexican carpeting;

---

[6]AASF, Accounts, Book XXXXVI, Box 1, Santa Cruz, 1782–95.

[7]*The Road to Santa Fe,* ed. by G. C. Sibley, 1825–27. Kate L. Gregg, U.N.M. Press, 1952.

Figure 120: The wheel used to spin yarn for jerga in New Mexico, still in use at Santa Maria Chiconcoac. (Courtesy of Pemex Travel Club)

Figure 121: Widths of jerga sewn together to fill floor area.

made of wool and colored black and white only. In short we may consider this great hall as two rooms for one half of it is carpeted and furnished for the parlor, while the other half has a naked floor, the dining table and all things attached to that establishment to occupy it."[8] Mrs. Magoffin's description of the black-and-white wool carpet unmistakably describes the checked jerga made with natural light and dark brown yarns. She also indicates that New Mexico domestic arrangements were still as adjusted to the problems of dining as those of the Middle Ages, "naked" floors being more practical in living areas where meals were served.

In many lengths of twilled jerga it is apparent that different weavers took turns at the loom, indicated by reversal of twilling direction, the relative tightness of the weaving and even complete changes in pattern which occur at random and, after going on for more or less distance, then revert to the original pattern.

After the idea of making rag rugs was introduced by eastern Americans, various experiments were made by local weavers, such as rag wefts on wool warps and wool wefts woven on cotton string warps. Neither durable nor attractive, most of these compromises were replaced altogether by rag rugs. Older weavers made these in large sizes for home use, and the few country-made looms still in operation produced nothing else in their last years except in the Chimayó valley where blankets are still made today.

THE RIO GRANDE BLANKET

The largest category of textiles made by New Mexico Spanish weavers that has survived is the Rio Grande blanket. The name was given by the late Dr. Harry P. Mera after long study of the material and available records to distinguish these blankets from those woven by Indians, and also in protest against a popular misnomer, current for many years, that of "Chimayó blankets." Nearly all Spanish families had looms on which they or their servants did the weaving. Spanish settlements were along the Rio Grande and its upper tributaries, hence the name Rio Grande is appropriate and inclusive. After commercial bedding and clothing had replaced homemade articles of the kind, the people of the Chimayó valley and its immediate neighboring villages continued to weave for curio dealers in Santa Fe and other tourist centers. While their products were largely designed by the dealers for speedy output, with pseudo-Indian patterns, and were made up of commercial yarns and dyes, the continuing activity in weaving there gave rise to the notion that all

---

[8]*Down the Santa Fe Trail and Into Mexico, 1846–47,* Susan Shelby Magoffin. Yale Univ. Press, 1926. (Paperback reprint 1962.)

blankets of the non-Indian class had been made in or around Chimayó, no matter how old they might be. In fact, weaving for home use persisted well into the 20th century in parts of Santa Fe, Taos and Rio Arriba counties in New Mexico, and in the San Luis valley in southern Colorado, where older weavers continued to exercise the skills they had learned in youth.

In prehistoric times Pueblo Indians had woven on both belt and upright looms. Pueblo refugees who fled to the Navajo-occupied San Juan river-Gobernador districts after the reconquest taught their Navajo neighbors to weave as well as to make pottery. As a result Navajos also worked on upright looms, which entails a method of weaving unlike that used on the European horizontal harness loom, and produces differences in the finished product. The Spanish used the latter, roughly made in the colony, but on the same lines and principles as those used in Spain by the 14th century. They are still to be found in some parts of North Africa. A refined example of these looms was shown in Diderot's Encyclopedia of 1763.[9]

Because no documentary mention of the horizontal loom has been found in regional archives before the middle of the 18th century, it has been argued that they did not exist and that all weaving in New Mexico was done by Indians on upright looms until around 1750. The Spanish loom, as large and cumbrous as a canopied fourposter bed, was probably never transported from New Spain to New Mexico but simply made of local wood on the spot. Like watering troughs of hollowed logs, corral posts and such objects, looms were not mentioned in wills or inventories which did include scarce articles of metal or other imported materials.

Another subject of uncertainty is the approximate date when Pueblo Indians began to weave with wool instead of cotton. While Spanish documents refer to textiles collected as tribute or taxes from Indian villages, their usual word for these articles was manta, a term used for pieces of Indian cloth since the first visitations among Pueblos when their textiles were of cotton or other vegetal fibres. In spite of the scarcity of 17th century records about New Mexico, one invoice, published in 1935, throws some light on both the use of the horizontal loom and of wool yarns.[10] The invoice, made out in Santa Fe, was of goods shipped by Governor Rosas for sale in Parral, Nueva Vizcaya, now the state of Chihuahua, Mexico. The first item is: "Nineteen pieces of sayal containing 1,900 varas." Sayal was a coarse woolen cloth used for wagon covers, tents, sacks and horse blankets. Bloom's comment on this entry was: "It would be interesting, for example, to know by whom, and under what conditions, nineteen pieces of sayal, each a hundred varas in length, were produced. Possibly the wool was prepared and the weaving done in the various pueblos, but more probably an

---

[9]*Encyclopédie ou Dictionnaire Raisonné des Sciences, des Arts et des Métiers de Denis Diderot, Recueil des Planches sur les Sciences et les Arts Méchaniques.* Paris, MDCCLXIII. Reprint, Dover, New York, 1959, Pl. 309, "Weaving, I."

[10]"A Trade Invoice of 1638," Lansing B. Bloom, NMHR, V. X/3, 1935, p. 242.

obraje, or workshop, was operated in Santa Fe with weavers secured from the pueblos under the encomienda system."

Bloom's interest was in enforced Indian labor but the existence of the European horizontal loom is also proven by the pieces of woolen cloth, each 100 varas in length, or, (if all were actually of equal length) 275 feet long. To have been woven on an upright loom the posts and frame of this would have had to be 275 feet high. The horizontal loom with its cloth shaft on which the finished goods are rolled could easily have turned out such lengths. Thus the invoice of Rosas establishes weaving with wool by, and obviously before, 1638 in New Mexico, and the use of the horizontal loom as well. Bloom further translated "mantas" as small blankets, which at least suggests that by 1638 they too were made of wool.

Another debated point in the study of Rio Grande blankets is their age. As yet there seems to be no way of pinpointing the exact age of a given specimen, in spite of some authorities who claim that none exists older than *ca.* 1860, and folksay which sometimes ascribes two or three hundred years to a family heirloom. However, a blanket may be dated within reasonable limits on the basis of materials, dyes and patterns. The strongest argument against great age for any blanket is the fact that they were originally made to serve as bedding and outer clothing and therefore had hard usage. When new blankets were obtained, old ones were converted into saddle blankets, wagon blankets or stuffing for quilts. Moths and mice were also destroyers of woolen goods.

With a few exceptions such as blankets containing handspun cotton combined with wool and others having some areas woven with yarns dyed in ikat technique, most Rio Grande blankets may be safely classified in four chronological groups:

Group I

Those woven with silky merino wool yarns spun in one or two ply and containing only natural dyes or colors. These are not necessarily all present in one blanket. The patterns may be of bands, stripes and ticked lines, or may contain small elements borrowed from so-called Saltillo sarapes imported from Mexico. Since little exists in print about the latter it should be kept in mind that these were finely spun and woven blankets or ponchos valued as much by Mexicans themselves as by New Mexicans and Anglos in the territory of the 1830s and '40s. These sarapes had complicated designs based on medallions and lozenges at the center, multiple, small interlocking lozenges or segments over the field and still more elaborately worked borders on four sides. In the extensive graphic material available that shows the dress of colonial New Spain, such as paintings and prints, there is nothing that depicts the Saltillo sarape until around 1830 and later. Prior to that time blankets worn by rich or poor are shown with patterns of plain stripes, wavy lines, or borders of flowers.

The influence of articles imported by the Manila galleons on handcrafts of New Spain had been powerful for two centuries. It is no surprise to find, as that royal caprice ended early in the 19th century, that other goods from the Far East still exerted an influence by way of trade with France and England. Chinese carpets, Persian hangings and hand-blocked cottons made in India were busily copied in French and English textile mills, and these copies reached New Spain. By 1826, it was said, Mexican artisans could imitate French block printed designs so well that it was cheaper to import plain cotton or linen yardage and hand print it in Mexico than to pay the higher prices and import tariffs on the fancy calicos from Europe. Of the Far Eastern designs, those with large central medallions or lozenges seem to have been adopted in Mexico by sarape weavers in the north. While the name Saltillo has been given this kind of design, similar designs were recorded as having been made in the towns of San Miguel de Allende, Guanajuato, Zacatecas and, farther south, Oaxaca. There seems to be no distinguishing character that might relate an old sarape to any of these centers at present. Like other textiles, those that contain only natural dyes may be presumed to be older than the 1860s. Mexican nationalism began to favor pre-Columbian symbols as the republic grew in stature, so that Aztec gods, the calendar stone and the national emblem of the eagle and serpent may be dated as later 19th century products or those of today.

Whatever the exact circumstances of its invention, the Saltillo sarape was evidently brought to New Mexico in the 1830s. While the finely spun warps and wefts of the Mexican product, whether of flax or wool, were beyond the ability of New Mexican weavers, the design elements began to be adopted by them in their own blankets. Many existing examples suggest that the weavers had little access to dyes other than indigo, logwood and vegetal yellows, thus limiting color schemes, and also that the intricate Saltillo designs were at first beyond their capacity. Presumably the earliest Rio Grande adaptations of imported Saltillos simply incorporated one or two motifs from a design on their usual striped or plain blankets. As the Saltillo patterns grew more familiar, or the weaver's skills increased in New Mexico, more elaborate patterns were undertaken, and sometimes were very successfully carried out. From these Saltillo sarapes was borrowed every design element that is found in Rio Grande blankets. At the same time Navajo weavers also adopted some design elements which they used in their own way.

It has not been proven, as some writers have stated, that the Spanish New Mexicans borrowed certain design elements, such as stepped or terraced lozenges, serrated elements, chevrons and so on, from Navajo weavers in the 19th century. All of these were taken from Saltillo sarapes after their arrival in the frontier and on a far more extensive scale than the borrowings of the Navajo.

Group II

Rio Grande blankets made with imported, three-ply commercial yarns dyed in the factory. These are commonly called Germantowns

Figure 122: Sarape of the second quarter of the 19th century, Mexico, showing direct influence of Oriental design. (Courtesy of the Field Museum of Natural History)

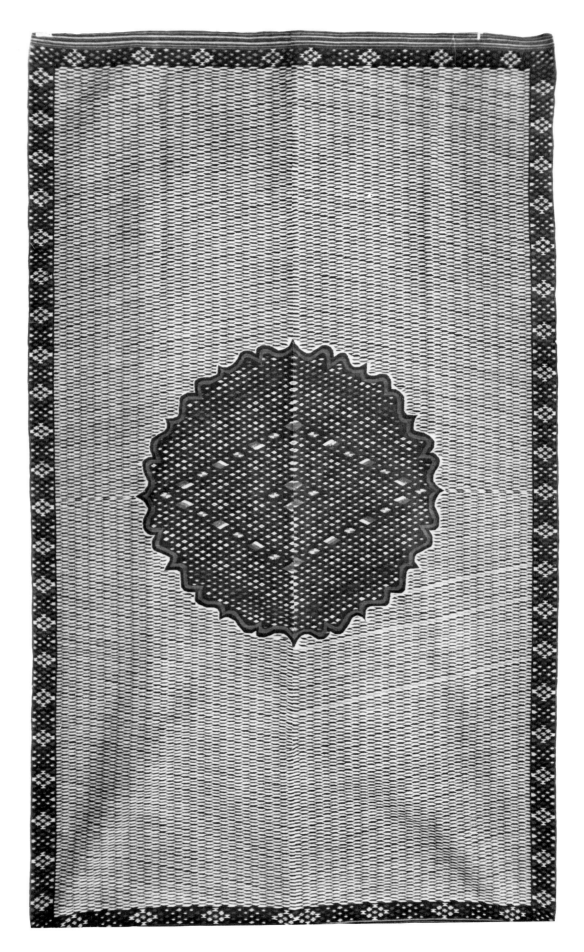

but were also of what is now called Saxony. Spun and dyed in eastern states, they were not necessarily from the kingdom of Saxony nor from Germantown, Pennsylvania, but had been given the names because those places were textile centers at the time, and produced quantities of similar yarns. These yarns were sold in a wide variety of colors which permitted a weaver more latitude in coloring than had the traditional dyes available in New Mexico. Although it has been accepted as fact that these commercial yarns did not reach New Mexico until the Civil War had ended there, or after 1863, it is to be noted that a few blankets worked in busy Saltillo patterns and composed of Germantown yarns contain red areas dyed with cochineal rather than with the new synthetic red dye. Since true cochineal was displaced as a commercial dye in the 1860s, it is possible that some Germantown yarns arrived in New Mexico prior to 1860. For instance, an invoice of goods bought by Richard Owens from the Spiegelberg Beuthner Company, Santa Fe, July 19, 1856, included "25 lbs. scarlet wool yarn @ 2.00 . . . $50.00."[11] With flocks of sheep numbering many thousands in New Mexico at the time, the price of $2.00 a pound for red wool yarn strongly indicates that this was imported from our eastern region. As 1856 was the year when coal tar dyes were first discovered, any red dyed goods shipped west before that time must have been colored with cochineal or madder or some equivalent natural product. Hence Owens' scarlet yarn, and probably other lots of predyed yarns, were already being sent to New Mexico before 1860.

An earlier date for blankets of imported yarns automatically opens the possibility that certain extant examples may be more than 100 years old. Some of the presumably earlier Germantowns are not only woven with wefts of three or four ply yarns, but also with bleached white wool Germantown warps. In view of the cheapness of New Mexico grown wool, a price of $2.00 a pound for imported yarn added greatly to the cost of making a blanket. Either the weaver had his or her own sheep, or the weaver's employers owned them; the annual shearings produced more than could be used in home weaving. It is easily understood why the Germantowns were never common and for the most part ceased to be made after about 1870 when packaged aniline dyes were brought on the territorial market to be used on home grown yarns.

Group III
These include blankets woven of hand-spun wool wefts and warps, many with the silky fibred Spanish Merino fleeces and often with mixtures of natural and commercially dyed colors, apparently determined by what was at hand. For example, one of these blankets might contain indigo, vegetal yellow and a clear vermillion red of commercial origin combined with light and dark natural yarns. Patterns continued to include bands, stripes and ticking together with some elements taken

---

[11]AASF, LDD, 1856, No. 6.

from Mexican sarapes. Borders on the long or selvedge sides tended to disappear, and design motifs grew larger as homespun yarns returned to use. The light, clear, commercial red dye found in these blankets is said by old-timers to have been used only in the 1870s. Unlike later packaged red dyes, this brand (name unknown) did not fade or run. If this folksay about the nonfading red dye having been sold only in the 1870s can be proved to be true, it gives a good ten-year range for blankets in which it is found.

Group IV

By 1880, when the railroad had come into New Mexico and larger quantities of goods could be imported than had been possible over wagon trails, factory-made clothing displaced blankets as garments, and the latter were homemade only for bedding. During the same period, enterprising non-Spanish immigrants had introduced other breeds of sheep that yielded more pounds of wool at a shearing than did the old Merinos. Unfortunately the new breeds, notably the Rambouillet, however productive, had short-fibred fleeces which, when spun, resulted in harsh, brittle and lustreless yarns. These of course could not be expected to make lightweight, silky textured blankets. At the same time commercial cotton warps made their appearance in New Mexico, and are to be found in some examples otherwise dated as having been made in the 1880s and '90s. A few older weavers, or those working in remote places, may have continued to use old designs, some vegetal dyes and wool warps, but for the most part the combination of the new materials prevailed, making these blankets easy to recognize. As herds of goats grew more numerous, mohair yarns were also used in blankets, sometimes combined with wool or with cotton warps. The variety of packaged dyes gave free rein to the weaver's fancy, and light and dark red, candy pinks, blues, greens, oranges and purples were worked up in dazzling discords. When new, one of these blankets, whether designed with stripes or a busy pattern, must have been distracting to look at, but fortunately most of the colors have faded and run into each other after repeated washings.

The new colors were popular in their time, to judge by the many blankets that were made in rainbow hues and busy patterns. The latter were basically continuations of Saltillo motifs, enlarged, removed from their original all-over compositions and coarsened, with large central lozenges and quarters of the same motif in four corners. More often the band or stripe was revived in combination with the lozenge. Folksay ascribes this style to the valleys of Peñasco and las Trampas, on the Sangre de Cristo mountains' western slopes, and to the decades 1880–1900. At el Valle, a tiny hamlet east of las Trampas, local residents tell of a crippled girl named Patricia Montoya, for whom her family made a loom with hand pedals instead of foot pedals. She is known to have woven during the 1890s, and is credited with the introduction of the eight-pointed star as a motif. In point of fact these had appeared many years earlier when indigo and cochineal dyes were still in use. The

Figure 123: A classic sarape of the so-called Saltillo design, Mexico, second quarter of the 19th century.

Figure 124: Rio Grande blanket, New Mexico, reflecting influence of Saltillo sarapes from Mexico.

blankets attributed to Patricia Montoya sometimes contain twelve to fourteen stars which are integrated into complicated patterns. Each star point is diamond shaped and composed of two colors. The starry blanket is now called a *Vallero* after the village where it is said to have been designed. There are so many of these *Valleros* in existence that it is doubtful if one woman could have made them all, but, like any novelty, the designs and color schemes were probably copied by other weavers (Appendix II-A, Names of Weavers).

From 1880 well into this century, stripes and ticked elements continued to be woven on traditional lines but with natural, undyed wool yarns and coal tar dyes. In the San Luis valley, where weaving continued into our own time, one or another of the vegetal yellows and a soft purple made from *capulín* (chokecherries) were combined with the packaged dyes. Perhaps from inability or disinclination to buy dyes, San Luis blankets often contained large areas of undyed white and dark wool yarns. The *sarape del campo* or camp blanket, was made for campers, herders and servants at all times since wool was introduced into New Mexico. It was of natural dark brown wool from "black" sheep, woven in random shades of light to dark yarns, sometimes without a single stripe. Regarded as of no value and given hard use, relatively few camp blankets have survived, but today we find them attractive.

Another fairly uncommon type of Rio Grande blanket was made for the bridal trousseau, either all white or white with a narrow dark brown border at each end. Traditionally these would have been supplied by the groom's family. One of these in the collections of the Museum of New Mexico has carefully spaced brown wool warps in it which appear faintly over the white field, giving the blanket a subtle texture. Either preference for coloring, or the monotony of weaving a solid, unvarying blank cloth, seems to have limited production of white blankets to those woven for ceremonial occasions. Urged to produce all-white rugs for modern markets a few years ago, Navajo women refused to make them on the grounds that it was too boring and that mistakes were too conspicuous.

Particularly in an elaborate design, it is a test of skill for a weaver to complete two widths and have the pattern match exactly along the central seam when it is sewn together. This is demonstrated in some blankets where not only the pattern but the color scheme differs on the two widths. Though names of weavers have been obtained from some families, their recollections did not specify whether one or more persons wove the entire blanket. Because country-made looms, cumbrous as they were, had narrow frames averaging between fifty and sixty-five centimeters, it has been commonly assumed that most old Rio Grandes were woven in two widths and then sewn together. This in turn was assumed to be a criterion of relative age, because modern looms allow wider widths of weaving. However, two samplings undertaken as tests are surprisingly inconclusive as to the relationship between age and the making of blankets in one width or two. The decision to weave a single-width blanket may have been one of professional pride. To do so, a

Figure 125: Printed sarape mechanically produced in Germany for cheap markets after 1880.

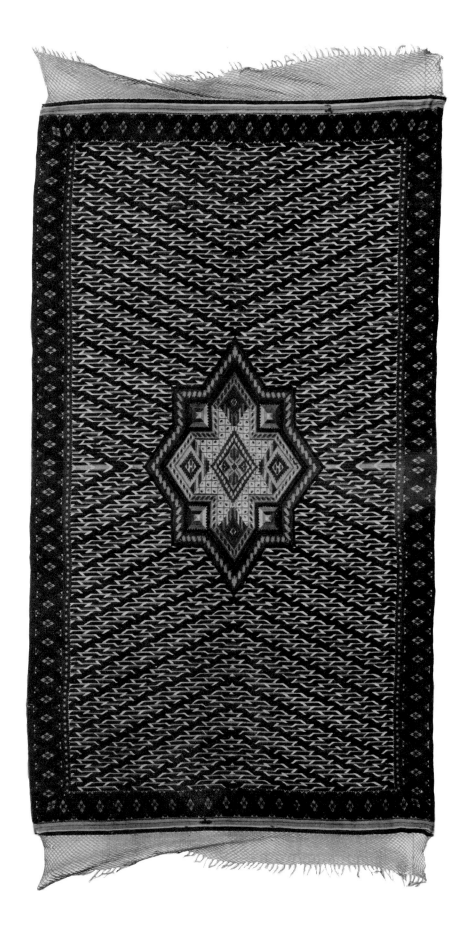

double harness was set up, the weaver began working the shuttle from the left side of the loom across the warps to the right, then down to the underside and back to the left side. If this was more physical labor than working in single harness it also eliminated the difficulties of matching the design on two widths, guaranteeing a continuously identical pattern from side to side.

Sampling One, random blankets in museum collections.

		One Width	Two Widths
Group I	Bands, stripes, ticking, indigo and other natural dyes	7	12
Group II	Saltillo derived patterns, natural dyes, Saxony-Germantown yarns	1	4
Group III	Stripes, Saltillo motifs, handspun yarns, commercial and natural dyes, some commercial cotton warps	10	2
Group IV	Coarse handspun yarns, mohair, commercial cotton warps, commercial dyes, crude color combinations	5	8
		23	26

Sampling Two,

	The Dr. H. P. Mera Collection of Rio Grande Blankets. (S.C.A. Society in Museum of N.M.)		The Charles H. Woodard Collection, (in Colorado State Museum).	
	One Width	Two Widths	One Width	Two Widths
Group I	2	6	7	12
Group II	1	7	2	0
Group III	0	7	10	2
Group IV	1	8	5	8
	4	28	24	22

Although the first sampling was taken from blankets that had not been collected by one individual, some of the figures are, surprisingly, the same (see the random sampling, Group I, and Woodward collection, also in Group I, and, again, the same samplings in Group III). The collection made by Dr. Mera was culled from many possible examples over a long period of time, and, where known, the blankets came from the general area between Taos and Rio Abajo, (south of Santa Fe to Belén). The nature of any collection is influenced by the personal selection of the collector; whether Dr. Mera had a preference for blankets woven in two widths, or whether those were the most numerous among the specimens that he thought best illustrated the sequence of Rio Grande blanket making, are debatable points. In the random sampling and the Woodard collection there appears to be little difference between the use of the two methods. Most of the Woodard collection was acquired in the San Luis valley, Colorado, where commercial looms with frames wide enough to allow weaving of blankets in single widths were introduced by 1890. This fact might account for the ten single-width blankets in Woodard's Group III, but the random sampling

Figure 126: Detail of Figure 127.

Figure 127: Rio Grande blanket, New Mexico, expertly dyed by the ikat technique. Probably made by Ignacio Bazan. (Photographs by Richard E. Ahlborn. Courtesy of Museum of History and Technology, Smithsonian Institution)

Group III did not include blankets all collected from the same region. Perhaps a number of New Mexico weavers had acquired commercial looms at the same time, but away from the Chimayo valley most of the home looms that have been seen in the past forty years, or even fragments of them, were the rough-hewn country-made models with small frames. In any case, the number of blankets woven in two widths from the 117 among three samplings is 76, indicating that New Mexico weavers over decades preferred this method except during the period of Group III; but the margin of difference between the two methods is not enough to prove any particular age for a blanket without reference to the other factors cited above.

There are a number of references in the literature to the master weavers Ignacio Ricardo Bazán and his brother, Juan, who were brought to Santa Fe under contract in order to improve provincial weaving. Whether the cloths were fresadas, mantas, bayetas, or sarapes, it appears that their technical qualities had become so poor that, when sent to Chihuahua for sale or exchange from New Mexico, they brought very small prices. Since New Mexico relied chiefly upon textile exports and tanned hides for credit, this had fallen very low in the outer market. In an attempt to correct the situation the Bazán brothers were engaged by a contract dated in Mexico City in September 1805. They were to live in Santa Fe for six years and teach weaving. No further reference to Juan has been found, but Ignacio appears in his marriage papers of 1807 where he gave his birthplace as Puebla, New Spain, and again when he filed a claim for payment as a master weaver in 1809. His daughter was baptized in Santa Fe; his son, Joaquin Alejandro Bazán, was married to an Ortíz, and their children were baptized at Tomé and at Belén, where Joaquin was buried in 1871.[12] Contrary to popular traditions, nothing has been found to prove that the Bazáns ever lived at Chimayó. The brothers were expected to bring samples of fine weaving, proper looms and other equipment with them, and to improve the value of locally made textiles. Pedro Bautista Pino referred to them, although not by name, in 1812: "A few years ago we saw introduced fine looms for cotton by an expert sent there by the government. He has taught many in a very little time. Although I call it fine this is in respect to that which was made before, for this fine cloth is coarse in comparison with the fine fabrics that we are accustomed to from China."[13]

Pino's comment shows that the weaving of cotton had fallen to as low a level as that of wool, and also indicates that Oriental textiles were a matter of fact even on the northern frontier. However, very little has been found of handspun and handwoven cotton goods in present day collections in the form of yardage or embroidery supports.

[12] Chavez, ONMF, 1954, p. 146.

[13] Pino, Pedro Bautista, "Exposición Sucinta y Sencilla de la Provincia de Nuevo Mexixo," Cádiz, 1812. In *Three New Mexico Chronicles,* transl. by H. B. Carroll & J. Villasana Haggard, Quivira Society, Albuquerque, 1942.

The outstanding specimens containing handspun cottons made in New Mexico are six Rio Grande blankets which, so far as is known, are mavericks among many hundreds of those recorded. The most typical in design as well as material is one in the H. P. Mera collection (L.5.62–74, in M.N.M.). It is 243 by 112 centimeters, woven in two widths of two ply handspun cotton warps and single ply handspun white cotton wefts combined with single ply handspun wool wefts in all areas worked in color. The coloring of the wool yarns is limited to cochineal and shades of indigo. The pattern refers to Saltillo sarape designs although the broken-line motifs relieve the heaviness sometimes found in solid color renderings of these.

During April 1967 I had the opportunity to examine the historic textiles in collections of the Museum of Northern Arizona, Flagstaff. Among their Rio Grande blankets is one two meters by 110 centimeters measured across wool bands, and up to 120 centimeters wide measured across cotton weft bands (MNA 2203/E 1870–272). This blanket is woven in two widths of handspun two ply white cotton warps and handspun two ply white cotton wefts in the white areas. There are paired warps on selvedges. Color areas are of two ply handspun wool. The brown wool stripes have a peculiar sparkle which suggests carefully matched natural wool yarns rather than a brown dye. These stripes are grouped with red wool stripes dyed with cochineal, spaced between broad white cotton bands in which are diamonds formed by small red dots, also cochineal dyed, of extra wefts of wool yarn.

Of particular interest is the original tag on it from the Fred Harvey Indian Department on which is a note saying: "Native cotton raised at Lemitar, N.M." The village of Lemitar on the Rio Grande is about forty-five miles south of Belén, a short distance north of Socorro. Its location is still another possible clue to the identity of the weaver of the handspun cotton blanket series as Joaquin Bazán, son of Ignacio, or some of his pupils. The Museum of Northern Arizona's cotton and cochineal dyed blanket may have been woven at any time between the 1830s and 1860s on the basis of its materials and design. Since Joaquin Bazán did not die until 1871 he could easily have been the weaver of this as well as of the others described here. The record on native cotton raised at Lemitar is of interest because the time period falls between pre-Spanish and colonial raising of cotton and the recent intensive cotton farming of today in the southern part of New Mexico.

Another of this group also is in the Museum of New Mexico (FA.-64.21-1), and was acquired in Santa Fe some forty years ago by the late artist, Olive Rush. This blanket is 206 by 128 centimeters, of two widths, with single ply handspun cotton warps and single ply handspun cotton wefts in the large white areas and of single ply handspun wool, dyed indigo by the ikat method, in the color stripes. A fourth, plain striped blanket now in the Joe and Emily Lowe Museum, Coral Gables, was described by Dr. H. P. Mera as having handspun wool warps, handspun white cotton wefts between stripes of "commercially dyed" red and green three ply wool wefts. Part of these red yarns were raveled and respun with white wool, according to Dr. Mera.[14] The remaining two of the six blankets discussed are in the collections of the Taylor Museum, Colorado Springs. T. M. 3772 is 225 by 123 centimeters, woven in two widths with warps of two ply handspun wool and white wefts of single ply handspun cotton combined with two ply German-town wool yarns in all color areas. All dyes are aniline, bright blue, yellow, two shades each of brown and green, except for areas of com-mercially spun wool yarn dyed with cochineal. The design is a typi-cally New Mexican combination of stripes with serrated and small dotted elements taken from Mexican blankets; the weaver managed a reasonably close matching of pattern and coloring on the two widths. The presence of a small amount of cochineal dye with commercial wool yarns suggests a possible date of the mid-1860s.

The last of this group, also in the Taylor Museum, was a bolder attempt at design and coloring, as if to give the illusion of looking at one textile through another. It is 240 by 115 centimeters, woven in two widths with two ply handspun wool warps and single ply handspun white cotton wefts in stripes spaced between colored areas of three ply Germantown wool yarns. These are worked into an all-over design of serrated lozenges with marked asymmetry in the finished product and equally faulty color matching of the two halves. Colored yarns were the same as in T. M. 3772, all commercially dyed except for small amounts of cochineal, also found in T. M. 3772.

The reflection of Saltillo sarape influence in three of this group of blankets suggests dates of making after 1830; the presence of com-mercially spun and dyed yarns in three, a dating of at least 1855; and the presence of cochineal dye in two, a dating of pre-1865. Number 3 (FA.64.31-1), however, might have been made early in the 19th century in view of its limitation to indigo dye alone and the presence of another foreign element, that of ikat dyed yarn. The technique takes its name in several languages from the Malayan verb *mengikat*, to bind, knot or wind around. The most elaborate textiles composed of ikat dyed threads came from Indonesian islands largely inhabited by Malayans. The threads, cotton or silk, were wrapped in bundles on warps strung on a frame. Where the threads were tightly tied the ensuing dyebath left those areas uncolored. Experts in this method could plan multi-colored designs by tying up enough of the threads to allow progressive untying as each different dye was applied. When the dye process was completed the weaver employed the thread, or yarn, in one continuous length and the pattern, however elaborate, worked itself out with no change in shuttles or bobbins. Both warps and wefts were dyed by the ikat method in some Indonesian textiles.

Like other imports from the Far East, the ikat method was adopted in textiles of New Spain where, even today, silk and cotton rebozos are made in this technique. Fragments of others of cotton and silk have

---

[14] "The Alfred I. Barton Collection of Southwestern Textiles," H. P. Mera, Santa Fe, 1949, p. 99, No. 521.

Figure 128: Rio Grande blanket, hand-spun white cotton warps and wefts combined with natural dyed wool yarns.

been found that were already in the possession of New Mexicans prior to 1830. However, the employment of ikat dyeing on wool yarns woven into Rio Grande blankets remained unnoted until recently when a fragmentary indigo dyed Rio Grande blanket was presented to the Spanish Colonial Arts Society by Mrs. Mabel O'Dell.[15] This, Number L.5.60-48, 186 by 112 centimeters, is woven in a single width with warps and wefts of two ply handspun wool. The design is of the most conventionally striped and ticked type except for five bands of indigo dyed in the ikat manner with simple serrated forms reserved in white. This method seems to have been attempted by a novice as the bands vary in width as much as five centimeters, thus varying the sizes of the serrated motifs. The weaving, however, is even and firm, indicating that this was not entirely the work of a beginner, but only that the dyeing process was unfamiliar. Number 3 in the handspun cotton group, supra, strongly resembles the indigo wool blanket in its ikat dyed striped areas and may have been the work of the same weaver. None of the six blankets just described suggests the work of an imported master weaver, but their peculiarly atypical materials and/or dye techniques do strongly suggest an influence from elsewhere than the upper Rio Grande valley. This might have been Ignacio Bazán and his instructions and example.

What may very well have been woven by Bazán himself is a Rio Grande blanket in the collections of the Smithsonian Institution (U.S.N.M., Acc. No.357.437) which is 279 by 143 centimeters, woven in a single width with four multiple warps down the center and a tightly twisted, three-ply cord along each selvedge. These are not characteristic of Rio Grande blankets. The warps are of single ply handspun natural wool spaced ten per centimeter; wefts are of the same and also woven ten to the centimeter. To quote Pino: "... although I call it fine this is in respect to that which was made before ..." This yarn count is fine for Rio Grande blankets but coarse in comparison to the best Saltillo sarapes. The overall design is of stripes and bands of indigo in two shades, divided by plain white stripes and broad bands dyed by the ikat technique which was woven into repeated white or negative figures closely related to those from Malaysia, a stylized, anthropomorphic form. The planning and spacing of both ikat dyed yarns and plain stripes are mathematically exact and the execution of both dyeing and weaving are professional in this unusually large blanket. At present no comparable Rio Grande blanket is recorded, but if one of this class was made in northern New Mexico, there must have been others. This blanket was collected in Chimayó about 1910. Perhaps similar specimens will come to light from unknown private collections in the future.

Although it has been postulated that the Bazáns were responsible for the introduction of Saltillo sarape designs in New Mexico, it is clearly proven by graphic sources that these had not as yet come into production in Saltillo or other parts of Mexico by 1806. What sort of

---

[15] "Ikat Dyeing in Southwestern Textiles," E. Boyd, *El Palacio,* 68/3, 1961.

patterns did the Bazáns bring with them then? Other than bands and stripes, or floral motifs, what more probable than the much admired Far Eastern ikat dyed designs? The Smithsonian blanket proves that the method could successfully be translated into wool yarns from more traditional cotton or silk. As for the other two Rio Grande examples containing ikating, they, like those containing handspun cotton, suggest that they were the work of a pupil of the Bazáns. The simple serrated indigo bands may have been dyed by a short-cut method, that of holding a hank of yarn doubled over so that both ends fall into the dye pot and the center remains undyed. This, when woven, can only produce simple angular elements like the two shown here. Such cloth is called *tela de lengua* (tongue cloth) in Majorca, where it was made into recent times. The art of ikat dyeing has spread into western South America as well as Mexico and, in the opposite direction, through the Middle East to North and West Africa as well as to textile-making centers of the Asian mainland. Its appearance in New Mexico, however, suggests an early 19th century date when Far Eastern goods, or imitations of these, were more familiar and before commercial goods began to cross the prairies from our eastern states.

How many of Bazán's pupils were volunteers and how many were the *criados* of well-to-do families, or Pueblo Indians, is unknown. Long before 1806 the wealthy New Mexicans had many servants, mestizo, Indian or Spanish, some of whom had the duty of weaving not only for family uses but to supply the tiendas or stores which nearly all landowners maintained. In a barter economy these shops served to provide outlets for the products of the owner's farms and ranches by exchange and in payment for other goods and services. They were not unique to New Mexico but were operated by landowners all over New Spain as well. While sarapes or blankets are mentioned frequently in late colonial New Mexican documents, an idea of the quantities in which they were made is given in the 1814 will of Rosa Bustamante. She was the widow of Antonio José Ortíz, a prominent figure in official and religious affairs in his time and owner of large ranches and herds of livestock. Clause 58 in her fifty-page will states: "I declare as mine two hundred and twenty sarapes made from this year's wool crop."[16] These with other assets were to be sold and the proceeds divided equally among Rosa Bustamante's heirs. Not only did the Ortíz family own thousands of sheep to supply wool, but, evidently, enough criados to weave two hundred twenty blankets between the spring shearing and July 8 of the same year, when the will was written. We would like to know what these sarapes looked like, but, as usual, there is no further notation.

Custos Josef Pereyro made a report on the missions of New Mexico dated 30 December 1808. In the final summary he stated that the Indians then had no other industries besides planting, except those of

---

[16]Ortíz Family Papers, Archives Div., New Mexico State Record Center, Santa Fe.

Laguna, Acoma and Zuni who, in addition to this and the hunting of buffalo and deer, "occupy themselves in weaving mantas, *cotones* (cotton goods) and tilmas to clothe themselves, and to trade with the settlers and Indians of other pueblos." This notation indicates that by 1808 Pueblo Indians on the Rio Grande were no longer weaving blankets for themselves or for trade. Evidently the Spanish weavers of Rio Grande blankets had already taken over the production of these except for the western pueblos. This definite date should settle many claims made by amateurs of the southwestern Indian textiles that certain examples of blankets had been made in one or another Rio Grande pueblo simply because they later had been acquired there.

A frequently repeated question is how a Rio Grande blanket is distinguished from one made by Navajos, especially in the case of simply striped blankets. With rare exceptions both kinds are woven in plain tapestry weave (the cloth is the same on both sides without having a "front and back" of different finishes). The weaving is weft faced with wefts going one over and one under each warp. Exceptions are the relatively recently made double-faced Navajo saddle blankets and rugs which present not only different colors but completely different patterns on each side.

It is quite easy to tell a Rio Grande from a Navajo for several reasons based upon the mechanical method of making one or the other. The Navajos adopted the Pueblo upright loom from their teachers around 1700 and still use it. This loom is strung on a frame between posts set into the ground. The completed work is planned and executed within the frame on which the warps are strung. Two extra warps are tied loosely on the outer sides of the loom; as the weaver comes to an outer side of the warps she passes the weft through one of the extra warp threads, giving both of them a half twist. This repeated process of twisting the outer warp pairs into loops as the weft is pulled through them takes up the slack in these warps and forms the decorative yarn finish along the selvedges common to Navajo weaving. The same finish is made on ends of rugs or blankets by pulling the loom frame pole out of the loops formed by stringing the warps over it in the beginning. This technique of stringing warps and twisting the outer ones with the wefts reinforces the fabric as well as making a decorative finish.

Another characteristic of Navajo woven textiles is the "lazy line." These are diagonal lines of open spaces between one part of the work and other. They appear at random and often have no relation to the figured design. They are formed by the weaver who sits on the ground while weaving. When she does not wish to move to the other side, or cannot reach all the way from one side of the loom to the other in throwing the weft, she simply weaves back and forth on one side for a while, keeping the top of the area at a slope so that the rest of the work, when she moves to it, will have a diagonal join and not a straight vertical lazy line between the two parts. Not all Navajo textiles contain lazy lines, but many do. In the case of small mats, where such lines are present we may assume that the mat was the work of a little

Figure 129: Rio Grande blanket of hand-spun cotton yarns and bands of wool dyed indigo by the ikat method; probably by a pupil of Bazan's.

girl. It is impossible to make lazy lines on the horizontal harness loom used by the Spanish. The presence of lazy lines and marginal warp-weft twisted finishes are two indications of Navajo weaving on an upright loom. Another is the stringing of warps; Navajo weavers often strung random colored yarns without regard for their spacing.

Rio Grande blankets often had warps spaced deliberately in blocks of white and dark yarns, or warps of both spun together. Blankets woven in two widths were strictly Spanish and may be identified as not made by Indians. Sarapes from Mexico were also woven in two widths but are distinguished by materials and designs from those of New Mexico. A Rio Grande blanket woven in one width is easy to recognize because of the multiple warps, usually two but sometimes more, that were strung at the selvedges and down the center. No Indian blankets contain these. On the horizontal loom the wefts are merely passed around these without a twist in the outer warps. The technique is not as durable as the Navajo method. Blanket ends were finished by cutting warps from the loom and tying the warp ends in knotted fringe. While old striped indigo blankets made by Spanish or Indians may look alike superficially, they can be distinguished by these mechanical components.

By 1900 the Navajos had ceased to weave true blankets. Pueblo weavers reserved their weaving for ceremonial garments or for strictly tourist articles like belts, place mats or pillow covers. The Navajos turned to making floor rugs and saddle blankets. The Rio Grande blanket continued to be made for use as bedding into recent times. However the misnomer, "Navajo blanket," persists as does the misuse of Rio Grande blankets for floor carpets. They were not intended for the purpose and soon wear out on floors.

The last rare exceptions to the four groups of Rio Grande blankets described here are popularly called slave blankets. The literal status of servants in New Mexico was often confusing. Spanish, Indian or mestizo might be referred to as criados (raised from childhood by their masters) and might be legally free or slaves. However, they were often wholly dependent upon or indebted to their owner or master to an extent that rendered them chattels. Indian children or very young women captured from nomadic or gentile tribes were more easily domesticated than adults. Navajo girls who had already learned to weave might prefer the upright loom to which they were accustomed. Blankets made on such looms with two, three or four ply yarns used by the Spanish, rather than Navajo-spun single ply yarns, often contain commercial dyes and busy designs which identify them as having been made after 1865. As might be expected, Mexican sarape designs, when adapted by Navajo weavers, reflect a different approach from that of the more familiar Rio Grande versions of the same source. Whether plain striped or lozenge centered, a slave blanket will not contain multiple warps, and may or may not show lazy lines. As a rule, they have the twisted warp-weft selvedges of Indian textiles. Occasionally a slave blanket has areas of wedge weaving, also one of a Navajo weaver's technical variations. The difficulty of weaving in diagonal blocks without producing a baggy cloth is great, and the successful execution of the feat was probably a feather in the cap of the weaver.

Slave blankets containing aniline dyed yarns may seem historically improbable, but Navajos were still owned by both Spanish and Anglo families in New Mexico as late as the 1870s, according to records. The slave blanket is prized by collectors for its rarity and is interesting for its exhibition of culture contacts.

While the use of old dyes such as indigo and cochineal in weaving today is confined to the esoteric contemporary craftsman, most often neither Spanish nor Indian, it can be shown how relatively recent or long ago the use of certain natural dyes was abandoned among New Mexico Spanish weavers by the folk usage of names for certain colors. Shades of indigo blue, instead of being called *añil,* are referred to as *azules viejos* (old blues). *Cochinilla,* or *grana,* (cochineal) has been forgotten. Samples of aniline dye powders sold in general stores fifty or so years ago have been produced by descendants of weavers as *carmesí* or scarlet dye. Anciently, scarlet was obtained from Kermes, *Coccus ilicis,* a parasitic insect raised for its coloring properties in warm regions of Persia and southeast Asia. Industrially it was superseded by the discovery of *C. cacti* (cochineal) in the 16th century. The name, scarlet, continued in popular usage for aniline red dyes but these ran and faded. Another synthetic, beet red dye, was locally named *sangre de toro* (bull's blood); old timers believe that this was a natural product whose secret has been lost. It is all too apparent, in many late blankets, that it is a synthetic product.

On the other hand, names for vegetal yellow dyes, which were still used in later blankets, are those of the actual plants from which the dyes were made. The most commonly used were *Canaigre* (dock root, *Rumex himenosepalus*), *Chamiso, Atriplex canescens Nutt,* Palo Amarillo, *Morus tinctoria,* and *Yerbavivora* (rattlesnake weed, *Myriadenus tetraphyllus*). One or another of these is available over northern New Mexico depending on the local terrain. The purple juice of chokecherry or *Capulin,* like the vegetal yellows, was combined in late type blankets with commercial reds, blues and pinks of synthetic origin. These color names have been remembered while those of cochineal and indigo have been forgotten except by traders or dealers.

THE COLCHA

The Spanish word *colcha* signifies a quilt or bedcover, but the New Mexican colcha is not a quilt in the sense of being a cover filled with inner material and tacked or quilted to hold the contents in place. Such a quilt in New Mexico is called a colchón. The regional colcha was first a hanging which was solidly embroidered with wool yarns so that none of its woolen support was visible. The stitch used throughout was always the same, a long stitch laid close to, and parallel to, the previous one, then caught down by small diagonal cross stitches at an angle of about forty-five degrees to the long stitch. In a way this is a quilting of the stitches, so the name may be taken to refer to the embroidery stitch rather than to the entire finished fabric.

Figure 130: Wool embroidery on wool support collected in Mexico in 1847. The New Mexico colcha stitch is not present. (Courtesy Denver Art Museum)

A baffling point about this regional embroidery is that pieces from Spain or Mexico, superficially comparable in materials and design and contemporary to the old colchas, do not contain this stitching technique. The only plausible origin yet found for the method is the Far East. Chinese embroideries in silk came to Mexico in large quantities in the 18th century, and some found their way to New Mexico in the form of altar frontals. These were worked with nearly invisible stitches of delicately shaded silk and in intricate designs that at first glance bear little resemblance to the New Mexico embroidered colchas worked with limited colors in coarse yarns. However, the basic colcha stitch is found on Chinese pieces, although always combined with other stitching techniques. New Mexico women, whose embroidering was confined to wool material, may have taken this stitch over from the Manila galleon export pieces, finding that it not only gave textural quality to their needlework, but served to hold their long, loose yarn stitches more firmly in place.

An early usage of the word colcha in New Mexico is in an inventory of Santa Ana mission where Fray Pedro Montaño wrote:

I, Frai Pedro Montaño, in 1743, placed a curtain before the picture of Lady St. Anne which is a colcha from Tlascalteca.[17]

The picture of the patroness of the mission was a gift from the royal mission fund in 1712, and is still in its place above the high altar, but the curtain has long since vanished. We do not know whether it was actually embroidered or only a woven textile. A later inventory added slightly to its description:

Ytem, one curtain or colcha from Tlaxcalteca of blue and white which serves as the veil of Lady St. Anne.[17]

Four embroidered wall hangings are listed by Dominguez in his inventory of the sacristy of the military chapel at Santa Fe in 1776 and one Chinese carpet, *alfombra* (Dominguez, p. 36). The term alfombra meant a woven carpet from some other part of the world. At that time the Castrense had been built for only fifteen years and was the fashionable chapel of the capital. The colcha is spoken of also at Santa Cruz de la Cañada, then the second town of New Mexico, where an all-wool colcha with white flowers on a dark ground was on the steps of the sanctuary. What was probably the same colcha was listed in the 1779 description of the Santa Cruz church.

By 1782 Santa Cruz had acquired another colcha of dark, multicolored wool, and in 1787 a new inventory was made. In this the

[17]Both citations, AASF, L. D. 1712, No. 1.

Figure 131: Eighteenth century altar cloth, New Spain, silk and metallic threads worked in seed, satin and couching stitches on linen gauze.

Figure 132: Fragment of wool embroidery in the colcha stitch, mid-19th century New Mexico.

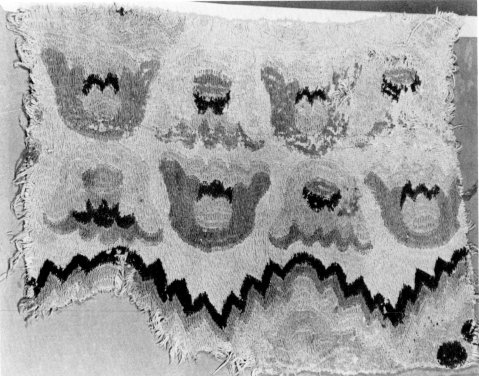

embroidered wool colcha and a "little, old carpet" in the sacristy were augmented by "a new colcha which serves as the carpet for the high altar which was given by a pious woman," as well as a new colcha for the chapel of St. Francis which had just been completed.[18] By 1818 there is an added notation to the Santa Cruz inventory: "Of the four carpets (alfombras), two are of jerga and one is of embroidery. Of the jergas one is worn out."[19]

Thus there is documentation of the use of the name and of the making and function of the colcha in 18th century New Mexico, primarily as a hanging and as a substitute for a carpet. It must be recalled that the Indian rug as it is woven today for covering floors was not made until the later 19th century when the demand by Anglo-Americans turned Navajo weavers to this type of textile. In colonial times Indian and Spanish alike wove blankets for clothing and bedding which were too soft and fine to serve as coverings for floors of packed earth. For lack of "Turkey" or Spanish or Chinese carpets, the ever-resourceful New Mexicans seem to have taken down their wall hangings to spread before the altar.

A colcha in the Museum of New Mexico suggests an 18th century age and a point of origin in or near Santa Cruz on the basis of its design. The Confraternity of Our Lady of Carmel was established at Santa Cruz in 1760, and was for many years the most popular and had the largest membership of any religious organization among laymen in New Mexico. To keep accounts of expenses, dues, and gifts, Father Francisco Campo Redondo set up two account books in 1760 and 1761.[20] On the title pages of these he drew in ink the emblem of the confraternity with ornamental scrolls and lettering. It is not difficult to imagine that a woman, tired of embroidering flowers or checked motifs on a colcha, may have taken this ink drawing as a model for her design and later presented the finished product to the Chapel of Our Lady of Carmel. This colcha suggests from its size that it was meant to be used as a hanging rather than as a carpet.

More often the colcha was designed in parallel wavy bands of color with a stylized clove pink spaced at intervals between them, or varicolored squares in a tiled effect, or of meandering leaf and floral patterns very carefully planned in composition. The motifs of rose, pomegranate, and pinks with cross-hatched filled elements are characteristically Hispano-Mauresque, while the scroll-shaped leaves, whose opposite halves are of different colors, reflect the Orient in form and color scheme. Like the bayeta or homespun on which they are worked, the yarns of Merino sheep fleeces embroidered on those which appear to be the oldest are fine and silky. The dyes employed are those traditional to New Mexico: indigo, cochineal, logwood for tan shades of rose, and

---

[18] AASF, Accounts, Book XXXXVI, Box 1, Santa Cruz.

[19] AASF, Accounts, Book LXII, Box 5B, Santa Cruz, 1818.

[20] AASF, Accounts, Book XXIV, Box 1, Santa Cruz.

several local vegetable dyes that made yellows, silvery greens and violet when combined with the two imported dyes.

One colcha of the wavy banded type is estimated, according to family information, to have been made in 1848. The decline of fine embroidery and good design and color in the colcha — as well as the deterioration of Rio Grande blankets — coincided with the introduction of new materials and techniques by the so-called Anglo newcomers. These of course include the usual mélange of non-Anglos, such as French, German, Polish and Syrians, many of whom engaged in commercial trade and sold Saxony and Germantown yarns and packets of aniline dyes in their stores or peddler's packs. The Anglo also introduced other breeds of sheep whose wool clip was larger per shearing than the leggy Merino's, but the fleeces did not spin into silky strands; instead they were short-fibred, harsh, and brittle. Trade yardage, wallpapers, oil cloth, and other innovations aroused interest in new, if meretricious, designs and color combinations, as did new forms of domestic busy-work. One textile specimen in the Museum collections reflects the influence of Anglo women. Its surface is covered with long parallel stitches of nonregional form with no cross-tacked or colcha stitches on it, and the large rosettes over it are worked in the hooked rug technique, unknown to New Mexican tradition. The yarns are handspun and dyed with commercial colors.

Three other specimens made use of salvaged materials. The first has as support pieced scraps of a Rio Grande blanket, and is crudely stitched all over with colored squares. The others are also of multicolored checked or tile designs worked on floursacks. All three of these are coarse and asymmetrical in design, but exhibit the true colcha stitch.

A different type of embroidered colcha is sold today in sizes varying from chair tidies to large hangings. These have been made by enterprising women in Taos County for fifty years, and are often worked on old homespun salvaged from woolsacks with handspun yarns raveled from old blankets, although some examples may combine handspun and commercial yarns and vegetable and aniline dyes. The designs include such subjects as saints, Indians, flagellant processions, covered wagons, stagecoaches, animals, adobe houses, fireplaces, seven-branched candlesticks, and various other motifs combined with Navajo blanket patterns of the 20th century. While neither old nor Spanish in tradition, these represent many weeks of handwork and inventive imagination, a 20th century cottage craft which in some cases has a distinct charm of its own.

Figure 133: Eighteenth century embroidery in wool on linen, Salamanca. (Courtesy Museo Nacional de Artes Decorativos, Madrid)

Figure 134: Embroidery in the colcha stitch on Trail trade cotton twill, second half of 19th century, New Mexico.

WOOL YARN EMBROIDERIES ON COTTON GOODS

In the past, wherever sheep and flax were raised, the making of woolen and linen fabrics naturally followed, and embroidering on these

with wool yarns was generally practiced in rural areas of Europe and England. When the East India trade brought fine cottons to Europe they were received as exotic novelties, and their hand painted, block printed, or resist dyed patterns were promptly borrowed by needle-workers and transferred to woolen, linen, or silken fabrics. Since the Far Eastern cottons came through the East India Company their patterns were dubbed "Indian," but many were basically of Persian designs adopted by Indian textile workers.

Seventeenth century English embroidery strongly reflected this style, and combined motifs such as the tree of life, pineapples, palms, leopards, tigers, elephants, and large medallions with small allover repeat elements. The large figures suited the hangings for great canopied beds, high doorways, and embrasured windows. The work is loosely called crewel work, signifying either chain or other outline stitching, which defined the figures while the interior areas of each element were filled with a variety of other types of stitching and colors. The embroidery formed the patterns but did not fill in the background or support.

American colonists of the northeastern states continued in the tradition to some extent, abandoning large figures in favor of rather thinly spaced allover floral patterns for their bed hangings. By the early 19th century the women of families which had migrated west into New York State made counterpanes of the same general design, incorporating small human and animal figures, boats, and so on.

There has been some question in the minds of students of New Mexico embroideries as to whether those worked on cotton twills were of Spanish colonial traditional origin or borrowed from the Anglo-Americans who came with their wives to live in New Mexico after the annexation in 1846. In favor of the latter possibility, it has been pointed out that the New Mexican embroideries on cottons have open, scattered, and principally floral elements, sometimes including small birds and insects, which are reminiscent of the rustic eastern American crewel work of the early 19th century as it had developed (or rather, retrograded) from the 17th century English hangings. On the theory that New Mexico embroideries in wool on cotton had been introduced by inhabitants of eastern states whose forebears came from England where the "India" or Persian designs had arrived in the days of Good Queen Anne, the passage of design elements in embroideries may be plotted as shown on p. 219 Fig. I.

However, several factors in the New Mexico embroideries and in history must be considered before reaching any conclusions. The production of cotton in 18th century New Mexico is here documented negatively. Its importation seems to have been equally nonexistent, and it is therefore unlikely that embroidering on cotton yardage was possible for the housewife. In the 18th century, shiploads of raw cotton went from the colonies to their mother countries, France or England, to be processed into cloth on the new mechanical (if still hand- or water-powered) looms of the scientific age. In Mexico hand spinning and weaving continued far longer without competition from mechanized looms. Early in the 19th century Mexico made trade agreements with England allowing cheap, mass-produced English goods to be imported at favorable tariffs. Some of these found their way to the annual fairs at Valle de San Bartolomé in Chihuahua which were first licensed in 1805.

To these fairs New Mexican caravans drove pack mules laden with hides, fresadas and flocks of up to 15,000 sheep, all to be traded for what was wanted from the outside. Cotton cloth was one of these, but the system of dual valuation kept New Mexican credit unbalanced. The Mexican silver peso was the official one, often called *un peso fuerte* or *un duro* (hard peso, or strong), which later on became the U. S. dollar standard.[21] Fractional units of this peso were eight reales, worth twelve and one half cents each, from which came our slang expression of being worth "two bits." The "old price" peso was more often the standard of value in rural Mexico, equalling fifty cents, but in the north the New Mexican received credit for his exports in the *peso del pais* or *de la tierra,* just as he did at home. His purchases, however, were charged against credits on the silver or hard peso basis. Coins were scarce and seldom changed hands; trade was on a barter basis with accounts kept by debit-credit entries which permitted usage of two rates of peso. It is obvious that if a goat was worth one peso of the country, or twenty-five cents, and cotton yardage cost one silver dollar a vara, cotton goods were in the luxury class, and New Mexicans did not benefit from the low tariffs on English goods agreed upon at Mexican seaports.

Apparently the Bazán brothers, in addition to instruction in weaving, were also expected to develop a self-sufficient cotton industry in New Mexico for domestic usage and export credit, according to Pino's comment: "There is no other industry known in this province than those of wool and cotton. Necessity has obliged them to weave." Suggesting that the tithes, the tenth of various products collected to send annually to the Bishop of Durango for support of the church, might better be kept at home, Pino noted that among other goods sent was cotton in the amount of 40 *arrobas*. In contrast to corn (3000 fanegas), wheat (2000 fanegas), and wool (1000 arrobas), it is clear that cotton was not a large crop; in theory it was produced only in the amount of 400 arrobas annually in the province of New Mexico, although the tithes, or *diesmas,* were not given as literally by the people as required.[22]

---

[21] The large silver pesos minted at Mexico City had become currency throughout the Far East during export trading years with the Chinese, and were accepted as truly international currency. It is startling to realize that since the Chinese Nationalist government has been confined to the island of Formosa, it has ordered from the National Mint of Mexico thousands of silver pesos, struck with the dies of the Spanish crown prior to 1821, because these coins are still held to be more valuable in Far Eastern trade than any others.

[22] Pino, Pedro Bautista, op. cit., p. 223.

Did the Bazáns teach New Mexicans to spin and weave cotton twills, canvas, muslins, or other yardage, as well as cotton blankets? Was this one beginning of the appearance of cotton goods in New Mexico after the turn of the century? If any cotton yardage was made locally it has not been identified as such. Cottons however did appear frequently on invoices and in inventories from then on. Not only santos had muslin and other cotton garments, but altar frontals of *indianilla* (printed calico) were repeatedly noted, as well as their "unsuitability." The Chihuahua fairs, of course, provided some cottons at whatever price.

After 1821, when the Santa Fe Trail trade was started, more factory-made goods came to New Mexico, including calicos and coarse muslins. The round trip from Missouri to Santa Fe, and then on to Chihuahua and return, was found to be more profitable by the Yankee traders than trade in Santa Fe only, while New Mexicans seemed to find the Trail goods cheaper or better for their purposes than the Chihuahua goods and prices. Today it is difficult to tell what place was the source of many cotton fragments left from early 19th century New Mexico. An exception are scraps of a printed cotton intended to be used as handkerchiefs or neckerchiefs which can be traced to English cotton mills of 1832.[23]

No cottons used as supports for wool embroideries in New Mexico prior to the arrival of aniline dyes were handwoven, at least none of those that have been examined by me. Most of these were of cotton twill in various weights. The embroidery designs were worked in the traditional colcha stitch, but did not follow the same patterns as those found on solidly worked wool colchas. The best of the pieces worked on cotton had a formal plan of border, corner elements, and a large central medallion or bouquet. Motifs were basically Hispano-Mauresque: the pomegranate, peony, clove pink, rose, and small birds, with leafy scrolls and sometimes a cornucopia. On the basis of these design elements it seems justifiable to assign these embroideries to Near and Far Eastern ancestry, but one that reached New Mexico by way of the Mediterranean to Spain, Mexico, and thence north. The embroidery stitch, however, seems to have gone from China to Mexico rather than by way of England and New England (See p. 219 Fig. II). It is fairly certain that embroidering on, or the use of, cotton yardage was a 19th century development in New Mexico.

Other examples contain the same indigo-cochineal and local vegetal dyes and colors as those in regional colchas and blankets, and later ones combined Saxony, handspun, and Germantown yarns and packaged synthetic dyes, as did later blankets. Stitchery declined in quality as did planning of patterns, which grew helter-skelter as whimsical inscriptions, animals, and symbols in gaudy colors replaced handsome older designs. Crochet, patchwork, feather-stitching, and prestamped patterns for cross-stitch literally stifled creative, free-hand embroidery in New Mexico by the end of the 19th century.

Figure 135: Aniline dyed wool yarns on muslin support, New Mexico.

---

[23]*Antiques,* Vol. XXV-3, March, 1954, p. 233. "A William IV Calico in New Mexico."

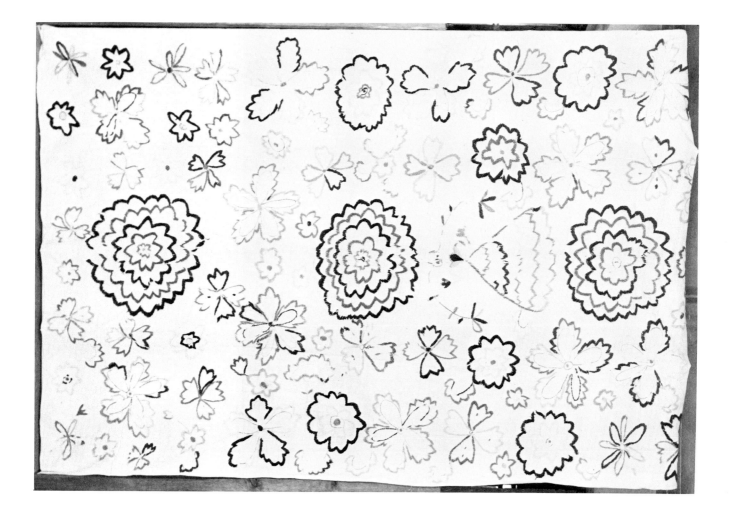

Wool Embroideries on Cottons

FIG. I

PERSIA
|
INDIA
THE EAST INDIA
COMPANY
|
ENGLAND
|
NEW ENGLAND
|
NEW MEXICO

FIG. II

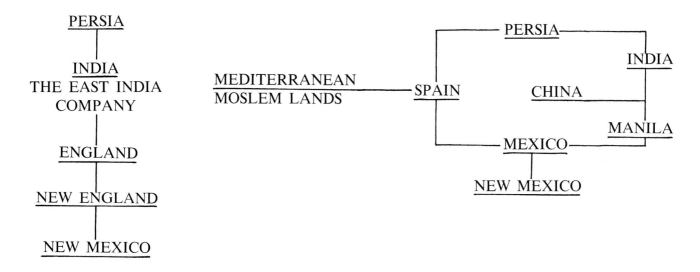

The Anglo-American introduction of glazed windows and bedsteads created a use for curtains and counterpanes, and as a result nearly all the surviving wool embroideries on cotton were made in suitable sizes and shapes for these purposes, a further support of the theory that such work was of 19th century origin, and done mostly after 1846.

COLONIAL DRESS

The popular myth that New Mexico was settled by cavaliers in full suits of armor with velvet breeches and plumed hats laced with gold, escorting ladies trailing brocaded satin gowns, is not proven by any known documents. Nor was this the case in the early period of colonization in New Spain. Although high-ranking officials did undoubtedly bring with them one or more suits of fine clothing for state and gala occasions, the average colonist was of humble birth, owning little and bringing with him tools of his trade rather than a wardrobe.

People who lead an active life and perform hard labor cannot be hampered by flowing robes. Even the European nobles wore simply cut, close-fitting garments of durable materials when hunting or traveling, no matter how extravagantly their dress might be designed when at home or at court. Robes of extreme length or fullness made of perishable materials proclaimed that their wearers were in sheltered circumstances and served by their inferiors. The dress of European peasants changed little over centuries, consisting of a linen shirt, collarless wool or leather jerkin and clumsy breeches for men. Women wore a laced bodice of some heavy stuff over a linen chemise with a full, ankle length skirt to allow the wearer to perform domestic duties and walk in all weather. The blanket or large square of cloth was more often the outer garment of the poor than a cloak, which was the mark of some social standing. Before the art of tailoring began to improve, clothing was composed of various sized pieces of cloth sewn together without fitting or tied on the body. By the time of the conquest of New Spain, such niceties as fitted sleeves and breeches had been developed as well as fancy trimmings for the well-to-do. The common man wore either a homemade wool cap, or a felt or leather broadbrimmed hat which might be allowed to flap or be cocked up at one side.

Spanish women, after 700 years of Moslem influence, went more covered in public than did those of other warmer parts of Europe, wearing deep, stiff collars, a veil over the head and face and an outer shawl or cloak. In fact, the habits of several orders of nuns, except that they are black and white, have preserved many features of the street dress of 16th century Spanish women. The long, narrow scarf or rebozo was an Arabic introduction into Spain, and went from there to New Spain, where it was so generally adopted by Indian women that it is now considered as a traditional part of many indigenous Mexican costumes.

When Hernan Cortés had finally defeated the Aztecs and taken possession of lakeborne Mexico City, his soldiers were suffering from such a shortage of arms, shirts, breeches and hose that he offered a full pardon to any Indians who would return any Spanish arms or clothing that they had captured. By 1528 twenty-five licensed tailors had come from Spain but, upon arrival in New Spain, most of them found it more profitable to trade in slaves, mules, hides or wine. Thus it was not the lack of textiles that made clothing expensive but the lack of artisans who understood European cutting and fitting. To native cotton and hemp the Spanish soon added flax, wool and silk. By 1550 it was stated that no Indian was so poor that he could not pay his tax with ten or twelve varas of linen.

Silk had for centuries been a highly prized importation from the Far East, brought by ship and overland caravans into Mediterranean Europe. The science of raising silkworms had been understood and practiced in Spain before the discovery of the New World. Mulberry trees, another Arabic introduction, were soon planted in New Spain in suitable locations. By 1540 there were 110,000 mulberry trees on one hacienda in the valley of Atlizco alone. Silkworms had been successfully imported, and Indians had been trained to tend them and to gather, unwind and respin the silk from the cocoons. It was predicted that New Spain would soon be the center of world trade as it could raise more silk than all the rest of the Christian world. In 1562 the annual shipment of silks raised in Oaxaca to Guatemala and Peru was valued at 400,000 gold pesos. The crimson silk velvets and iridescent taffetas made by Indian weavers were claimed by colonial officials to be as fine as any from Spain or Venice. Thus, forty years after the conquest, New Spain was producing every class of textile, as well as gold and silver cloth, furs and feathers in sufficient amounts to supply local demand and for profitable export.

A fatal blow to the western silk business was dealt by the successful establishment of the Manila galleon line, a favorite project of Spanish ambitions. In the last quarter of the 16th century Spain made satisfactory agreements with Chinese traders who brought shiploads of silks to Manila although the Spanish were not welcomed on the Chinese mainland. As early as 1582 an official reported that it was no longer necessary to grow silk in New Spain, even though it was of very fine quality, because so much silk now came yearly from the Philippines. Almost a hundred years later, in 1679, the ailing, irrational King Carlos II signed a decree that all mulberry trees, or any other trees that might nourish silkworms, should be torn up by the roots. Indians of New Spain could better be employed in the mines from which the Royal Fifth was greater than that derived from the raising of silks. While large-scale production of silk was officially abandoned in New Spain, the royal edict must have been imperfectly obeyed in some parts of the colony. Native silk is still raised in suitable areas of Mexico and is distinctive in its slightly rough texture when woven into fabric.

No fragments of clothing brought by early New Mexican settlers are known to exist. However, some clues as to how they may have looked can be found in contemporary prints and paintings of New Spain. Although artists more often painted official or ecclesiastical dignitaries, or religious subjects, a number of pictures of gala processions show us the garments of the bystanders, the common people. Other sources of knowledge of ordinary dress are engravings showing miraculous rescues or cures of contemporaries (as those showing the first recorded miracles performed by the image of Our Lady of Guadalupe), painted ex-votos of the same class of happenings, usually with the date of the event itself, and the paintings commissioned to depict what kinds of clothing might legally be worn by various degrees of mixed-bloods. The latter, showing *trajes de castas* are of the 18th century, and give a wide range of types of clothing used by persons whose biological makeup varied from half European and Indian through mixtures of Indian, Negro and Oriental. Those with only a quarter of white blood or less were prohibited from wearing certain classes of materials, with more prohibitions in the cases of full blooded Negroes or Indians. On the other hand, the Spaniard with an Indian wife or mistress is shown in the clothing of a gentleman of his day with equally fancy dress on their children, while the Indian preens herself in clothes like those of Spanish ladies of New Spain at that time. From such sources we may draw some conclusions as to how the early Spanish New Mexicans looked.

The importation of Chinese silks had a strong influence on other textiles and even the shape of some garments in New Spain. Far Eastern design elements were copied in other embroideries and woven goods, just as Chinese porcelains were imitated in common pottery in New Spain as well as in Europe. Early inventories of New Mexico missions after the reconquest mention vestments and altar frontals from China. They may well have had some effect upon embroidered articles made on the frontier, of which we have no visible remains.

It is no problem to imagine the Franciscans of the colonizing period in their blue homespun habits with a knotted cord girdle, broad-brimmed, low-crowned hats and leather sandals. Every two years each missionary was sent a new linen shirt by the supply caravan, and another for the use of the sick in his infirmary. Mass vestments, whether of Chinese or other silks, came from New Spain and resembled the Spanish vestments of their day in that the chasubles were of Spanish or "fiddleback" cut, unlike those used in Italy. Spanish Franciscans serving in foreign missions had been conceded the privilege of wearing blue habits in honor of the Virgin Mary instead of the original gray, or undyed, unbleached habit worn by the founder of the order. They also had the privilege of using certain blue vestments and frontals on special feast days honoring Our Lady. These blue ornaments, by then worn out, came in for caustic comments by the 19th century secular clergy in New Mexico, and automatically became obsolete when Mexico and New Mexico ceased to be Spanish possessions.

Military equipment underwent changes in the New World in many ways. Metal armor was scarce for the rank and file, as is indicated by equipment listed for exploratory expeditions that supplied suits of half armor for half of the men on the muster roll on the theory that the armor could be used by each duty shift, but making no allowance for an all-out alarm. In addition to its scarcity, metal armor was heavy. It was soon replaced by quilted cotton coats, already in use among some New World tribes. These were light in weight, cheap and easily obtained. Chain mail shirts or a breastplate were worn over these by those who could afford them, but they also were too heavy for long marches on foot or for men who had to ford rivers. Officers continued to use metal helmets, cuirasses, and arm and leg pieces until these were too old to be service-able. The metal shield was discarded for others of buffalo or bull hide, laced together in layers while fresh and flexible. The lacings were spaced in a geometric pattern which drew the shield into a convex form when it had dried. The insides of these shields had buckskin linings, hand grips and loops by which to hang the shield on the saddle. Once dried and set in shape, these shields could resist arrows and spears. Firearms were so few and ineffective during the Spanish period in New Mexico that bows and lances as well as rawhide shields were still in use among New Mexican militiamen in 1846 when General Kearny annexed the territory for the United States.

The Spanish hide shields were made in two shapes: a round one called *la rodela,* and a kidney-shaped one known as *una adarga.* According to records they were made on the large, mission cattle ranches of pres-ent day Chihuahua and Sonora by Indian converts for the use of the military. As the coats of arms of Spain and other heraldic devices were not subjects of ecclesiastical study, the mission fathers sometimes designed the royal arms on these shields with frames of posies instead of the collar and emblem of the order of the Golden Fleece. Whether similar shields were ever made in New Mexico is uncertain although the tradition that some were of bull buffalo hides would suggest that they could have been made on the frontier. Most of the rawhide shields now in recorded collections have come from Indian pueblos where they had been kept for generations as symbols of enemy power.

Complete pieces of early colonial armor, on the other hand, have not been found in New Mexico except according to folksay. The crown of a salade which was found at the ruins of San Gabriel del Yunque, west of the Rio Grande opposite San Juan Pueblo, is the most convinc-ing specimen of early Spanish armor as yet found in New Mexico. Oñate and his colonists settled at San Gabriel in 1599 by permission of the Pueblo of San Juan and remained there for some eight years. By 1610 the Spanish had moved to the present capital, Santa Fe. According to Harold L. Peterson, an authority on colonial arms and armor, this shape of helmet was used by common soldiers in Europe around the date of the discovery of the New World by Columbus, or a hundred years before it was carried to New Mexico. The custom of sending obsolete equip-ment to remote outposts has continued in many instances until today.

No whole pieces of chain mail have been found either, but only single links or chunks of links rusted together, in historic sites. It is thought that they came from the protective curtains or collars that were hung around the bottom of a helmet to protect the neck, or from the bottom of a cuirass. Some of the fragmentary chain links found are of the smallest size made by European armorers, with a tapered end riveted to the head end. Each link of this kind was riveted to five others, forming a close mesh.

The *cuero,* or leather coat, was also worn by the military in place of metal armor; stitched in layers, it also withstood spears and arrows. In New Mexico there were few regular troops from New Spain; the defense of the colonists was expected to be performed by the militia after the early settlement phase. Regular troops came and went as escorts to officials traveling to and from New Spain and to supply caravans and new groups of settlers. Except for the governor and his few aides, whose highest rank was that of captain, the militia was composed of able-bodied male residents who were required to serve for regular tours of duty. They apparently were not issued uniforms, but had to clothe themselves as best they might and to bring their own arms and horse gear. The abundance of buffalo, cattle and deer hides in the province supplied materials for locally made leather coats, hats, and saddles as well as breeches, boots and bridles, however provincial they might be in shape and ornamentation.

When the Spanish removed from San Gabriel to Santa Fe in 1610, they must already have learned how little in the way of replacements to their wardrobes would come from New Spain, and how much they must rely on the products of the country and their own ingenuity. With the oft-cited Indian mantas, plenty of animal hides and pelts and the expanding wool crops from their own sheep, a pattern in New Mexican clothing was set for about two hundred years with minor changes from time to time when some imports or new ideas reached the colony. Nearly everything was made of wool, buckskin or leather. The frontier did not attract, and would not have supported, professional tailors or cobblers. The cutting and stitching of clothing and shoes were parts of domestic life like cooking, spinning and weaving. As growing of cotton seems to have been abandoned, kerchiefs and undergarments of "holanda, ruan, bretaña, or cambrai," all place-names from which linen was exported, came from New Spain.

After the middle of the 17th century, men's breeches were no longer padded or puffed but fit closely, their outer sides slit open at the bottoms and trimmed with braid and fancy buttons which were never fastened. Even the poor man sported brass, bone or copper buttons on his breeches, in imitation of the silver or gold ones in the form of pomegranate blossoms worn by his masters. A sleeveless surcoat which was conveniently loose and had pockets replaced the doublet of the 16th century. It was worn over a shirt and under the outer greatcoat, or cloak. With time, the surcoat evolved into the modern vest. The greatcoat with long waist and full skirts was made in New Mexico in the 18th century of hemp embroidered leather or of blue homespun wool with red facings.

Shoes in New Spain were like those from the old country, with leather soles, medium heels and soft uppers cut in three pieces, the front with its tongue and two sides stitched together at the back with ears that were buckled over the instep. When French fashions reached New Spain in the later 18th century, high heeled pumps came into favor in wealthy circles. In New Mexico, people, except for a few *ricos,* had taken to making and wearing *gamuzas* (buckskins). These were something like Indian moccasins with rawhide soles and soft tanned uppers, but they were tied over the instep instead of being buttoned at the sides like those of their pueblo neighbors. As late as the 1930s older New Mexico countrymen were still making their own gamuzas as they had learned to do in boyhood. By 1846, pegged shoes from St. Louis began to come into the territory, sometimes known today as "Forty-Niner's boots" but in style at the time. These, sold in general stores, became fashionable for New Mexicans to wear to church and on public occasions, but their lack of difference in shape between right and left feet must have almost canceled their prestige value.

Among ordinary people there was little basic difference between the woman's dress of the 17th and 18th century; a boned bodice laced over a chemise and full skirt of homespun wool, sometimes with a length of contrasting colored cloth tied around the waist as an overskirt. In summer a gauzy kerchief was tied over the hair, and the indispensable rebozo from New Spain served as head covering, scarf or burden carrying cloth. In winter women wore a *tapalo* or shawl, or a blanket, for warmth. The wealthy woman had a hooded cloak.

Roads in colonial New Mexico, in spite of the official name, Camino Real, were no more than horse trails, following or crossing streams and quite unimproved. To escape the discomforts of jolting in heavy baggage wagons both men and women of all classes rode a horse, if they could procure one, or walked when on journeys. The mobility and equestrian prowess of the colonial New Mexican woman is proven by numerous documents which show her acting as a godmother at a christening, as witness at a wedding, buying land, or selling livestock, all of which papers were signed by the same woman at places a hundred or more miles apart within a year or so. Such ladies were escorted by one or two female servants as well as by male relatives as a matter of course; the habit of travel for women as well as men seems to have been a part of New Mexico colonial life. Whether for riding, walking, hoeing in the fields, plastering, or for other domestic labors performed by women, practical dress was more important than the fashions of distant cities. The short skirts which so shocked English-speaking eyewitnesses in mid-19th century were a part of the frontier way of life as was deerskin clothing for the New Mexican men.

While gold and silver jewelry was scarce until the discovery of these metals in New Mexico, we know that some women did have necklaces, earrings and brooches of gold, silver or pinchbeck, set with pearls, false pearls, paste or corals. Their existence is recorded in church inventories after they had been given as tokens of devotion to a favorite image of Our Lady, especially those of Carmen at Santa Cruz de la Cañada, and of la Conquistadora at Santa Fe. The statue of Carmen even owned

Figure 136: New Mexico bulto, San Ysidro, in men's dress of the time — breeches, braided vest and kilted coat.

a little silver dog and silver toothpick, indicating that the latter was also a convenience on the frontier. Incumbent priests exercised their prerogative, as they continue to do today, to collect these offerings from time to time and send them to Durango or Chihuahua to be melted down and refashioned into a chalice or cruets. Although it has been said that true Mediterranean corals entered our southwest only as trade goods early in the 19th century, documentary records and evidence from excavated historic sites prove that they were brought to New Mexico as personal property in the 17th and 18th centuries. If not all colonial settlers owned elegant jewelry nearly every woman could boast a brass or silver cross, a few glass beads and a religious medal of bronze or brass.

While New Spain continued to formulate regulations for the clothing and jewelry of mixed-bloods, these were virtually unnecessary in New Mexico where little or no occasion was offered to acquire articles of dress above anyone's station in life. Limitations of the frontier had the democratic effect of reducing differences in dress between landowners and criados, with the probable factor of degrees of raggedness as a major distinction. Many colonists had been peasants, servants, soldiers or convicts before they came to New Mexico. Their previous conditions served to adapt them to the rough and ready frontier life and simplicity in dress, even when some of them became landowners of importance.

In the absence of descriptive material by Spaniards, we have an account of the typical clothing of the Spanish inhabitants of the frontier province of Sonora, which would as well represent the frontier New Mexicans of the same time. This was written by the German priest Ignatius Pfefferkorn, who served in Sonora from 1756 until the expulsion of the Jesuit Order from New Spain in 1767. The Spanish people that he refers to were then living in the mining camps of the Sierra Madre. Among other details of dress noted by Pfefferkorn was the same shortage of linen which is familiar from the conquest to the end of the 18th century. From *A Description of the Province of Sonora,* by Ignatius Pfefferkorn, University of New Mexico Press, 1949, Coronado Cuarto Centennial Pubs., 1540–1940, (ca. 1765), pages 286–288:

> Except for some of the wealthier most Spaniards in Sonora dress poorly, though the style is about the same for all classes. The men generally wear coats of red or scarlet cloth which are so short that as a rule they hardly reach a quarter of an ell below the hips. The coats are trimmed in front with little copper or silver buttons, which are for decoration only because the coat is always open. The sleeves are sewed only up the back, beginning at the shoulders. They are open in front so that they hang straight down. Under the coat is worn a jacket of blue cloth having long sleeves. The pants are of blue or red plush. This material is chosen generally because of its durability, which is all the more necessary because a day rarely passes that the wearer does not make a tear. Those who can bear the expense or have the credit trim their suits all over with silver borders. With their costume belongs also a little, round, stiff hat, trimmed with silver borders and a blue mantle which is decorated in front with a fine red material about an

ell in width. No Sonora Spaniard appeared in church without his mantle, even if the heat were practically unbearable. Outside of church the mantle is not used except on the journey. Then it serves to keep off rain and as a cover at night if there is no other at hand.

The Spaniard's shoe, instead of having a solid piece of toe leather, has several inch-wide cross strips with slits between. Since Sonora stockings are footless, ending at the heel, the toes and the front of the foot would remain bare except that the Spaniards wrap the bare part with red cloth, which then shows through the slits, and, in their opinion, beautifully decorates the foot. Over the cotton stockings, instead of boots, they wear a kind of deerskin legging.

The Spaniards tie their hair close to their heads or braid it into a long plait. The merchants, gachupines, and all those who wish to hold themselves above the rabble, have their heads shaved and cover them with caps of muslin. The wide fold of such a muslin cap stands up stiffly and is trimmed with fine lace.

On the whole, the Spaniards in Sonora are extremely ambitious for position. A large number arbitrarily give themselves the title of Don, signifying noble origin, although their grandfather may have been a farmer or an artisan. Many will go up to their ears in debt simply to satisfy their pride in putting on a grand appearance. As it is, no matter how splendid the appearance of a Sonora Spaniard, he always suffers a secret shortage of necessary linen. Few there are who have more than two shirts. One shirt must always be in the wash if the wearer is to appear in clean linen on Sunday.

The gowns of the Spanish women in Sonora are pleated around starting from the belt. There are three rows of pleats covering a third of the gown. On the upper part of the body is worn, in most cases, a shirt-waist which, for the sake of modesty, is closed at the neck with a collar. When the women are dressed up they wear a shirt-waist whose sleeves, collar and upper part are embroidered to the width of two hands with silk, often mixed wth gold and silver. Jackets are worn only by those who especially wish to set themselves apart from the common crowd. On feast days the jackets worn are usually of silk, sometimes also of gold and silver. Gowns worn with these jackets must always be of the same material as the jacket. It is easy to imagine that in a country where all European goods are so excessively expensive such finery must cost more than many can afford to pay. But that is no obstacle; the desire for beauty is just as strong in the women of Sonora as it is in German women. Their position must be maintained. The result is that either their household must suffer, or else they must give up their display and languish secretly.

All Spanish women without exception braid their hair as do the men.

Thoses of the nobility add an ornament in the form of a silken ribbon, embroidered with gold and silver, wrapped on the end of the braid.

Whenever she leaves her house the Spanish woman covers her head with a rebozo, that is, a cloth three ells long and about one and one half ells wide which is worn in about the same way that our women wear the scarf.

Rebozos are worn by all Spanish women in Sonora and in New Spain generally. They serve both as a covering and as an adornment. These cloths are elaborately worked with all kinds of pretty vari-colored figures.

Some rebozos are made of pure cotton, others of mixed cotton and silk and still others of pure silk. The most costly are made of the finest silk with beautiful flowers and other ornaments of gold and silver woven into them. On the ends of all rebozos are long fringes of cotton, silk or gold and silver, according to the quality of the rebozo itself. Cotton rebozos are worn by the common people, the silk ones by the gentler folk and the wealthier.

In New Mexico after about 1780, three saints were represented by santeros in the garments of contemporary New Mexicans instead of those of Biblical or medieval times. These saints were Santiago (St. James Major, patron of Spain), San Ysidro Labrador (St. Isidore the Farmer, patron of Madrid), and San Acacio (St. Achatius). The latter was one of the fourteen Holy Helpers, saints accredited with performing "the impossible" for their devotees, but recently Acacio has been declared apocryphal and an invention of the chroniclers of the Golden Legends, formerly popular Gothic tales of miracles written by various monks.

After the remains of St. James the Apostle had been claimed to repose in Compostella in northwestern Spain, they became a great magnet for pilgrims. Many of these came from all of Christian Europe as well as from Spain; the emblem of the cockleshell found on the shores of nearby beaches was worn to show that a pilgrim had accomplished his journey to Compostella. The order of Caballeros de Santiago was formed in Spain; its members were of the aristocracy. The alleged apparitions of the apostle during battles between Moorish and Spanish forces during the long struggles to expel the Moslems from the Iberian peninsula, with Spanish victories resulting each time that Santiago appeared, gave the order both military and religious significance. Although images of St. James had at first shown him in apostolic robes, after the miraculous apparitions in battles he was depicted in the military dress of knights of the time. Members of the order, engaged in conquest and pacification of large Indian populations in Mexico and Peru during the 16th century attributed some of their victories to the apparition of Santiago in the sky, mounted on a white charger. According to Villagra, Governor

Oñate's handful of soldiers succeeded in taking the Pueblo of Acoma on its sheer-walled rock in 1599 due to the appearance of Santiago and the most holy Mother in the sky.[24]

Fourteen "authorized" apparitions of Santiago during battles in the New World have been published. There is a folk legend, apparently not authorized, that the apostle made an appearance during the Mexican revolution of 1910-16. The cult of Santiago was assimilated by Christianized Indians, many of whom still represent the armed and mounted warrior in annual ceremonial dances held in his honor. Such feast day dances are scattered all over Mexico, Central and South America and the formerly Spanish Caribbean islands, as well as in several pueblos of New Mexico. Earlier colonial folk images of Santiago are easily traced to one or another edition of the Hispanic missals printed at the Plantin Press in Antwerp for four centuries and distributed throughout Spain and her colonies. The Hispanic missal contained masses and prayers of devotion to particular Spanish saints not included in Roman missals and often had an engraving of Santiago as patron of Spain on the title page. While few New Mexico governors were members of the order of Santiago, the constant menace of nomadic Indians kept the colonists' devotion to their miraculous military protector active until the United States succeeded in removing the hostiles to permanent reservations. New Mexican santeros who simplified their models and concentrated on the saintly image and its symbols still included certain details of the horseman's dress and equipment which give us a clear picture of the New Mexican man's appearance, whether at the close of the 18th century or during the period of the Mexican Republic. The small figure of Santiago at El Santuario in Chimayó is a well known example. Another in the Museum of New Mexico faithfully shows the homespun blue breeches and coat, stiff leather hat and elkskin *botas*, or leggings, worn on the frontier in the early 19th century.

San Ysidro Labrador, whose life history as a farmhand stresses his piety and not military feats, was represented in New Mexico in the same clothing as Santiago of the 1780–1830 period, but on foot and without botas, shield or sword. Ysidro was the servant of a Madrid landowner of the same de Vargas family that some four hundred years later produced the general and governor, Diego de Vargas, the reconqueror of New Mexico in 1693. Ysidro's habit of kneeling to pray in his master's fields was rewarded by angels sent from the heavens who drove the oxen while he prayed. He is also said to have struck the ground with his ox goad, causing a spring of fresh water to gush forth where it was needed. As an intercessor for rains in arid lands he was highly venerated by New Mexicans as well as Castilians. His images were taken in procession to bless spring plantings and to visit them when they suffered from droughts.

---

[24]*History of New Mexico,* Gaspar Pérez de Villagra, Trans. by Gilberto Espinosa, Quivira Society, Los Angeles, 1933.

Images of San Acacio in New Mexico, with few exceptions, were in the contemporary dress of the santero's day, a custom evidently already in vogue in Spain. The legend of the saint was assigned to the first century A. D., when he was said to have been a general in command of Roman legions, on the eve of a battle with pagan armies who greatly outnumbered his troops. An angel appeared to him that night, promising him that if he and his men became Christians they would win the next day's battle in spite of their lesser numbers. He accepted the offer and was the victor. It is said that he retired as a hermit on Mount Ararat, but was recalled by the Roman authorities and ordered to recant his conversion. Christianity was then regarded as a cult of slaves and unsuitable for one of noble rank. Acacio, however, affirmed his Christianity and was sentenced to be crucified with his converted soldiers. Unlike the Spanish perspective of a field of crucified men New Mexican santeros suggested the soldiers by a row of small figures, mere onlookers, and sometimes only painted a sword, gun or drum as symbols.

A bulto of San Acacio, for whom a street in Santa Fe, New Mexico, was named in 1924, gives a very complete picture of the military dress in New Mexico in the 1780s (Pl. 24).

When repairs to the cathedral of Arizpe, Sonora, were made a few years ago, the priest in charge invited anthropologists from the University of California at Berkeley to try to locate the lost grave of Juan Bautista de Anza. Arizpe was once the capital of the state of Sonora although it is now a small town on a mountain road. De Anza's father had been governor of Sonora; he himself was born at Arizpe and was brought up as an effective Indian fighter. He had pioneered an overland route from Sonora to San Gabriel in California and in 1776 he led a party of colonists from Sonora across the mainland and up the California coast to found the present-day city of San Francisco. In 1778 he was appointed governor of New Mexico with instructions from the viceroy to suppress the raids of Comanches that at the time had nearly wiped out New Mexico. In the next year de Anza succeeded in defeating a band of Comanches in their own territory and in killing Cuerno Verde, their leader. As a result the Comanches allied themselves with the Spanish, Pueblos and Navajos against their common enemy, the various Apache groups. For some years New Mexico enjoyed more security and expansion than it had ever had, as a result of de Anza's strategic successes. He set about the fortification and relocation of several towns and villages, even proposing to move the capital, Santa Fe, to the south side of the river. Another of his projects was secularization and removal of the Franciscans. These innovations were so fanatically opposed by the traditionally insubordinate New Mexicans that he was retired by the viceroy in 1787. Returning to his home at Arizpe he died in the following year; church records stated that he had been interred in the sanctuary of the cathedral.

Excavation of the stone paved sanctuary in February 1963 exposed coffins containing human remains that were too old, or too young, to have been that of de Anza. A third coffin contained bones described by a physical anthropologist as those of a robust man in his early fifties. De Anza was fifty-three when he died. The well preserved skeleton wore:

> a blue coat, with a high military collar embroidered with silver thread. The coat had brass buttons. Beneath the coat was a red vest, and the skeleton wore dark trousers that came just below the knees. The shoes were of black leather and were cut low like pumps.

> The clinching evidence to the experts . . . were two insignia of the Third Order of St. Francis, the Franciscan order for laymen to which de Anza belonged. Over the chest was the remnant of a scapulary and a Rosary. Around the waist was the cord worn by members of the Franciscan (Third) Order. (The *San Francisco Chronicle,* March 4, 1963)

While the New Mexico bulto of San Acacio has neither silver embroidery on the coat nor Tertiary insignia, and does wear horseman's *botas*, a pouch for powder and a crown of thorns, the uniform is remarkably like the description of de Anza's.

Persistence of the cult of San Acacio in northern New Mexico is proven by a number of bultos made by José Benito Ortega, who was working until 1907, according to his relatives (p. 420). Ortega clothed his figures in the same vest, coat and breeches of a century before but painted them in his own manner in bright red, yellow, green and blue.

Just when breeches were replaced by long trousers in New Mexico is uncertain. In Mexico the transition had already taken place by 1826 when Claudio Linati made his invaluable on-the-spot drawings of all classes of Mexicans. Only the most abject beggars or *leperos* were shown by then in short breeches. Conservative Alta California hacenderos, it is said, first beheld long trousers in 1834 when a ship brought passengers wearing these from Mexico.[25] On the other hand, the infiltrations of trappers and traders from the eastern United States after Mexican independence and, in the case of trappers, before 1821, may have introduced newfangled long pants somewhat before 1834 in New Mexico. Early sketches of mountain men and nomadic Plains Indians depict these wearing long buckskin trousers, usually fringed. A rare painted panel from an adobe house in the village of Santa Cruz de la Cañada shows the dress of the *cibolero*, or buffalo hunter, as faithfully as any early sketches made by foreign visitors to New Mexico. Although undated, the regional folk style of the painting places it in the first half of the 19th century.

---

[25] Woodward, Arthur, Los Angeles County Museum Quarterly, V. 6/3, 1947.

In general, New Mexican men seem to have adopted the wide bottomed, slashed trousers worn in Mexico rather than "stovepipe" English and American models. Tight at the seat and trimmed with braid and fancy side buttons, these trousers, like the slashed breeches before them, were left open at the sides to display linen underdrawers.

The colonial female dress, like nearly everything else related to fashions in design, reflected the impact of French Directoire and Empire styles before reverting to short, full skirts, such as were described by various American writers in the 1840s in New Mexico. By the middle of the past century the impact of imported female styles began to erase the graceful and untrammeled dress of New Mexico women. Stays, crinolines and, later, bustles, high boned collars and stiffly wired millinery creations were adopted by degrees. An impression of acutely uncomfortable determination to conform with the new standardization is to be sensed when one examines portraits of New Mexicans made during that era of transition. The last survivals of the New Mexico Spanish woman's dress were the rebozo and shawl which most women wore in place of a hat or coat until 1941. After 1945 conformity with mass-manufactured national products became total.

APPENDIX
Mantas

As an illustration of the use of the Spanish noun *manta* to include any number of kinds of textiles of feathers or fur, the following notes are given in translation from the Spanish. They have been abstracted from *El Traje En Mexico,* Abelardo Carillo y Gariel, Mexico, 1959.

After the conquest by Cortéz of the Aztec and other contemporary peoples of Mexico in 1520 the Spanish levied tribute from Indian

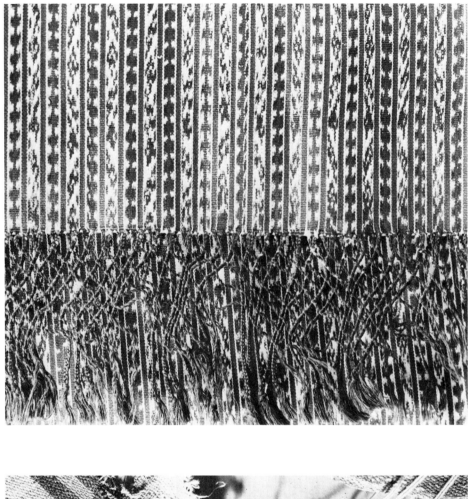

Figure 137: Silk rebozo dyed by the ikat technique, Mexico *ca.* 1840.

Figure 138: Fragment of cotton rebozo dyed indigo by the ikat technique, found on a New Mexico bulto of *ca.* 1830, reused.

villages, based on the kinds and amounts of things that each produced. This direct taxation was later changed to the encomienda system which assigned certain villages and lands to a Spaniard. As manager of land, products and people he could exact a proportion of the crops, textiles or whatever was produced for tax payment to the crown, and then for his own benefit. Some villages paid taxes in cotton cloth, (manta) intended to be made into clothing, and also in completed garments such as shirts, petticoats, shawls, kerchiefs, sheets and bed hangings.

In New Mexico it has for long been taken for granted that mantas were woven in sizes commonly worn by Pueblo women as a dress or shawl, but it appears from Carillo y Gariel's quotations from 16th century documents that to the Spanish of that time the word was all-inclusive as is our definition of the English noun, cloth. A memorandum of 1553 noted that the Indians of Panuco were heavily taxed. At first they made small cotton mantas that were of little value, but, in later years, the encomenderos had insisted that the mantas be longer, wider and more tightly woven so that one of these was worth three of the old kind. However, the same number of large mantas was required from the Indians as had been before. The population had diminished, the weaving was done by women and their looms were no wider than their own arms. The people were discontented by being forced to work too much. The mantas were made up of four to six *piernas*, or widths sewn together. The pierna was not a specific measurement, and was varied according to the demands of the encomendero. A landholder of Metatepec, thinking that his Indians were unjustly burdened, told them that they might shorten the length of each manta by one-half vara and reduce the width of each pierna by one-half *jeme*, (the distance between the extended thumb and forefinger). In 1554 Indians of Meztitlan were instructed to make their cotton mantas of four widths, each six varas long and two-thirds of a vara wide. Each manta was to be "well and tightly woven and pure white"; twenty-eight bundles of these were to be delivered every two months. The Indians did not have to take them to Mexico City nor any other place but had merely to bring them to the warehouse at Meztitlan.

In other places the pierna or width was from two to four and one-third varas with as much variation in the required lengths. Cotton mantas then had a cash value of from two to four tomines, equal to two and a half reales, when regarded as tribute, but were sold for better prices by the encomenderos. As the Spanish population and the mining industry both increased, inflation raised the value of a bundle of mantas from five pesos in 1550 to that of eighty pesos in 1565.

That the manta was not made only of cotton is noted in descriptions of 16th century markets in New Spain.

"The richest merchandise in these markets is that of mantas of which there are many different kinds. They are of cotton, some finer than others; white, black and of all colors, some large, others little, some for beds, richly damasked, others for cloaks, others for quilting or to be made into breeches, shirts, hats, mantles, kerchiefs and many other things. They weave rich mantas in colors, since the coming of our people some of these contain threads of gold or colored silks. Those that are already made up have in them rabbit skins and tiny bird feathers, a thing worth seeing. Mantas are also sold for the winter time made of feathers, or rather, down, some white, others black or of many colors; these are very soft and warm; they would adorn the bed of any lord. Others are sold of threads of spun rabbit fur, cotton and flax."

The first sheep sent from Spain had been scrubs yielding coarse fleeces. In order to improve the breed and the wool, Don Antonio de Mendoza, first viceroy of New Spain, (1535–50), sent for Merino sheep for his estates at Tlaxcala. His efforts to improve sheep raising and the textile industry were supported by his successor, Viceroy Luis de Velasco. A fiscal administrator noted in 1544 that the Indians were making mantas of wool that improved each day. "Some are as good as those from la Mancha or Aragon . . . they weave some which are great undertakings . . . and others of common quality." By 1560 Gonzalo Gomez, first encomendero of the pueblo of Istapa in the province of Michoacan, collected tribute in wool yarn worth one thousand pesos, two hundred pounds every eighty days. Other pueblos paid their taxes with woolen mantas.

These excerpts from Carillo y Gariel suggest that the colonial usage of the word manta should not always be taken by us today to mean cotton cloth or shawls. Spanish importation of sheep and the development of woolen textiles in New Mexico, together with their introduction of new dyestuffs, most probably had effected sweeping changes in the weaving of textiles in New Mexico fairly early in the 17th century.

APPENDIX
Names of Weavers

It is evident that there was no tabu on weaving by members of either sex among Spanish New Mexicans. The information below was collected from the families of weavers or is based on presence or absence of aniline dyes in blankets claimed to have been made by a certain individual. As the San Luis valley in Colorado was settled by New Mexicans after 1851 the Colorado Spanish may be regarded as members of the same social and cultural group.

Manuelita Apodaca, Watrous, N. M., wove a blanket containing indigo and an aniline red dye, about 1880 (L. 5.56-35). Information from her daughter.

. . . Garcia, La Isla, Colorado, wove a blanket containing vegetal and aniline dyes (L. 5.54-75). He was a weaver from about 1880 to 1900 according to his granddaughter. She did not remember his first name.

Antonia Lopez, Park View, N. M., born 1834, died 1923, wove blankets and jerga. A large jerga contains indigo and aniline red dyes (L. 5.57-34). Information from grandson.

Martina Lopez, las Trampas, N. M., wove blankets containing aniline dyes and busy, Saltillo motifs with striped ends, 1875–90. Information from grandson. (No identified examples produced.)

Luisa Manzanares, Los Brazos, N. M., born 1864, died 1949, made a blanket containing vegetal and commercial dyes (A. 5.57-34).

Patricia Montoya, El Valle, N. M., wove blankets containing eight-pointed stars, busy patterns and only aniline dyes in the 1890s. Information given by her family to Mr. Elmer Shupe.

Martín Roybal, Jacona, N. M., born ca. 1860, wove jerga using aniline red dye and yellow dye made from local "yerba vibora" or rattlesnake weed. Information from grandson.

The following names are given here by courtesy of the Colorado State Historical Society Museum, Denver. They were among the records of the late Charles H. Woodard on his collection of Rio Grande blankets which he bequeathed to the State Museum.

Damian Duran, Los Pinos, Colorado, wove a blanket containing Germantown yarns in Saltillo sarape pattern (E. 2018-10) about 1865 or 1870.

Felix Esquibel, San Pablo, Colorado, made a blanket containing aniline dyes and Mexican pattern (E. 2018-46) after 1880.

. . . Gallegos, mother of Gaspar Gallegos. She was born in the San Luis valley in 1867. She is said to have woven blankets and 300 yards of jerga, samples of which contain commercial red dye (E. 2018-51). Her first name is forgotten by descendants.

Pablo Garcia, Conejos, Colorado, made blankets containing aniline dyes with lozenges and stripes in design. No dates given (E. 2018-1 and E.2018-43).

José Lovato, Chama, Colorado, wove blankets containing only aniline dyes, no dates given (E. 2018-34).

Juan Miguel Vigil, San Luis, Colorado, wove a classic blanket of natural yarns and indigo dyed stripes (E. 2018-3). Only date given was that his grandson was born in 1874.

Figure 139: Fringed leather jacket worn by hunters such as the one in Plate 15.

APPENDIX
A Colonial Student's College Outfit, 1792

Carlos IV of Spain founded the "Royal College for American Nobles" at Granada in 1792. The college was intended for the education of colonial youths from all Spanish holdings in the Americas and Philippines. Boys were to be of pure Spanish blood or of "pure blood of Spanish and Indian" if the Indian ancestor was a cacique or cacique's daughter. Courses offered included political, legal, military and religious studies to fit students for colonial careers, as well as modern languages, painting and music.

Except for theological students they would be given exercises in riding, fencing and dancing. The director would offer other activities according to the season in the interests of health and to "relieve animal

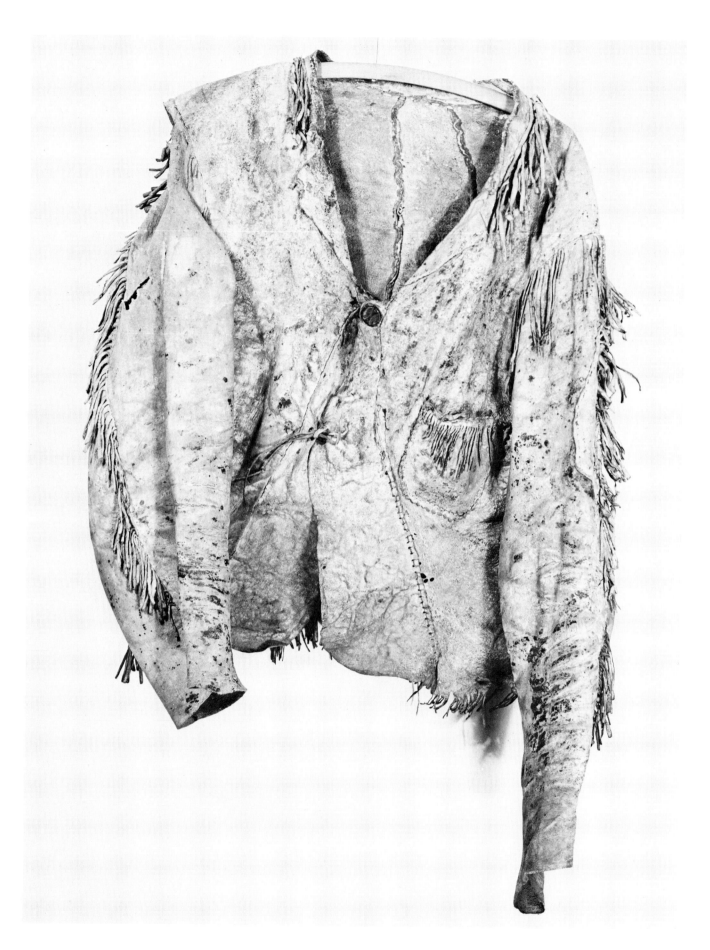

spirits." Applicants would have to pass physical and Latin examinations. No student could keep slaves or servants at the college but would be cared for by servants of the college, proctors and doctors. No group of students was permitted to sit at the same dining table regularly but had to change places daily. All were to be taught proper use of the knife and fork. Students might enter college between the ages of twelve and eighteen to study for an M.A. law degree and doctorate.

In view of the French invasion of the following year it is doubtful if this liberal, if belated, program for colonial youth had many candidates. Three boys are recorded as having been enrolled from Guatemala, but there is no evidence of any having gone from New Mexico. However, the instructions for clothing and equipment to be supplied by the students give us an idea of what was then in use and regarded as basically necessary for young men of the upper class.

Item 5 – Utensils and clothing that must be brought to the college by students. A trunk and litter to carry it, a metal writing desk, a complete service of silver [a service consisted of knife, fork and spoon, and a place plate] with the monogram of the owner's Christian and family names, a silver cup with the same cipher, a cup of majolica or porcelain. Two combs, one coarse toothed and one of ivory, two brushes, one for clothes, the other for shoes and boots. A pair of scissors, a pocket knife and case for quill pens. Two cloaks, one of white wool for winter, the other of mohair for summer. Twelve light-weight shirts and others with cravats. Two light shirts to sleep in. Six pairs of silk stockings, two pairs of shoes, twelve kerchiefs, eight colored and four white, four cot sheets and four pillowcases. One cloth, six napkins, four towels, two hair combing towels. These last effects may be obtained in Granada so that all will be alike.

A suit for winter or summer, according to the season when the student enrolls, should be of light weight and made of cloth or wool. A small sword, pair of buckles, a folding cot, two mattresses, a quilt and bed cover. Two night caps, a stand with its folding table for books. A curtain for the bed alcove.[1]

Figure 140: Spanish-style moccasins tied at the front, and leather cartridge box embroidered with hemp thread.

---

[1]From "El Real Colegio de Nobles Americanos de Granada," Hector Humberto Samayoa Guevara, in Antropología e Historia de Guatemala, VXVII/2, 1965.

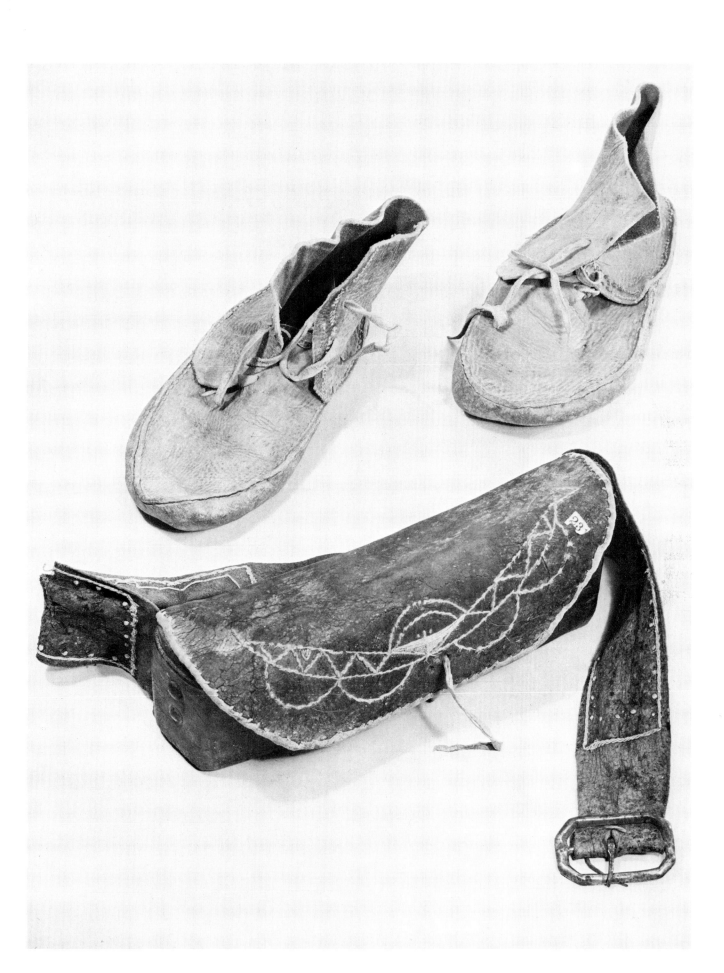

TEXTILES IMPORTED INTO COLONIAL NEW MEXICO AND RELATED TERMS AS FOUND IN AASP AND REFERENCE NO. A PARTIAL CHECK LIST.

Mss. Word Form	Spanish Dictionary Word Form	Definition	Word Root	Usage of Item	Date of Mss. Reference
alamares	alamar	thread loop and button sewn on edges of garments to fasten or as ornaments	Ar. alhamir	ornamentation of litter	1710
alepin	alepin	fine woolen, probably like broadcloth	Ar. halebi, from Aleppo	tunic of statue	1820
alfombra	alfombra	woven carpet of wool or other material	Ar. aljomra	usually in reference to a substitute for	1712–1820
algodón	algodón	cotton cloth	Ar. alcoton	cord girdle chemise of statue	1712 1818
arpillera	harpillera	sack cloth	Sp. herpil, loose carrying sack	payment to laborer	1710
bretaña	bretaña	fine bleached linen	from Brittany	tunic of statue, lace trimmed alb and amice chemise of statue	1710 1712 1818
brocatel	brocatel	silk damask woven with metallic threads	Lat. dentate, toothed	palium altar frontal	1710 1712
brocato	brocado	multicolored silk with or without metallic threads, this reference to brocato de Sevilla	Same as above	altar frontal	1712
cambrai	cambray	cambric, fine bleached linen	from Cambrai, France	amice	1712

Textiles Imported Into Colonial New Mexico and Related Terms As Found in AASF and Reference No. — (Continued)

Mss. Word Form	Spanish Dictionary Word Form	Definition	Word Root	Usage of Item	Date of Mss. Reference
cañutillo	cañutillo	either tubular glass beads or thread used in decoration of garments with passementerie	Sp. canuto, pipes	altar ornamentation trimming of statue robe	1710 1818
coquillo	coquillo	cotton cambric	from Cuba, used prior to introduction of drill	chemise of statue	1818
chapaneco	chapaneco, also chapaneques	yardage — type unknown	of, or from, Chiapas, Mexico	payment to laborer	1710
damasco	damasco	silk damask, specified as Chinese in this reference	from Damascus	altar frontal	1712
encaje	encaje	point lace, in this reference, silver	Sp. en, and caja, to catch or engage	trim on statue garments altar ornaments	1710 1818
espolinada	espolín	silk and metallic brocade woven with scattered multicolored flowers	Sp. espuela, spur	chasuble	1826
felpa negra	felpa	a type of velvet	Ger. felbel	lining of tabernacle	1826
flecos	flecos	colored silk fringe or cord used in passementerie	Lat. floccos	trimming of baldaquin	1710
galón	galón	galoon, braid, usually metallic, in this reference, "false silver"	Sp. gala	trimming of standard	1712
ylo hilo	hilo	thread	Sp. filo	reboso of, and payment to a laborer, one peso of-	1710

Textiles Imported Into Colonial New Mexico and Related Terms As Found in AASF and Reference No. — (Continued)

Mss. Word Form	Spanish Dictionary Word Form	Definition	Word Root	Usage of Item	Date of Mss. Reference
indianilla yndianilla	indiana	linen or cotton cloth printed in colors on one side only	from East Indies	altar frontal	1818
lantejuela	lentejuela	silver sequins	Sp. lentejas, lentils	ornamentation of baldaquin and statue garments	1710
lienzo	lienzo	cloth of linen, hemp, maguey, cotton or mixtures of these	Lat. linteum	canvas of painting	1712
lino	lino	linen	Lat. linum	sheet	1820
musuelina	muselina	cotton muslin	Ar. muceli, from Mosul	chemise of statue	1818
pacillo	pasillo	long stitch used in certain embroideries	Sp. paso	on tunic of statue	1820
palmilla	palmilla	cloth woven at Cuenca, Spain, usually blue	— — —	payment to laborer	1710
pelo de camello	pelo de camello	camels hair cloth or an imitation of it	— — —	payment to laborer	1710
pita	pita	fibres of vegetal material	— — —	payment to laborer	1710
razo de china	raso de china	satin, in this reference, Chinese	— — —	material of baldaquin and cover of processional litter	1710
revezillo	rebocillo rebocino	sheer white cloth used to cover woman's head as shawl, cap or wimple	Sp. rebozo	payment to laborer	1710

Mss. Word Form	Spanish Dictionary Word Form	Definition	Word Root	Usage of Item	Date of Mss. Reference
revoso reboso	rebozo	shawl, long and narrow, to cover woman's head and face, of plain silk or of thread in these references	— — —	payment to laborer	1710
ruan	ruan	bleached linen	from Rouen, France	amice loincloth of crucifix corpus	1712 1743
ruan florete	ruan florete	linen with floral print	from Rouen, France	payment to laborer	1710
seda	seda	any silk fabric, usually with qualifying adjective — also silk thread	Lat. sela	various	1710 plus
serreja	serreta	metallic braid with one edge dentate, formerly worn by Spanish officers of auxiliary corps to distinguish them from those of regular armed forces who wore straight edged braid on uniforms	Lat. serra	galoon trim on standard	1712
tafetán	tafetán	silk taffeta	Pers. tafta, weaving	altar frontal gown of statue	1818
tela	tela	a textile, usually followed by an adjective	Lat. tela	various	latter 18th c.
terciopelo tlascalteca	terciopelo tlascalteca	silk velvet blanket or shawl?	Sp. tercio and pelo from Tlaxcala, Mexico	tunic of statue blue and white veil or curtain for oil painting in mission	1820 1743

All items under date of 1710 from The Rebuilding of San Miguel at Santa Fe in 1710, George Kubler, 1939, Colorado Springs, Colorado, taken from the Spanish text of that publication. Other items from the AASF.

WOODWORKING

The fact that New Mexican furnishings, as well as structural woodwork, continued to repeat Spanish 16th century forms during the 18th century is the most significant indication of what the 17th century, or prerebellion, styles were in the colony. A few fragments of ceiling timbers, door frames, benches, and altar ornaments retrieved from excavations of the early missions confirm this hypothesis. Whether for felling and dressing tree trunks or for making small, fancy pieces the woodworking tools were the same. Primary in importance were the adz and long, narrow Spanish ax, a crude auger for boring into wood, the awl, chisels and gouges, the froe for splitting staves, thin sections, or reaming out the interiors of logs, the hammer, knife and two types of handsaw. The single hafted saw or *serrucho* was small, often no longer than a kitchen knife, while the *sierra*, much like a bucksaw, appears absurdly frail for its long history of usage. The identical form of saw is shown in a Romanesque fresco from Catalonia.[1] It was also represented in colonial Peruvian paintings and, although it has been discarded in New Mexico for hardware from the eastern United States, the same two-handed saw was still in use in parts of rural Spain in 1963.

Woods commonly used for construction and for cabinets were pine and red spruce with pegs and dowels of scrub oak. Cottonwood served for making hollowed-out troughs, barrels and the long sections of hollowed logs that carried irrigation water across gulleys and ravines but was too tough and fibrous to work into more precise shapes.

Kinds and forms of domestic furniture made in colonial New Mexico were those common to the poorer classes of Spain at the time of migration; the *trastero* or dish cupboard, various boxes and chests, hanging shelves, small stools or backless benches. Since Spain was barely emerging from the Middle Ages by 1500 the effect of Renaissance and Baroque styles upon rural Spanish design was negligible. Isolation of

---

[1] UNESCO World Art Series; "Spain, Romanesque Paintings," New York Graphic Society, 1957, Pl. IV, "Martyrdom of St. Juliet, ca. 1100 A.D."

Figure 141: Interior of 18th century chest.

Figure 142: Exterior of paneled chest above. (Photographs, Ernest Knee)

Figure 143: Chest on stand
with lions and pomegranates.

Figure 144: Chest with braced legs, *ca.* 1800.

Figure 145: Vesting table showing Neo-Classic influence, made 1815 for the Santuario de Esquipulas, Chimayó. (Photograph by Richard E. Ahlborn)

Figure 146: *Trastero* or cupboard, 18th century, with hand-shaped spindles, eyelet hinges and secret compartments within.

frontier New Mexico from style innovations is underlined by the persistence of archaic forms over so long a period.

Joints were made by mortise and tenon or dovetailing, although the latter, due to poor tools, was clumsy. Large storage chests for household purposes, like those in church sacristies, were composed of single, hand-adzed slabs of lumber on four sides, lid and bottom. The front and ends had relief carving produced by chiseling away background areas; dovetailed corners were concealed by applied moldings. Design elements were limited to rosettes, pomegranates, lions, meandering vines, and, occasionally, a hare or gryphon. In recent years local folksay has claimed that New Mexicans devised an original motif representing an indigenous wildflower, the scarlet penstemon. This notion was based on ignorance of traditional Hispano-Mauresque design which had employed the pomegranate in all aspects of tree, twigs, leaves, buds, blossoms, and fruit for centuries. As the pomegranate will not live in the upper Rio Grande valley, woodcarvers in time developed a non-representational form, or perhaps forgot what their prototypes had been, but their stylization is still easily related to the Old World motif. The generally humble level of New Mexican colonists is reflected by the absence of armorial devices on woodwork except for those on religious properties.

Dower chests, like those for religious vestments, sometimes had a few oblong boxes at one end of the interior. The chest stand was as a rule a pair of low, unconnected trestles until near the end of the 18th century when chests began to be made with legs. Hardware was kept to a minimum with eye hinges for the lid, a short hasp and small lock. If these had any pretensions to ornamentation they, like the cast metal keys, were made in New Spain. Grain chests of the 18th century were large enough for playhouses with simplified geometric panels. Survival over each winter was largely dependent on supplies of grain, so the storage chest was appropriately designed as a possession of importance.

Although the evolution of the free-standing cupboard may be traced from the chest-on-chest, New Mexican cupboards were made in one piece, sometimes two meters in height. The sides were plain wooden slabs with ornament concentrated on the front, topped by a cornice of one or three carved shells. In *mudéjar* tradition the upper doors had grills of handcarved spindles so that the contents were visible; the lower pair was of solid wood. Behind these were shelves or rows of wooden boxes alternated between blind panels. An equal number of these *caxones*, then called drawers, were fitted behind the stationary panels and were only accessible from the back of the cupboard, thus perpetuating the old custom of making "secret" drawers in cabinets. Less imposing trasteros had one pair of doors composed of small panels in frames; both styles had the usual iron eyelet hinges and small wrought iron hooks or hasps to close them.

Officials, like missionaries, had need of writing desks and it is probable that the old Spanish *vargueño* or traveling desk was brought to New Mexico by various persons in authority. However, they were either taken back with the visitors on their return to New Spain or have been lost. No whole or fragmentary desks have as yet been found which can be said to have been made in New Mexico at any time during the Spanish period.

The most prominent and prosperous family of the time in Santa Fe owned several writing desks, according to the will of Rosa Bustamente which was written in July 1814.[2] She was the widow of Antonio José Ortíz who had died in 1806. To children and grandchildren Rosa left a desk, or a small desk, a desk of middle size, or one with its little table. As was customary her will was written by a professional secretary whom she humbly begged to sign her name for her, with witnesses to her identity, because she did not know how to write. The desks were probably used by her former husband and his business secretaries or accountants. The widow Ortíz also disposed of twelve stools covered with cowhides, two tables, a wardrobe and two *camapes* or sofas. While these exotic pieces of furniture were marks of social standing in Santa Fe of the period, they were probably rustic in comparison with others owned by wealthy families of New Spain.

The Mozarabic and Medieval customs of the Spanish required no bedsteads, chairs or tables except among upper class families and religious. Mention of such pieces in 18th century New Mexican documents is scanty and refers to belongings of governors, ecclesiastics or recently arrived newcomers. Tables for specialized purpose were made to serve dishes to diners who sat or reclined on woolsacks. They were therefore appropriately low; for a long time examples of these were classed as footstools but lately they have been rediscovered as colonial precursors of the currently fashionable coffee table. Dominguez' 1776 report on missions of New Mexico noted the following furnishings of conventos (p. 28, Santa Fe): "An ordinary table without a drawer. Four crude little armless chairs. Two crude armchairs. A wooden bed with legs like pillars. Father Zarte provided all this." (Father Zarte was assigned to service in New Mexico from Puebla, Mexico, in 1772.) Page 56, Nambe: "Two ordinary tables, without drawers and very poor. Two rough chairs, an ordinary bench, badly made. Three bedboards on adobe legs." Page 69, San Ildefonso: "The board alcove and bed. A very large, strong table and drawer that Father Irigoyen made. Two small chairs and a little bench that Father Vega installed."[3] If the missionaries from Mexico had such austere and scanty furnishings that were so seldom replaced, it is obvious that they were not commonly in use among the laity.

Possession of a chair in a private home was a status symbol indicating that important officials or priests were received by the family.

---

[2] Ortíz Family Papers, op. cit.

[3] Father Irigoyen was at San Ildefonso at intervals between 1730 and 1736, while Father Vega visited there between 1769–77.

Figure 147: Serving table for dining at floor level.

Figure 149: Eighteenth century armchair, New Mexico, commonly called a priest's chair.

Figure 148: Seventeenth century armchair, Spain. (Courtesy Museo Nacional de Artes Decorativos, Madrid)

Such chairs resembled those used in church sanctuaries, and, although rudely mortised of unadorned pine, repeated the design and construction of Romanesque thrones of eight or nine centuries before. The persistence of this archaic chair pattern in New Mexico into the 19th century is in itself proof of the New Mexican's preference for woolsacks, small stools or built-in adobe banquettes as domestic seating conveniences.[4] The same was true of decorative benches with back rail and arms, which were originally made for use in the church sanctuary and by selected dignitaries attending Mass, or for seating ladies at dances in the sala. Until very recent years New Mexicans stood or knelt upon packed earth floors in church with the exception of the privileged few who heard the Mass from seats. As tools, woodworking and transportation improved in the 19th century more enterprising families began to make and own their private pews in churches. Since each bench was made by or for a family, they were of all sizes and patterns. Variety in rails, splats, and aprons was often handsome with a feeling for proportion and restraint in ornament which was typical of the best of Spanish New Mexican woodworking. Needless to say the pews were first replaced in town churches by standard rows of commercial design, at first Neo-Gothic, after the advent of the new Bishop Lamy, and more slowly in village chapels and Indian missions. The conservative pueblo of Santa Ana is one that has retained the ancient earth floor with no pews or seats in its mission.

The single or double wall shelf was generally used, as it was and is in Spain, to hold small articles. It was made of two wedge-shaped brackets into which a shelf was tenoned. A stepped or decorative cornice was pegged along the shelf front but as it hung down. unlike European counterparts, it had no practical use in keeping things from falling off the shelf.

Small treen was made to some extent in the form of bowls, dippers, ladles, spoons, and saucers for weigh scales or *balanzas*. A few baptismal fonts were scooped from cross-sections of logs for chapels where those of copper were lacking. Perhaps the most ingenious, if inefficient, attempt to provide substitutes for iron locks was the New Mexican wooden lock disparagingly mentioned in more than one 18th century church inventory, and also in use at Indian pueblos.[5] The "key" of these slab-faced locks was intended to displace the wooden tumblers, on the same principle as that of a metal lock, but lacked precision contact and was hardly effective.

Preceding Page:
Figure 150: Eighteenth century side chair, Spain. (Courtesy Museo Nacional de Artes Decorativos, Madrid)

Figure 151: Eighteenth century chair and table, New Mexico, made for use in church sanctuary. (Photograph by Laura Gilpin)

Figure 152: Pine chair showing Federal style influence.

Figure 153: Pine armchair reflecting influence of Trail traders from the East.

Figure 154: Museum exhibit of a 19th century chapel, New Mexico, showing family-owned benches.

Figure 155: Scoops and ladles of wood.

---

[4] Magoffin, Susan Shelby, *Down the Santa Fe Trail and into Mexico, 1846–47,* Yale University Press, 1926, reprint 1962.
[5] Dominguez, p. 50: In speaking of dwellings at Tesuque Pueblo: "The fastenings (of these rooms) are a wooden lock and key."

Handcarved candlesticks,[6] sconces, *arañas* or chandeliers and wooden lanterns[7] were principally for church or private chapel usage, for lack of metal ones. They must have burned quite often, and it is understandable that they were soon replaced after scrap or salvaged tin became available in the second quarter of the 19th century by tin sconces and chandeliers and, a few decades later, by kerosene lamps.

Wooden musical instruments that were made in the colony were the drum, flute, rattle and violin. The Spanish drum was composed of thin sections of wood laced together with thongs, covered with gesso and painted. The rawhide heads were tightened by a network of thongs stretched around the box. It is quite different from the hollowed, solid logs used by Pueblo Indians in making their drums and was undoubtedly modeled after military drums that came into the colony made with brass nails, lacquer and more gaudy materials. Only a few small chapels in New Mexico still keep their old drums, but in Spanish times, when religious feast days were celebrated by the firing of guns, drums and violins provided music for processions, Mass and social dancing.

Rough, undecorated pieces of functional importance that required labor and good sized pieces of wood to make them included the sawhorse type of spinning wheel and the harness loom. Sometimes made from a fortuitous forked tree, the New Mexican wheel was similar to one shown in more finished state by Diderot:[8] The massive loom, as large as a four-poster bed, was roughed out with ax and adz so that the post and slot construction could be easily taken down and reassembled by two men. In spite of its unpolished appearance the New Mexican loom contained all of the necessary features shown by Diderot in his drawing of the "horizontal frame loom" (ibid, V. II, Pl. 309, "Weaving, I").

Making of farm implements in addition to *canoas* or troughs also required heavy labor in woodworking. The wooden plough or *arado*, used in New Mexico until seventy-five years ago by most farmers, was of the same form as that used in Biblical times. It was, and is, used in India, the Andean regions of South America, and other parts of the world where agriculture has figured importantly. The wooden plough achieved pictorial documentation in connection with the life of St. Isadore the farmer, patron saint of Madrid, and was duly reproduced with images of him not only in Spain but into the 20th century in New Mexico. To southwestern Indians the wooden plough was a notable

---

[6] Dominguez, p. 53, Nambe Mission: "Two dozen ugly old candleholders of rough wood which Father Toledo provided." (Father Toledo was at Nambe, Oct. 1753–55; Archives of the Archdiocese of Santa Fe, Chavez, ed., p. 257.)

[7] Santa Cruz Inventory, 19 May 1779, "Una farol de madera con tres vidrios" (A lantern of wood with three panes).

[8] "Recueil des Planches sur les Sciences, les Arts Méchaniques," from the *Encyclopedia of Denis Diderot,* Paris, 1763, Dover Publications, Inc., New York, 1959, V. II, Pl. 306, Fig. 9, "Wool Spinning Wheel."

Figure 156: Wooden lantern with container for tub weights used as a grease lamp.

Figure 157: Exterior of wooden lantern with selenite panes.

II-B

257

improvement over their prehistoric digging sticks until it was replaced by factory-made metal ploughs with other modern farm machinery. Stake-sided farm carts had solid wooden wheels intended to revolve although the wooden axles did not. At a result the wheels soon wore into polygonal shapes so that carts dragged along the ground like sledges.

The making of molasses, locally called *miel*, or honey, required a barrel, a trough hollowed from a log, a disc-shaped press, and wooden mallets. Except for wild bee's honey, corn syrup was the only sweetening available to New Mexicans. The annual crushing and straining of cornstalks was a communal event when each family brought its supply to the *mielero* for processing and took turns helping others in the work[9].

Around the turn of the 19th century several changes in woodworking methods appeared in New Mexico. One was the making of chests on legs, and another the use of geometric decoration instead of the old lions and pomegranates. Mozarabic motifs in chip-carving or gouged patterns had been used on beams and corbels from the beginning of the colony, but not, apparently, on movable furniture until the end of the 18th century. Also the influence of the late 18th century neo-Classic fashion was reflected in a few cornices, pediments and furnishings.

A brilliantly colored novelty of the period was a series of plain wooden chests painted in oils with amusing scenes. It has been stated that these were made in Mexico and brought north from the Chihuahua fairs after 1805 as containers for purchases made there. Tree-ring tests, however, proved that their wood was pine from the upper Rio Grande valley.[10] They were made before the advent of hand tools from the eastern United States, and, like earlier carved chests, were composed of solid slabs for sides, bottom and lid, dressed by adz rather than plane, and had crude, handwrought iron hinges, hasps and locks. As their subjects featured exotic, or semitropical flowers around borders and scenes of helmeted dragoons, people in boats, and turreted architecture, they were probably painted by an emigrant from Mexico who brought his oil pigments with him. A panel showing a fishing party catching large red snappers indicates that the artist knew the west coast, or Gulf of California region. The repetitious but competent proficiency of his brushwork suggests that he had had experience either in painting wooden boxes in Mexico or, even more probable, in painting majolica wares.[11] The chief interest in these boxes aside from their

---

[9]Appendix II-D, Wills, and *Shadows of the Past*, Cleofas M. Jaramillo, Santa Fe, 1941, p. 38, gives a description of the old method of making syrup.

[10]Personal communication, W. S. Stallings, Jr., dendrochronologist, 1941.

[11]Erwin O. Christensen, *Popular Art in the United States*, Penguin Books, London, 1948, Pl. 29, and Fales, Dean A., *American Painted Furniture 1660–1880*, Dutton, New York, 1972, p. 251.

Figure 158: New Mexico
painted chest, *ca*. 1830.

decorative quality is their record of contemporary dress, already discussed in Section II-A.

Unsuspected at the time, a revolution in methods of construction, in forms and kinds of woodworking in New Mexico was to be created by the Santa Fe Trail after its opening in 1821. With the eastern-made, small hand tools which were among the trade items, New Mexicans began to learn shortcuts in the preparation of utilitarian pieces and application of fancy trimming and, above all, to indulge in the use of square cut nails to put parts together. The construction of a door, for example, completely changed. Mortise and tenon joins, true panels and the puncheon post disappeared. The battened door was composed of narrow, parallel strips of lumber on the back and the face was made of boards running in other directions, all assembled with nails. Over the face, moldings cut with a hand plane were arranged to simulate one or more panels; New Mexican taste often planned these in cruciform patterns. The door swung on cheap, factory-made hinges, and sometimes had its moldings picked out in colors.

Trimming saws, molding planes and mitre boxes were responsible for the rapid changes in woodworking after a period of more than two centuries of repetition of ancient methods and styles. The traditional chest was replaced by plain wooden trunks with hutch tops copied from wagon boxes brought by the traders; cheap factory locks and hinges made them desirably mouseproof.[12] Grain chests grew even larger, but were constructed with numerous boards instead of single slabs, and had the same trimming of fancy moldings and simulated bosses as those used on doors.

When the three-way trade between the Missouri, Santa Fe and Chihuahua had been profitably established and cooperation of the Mexican Republic appeared secure, several traders found it convenient as well as agreeable to make Santa Fe or Taos their residence and to marry daughters of prominent New Mexican families. These men adapted their habits to the language, religion, social customs, and diet of their brides, but insisted upon having the accustomed amenities of home such as glazed windows, bedsteads, tables, chairs, washstands and wardrobes. By 1830 beds and chairs were made in New Mexico in the style known as American Federal, or Duncan Phyfe; the use of local pine instead of hardwood gave such pieces a rustic air, but it is obvious that they were designed or made by Americans from the eastern states. Except for a few simple looking glass frames, no examples of this style have been found that have been proven to have been brought to New Mexico at the time; the local pieces must necessarily have been made from memory.

While the wagon trains rolled under dust clouds over the prairies,

---

[12]Workman, William, "A Letter from Taos, 1826," Ed. by David J. Weber, in New Mexico Historical Review, V.XLI/2, 1966.

Figure 159: Left, door carved by Jose Dolores Lopez *ca.* 1930. (Photograph by John Waggaman)

Figure 160: Right, battened door from the Penasco valley *ca.* 1900.

the newly fashionable neo-Gothic style had arrived in cities of the eastern seaboard, and in due time made its way into New Mexico, five thousand miles from Horace Walpole's Strawberry Hill in space, but infinitely farther away in cultural consciousness. While the lathe-turned spool rails and Gothic finials of the style were attractively new to easterners, they were rather a familiar extension of the traditional mudéjar grills in the Spanish west where carpenters, as yet unaware of machine lathes, were content to whittle spindles by hand as in the past and to construct rustic day beds combining sleigh ends and spool rails. Some of these had a back rail and were called camapés or sofas. While it became a matter of prestige to display such a bed in the sala of self-respecting homes the majority of New Mexicans, particularly in the country, continued to prefer to sleep on the floor with their wool-sacks, blankets and sheep pelts. The bedstead was reserved for honored guests, bridal couples on their wedding night, for reception of visitors by mothers after a lying-in, and the corpse between decease and the funeral Mass at the church. The obvious discomfort of these hard, narrow beds was a matter of indifference when they were not in regular use.

Figure 161: Bedstead made for the visit of Bishop Zubiria to Chimayó in 1845. This is identical to beds in convents described in the Dominguez report of 1776.

Figure 162: *Careta* or farm cart drawn by oxen.

Contemporary letters or journals record the conservatism of the Spanish New Mexicans in their use of the new forms of furniture. The precise descriptions given by Susan Magoffin of her visits to Santa Fe homes include a dinner party given by the Eugene Leitensdorfers for General Kearny, his officers and several Santa Fe traders on September 19, 1846. Leitensdorfer, a Trail trader, had married Doña Soledad Abreu of a well-known Santa Fe family. After two or three hours at the table the ladies left for another room where they "took seats on the low cushions placed around the wall."

On the same day Susan and her husband Samuel Magoffin, also a trader, visited the home of Don Gaspar Ortíz and were received by his wife. "Her house I suppose is one of the best in the city . . . The long salon to the front is the sitting room. This is furnished with cushions, no chairs, two steamboat sofas, tables, a bed and other little fixtures."[13]

While the Magoffin caravan toiled over the rough road from Pecos into Santa Fe on August 30, a Sunday, Lieutenant Colonel W. H. Emory[14] attended Mass at the Santa Fe parroquia which he briefly described: "Today we went to church in great state. The governor's seat, a large, well stuffed chair, covered with crimson, was occupied by the commanding officer. . . . Except the governor's seat and one row of benches, there were no seats in the church. Each woman dropped

[13] Magoffin, op. cit., p. 137.
[14] "Notes of a Military Reconnaissance from Fort Leavenworth, in Missouri, to San Diego, California, including part of Arkansas, Del Norte, and Gila Rivers," Lt. Col. W. H. Emory, made in 1846-47, with the advance guard of the Army of the West. Washington, 1848. Report of the Secretary of War, 30th Congress, Executive Document 41.

on her knees on the bare floor as she entered, and only exchanged this position for a seat on the ground at long intervals, announced by the tinkle of a small bell."

At Bernalillo, which Emory noted was "a small town but one of the best built in the Territory," he and his aides visited the home of a wealthy man. "We were led into an oblong room, furnished like that of every Mexican in comfortable circumstances. A banquette runs around the room, leaving only a space for the couch. It is covered with cushions, carpets and pillows upon which the visitor sits or reclines. The dirt floor is usually covered a third or a half with common looking carpet." (This was country-made jerga.)

Parts of the Report, Executive Document 41, were written by junior officers including Lieutenant J. W. Abert who noted that: "The houses throughout the country are furnished with mattresses, doubled up and arranged close to the walls so as to answer for seats."

A bed frame made for the visit of Bishop Zubiría y Escalante of Durango in 1850 by the Chimayó family which was to be his host shows that notions of bed construction at the time were the same as those of the 18th century Franciscan missionaries: "bedboards" in fact. Although the bedstead was piously preserved as a memento of the Bishop's visitation it was said by the former owners that it had never been used after his departure. In fact, until World War II, most rural New Mexican families still kept one bed in the parlor while old and young slept on the floor.

The Anglos preferred to sit on chairs and dine from tables, hence these were made at normal levels, and the American country style table with round top and square frame found itself decorated with Moorish patterns of chip-carving in New Mexico. The fate of the trastero was sealed by the introduction of American kitchen meatsafes; squatty, plain wooden frames with panels of punched sheet tin. Already delighted with salvaged tin containers which they remodeled into decorative frames for santos, New Mexicans took over the tin paneled cupboard until standard factory cabinets became commonplace.

By the end of the Civil War cheaply made commercial sets of Belter style furniture began to reach New Mexico, to be succeeded by "General Grant" and "Eastlake" of the same inexpensive grades. The prestige of owning such importations was sufficient to induce poor country people to make their own renderings of these, often of salvaged lumber and packing boxes from St. Louis. After 1865 young Southerners in seach of fortune in the West introduced the so-called plantation overseers' desk. It was copied in quantities as by that time the territorial population included officials and military, legal, commercial and other professional men who required the conveniences of a desk in their business. A contribution to domestic furnishing by incoming non-Spanish housekeepers was the once popular ironing table whose top turned up to make a bench. No longer in use, these rustic laundry tables have recently been described by local folksay as "priest chairs," another example of the unreliability of folklore.

Rural woodcarving of nonreligious pieces did extend into the present century, but was chiefly confined to ornamental wall shelves and parlor stands inspired by those popular at the Philadelphia Centennial, and therefore most of these were stained or painted black. The most original and competent maker of such pieces was José Dolores Lopez of Cordova, New Mexico, 1868–1938 (Sec. Appendix IV-B), who began by supplying them, as well as santos and fancifully carved gravemarkers, for his neighbors. Some of his shelves and decorated boxes are logical extensions of the regional style while others were attempts to graft Moorish chip-carving upon forms then being released from Grand Rapids.[15] Either type, however, has the stamp of Lopez' personal touch and sense of proportion. After his work was discovered by artists and writers in the 1920s his market extended to Santa Fe where he even made several fancy doors for private homes. With few exceptions, however, woodworking declined as carpenters used standard mill lumber, tools and construction methods, and found it more profitable to work on buildings for regular pay. Attempts at reviving traditional designs made by hand labor have proved too expensive to succeed, and all too often the product was a bowdlerized version rather than a serious reproduction of an old piece.

---

[15] Lopez family tradition says that José Dolores was using the designs of filigree jewelry in his woodcarvings.

METALS, THEIR USES
AND RE-USES

BELLBRONZE, COPPER, IRON

Missions received bronze bells from New Spain in the 17th century. These were typically Spanish in shape, slender and long waisted with a heavy crown at the top by which they were lashed to the yoke on which they were suspended. It has been argued that some were saved from destruction in 1680, but if this was true it is not proven in the case of any specific bell. Others were recorded as broken by the Indians; fragments of those have been recovered during excavations at Pecos and Awatovi pueblos.[1] These fragments will overlay whole bells brought to New Mexico after the reconquest, fitting perfectly, proving that there was no change in bell shape and decoration in New Spain between the 17th and early 18th centuries. (See "Awatovi," Fig. 6). Decoration consisted of the so-called diamond cross, banding, the name of the church's patron saint and/or a date, done in low relief. The raised areas were impressed into the sides of the sand-adobe mold and sometimes inscriptions were reversed, or partly lost.

Eighteenth Century Bells of the Same Shape and Decoration as Bells of the Seventeenth Century, Made in New Spain and Sent to New Mexico.

---

*   Indicates that I am quoting information given by Miss Jane Howe, Norman, Oklahoma.

**   Indicates information from records of the Fred Harvey Company. (I am indebted to Byron Harvey, III, for making these available.)

* 1. Bell at mission of San Esteban, Acoma Pueblo: "SAN PEDRO ANO DE 1710."

---

[1] "The Artifacts of Pecos," A. V. Kidder, Papers of the Phillips Academy Southwestern Expedition No. 6, New Haven, 1932, and "Franciscan Awatovi," Montgomery, Ross Gordon, Watson Smith and John Otis Brew, Papers of the Peabody Museum, Harvard University, V. XXXI, Reports of the Awatovi Expedition, Peabody Museum, No. 3, Cambridge, Massachusetts, 1949.

2. Bell in Old Candelario Curio Shop, Santa Fe, origin unknown: "SAN IOSE 1710." The spelling of José is possibly the foundryman's abbreviation as Spanish academicians only adopted the modern form in the late 18th century. Before then it was written Joseph, or Josep or Josef.

* 3. Bell in new mission of Santa Clara, Santa Clara Pueblo: "SAN-TIAGO. D. ANO DE 1710."

* 4. Bell in mission San José, Laguna Pueblo; (mission said to have been begun in 1699) "SAN CHRISTOVAL X ANO 1710." There is a second bell in this church of the same shape but undated.

5. Bell at mission San Lorenzo, Picurís Pueblo: "SANTO DO-MINGO DE 1710." Prior to recent rebuilding of this mission the bell was hung by ropes from a pole framework planted in the ground at the west side of the church. It had no clapper and was struck with a rock by the bellringer.

* 6. Bell at mission Nuestra Señora de la Asunción, Zia Pueblo: "SAN PABLO ANO DE 1710."

7. Bell in Museum of New Mexico: "NSETRA SENRA DE GVAD-ALVPE SIENDA DEL GABINO" "A MARZO L O 17x8" (third numeral lost).

8. Bell in Museum of New Mexico: formerly in a village church, state of Chihuahua, Mexico: "SAN INASIO 172x" (fourth numeral lost. If we allow the lost numeral on Bell No. 7 to have been either 0, 1 or 2, all of the above eight bells share form and mechanical construction, style of lettering, ornate decoration in relief; all are dated before 1730. Apparently the bellcasters of New Spain began to mold bells in a different shape sometime after this date, whether by intention or accident. The profiles of bells dated later than those of the first group, although still long and slender, lack the clean angles of shoulder and lip, and the slightly concave silhouette of the skirt of the earlier bells.

**9. Bell bought by William Randolph Hearst from the Fred Harvey Company, now at San Simeon, a California State Park: "NVESTRA: SENORA: DEL PILAR: ORA PRO NOBIS: ANO DE 1735."

10. Bell in Museum of New Mexico, well cast but of pure copper content, no relief decoration, inscription incised after casting. AD 1741: VIVOS INVOCO   MORTUOS PLANTO   (I call the living, I lament the dead).

* 11. Bell in new church of Santo Tomás, Abiquiu: "ANO DE 1744." The previous church at Abiquiu was under construction at the time. This bell has the later style profile but retains relief cross and ornaments.

**12. Bell at San Simeon, California: "SE HIZO EL ANO DE 1751" (? possibly 57). "S. LVIS GONZAGA, ORA PRO NOBIS. JHS." The original New Mexico location of this bell is not given in the records. St. Louis Gonzaga was a Jesuit and so is the "JHS" emblem on the relief inscription.

There are two possibilities as to how or why this bell came to New Mexico; the first is that it was obtained by Governor Marín del Valle for his chapel of Our Lady of Light, the Castrense in Santa Fe, which he and his wife had built in 1760-61. The stone altar screen in that chapel depicts St. Ignatius Loyola, founder of the Jesuits, and it is said that Marín del Valle had been educated by Jesuit teachers. He may have had a bell inscribed with the name of another Jesuit saint for his Santa Fe project. Fray Dominguez mentioned "a good middle-sized bell" in the central bell arch of the Castrense facade; his adjective "good" implies that the bell was from New Spain (Dominguez, p. 34). After the expulsion of the Jesuits from Mexico in 1767, Franciscans were placed in charge of the former Jesuit missions, as was the case in Pimería Alta. Franciscan patrons replaced those of the Jesuits in Sonora, and a bell (no matter whose saintly name was on it) after being replaced by another could have been sent to New Mexico missions where bells were always lacking.

The extreme degrees of heat and cold within a few hours that are common to northern New Mexico winters caused the cracking of many bells. Collapse of belfries and the breaking of rawhide lashings by which bells were suspended accounted for damage to others. Since a number of bells were cast with no provision for a clapper they were struck by hand with a rock. Some bells hung in a belfry, others were hung from poles planted in the ground before the church. The bell ringers seem always to have struck the clapperless bells on the same spot in the lip so that some bells were worn so thin that they cracked or broke.

Figure 163: Sand-cast bell from Zacatecas of early 18th century is the same as those sent to New Mexico before 1680.

Figure 164: Bell sand-cast in New Mexico. (Courtesy of the Smithsonian Institution)

In addition to these vicissitudes the ancient custom of passing on church furnishings, including bells, from cathedral city to village and from town mission and so on to the frontier, which still continues, is the logical explanation for the presence of many bells in their locations of today. The named bells listed above have no relation to the patrons of the churches where they are now. An undated bell at San Francisco de Nambe Pueblo is lettered "SAN DIEGO." In view of the passing on of bells from place to place when one church was abandoned, or received a new one, the notations made by Dominguez in 1776 may not always prove that he saw the same bell or bells that we see in a given place today.

The Spanish searched for deposits of lead, tin and mercury as well as gold and silver, and did locate small copper deposits both in the Ortíz mountains south of Santa Fe, near Abiquiu, on the north side of the Peñasco valley not far from Picurís Pueblo. The old copper diggings near modern Cerrillos had also been mined for turquoise since prehistoric times and were only a few miles from the village of Ciénega where remains of a so-called smelter have been located.

The existence of an old Spanish smelter at Ciénega had been spoken of more than once by descendants of the Baca and Montoya families who had been landowners in the valley of the Ciénega river in colonial times. The valley has a permanent water supply and formerly had

many little placitas along its green banks; the remains of some are easily found, often superimposed on earlier Indian sites. At the western end of the valley the canyon narrows to a gorge where the river has eroded a channel through the lava beds to descend the western slope of la Bajada Mesa on its course to the Rio Grande. With the kind assistance of Mr. Ricardo C. de Baca of la Ciénega, my assistant, Alan C. Vedder, and I inspected the traditional smelter in the summer of 1962. The location is close to the river bottom on suitably sandy soil and surrounded by steep, heat-reflecting lava cliffs. It is in the middle of a prehistoric pueblo site, now deeply eroded by the river (LA. 149). An area of dark, burned soil contained lumps of slag with corn cob forms in them. Digging to a depth of 60 centimeters exposed consistently burned soil in spite of recent erosion.

Samples of the slag were sent to the New Mexico Institute of Mining and Technology at Socorro, New Mexico. I am indebted to Dr. Arthur Montgomery for having arranged to send the samples there, and to Dr. Frank E. Kottlowski, Economic Geologist, for his report on the specimens, and for his having made a trip to the site to personally inspect it. His report follows:

August 22, 1962

State Bureau of Mines
New Mexico Institute of Mining and Technology
Socorro, N. M.

Description of Assay Report

The two samples of material you believed to be slag with corn cob impressions are indeed furnace slag. The brick-colored sample does not resemble any rock, and therefore, you can be reasonably safe in calling it brick.

Dr. Kottlowski added:

The imprints do seem to be corn cobs; such were used by the Spanish as a reducing agent in some types of smelting.

The presence of fragments of fired brick was probably caused by the extreme heat of the burning corn on lumps of clay as the Spanish are not known to have made fired bricks in New Mexico. Prehistoric granaries that had burned by accident or enemies often contain casts of both corn cobs and roof materials that are fired to a bricklike hardness due to the intense heat produced by the dried corn in burning. No evidence of any building foundations was found in connection with the smelter at Ciénega. It is probable that it was simply a pit, like those used to sand-cast large bells in Mexico, over which the necessary pole scaffolding was raised to hoist up the completed work.

Although la Ciénega was inhabited by Spanish families in the 18th century its recorded importance seems to have been in the first half of the 19th. The now demolished first chapel of San José was licensed in 1817; it stood not far from the site of the smelter.

Francisco Luján was described in 1915 as an itinerant bell caster by Rafael Chacón, an old resident of New Mexico (*El Palacio*, V. 67/4, 1960, p. 139). Luján, according to Chacón, made a good bell for the chapel of Santa Cruz at Chamisal, in 1855 or '56. Like the santeros, the bell maker went to the village wanting his services and did his work on the spot. The use of local copper from the nearby mine is not mentioned in the Chamisal account but only ". . . old discarded copper pots contributed by the women to be melted for the purpose." After the molten copper had been poured into the sand mold Luján added "pieces of gold and silver . . . valuable rings and other jewels . . ." to give a clear tone. The dates of 1855–56 coincide with those of several other New Mexican bells that may have been made by Luján. All are thick walled and squatty, often defective in casting and predominantly of copper. They are inscribed sometimes with saints, names or a date or both in Spanish wording and Arabic numerals, frequently reversed as in mirror writing. Casting defects have led romantic persons to believe that some of these bells are dated 1356 although the numeral 3 is merely a defective numeral 8. In the 14th century, bells and other religious properties were inscribed with Latin wordings and Roman numerals, and the Spanish bell of the earlier period was markedly slender in silhouette.

The chapel of San José de Chama, completed in 1850, is said to have had, when new, three bells bearing the names of the donor's three daughters (*El Palacio*, V. 60/4, 1953, p. 159). These bells may also have been cast by Francisco Luján.

In an earlier letter from Chacón to Read dated November 13, 1915, Chacón gave further information as follows: that he was then aged eighty-two years, six months and twenty-two days, that he could read and write, did not use eyeglasses nor a cane. He said that Francisco Luján was from Embudo and that he had made a bell for the Chamisal church. Chacón thought that Luján's son, José Miguel Luján, a good silversmith then living in Clayton, Union County, New Mexico, would have more information. Chacón thought that Francisco Luján had moved to Embudo from Peña Blanca but said that the son would know better. He said that "Francisco was a silversmith and blacksmith, a very industrious man" (Benjamin M. Read papers, No. 121-a-13, New Mexico State Records Center). Perhaps the son, here named as José Miguel, was the same silversmith named by Carmen Espinosa in her paper on New Mexico smiths as José Manuel Luján (Carmen Espinosa, "Fashions in Filigree," *New Mexico* Magazine, V. 17/9, 1939).

Another statement in the Read papers, all in a folder entitled "Bell of San Miguel Controversy, 1914," was written by Clemente Ortíz of Santa Fe, dated November 14, 1914. Mr. Ortíz was eighty-three years old; he said that in 1856 he had seen two bells cast by a man who lived near Taos. The casting took place in front of the old Santa Fe parish church on the side next to San Francisco Street. Ortíz went several times to watch the process. Later on he saw the larger of the two bells lifted over the wall of San Miguel chapel on College Street and hoisted into the tower of the chapel. The tower was the three-tiered one of adobes and wooden framework which collapsed in 1872.

The correspondence on the subject of the allegedly oldest bell in San Miguel chapel, whose cast inscription was interpreted as reading in the year of 1356 at the time and still is, was initiated by Read in order to dispose of the myth, as well as the legend, that it had been shipped by sea and carted overland from Spain to Santa Fe. The bell in question was successfullly cast and has a sweet tone, but it is lettered in modern Spanish with Arabic numerals. Aside from the improbability that such a heavy bell would have been hauled from Spain when equally good or better bells were being made in northern New Spain, no church bell of the 14th century would have been lettered in anything but Latin and with Roman numerals. The numeral eight in the date on the San Miguel bell was defective in its casting and there-fore resembles the numeral three. The same defect appears on a contem-porary bell now in the Museum of New Mexico.

The historian Benjamin Read correctly assumed that in 1914 he would be able to find living eyewitnesses to the making of the bell and its installation at San Miguel chapel. All of these events, as stated by his witnesses, took place before the Christian Brothers took pos-ession of the chapel and opened their school for boys in 1859.

Clemente Ortíz went on to state that before the San Miguel bell was cast other bells were made in Santa Fe. "One of these was placed in the belfry of the church of Our Lady of Guadalupe in this same city. I believe this is true because it was told to me by persons of veracity who saw the bells made. I did not see it." According to his statement, Clemente Ortíz would have been twenty-five years old when the San Miguel bell was cast and well able to remember the episode.[2]

Among other documents in the Read file on the "Bell of San Miguel Controversy" are letters from individuals and the Santa Fe Chamber of Commerce, another from the Superior of the St. Michael's College at that time stating that he regarded the claim to antiquity as nonsense, and clippings from the Santa Fe *New Mexican* dated October 14, Novem-ber 3 and 12, 1921. In the latter New Mexico's other leading historian, Ralph Emerson Twitchell, Benjamin Read and Charles Lummis are quoted as being mutually satisfied that the witnesses located by Read had finally settled, for all time, the real history of the San Miguel chapel bell, and laid to rest the myth of its Spanish origin and antiquity. Lummis noted that romantic falsehoods tend to survive while facts are ignored and forgotten; his comment has proved to be correct.[3] I am

---

[2] Benjamin M. Read Papers, No. 235-a-1, New Mexico State Records Center.
[3] Lewis, Brother B., "Oldest Church in U.S., The San Miguel Chapel," 1957.

indebted to Dr. Myra Ellen Jenkins, senior archivist of the New Mexico State Records Center, for calling my attention to the Read papers.

The fate of the bell said to have been cast in Santa Fe for the old Guadalupe church, prior to the casting of the San Miguel chapel bell, is briefly recorded in a bill of sale dated March 9, 1929, signed by the incumbent priest of Guadalupe church at the time as vendor to an agent for the Fred Harvey Company. The bell was described as "an old Spanish bell, embossed with the following inscription: JUAN SENA Y Da. MARIA MANUELA DE ATOCHA – SANTA FE AGOSTO 21 DE 1856." Juan Sena and Doña Maria Manuela de Atocha were obviously the donors of the bell, which must have been well enough cast to enable the inscription to be transcribed on the bill of sale. It was purchased by William Randolph Hearst, with other bells sold out of New Mexico churches in the late 1920s, and sent to his home at San Simeon, now a public park operated by the State of California.

Long-waisted bells of the Spanish shape had been sent to New Mexico as late as 1789, when Fray José Carral sent a "fine, large bell for the tower" to the church of Santa Cruz de la Cañada after he had returned to New Spain.[4] This bell was sold on March 20, 1928, by the incumbent pastor, with the consent of the Archbishop, to the Fred Harvey Company together with two other bells from the Santa Cruz church and described as "The Cross, dated 1851, The plain one is Maria del Carmel. The other was Santo Christo. All three bells hung in the same tower at the old church at Santa Cruz, N. Mex." Although we have no dimensions or pictures of these it is probable that the Maria del Carmel bell was that sent by Fray José Carral, as in that time the confraternity of Our Lady of Carmel was flourishing at Santa Cruz; the 1851 bell was probably another cast by Francisco Luján.

From the records of the Fred Harvey Company, the documents in the Benjamin M. Read papers in regard to the San Miguel chapel bell, and the dates cast, or miscast, on New Mexico bells of the 19th century, it is possible to follow the traces of the bell casters. Whether all of the bells made between 1817 and 1868 were cast by Francisco Luján, it would not be possible to say without establishing the dates of his birth and death.

** 1. Bell from Ojo Caliente inscribed "Arsina Duro Arsina – 1817," wide and squatty shape. The chapel of Santa Cruz at Ojo Caliente was built in 1811.
** 2. Bell of same squat shape lettered above: "Año de 1817" and, below: "GVADADLAEJAPE" — possibly intended for Guadalupe; no place of origin recorded.
** 3. A bell of same squat shape, has old repairs at the top. It is

---

[4]AASF, Accounts, Book XXXXVI, Box 1, Santa Cruz, 1782–95.

inscribed on the replacement: "se yso este [c] ampana . . . 1819," Below was cast "ANO DE 1817" with the N reversed, a frequent error. Below this: "SE HISO ESTANDO YO MTRO EL R. P. OZIO." ("This was made, I being the minister, the Reverend Father Hozio.") The lowest inscription on this bell reads: "MARIA ANTONIA DE LA CRUZ. D. S. S." Father Francisco de Hozio had been in New Mexico since 1780 and was attached to the chapel of Our Lady of Light, (the Castrense) in Santa Fe in July 1787 and again in 1823. He was also connected with the Santa Fe parroquia during the intervening years.

** 4. Bell from Village of San Miguel, Doña Ana County, "marked the year of 1830"; size and shape unknown. Sold to Hearst.

* 5. Bell in church tower, Santo Domingo Pueblo, "SANTO DO-MINGO 1850." The present church replaces one washed away by the Rio Grande in 1886. From the shape of this bell it would not have been cast after 1886 when commercial foundry bells were coming into use. Did it survive the river flood to be hung in the present new church?

** 6. Bell from church of Santa Cruz de la Cañada, "La Cruz, 1851."

7. Bell in Museum of New Mexico, "Maria Jocefa AÑO D 1355" (1855, defective).

** 8. Bell from church of Our Lady of Guadalupe, Santa Fe, "Juan Sena y Da. Maria Manuela de Atocha. Santa Fe, Agosto 21 de 1856."

9. Bell in San Miguel chapel, Santa Fe, "San Jose Rogad Por Nosotros Agosto 9 de 1356" (1856, defective, Benjamin M. Read papers, op. cit.).

10. Bell in collections of Archdiocese of Santa Fe. "J. Maria D?an Juan AÑO 1860."

11. Bell in Museum of New Mexico, "J.S. MA. Y JE. ANO D 1865."

**12. Bell from "Capilla del Alto del Talco, commonly known as La Capilla de Señor Santiago, dated 1864." In books of Baptisms in the parish of Mora after 1856 there are references to Santiago Arriba and to Santiago de la Cebolla.[5]

**13. Bell from Arroyo Seco, Taos County, "esta campana se yama Maria Soledad de Jesus, Año 1866."

14. Bell, origin unknown, "N. Iosefa, Xbre 23 . 1867," private owner.

**15. Bells from Questa, Taos County, "One old mission bell, dated 1868."

**16.   One   Do.
date 1868
Large and small bells."

These bells are dated by the caster while several others that resemble

---

[5]AASF, "Libro de los Bautismos de la Parroquia de Sta. Gertrudes de lo de Mora, N.M. el Dia 25 de Enero Del Año 1856. Teniendo por primer parroco el Señor Don Pedro Juan Munnecom."

them in shape, rough surfaces and general defects are not dated but simply bear a crude cross, illegible lettering or "Maria." They may well have been cast within the time limits of the dated bells. The first three bells listed above dated from 1817-19 are similar in appearance and shape. The bell from Doña Ana County dated 1830 may not have fitted into this series as it might have been sent from Chihuahua. Leaving it out of consideration, there is a wide gap between 1817–19 and the next series of twelve dated bellls: 1850, 51, 55, 56, 60 and on to 1868. The latter may have been cast by Francisco Luján.

However erratic the inscriptions may be, some of these are of an alloy closer to true bronze than others. The bells of bronze quality were undoubtedly cast from the molten metal of an older one from New Spain that had cracked or broken. Some of the latter series of bells also were intended to repeat the long waisted Spanish shape of the 17th and 18th centuries, but lack the correct proportions and cleanly turned angular planes of the older bells which the bell caster may have observed before melting them down.

Unlike Spain and her iron-rich colonies, New Mexico did not produce iron, and as it was only imported in scanty amounts, decorative ironwork was unknown. As a result iron articles were prized, and the metal was reworked when its first usefulness was gone. Where possible, other materials were substituted for it, such as wooden grilles, locks and dippers (Sec. II-B), or rawhide lashings in roof construction, rawhide buckets, strainers, sieves and funnels. In making iron objects, New Mexican blacksmiths reduced them to the smallest possible size and style. Hinges were of eyelet type when used on trasteros, chests and small boxes. The basic tools, adz, ax, froe, hammer and saw, were shaped over and over from old metal, worn down from use, and thus gradually grew smaller in size.

Mission supply records, itemizing how many nails were allowed a friar to build a mission, with "two axes, two hoes, two locks," give the impression of frugality, and when organized supply deliveries had ceased, construction was adapted to thoses methods which required no nails or bolts. Dependent upon farming for indispensable grains, the main winter food supply, the population kept iron points on their wooden ploughs, but these were minuscule in view of the heavy bottom clays and stony highland fields they had to plant.

Because there was neither iron nor armorers in New Mexico the use of protective leather coats and shields had become general. Lances, spears and knives were hammered out by the same blacksmiths who made plough points, ox goads, branding irons, griddles, crude locks and spoons. The buffalo spear, with its oversized blade on a short haft, was developed as an improvement over Indian arrows for the hunter who had the nerve and a fast horse to ride close enough to a buffalo and strike it in the one vital spot exposed to a man at full gallop. The ox goad, known in Spain as *aguijada* or *gavilán,* and in New Mexico as *un punto de buey*, was made after the Spanish models, except that the curved end for cleaning the ploughshare was often reversed. The black-

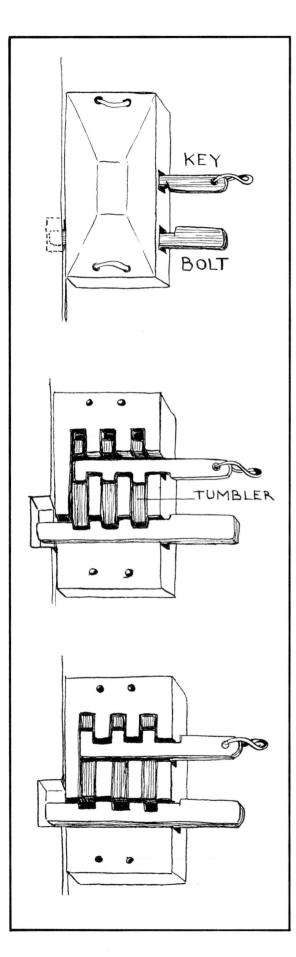

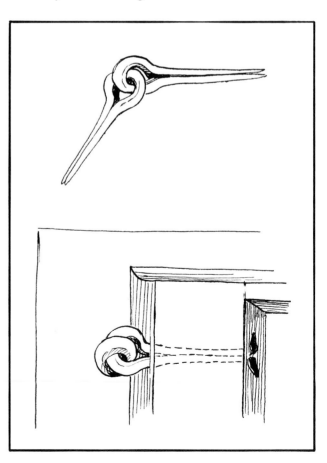

Figure 165: *Goznes* or eyelet hinges used in both Spain and New Mexico. Left, wooden lock with tumblers and key; these were tied to the door or shutter by rawhide thongs.

Figure 166: Old style wood plough and several forged points.

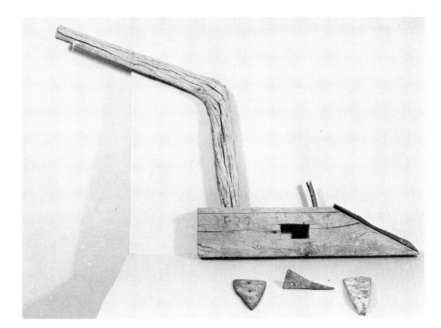

Figure 167: Mortars of metal, ceramic and wood from Spain, except the fourth from left which was sand-cast on the Santa Fe River, 19th century.

Figure 168: Copper baptismal font and lid, standard church equipment in colonial times. (Courtesy of Fred Harvey Foundation)

II-C

277

smith could expand his productivity and, at the same time, his own tools, after the Santa Fe Trail traders began to bring in bricks, or pigs, of iron. The ponderous, hand-forged chains and hooks with which oxen dragged timbers, harrows or farm carts were made in New Mexico after this time. Some oxen were still in use until about 1912, but the iron tips of common goads have so completely disappeared since then that hardly anyone living in New Mexico today can guess what these once familiar implements were for.

Livestock brands made for Spanish colonials did not have the heavy iron sockets for a long wooden haft common to Mexican irons, but were slender, fairly short and were branding marks more often than alphabetic letters. The older brands were forged in a continuous piece without the rivets of modern pieced irons.

Farm wagons, saddles and stirrups were made of wood without iron parts, but the horseman demanded extravagant amounts of metal in his bridle bit and spurs. The best of these came from New Spain, but plain country-made specimens were still unduly large.

An indispensable article was the steel to strike on flint to make sparks, or strike-a-light. Known in Spain as the *chisquero* (spark maker), in Mexico as an *eslabón* (link in a chain), and in New Mexico as a *chispa* (spark), these were carried about with a flint and wad or roll of tinder to light fires, candles or cigarettes. Today the public has forgotten the strike-a-light but many of us are still using its direct descendant, the cigarette lighter, which acts with less effort on the same principle and is regarded as a modern invention. The Spanish steel was commonly of a horizontal oval shape with a thick striking edge at the bottom and outcurving rat-tail ends. Like so many other "Spanish" design motifs, it is a stylized rendering of the scorpion still used as a clan or tribal symbol by Moslem groups living in Asia Minor and the Caucasus, where it frequently appears on rugs. Mexicans, like the people of Spain and South America, had fanciful strike-a-lights for the well-to-do, but the common Mexican shape was a closed link or a long, open oval with outcurving ends, while New Mexicans preferred a narrow, incurving oval.

Small tongs to take live coals from the fire and spits and skewers for broiling meat had austerely elegant lines. Regional corner fireplaces had no space for built-in cranes or spits; cooking of large meats was done in outdoor fire pits or adobe ovens. Beans and other foods needing long boiling were cooked in kettles set on a trivet. The trivet also went on journeys to be used at the campfire. The New Mexican name for a trivet is an interesting example of the survival of the pre-Cortesian Aztec language: *tinamaíste* (Aztec, *tenamaxtle-tetl,* stone, *namicíta,* equalizer, from the ancient open fire pit which had three stones set in it to make the cook pot level). Other pre-Columbians made tubular tripods of fired clay for the same purpose.

While iron cook spoons were prized and worn to stumps, they resembled those made all over the western world with a plain bowl and rattail handle. I have not been able to trace the origin of the two-bowled spoon

Figure 169: Wrought iron candelabrum, New Mexico, 19th century.

Figure 170: Forged shears, 18th and 19th centuries, New Mexico.

which seems to have been a popular New Mexican kitchen tool. It is possible that this, too, was a device to save the iron required for two spoons by making one handle with two bowls. Old timers say that these were used in cooking *chicharrónes,* or fried scraps of pork fat, the "chittlins" of Anglo Saxons. However, no explanation for the fact that the two bowls always face in opposite directions has yet been proposed.

Iron locks made in New Mexico were of the crudest, cold-chiseled from a flat plate and die-stamped with tiny stars or crescents in random arrangements. They were probably composed of reused parts of locks and slide bars from New Spain.

The unwieldy iron molds to make altar breads which were kept, in theory, in each church for its own use, were obviously forged by blacksmiths. They were of scissors shape and used like a waffle iron. The primitive Crucifix engraved on the inner face of one mold seems to have been scratched by an amateur hand. Inventories of church belongings contain dry comments by visiting church officials on the whereabouts of the wafer mold for a given church such as, "the woman who makes them for a year . . . always keeps the iron at her house although it belongs to the mission" (Dominguez, p. 20). Also, "although the iron belongs here it is, for reasons unknown, now at the mission of X."

The failure to find gold in New Mexico in Spanish times did not have as much effect upon the lives of the settlers as the lack of iron which restricted their activities and their possessions to a pattern experienced by European peasants of the Dark Ages. Contemporary wills, in their itemization of household articles, vividly point up the values set upon iron or steel objects and also wooden ones which required metal tools to make them (Appendix II-D, Wills). A notable exception is the mention of "una cama alta también de fierro" among the possessions of Rosa Bustamante in 1814 (p. 445). The bed is listed after the usual pots and pans of copper, iron ax, adz, chisel, griddle, grill and spoon, which items were still in short supply evidently, although the widow Ortíz had inherited ample lands, livestock, sets of silver dishes and tableware from her husband. The high bed, also of iron, is the only bedstead of any kind listed in the fifty-page will. Since the overland trade from Missouri was not yet in existence, this bed must have been a prestige symbol in its extravagant use of iron, as well as by its mere existence, in New Mexico at the time.

GOLD AND SILVER

Legends of lost Spanish mines, of veins, nuggets and placer locations which have multiplied over the years, have little foundation in colonial records. After early exploratory expeditions had made negative reports on the riches of the north, New Mexico was considered a field for conversion of souls and a buffer between peaceful and hostile Indian groups.

Emphasis was on the protection of the richer provinces of New Spain to the south rather than the defense of the indigenous pueblos of New Mexico itself. Alarms of French intrusion from the Mississippi and of Russian expansion down the coast of Alta California, both in the 18th century, led to instructions from the royal court of Spain to viceroys of New Spain to increase colonization in the north and to defend the colonists. Development of mining resources in the north, however, was as neglected as the military protection of New Mexico, in proportion to the size of the area involved. It was taken for granted that hard coinage did not circulate in New Mexico in the 18th century and that business was conducted by payment in goods or services.

Mention of silver ornaments made in 1776 among religious properties are few and, where they occur, are emphasized. At Taos Father Dominguez said that the incumbent priest, Father Olaeta, had removed all bits of silver in the form of crosses, crowns, medals or reliquaries and other gifts of the faithful to the statue of Our Lady of Sorrows to be remade into "a small silver ciborium and cruets." With the approval of the Alcalde Mayor, his assistants and the principal Indian men of the pueblo, the silver was weighed in the presence of the said men, amounting to eighteen ounces. Father Olaeta assumed the cost of having the new pieces made; with the permission of the Vice-Custos of the province, the eighteen ounces were sent to Chihuahua to one Carlos de la Tornera, who was asked to see that the new pieces were made. A year later Olaeta wrote again to Chihuahua, and was informed that Tornera had died. His executor stated that the reliquaries and other items were on hand together with a memorandum by the deceased stating that they belonged to Father Olaeta. This reply was dated February 4, 1776. What finally became of the silver pieces is not related, but the procedure indicates that eighteen ounces of silver were regarded as valuable at the time, and that silversmiths were not then working professionally in New Mexico (Dominguez, p. 105).

Dominguez in his inventory of San Miguel chapel at Santa Fe noted only two pieces of silver: "a small nimbus, a little sword, like a dagger, eight inches long" (Dominguez, p. 39). Both belonged to the statue of the patron, which is an excellent example of the finest period of *estofado* surfaced woodcarving in New Spain. It was already in Santa Fe in 1709 when it was carried in processions around New Mexico to attract donations in materials or labor for the rebuilding of San Miguel chapel. By 1776 the more fashionable new military chapel of Our Lady of Light on the plaza had apparently drained the former congregation away from San Miguel chapel. Dominguez noted that contents of the sacristy were kept in the house of the majordomo of the chapel. The present silver headpiece of the image of San Miguel can hardly be described as a nimbus but is a helmet of the colonial style, rather resembling a bishop's mitre from the front, which was made for the adornment of images of archangels at the time and later on copied in tin in New Mexico. The design suggests that it was made in New Spain in the 18th century.

A comparable silver helmet belonging to another statue of St. Michael is now in the Taylor Museum. The bulto, of New Mexico 19th century santero style, was probably modeled after the prototype in San Miguel chapel, Santa Fe, as were many others of the same subject at the time. The second San Miguel is said to have been owned formerly by the church of San Miguel del Vado on the Pecos river, an eastern frontier outpost founded in the late 18th century. License for the church was requested from Durango in 1804 with the notation that the building was already started (AASF, L.D. 1804, No. 14).

The statue, now overcoated with oil paint, and its heavily decorated silver helmet, studded with paste and turquoise sets, reflect the prosperous years when the town of San Miguel was the first stopping place of any size for the Trail trade caravans of the second quarter of the 19th century. The silver helmet suggests by its exuberant design that the smith was Mexican and very likely was living in New Mexico. Mexican smiths were reputedly the first teachers of the Navajo silversmiths, and by the end of Mexican Republican rule were present in various parts of New Mexico (Wilder and Breitenbach, pl. 28).

A peace medal found during excavation of a historical period Indian burying ground in Nebraska and now in the Nebraska State Historical Museum, may very possibly be a specimen of Santa Fe silverworking. The convex silver gorget has a peso of Carlos IV, dated 1797, set into the face. The silver gorget is engraved lightly, or perhaps might better be described as having been gouged with a graver, outlining a freehand design of a three-lobed crown above the coin, massed banners with crosses and tassels on the tips. Below is a Spanish drum and two bugles. The whole is framed by small leaves. The reverse shows the same crown above crossed olive branches encircled by small, die-stamped ring and dot motifs. The execution is amateur, and the design suggests that it might have been copied from a painted rawhide military shield of the time.

The presence of the peace medal in Nebraska suggests that it may have been one of several medals given to Pawnee war chiefs by Lieutenant Facundo Melgares during his expedition from Santa Fe in 1806 into the plains between New Mexico and the Missouri. Rumors of an incipient invasion by the United States determined authorities in New Spain to attempt to cement Spanish and Indian alliances against foreigners. The exploratory party sent westward by the United States was led by Lieutenant Zebulon Pike, whose eventual arrest by a Spanish party from Santa Fe on grounds of his having invaded Spanish soil is a matter of history. Before he had been discovered on the headwaters of the Rio Grande, Pike had held meetings with many Plains Indian groups, covering much of the same ground that Melgares had covered just before him. Pike noted that the Spanish party was outfitted at Santa Fe and in addition to diplomatic speeches made presents to heads of Indian nations of Spanish flags, grand medals and mules. Pike, in his dealings with the same Indians, made an issue of their display of the Spanish flags on the grounds that they were in the territories of the

United States and that Americans, not the Spanish, were their friends and protectors.[6]

On the other hand the Nebraska medal might have been one like that presented by Governor Manrique, along with a Spanish flag and a baton or staff of official authority, to Lobo Blanco, a "Cuampe" chief, on the occasion of Blanco's visit to Santa Fe in 1809. *Cuampe* and *Cumpe* seem to have been Spanish approximations of the name of a Plains Indian group now lost (SANM, Doc. 2206, March 3, 1809). The 1797 peso does not necessarily establish the year that the peace medal was made. It was simply a coin available to the silverworker at the time. Although a number of such medals were given to Gentile Indians by the Spanish it is a freak of circumstance that one was found in Nebraska and not, as yet, in New Mexico.

That the colonial period had not developed gold or silver mines to any extent, if at all, is shown by the following excerpt from AASF L. D., 1800, No. 16, n. d., not signed, among loose documents from Santa Clara mission:

"Producciones Naturales que se advierten gral'y particular en ésta Provª del Nuevo Mexico, dividas en Arbustos, Vegetales, Minerals y Animal . . . tenien otras barrias Minerales, se encuentran vetas de cobre, de plomo, de antimonia, y algunas que manifiestanse de Platas, el cobre por barios partes, hay con abundancia, vetas de yeso, de barios tierras, de colores come ocre, almagre y también piedra-alumbre, caparrosa, azufre, sal, se encuentran diversos barros de que fabrican losa, casi en todos los Pueblos, aunque tosca, y, no con abundancia, también carbón Piedra, clavos de Azabache."

(Natural products in general and in particular in this Province of New Mexico divided into shrubs, annual plants, minerals and animals . . . There are mineral locations, veins of copper are found and lead, antimony, and some that show signs of silver. Of copper there is an abundance in various places, also veins of yeso, of various colored earths such as ochre, iron oxide and also alum, copper sulfates, sulphur and salt. Diverse clays are found of which they make pottery in all of the Pueblos, although coarse. Also, but not abundantly, there is coal-stone [or] lumps of jet.)

In Pino's account of New Mexico of 1812, under the heading of "Producciones Minerales," he said that some mines had been intentionally abandoned at an unknown time in the past; who discovered or worked them was unknown. Pino said that there were mineral veins in the mountains containing silver, gold, copper, lead and so on, of which assays had been made. "If the province were even half protected these and other mines could be worked and the treasury would receive many thousands in taxes which it now loses by this neglect."[7]

---

[6] *Exploratory Travels through the Western Territories of North America,* Zebulon M. Pike, London. 1811.

[7] *Three New Mexico Chronicles,* tr. by H. Bailey Carroll and J. Villasana Haggard, Quivira Society Publications XI, Albuquerque, 1942, p. 221.

Pino's report to the Spanish Cortes was published at Cádiz, Spain, in 1812. His reference to silver and gold does not indicate any production of either metal in New Mexico by that time. Presumably, silver objects, as well as gold ornaments, if there were any, were still coming from New Spain. The few large landowners, by virtue of royal grants, could convert the products of their pastures, ranches and servants into goods for exchange at home and in Chihuahua, Durango or Zacatecas, where they could obtain luxuries such as fine clothing, horse gear and silver tablewares. An example of such late 18th century prosperity in New Mexico is to be found in the will of Antonio José Ortíz, dated August 12, 1806. He itemized as his "a silver service consisting of thirty plates with all that accompanied them, six platters, twenty-four place settings of knives and forks of marked and unmarked silver, twelve table knives and eleven place settings more, a salt, a *zarzena*, a tureen, two serving spoons, a carving knife, a cruet, two crystal vases with handles, three large decanter cases, incomplete, and two candlesticks."

This imposing list of silver pieces is a markedly different one from most New Mexican 18th century wills that itemized domestic belongings.

That mining of gold or silver in the area of the Real de Dolores and other mines around Cerrillos was not even thought of by the colonial Spanish in the 18th century is indicated by the negative evidence of certain deeds of which copies are to be found in Book D, Land Deeds, Territory of New Mexico, New Mexico State Records Center, Santa Fe. In April 1788 José Miguel de la Peña stated that the piece of land in the place called los Serrillos had been given at the conquest of this kingdom to the grandfather of Peña's wife, Don Alonzo Rael de Aguilar. The reconquest by de Vargas was the date referred to. ". . . having been unpopulated for so many years and having lost the deeds to the land," Peña begged for reconfirmation and for exits and entrances to the lands for the heirs of Rael and their servants in order to plant and keep animals. Governor Fernando de la Concha ordered the alcalde mayor of Santa Fe, Antonio José Ortíz, to make out formal papers in favor of the petitioner.

On June 12, 1788, Ortíz did so, ordering petitioner, José Miguel de la Peña, to pull up grass, throw stones and shout "Long live the King" in a loud voice, thus taking formal possession of the reconfirmed royal grant. The soldier, Juan Antonio Anaya, heir to grants given at the time of the reconquest, was selling parts of his land at Cerrillos to others in 1793. On October 19, 1803, Don Cleto Miera y Pacheco, alcalde mayor of the jurisdiction of Alameda, received 1,200 pesos de la tierra, 100 ewes, 1 she-mule, 1 mule, 2 horses, 100 pesos in silver and 200 pesos in goods for his ranch of los Serrillos which he had sold to Don Miguel Delgado, and with which he declared himself satisfied. Anacleto Miera was a son of Bernardo Miera y Pacheco, soldier, map- and santo-maker; by 1803 he had left the presidio at Santa Fe and moved to Alameda, north of Albuquerque. His Cerrillos property

Figure 171: Silver tabaquera, New Mexico, with engraved tobacco plant. (Courtesy of Fred Harvey Foundation)

adjoined that of the Peña grant originally given to Rael de Aguilar. Anacleto's sons by his second wife married two Rael sisters. None of these landowners in the Cerrillos area had, apparently, any interest in their holdings except for ranching purposes.

In the same Book D, Land Deeds, is a transcription of a petition made by Dolores Palomo, a citizen of the state of San Luis Potosí, Mexico, now a resident of New Mexico, for a claim to a virgin vein of gold that he found in the little mountain, in the Cañada of the springs of waters of gold above. The said vein faced to the east, its direction ran from west to east as did also the mine that was in the same hill of the said vein that, by tradition, was called the gold mine in ancient times. Not knowing who was the last owner, Palomo claimed the location for gold, silver, copper "or the metal that God shall be pleased to give me." Public notices were duly circulated notifying any heirs to the mine and vein to appear in their own behalf. No one appeared except the citizen Luis Lovato who justified his claim as owner of the land, and harmoniously agreed on December 30, 1831, to permit the petitioner to claim three varas for development. This was apparently the Real de Dolores which, later on, produced enough gold to support a camp. The transcriptions in Book D, Land Deeds, were entered as historical evidence by various mining claimants in the 1850s when the mining craze had started in New Mexico among enterprising Anglos. The silver dishes and other articles so lavishly displayed by New Mexican ricos and described by early Trail traders and military diarists, were still being bought in Mexico, as well as the Mexican silver pesos and ingots which the traders took back to the United States mint on their return from Santa Fe and Chihuahua.

The colonial silver collection presented by the late Mary Lester Field to the University of New Mexico includes examples of late 17th, 18th and 19th century styles.[8] In spite of guild regulations and official inspections, hallmarks were not always applied in New Spain, nor were they in other silver-rich colonies such as Guatemala and Peru. The silver pieces collected by Mrs. Field in New Mexico were for the most part made in New Spain and the later Republic of Mexico with the exception of a few simple, heavy shapes which might have been the work of silversmiths who had migrated up the Rio Grande around 1830.

The prosperity developed by the Santa Fe Trail trade had made a marked difference in household belongings by 1846. Lieutenant Colonel Emory noted at Bernalillo: "The plates, forks and spoons were of solid silver, clumsily worked in the country . . . at close intervals were glass decanters of Pittsburg manufacture, filled with wine made on the plantation." In the same report Lieutenant Abert wrote: "All the hidalgos

---

[8]Edward Wenham, "Spanish American Silver in New Mexico," International Studio, V.XCIX/410, July 1931, and "A Study of the Mary Lester Field Collection of Spanish Colonial Silver," Leona Mae Boylan, unpub. thesis for an M.A., Univ. of New Mexico, 1967.

pride themselves on allowing nothing but silver to approach their tables; even the plates are of silver."[9] The three-way trade with Missouri and Chihuahua had at last enabled New Mexicans to satisfy prestige standards by owning a few luxuries which the wealthy familes of Mexico to the south had enjoyed for centuries.

With the annexation of the territory to the United States the economy changed rapidly. The barter system was replaced by cash with short-term credit. Land mortgages were written for thirty or sixty days; default in payment of the interest put the property up for public auction. The old custom of lettting debts run on for years was canceled by the new laws, which gave an opportunity for easy profits to those shrewd enough to pay cash down. Old families, unaccustomed to Yankee legal customs, thus lost large landholdings and often were forced to convert their silver and other valuables into bullion to obtain ready money. As a result very few colonial or republican silver objects have escaped the melting pot.

There is a story about a silver cup, now in the Museum of New Mexico, that was inherited by descendants of one of the old Spanish families when their circumstances had been sadly reduced. Unable to distinguish between cheap plated ware and hand-hammered silver, they had kept an old silver mug on a bench in the back porch together with the bucket of drinking water. Whoever drank would briskly bang the mug on its bottom in order to empty the last drops for the next comer until the bottom rim finally broke, after which they peddled off the now-useless mug to a Santa Fe visitor. There is another similar story about an old silver basin now in the Field collection which, it is said, was sold by the former owner after he had used it for some time as a water trough for his chickens.

In spite of Colonel Emory's comment in 1846 that certain New Mexico silver pieces were "clumsily worked in the country," it may be questioned whether all of them were. By chance a passerby on the Santa Fe plaza saw a workman, digging a public utility trench along the street in front of the old Palace of the Governors, toss some oddly shaped objects onto the dirt pile with a shovelful of soil. Although the Santa Fe plaza had been repeatedly trenched for some fifty years before, no one had, or has, made any formal excavations to learn what remains of cultural materials might be retrieved from the subsoil of this nerve center of the old kingdom, province and territory of New Mexico. The bystander, a professional and technical metals worker, picked up the objects from the dirt and saw that they were of metal heavily encrusted with lime and soil deposits. He asked the workman if he wanted them and was told no, with some amusement. He took them home and cleaned them and came up with forks of the kind described by Emory, three of "clumsily" made silver, and one of what appears to be a silver and cop-

---

[9]"Notes of a Military Reconnaissance from Fort Leavenworth . . . to San Diego, California," Lt. Col. W. H. Emory, Ex. Doc. 41, Washington, 1848, pp. 40 and 452.

per alloy like the widely used *tumbaga* of the Spanish colonies. Two of the forks, however, bear marks used after the establishment of the Mexican Republic, and well into the mid-19th century there, although the shapes and quality of workmanship of marked and unmarked forks are the same.

The gold camps of New Mexico mushroomed in the post-Civil War era and even after 1900, but none of them lasted very long. The craft of goldsmithing seems to have been limited even more narrowly to the years between 1860, or later, and the coming of the railroads in 1880 when more New Mexicans traveled to eastern cities and adopted the fashions of New York in preference to those of Mexico.

The tradition of working gold or silver wire into filigree is as old as the Phoenicians who introduced the art into southern Spain some 3,000 years ago. Filigree jewelry was made in New Spain and certainly reached New Mexico in the 18th century if not earlier, according to the inventoried ornaments of various statues of Our Lady. Given as votive offerings, they had been the property of the ladies who gave them and undoubtedly had been worn by them. The mining of raw gold in New Mexico after the first working of the Real de Dolores near Cerrillos seems to have stimulated the making of gold ornaments on the spot.

The discovery of and working of gold in New Mexico happened to coincide with the rise of the Second Empire in France. The wife of Napoleon III, Eugénie, was Spanish and brought with her to Paris many Spanish styles which became international fashions. Among these were large shell combs, lace mantillas and elaborate filigree jewelry. The Empress favored very decolleté gowns which showed off sets of ornate, gem-studded collars, necklaces, bracelets, brooches and dangling earrings. Portraits of Eugénie and her ladies-in-waiting by Winterhalter show such sets in detail. Soon after, the intrigues of European powers installed the Archduke Maximilian of Austria as emperor of Mexico in 1864. He and his wife, Carlota, brought the tastes of the French court with them, and in the matter of female fashions the Spanish-oriented dress that Eugénie had launched in Paris. This included extravagantly jeweled and enamelled filigree sets which the skilled gold and silver-smiths of Mexico were well able to execute. The design of filigree jewelry made in New Mexico of twenty-carat soft, native gold in the 1870s and 1880s, although quaintly provincial in some examples, clearly reflects the styles of France and Mexico at the same time. Despite the purity of the gold, the New Mexico settings were of paste.

By the time such extravagances had become available in New Mexico, it became customary to expect that the well-to-do suitor for a young woman's hand would include in the trousseau he was obliged to provide a set of *gargantilla* (elaborate necklace with central pendant), bracelets, brooch, ring, earrings and a rosary, all of gold filigree. It was said by old timers that the smiths, like the santeros, traveled about equipped with their small tools, glass or paste "gems" and a certain amount of preconstructed elements of gold which could be worked up with others to form earrings, brooches, pendants and so on. The smith might visit a family where he had heard that the son was betrothed and there make up the gold jewelry for the prospective bride. The groom's family might supply part of the gold in the form of old or broken ornaments. The itinerant smiths apparently did not depend on this trade alone but worked at it with other occupations. J. Nestor Ortíz, an early settler of Los Pinos, Colorado, was said to have been a skilled artisan of filigree work and became rich by combining this skill with a mercantile business and grazing large flocks of sheep.[10]

Carmen Espinosa recorded the names of freelance or itinerant plateros in northern New Mexico and the San Luis valley, Colorado. According to her, one was named Juan Bautista Bueno, a silversmith and blacksmith of Taos. His son-in-law, Rafael Luna, and Luna's children, Antonio and Hilaria, were his assistants or pupils. Another smith was José Manuel Luján of southern Colorado, according to Miss Espinosa.[11] It is possible that the latter was the José Miguel Luján, son of Francisco Luján the bellcaster, mentioned in the Benjamin M. Read papers in regard to local church bells (p. 271). In 1915 José Miguel Luján was described as a good silversmith then living in Clayton, New Mexico; his father, Francisco, was said to be a silversmith, blacksmith and bellcaster. Francisco was casting bells in the 1850s and, on the evidence of similarities of bells, the 1860s. His son José might very well have been a goldsmith during the period of making local New Mexico filigree. The making of gold or silver work by blacksmiths was not peculiar to New Mexico; the same process was usual on the great cattle ranches of northwestern Argentina in the colonial period. A blacksmith was a part of the hacienda personnel, and, as the silver mines of Alta Peru were not far off in the Andes, he also hammered out silver dishes and vessels, shaped like Indian pots or wild gourds and barbarously heavy in weight.[12]

That New Mexico had smiths by the 1860s who worked in iron and silver has been documented by research on the beginnings of Navajo silversmithing. Unfortunately, as Navajo informants recalled early Navajo smiths, the names of the "Mexican" smiths who taught them were not given, but they were said to have been living along the Rio Grande and as far west as Cubero, New Mexico.[13]

The vogue for filigree jewelry persisted in western Europe and the United States until World War I, while in Arabic countries and Italy, Spain and Mexico it has never been abandoned. In Santa Fe local mer-

---

[10] Doc. 349/48, CWA project, 1933–34, "Interviews with old time residents of Alamosa, Conejos and Costilla Counties," Charles E. Gibson, Jr., Colorado Historical Society Library, Denver.

[11] "Fashions in Filigree," Carmen Espinosa, op. cit.

[12] *Platería Sudamericana,* A. Taullard, Buenos Aires, 1941. "Colonial Silver from Latin America," E. Boyd, *El Palacio,* V.69/2, 1962.

[13] "A Brief History of Navajo Silversmithing," Arthur Woodward, with Field Notes by Richard Van Valkenburgh, Museum of Northern Arizona, Bulletin No. 14, Flagstaff, Arizona, Aug. 1938.

chants hired filigree workers to make gold and silver jewelry in their stores. Late in the 1890s or around 1900, the Yontz store in Santa Fe is said to have hired ten filigree workers, while the firm of Spitz employed six men imported from Naples. These Italians had a strong influence on designs, producing pieces that were delicate and traditional in the somewhat nondescript, international style of the period. They made pieces copied from their own country, France and New York: chatelaines, watch fobs and vinaigrettes as well as the usual pieces of jewelry.

A unique method of prestige rating was that of the management of the Denver and Rio Grande railroad which ran from Colorado into Santa Fe. Presidents and high officials were given lifetime free passes over the railroad lines. Passes of engraved gold were provided for those of top rank, and silver passes for lower dignitaries. They were made by the Spitz jewelry firm in Santa Fe. Still another local merchant who employed native smiths to make filigree for his shop, John S. Candelario, kept his stock-in-trade stored by the barrelful.

Although Tiffany of New York sold gold and filigree jewelry like other famous gem dealers, and did incorporate turquoise into some pieces, the legend that they once owned the old Cerrillos turquoise mine in New Mexico is purely a legend. Tiffany's bought some turquoise from this mine which had been worked by prehistoric Pueblo Indians, according to another legend, but did not use Cerrillos turquoise exclusively and never had title to the mine. Tiffany designers, using turquoise, cut and polished the stone into symmetrical shapes set with pearls or gold ropes. The same styles were imitated in the West.

Visitors to Colorado or New Mexico were expected to bring home souvenirs of filigree ornaments set with small corals or small polished turquoise. As late as 1915, the rare collector in search of Navajo silver work had to go to the reservation or to Gallup or one of the Fred Harvey shops along the Santa Fe railroad line in order to buy any. Navajo silver work became popular among non-Indians after the first World War when artists and writers moved into northern New Mexico. The average customer learned to admire standardized commercial pieces sold all over the country or their dime store imitations.

The last filigree smith, Adolfo Ortíz, who practiced his trade in Santa Fe until 1966, was a son of Francisco Ortíz, who learned his skill in the Yontz store in the 1880s. In 1910, when Adolfo was sixteen, he went to work for Yontz as apprentice smith and general cleanup boy for the remuneration of one dollar a week. Although Mr. Ortíz could make fine filigree pieces until he closed his shop, most of his business in its last years consisted of engraving class rings, the sale of rosaries and tourist items.

Soon after the placers were first worked, reportedly in 1828, a vein of gold in rock was developed by Damasio Lopez in the same Cerrillos neighborhood. As Lopez understood the extraction of gold from hard rock with quicksilver, the vein was profitable enough to remind Santa Fe officials that Lopez was a Gachupín or European-born Spaniard, and that they were guilty of breaking the law in allowing him to own and

Figure 172: Filigree necklace and earrings of twenty-carat gold with paste sets, mid-19th century, New Mexico.

operate a mine. He was duly expelled from New Mexico. His partner, of the Ortíz family, and his workmen did not know how to process the ore, and the mine was temporarily abandoned.

The placers or gold bearing sands and gravels of stream beds in the region were the chief source of gold in dust form that was recorded as part of the goods taken back to Missouri by homeward bound traders in the later years of the Mexican Republic. References were made to accidental finds of pure gold nuggets on the ground. When Adolph Wislizenius visited New Mexico in 1846 he noted one gold mine of from two to four feet in width and forty feet deep across the vein, running south-south-east to north-north-west. The vein was then worked by a Frenchman named Tournier, and had been worked before him by the trader Roubidoux. Whether this was the same vein described by Palomo in 1831 in his claim to it is uncertain, but Palomo's and Wislizenius'[14] descriptions agree, and only one hard-rock gold mine appears in documents in the Cerrillos area during the Mexican period.

Gold bullion of no great value is entered as a credit item in an account of one of the most prominent merchants of Albuquerque in 1854. It appears on the balance sheet of the brokers of Glasgow and Brother, St. Louis, dated April 27. Of the total invoices in dry goods, hardware, groceries including spirits, and the expenses of the merchant's son while at school in St. Louis, the account of more than $10,000 was paid by a cash note with the exception of "the value of the gold sold for credit to your account" – $565.69 (Appendix II-D, Yrisarri, 1854).

What is more in the nature of folklore than history is a description of the property of the former governor, Manuel Armijo, after his death in 1853. "At his death he left $10,000 to Santa Fe churches and $2,000 to others. His daughters had $30,000 worth of old gold and plate coined and had a still larger amount left. His bath tub, eight feet long, was of solid silver. He had a bedstead the posts and sides of which were of silver with garlands of flowers in hammered gold. Around the posts of the bed were silver grape vines which formed a compact canopy overhead, and clusters of grapes of natural size were of gold. Everything about his place was the finest gold or silver could buy."[15]

This description was given in connection with an account of high taxes imposed by Armijo on wagons of goods brought over the Santa Fe Trail, the proceeds of which he put into his own pockets. Previous governors had been more moderate, or had been more lenient in collecting. Taxes on wagonloads of imported goods were not Armijo's only source of income; he was capable of exacting "donations" from his political friends and enemies as well as from foreigners.

---

[14] *Memoir of a Tour to Northern Mexico Connected with Col. Doniphan's Expedition, in 1846 and 1847,* Adolph Wislizenius, Washington, 1848.

[15] "Captain Charles Deus on the Frontier," Colorado Historical Society Library, Doc. XII/5; reminiscences of family of Charles Peter Deus who came from Germany to Santa Fe with the U.S. Army in 1846 and remained in the area.

According to the same account, the firm of Deus and Co. claimed credit for the first distillery in Santa Fe. "In 1847 the food supply in Santa Fe was so limited that the army was starving and suffering from scurvy. All food had to be hauled in for the first year from the states as food bought from the Mexicans was poisoned. There was no vinegar to be had. Deus said he could and would make vinegar at $1.50 a barrel, he received a contract and did so. He furnished vinegar to the army for four months, scurvy did not continue, the army told him it had enough vinegar. In a year or so he went to St. Louis where he had machinery made for a distillery, copper boilers and all of the other metal as light but strong as possible for shipment. He brought it out in wagons and set up a distillery on the river at Santa Fe. . . .

"He ran a saloon in town and made from $400 to $500 a night. He made the liquor (whiskey), of corn and wheat, native grown, it was very cheap to buy those things. He did very well but a spring flood washed away most of his distillery. He sold the remains of it and his business to Spiegelberg and moved to Socorro where he ran a hotel and made wine. After a year there he perceived it was not profitable and returned to the hotel business in Santa Fe."

The distillery was on what is now Water Street in Santa Fe, then called the Rio Chiquito since the river often shifted its banks in flooding and moved northward through the town. The shifting of the river-bed continued until recent embankments were built to control the channel.

The spring flood that wiped out Deus' business must have been in 1852, for on June 19, 1852, Jacob Spiegelberg took over a mortgage on property of John May, Alex. W. Reynolds, Peter Deus, Deus and Co., from John Stein and wife, given on January 5, 1852. The mortgage was on property

". . . on the south side of the Rio Chiquito, one half mile above the city. It is bounded on the east by land of Juana Ortiz, on the south by the Acequia Madre, on the west by an arroyo and on the north by the Rio Chiquito. It is 72½ varas from east to west with distillery, brewery, grist mill and so forth, and with all the tools and implements and utensils now in or about the premises for use in the business of conducting, working and carrying on said distillery, brewery and gristmill, and all materials now on hand for purpose of manufacturing beer. Also three wagons now at said premises, four mules, one horse, two billiard tables with balls and cues, one soda fountain with all the oils, essences and syrups and other things required. . . ." The sum due was $1,317.69.[16]

While not directly connected with mining or goldsmithing, the foregoing transaction and account of equipment reflects the rapid

---

[16] Book A, Territory of New Mexico, 1852, p. 38, in the New Mexico State Records Center, Santa Fe.

change in the economy in two decades, from the barter system to one of cash. Not only hard liquors and gambling tables but billiard tables and a soda fountain in Santa Fe in 1852 underline the new standards of luxury, if not elegance.

TIN WORK IN NEW MEXICO

It is true that tinned articles, such as a few plates, lanterns or boxes for storing altar breads, came to New Mexico in the 18th century, but they were not at all like the familiar sheet tin known today. These early tinned pieces were usually made of copper over which liquid tin was poured on whichever side it was wanted. Plates, such as were carried by soldiers and travelers, were lined with tin in this way, and as it was apt to peel away from the copper, the outer rim of the plate was rolled and hammered down to hold it firmly in place. In time the tin wore off except for fragments clamped under the rim.

In spite of a local tradition that, for lack of silver, Franciscans taught Indians to make ornaments of humble tin, it is obvious that there was no tin available in New Mexico. What started the popular native craft of making these bright and often attractive trifles, and even quite monumental pieces, was the arrival of tin containers for lard, lamp oil and other commodities over the Santa Fe Trail, mostly after 1846, as much for military as for mercantile uses. Machine-made sheet tin, of which most cans were made until the recent development of aluminum cans, was an invention of the turn of the 18th century, and was perfected for the use of Napoleon's armies while they overran Europe. Finding that the old custom of living off the enemy country was impractical because his troops were too numerous for available raided supplies, or were poisoned by the conquered populations, Napoleon commanded the invention of a safe way of carrying meats and other perishables with the armies. The first large-scale production and use of tin cans was for him. The process was soon known and adopted elsewhere, including the United States. Discarded empty tins were salvaged by New Mexican craftsmen and made into ornamental articles intended for religious decoration; candleholders and a few small boxes were also produced. All earlier tin pieces are distinguished by the many small scraps of tin cut and soldered together to make them of the size and shape desired, thus doubling the labor of making them.

Trail traders had introduced looking glasses framed with wood or tin, and their popularity was already great when Emory noted that in churches and private homes they were "without number," and hung up so high that no one could look into them. The added reflection of light indoors was the reason for New Mexican fondness for mirrors, not vanity.

Fifty years before the Trail trade began, small mirrors from Mexico had been used as candle sconces in a few churches, thus doubling the candle's lighting power, but looking glasses in New Mexico were still rarities. The wooden candle sconces, lanterns and chandeliers inevitably were charred or actually burned during the colonial period; tin candle holders offered a safer as well as brighter substitute. Candle sconces were decorated with birds, scrolls and finials. Some of these used the traditional Spanish double-headed eagle although it became so conventionalized that it is often barely recognizable. Other candle holders look as if they had been shaped in a few minutes for immediate use and with no interest in decorative effect. *Arañas* or chandeliers for chapels and large salas were made much like those of silver or brass combined with wood in our rural eastern districts although much more crude in construction. They are the opposite extreme in design from the crystal chandeliers that were fashionable at the same time in Europe and Mexico. In order to clean off the wax and replace candles the araña was hung from the ceiling by a rope and pulley.

Figure 174: Double headed eagle on candle sconce.

Frames, however, were in the majority for prints of all kinds, Mexican, French and N. Currier, eventually to be followed by Benziger Brothers' chromos from Cincinnati. The traditional santo sometimes received a new tin *nicho* if glass and equally novel wallpaper scraps were available with which to decorate it. Unfortunately, the impulse to provide the latest fashionable housing for family santos resulted in the chopping off of bases or feet, and maiming of hands, in order to fit the bultos to the fortuitous measurements of the little shrine. If a retablo was given a new tin nicho, neither was measured beforehand, or the tin scrap at hand was insufficient. The solution was to crop corners from the retablo or otherwise make it fit the new tin, rather as female modernists determined they would wear newfangled shoes whether or not they happened to be of their size. The New Mexican santo of the period of tin, and the distaff side of the human population, had equal reason to quote the adage, "Il faut souffrir pour être belle."

The earliest tin frames have crisp lines, following the design of eastern Federal styled mirrors, with a crest or cornice at the top and corner bosses between convex pillared sides. The resemblance is marked if we realize that tin was substituted for mahogany or rosewood and gilding. Later on, the eastern multiple family photograph frame was also reproduced in tin, but with wallpaper scraps and engraved saints occupying the medallions instead of Papa and the Aunties.

By 1900 red and green house paints were commonly sold in stores and had a regrettable effect upon tin work. Designs flattened and coarsened, relying upon daubs of opaque color for brightness. These not only dulled the lustre of tin but abolished the delicate stamping and chiseled designs that had previously given native tin work distinction and interest. The New Mexican processes of tinsmithing were markedly different from those used elsewhere. Since solder was not available, tin was assembled with pine rosin. When heating was needed it was probably done at the blacksmith's forge until blowtorches were brought out. Tools, to judge from the pieces themselves, seem to have

Figure 175: Tin can stamped "N. K. Fairbanks & Co., Prime Refined Family Lard, Chicago & St. Louis," reworked into a frame.

Figure 176: Federal styled tin frame with Currier and Ives print of Pope Pius IX.

Figure 177: Tin chandelier.

Figure 178: Tin and glass nicho
or shrine with painted panels.
(Photograph by Arthur D.
Taylor, Jr.)

been snips, or merely a cold chisel and hammer. Decorative designs were largely made with a nail, the cold chisel and a few small dies which were the same as those used on country-made escutcheons, on bridle bits and on leather. The same basic motifs are found on early dies made by the first Navajo silversmiths: small crescents, circles and dots which could be combined to form a variety of other design elements. As it is a matter of record that the Navajo learned silverworking from Mexican smiths at the same time that a great deal of tinworking was being done by the Spanish New Mexicans, it is logical that the same dies were used by Spanish and Indian on iron, tin, silver and leather.

The eastern tin candle mold was not very popular in New Mexico as it was an ancient Spanish custom to make candles by dipping. A few examples of candle molds in museum collections suggest that they were made in the territory because they were pieced from scraps rather than cut from whole tinned sheets. It is probable that most of the candle molds found in New Mexico were brought there by Anglo immigrants. When lamps began to be introduced, at first burning lard oil and then kerosene, candles disappeared from homes except on festive occasions, and were reserved for chapels and churches. Church candles like other church ornaments were then bought from religious supply firms, and the art of making candles at home was forgotten.

Utilitarian tin pieces, other than candle sconces, seem not to have been thought of; New Mexicans reserved tin for the beautification of religion. That a saint was framed with tin stamped "Fairbanks Pure Family Lard," or "Open Here," was immaterial; the letters meant nothing, but the rich pewter color of the earlier tin had a depth and glow which pleased a people long deprived of gold, silver or even gilding. It is still more attractive than modern sheet tin which has a thin, white color lacking in texture.

The older, traditional craft of making decoration with straw and corn husks, the poor man's gilding, was quickly abandoned when salvaged tin containers became available, but tin was extensively shaped into ornamental crosses as the straw had been used before. A cross of pure sheet tin, although handsome, did not appeal to New Mexicans as much as those composed of tin, bits of window panes, wallpaper, gold paper, calico scraps, cuttings from Sunday School certificates and other magpie materials. These "found" ingredients, although commonplace in our eyes, were all novelties to New Mexicans and represented values of exotic rarity at the time. When wallpaper was not to be had the substitute was to paint combed patterns and roses on paper which was laid under the glass panels. These, often erroneously said to be painted on the glass, were probably considered less desirable than real wallpaper, but are now regarded as more attractive. The legend that painting on the reverse of glass was an old New Mexican craft is of course disproved by the historical notation that in 1846 the only building in New Mexico that had glazed windows was the Palace of the Governors. No example of painting directly behind glass has been found among frames, nichos or crosses containing such decorated panels. Artists who settled in Santa Fe and Taos in the first quarter of this century were in fact responsible for a regional vogue for painting similar designs on window panes on the theory that this reproduced a traditional form of decoration.

Trinket boxes were extensions of tin, glass and paper nichos in construction and another adaptation of these materials to the older trinket or candle boxes that had been made of wood or leather. These were evidently made as late as World War I to judge by their decorative insets of greeting and trade cards, fashion plates and recent styles of wallpaper.

A few processional staves were made of hollow tin to replace older ones of wood, with tin crosses, crown or banners at the top. The fragility of the material and its inefficient soldering led to disintegration except for a few examples that were rescued from devout hands.

In later years tin match holders were devised and tin racks for combs and brushes; still later, electrified lighting fixtures, trays, tissue boxes and other utilitarian articles have been made for commercial sale. These are as a rule symmetrical, conventional and well constructed to withstand hard usage. The tourist is attracted by restaurant serving trays, stands and fireplace hoods of glittering tin stamped with scenes of saguaro cactus and longhorn steers. Although tinworking was not an old Spanish craft it has become a New Mexican trademark.

Figure 179: Tin and glass trinket box with commercial cards.

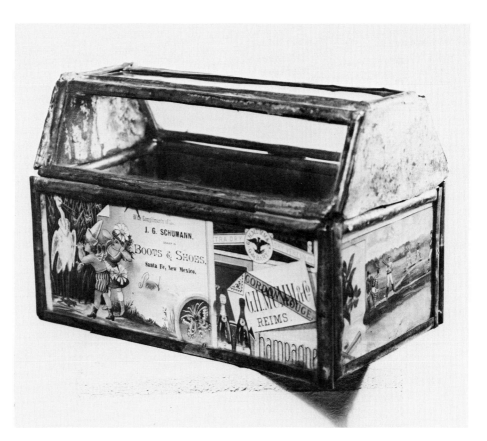

OPAS Y RAMILLETES, MINOR CRAFTS

Plate 16: Multiple cross with straw decoration.

Visitors to New Mexico who wrote of their impressions during the past century often mentioned paper flowers and decorations in the churches, describing them as gaudy, cheap or childish. This type of decoration continued until the end of World War II, and was assumed by tourists to have a basis of poverty, poor taste, and dime store influence. In a few cases this was true, but the homemade paper and other altar ornaments have a long history, beginning before written accounts, when men placed fresh branches, wreathes, and vines on the altars and holy places of their particular religion.

While Spain was squandering the wealth of the Indies during her great colonial period, it became the fashion to place sprays of gold blossoms, sometimes gem studded, on the altars of churches which were attended by the nobility. Simple folk, equally devout and anxious to give offerings, made altar flowers of what they had on hand: silk, straw, feathers, shells, wool, gourds, or paper. Whether of fresh blossoms or of gold, the Spanish name for these was *ramillete* (Spanish – *rama*, a branch), but the distinction made by gentry in colonial America between these offerings and those of the poor resulted in their referring to the latter's handwork as *opas*. (Quichua — *upa*, a mute, by extension from foolish or dull-witted people, to the acts or things typical of such people. Thus opa came to be a Spanish-Americanism for trifles).

New Mexican climate has more cold months than warm, so fresh flowers were available only from May through early fall. Artificial altar ornaments with evergreens were used instead. The inventory of Santa Ana mission, which began in 1712 and continued for thirty years, contains a separate heading: "Opas y Ramilletes y Antas," noting two opas worked in orange colored wool and "six ramilletes of paper on a green field in wooden jars."[1] In 1776 the Santa Fe parroquia had six little branches of small paper leaves curved like the rainbow (Dominguez, p. 16). In the Santa Cruz church in 1787 there were in the

---

[1] AASF, L. D. 1712, 1.

Figure 180: Chest with decoration of corn husks. (Courtesy of Detroit Art Institute)

Figure 181: *Petaca* or traveling trunk of rawhide with panels of colored baize and rawhide lacings.

Figure 182: Candle sconce, wood with applied straw and candle box with applied corn-husks. (Photograph by Ernest Knee)

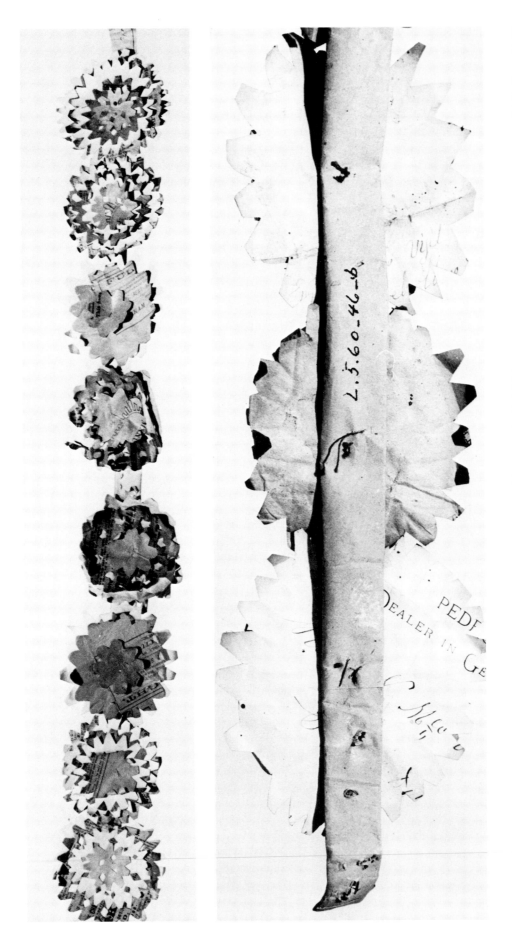

Figure 183: Ramillete or paper altar ornament.

Figure 184: Right, reverse of ramillete showing commercial letterhead dated 1880.

Figure 185: *Botas* or buckskin leggings embroidered and perforated; from a Taos family about 1840.

Figure 186: Containers made of gourds and rawhide.

II-D

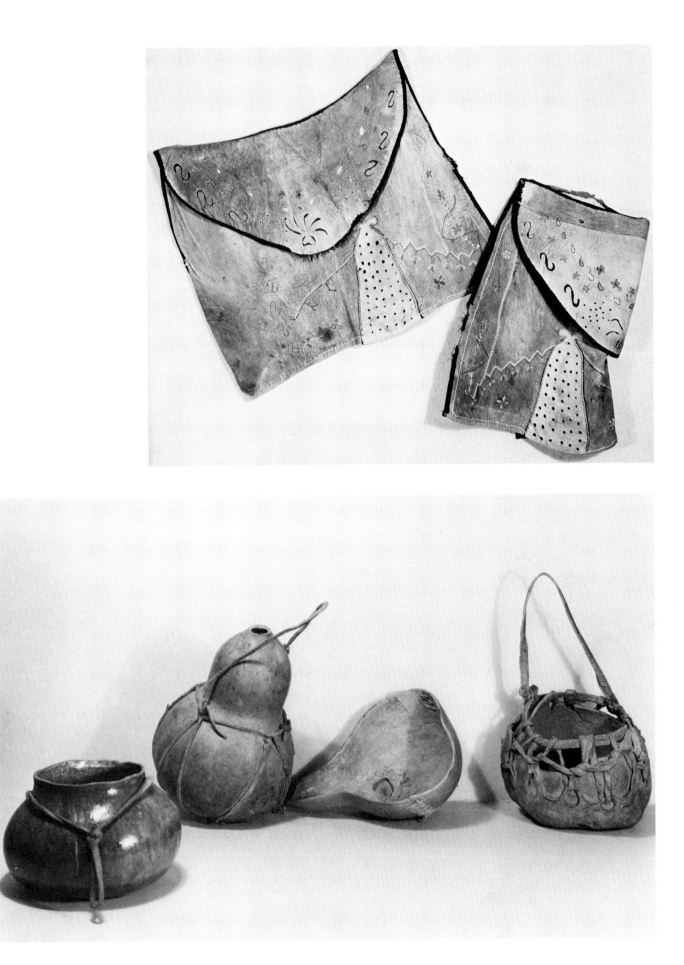

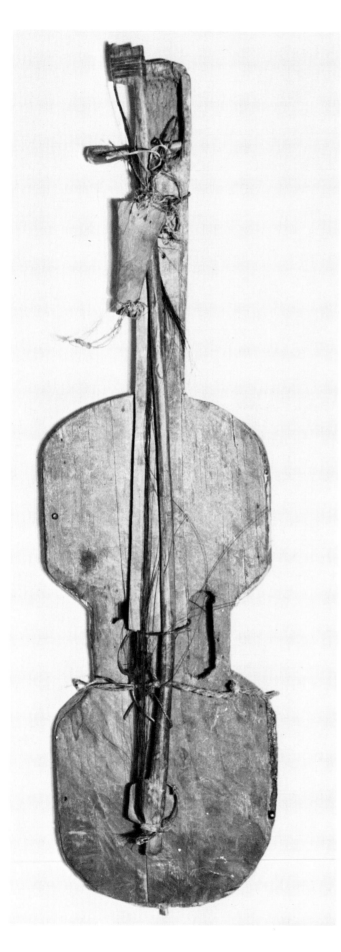

Figure 188: Chip carved New Mexican stirrup.

Figure 187: A New Mexican violin.

sacristy, "Twelve old rosettes of silk and forty-two multicolored roses" which were for ornamentation of the Virgin on special feast days.[2] Another inventory at Santa Cruz in 1826 included "tres opas de sabanilla morada" (three trifles of violet wool) in the sacristy.[3] In 1818 the Santuario de Esquipulas, then in pristine condition, owned forty-two "ramilletes de papel" as chapel ornaments. By 1826 there were 119 *rosas* among the goods in the little storerooms for sale to provide maintenance for the building (Appendix, I-B).

Among the contents of the now ruinous Duran family chapel at Talpa was a paper ornament folded and cut from blue and orange commercial soap wrappers to form a rosette. The folded and stitched backing of this opa was a mercantile bill dated December 25, 1880 (In the Museum of New Mexico). Colonial paper supplies were limited to official sheets of rag paper, sent from New Spain and watermarked with the emblem of the order of the church or governing department for whose use it was intended. Such sheets were numbered and issued to missionaries in amounts sufficient to make new record books, or on which to write reports or letters. Official paper sheets were often stamped, and the citizen requiring deeds and other documents was charged for both the sheets and the use of the government seal. Until it became commonly available from the eastern states, paper was in short supply and therefore not to be wasted on opas or ramilletes. Then, like wallpaper scraps, colored advertising matter as well as religious prints became desirable salvage material.

Once paper supplies were common, New Mexican ladies became skillful in making gorgeous flowers, usually dipped in wax, for altar vases and the *arco,* or arbor over images, bouquets and garlands.[4] Mixed with these were dried flowers and seed pods, but they did not allow the imaginative range of waxed paper in unlimited color schemes. In village chapels, including the Santuario, this custom was still to be seen during the 1930s. Housewives who made these ephemera in the country used to send their small children to the neighbors to sell or trade baskets of wax flowers, improbably gay and delightfully decorative.

Not always confined to religious ornamentation was the craft of decorating with wheat straw and corn husks, another skill adopted from the Arabs by the Spanish. In combinations of tiny particles of straw the variations of yellow produce a golden glitter which satisfactorily resembles gold leaf, literally poor man's gilding. The use of straw for trimming small boxes, frames, and even making pictures of colored straws, continued in southern Europe and Mexico. By the 18th century in the Old World it was as professionally done as marquetry

---

[2]AASF, Accounts, Book XXXXVI, Box 1, Santa Cruz.
[3]AASF, Accounts, Book LXII, B.
[4]Appendix, III-A, Truchas Inventory, 1826.

by means of dyeing straw in all colors. Straw-covered frames and perspective scenes are still made in Mexico. In New Mexico the straw was laid on to form patterns, usually against a black ground, although red was sometimes used. Candle boxes, small trinket chests, shelves, and sconces were popular articles to be trimmed with straw or husks, but straw-decorated crosses were made most often. The seemingly frail ornamentation has survived better than paint or gilding, probably because of the material used. For both glue and paint a mixture of pine rosin, soot, wax, and water was boiled up together to form black adhesive.

When the tin can reached New Mexico the old straw work went into the discard except, it is said, in the San Luis valley in southern Colorado which was settled by Spanish New Mexicans in the 1850s. Four santeros, whose skill in making straw mosaic was better than their efforts at making santos, are said to have worked there after 1875.[5]

The experimental nature of José Dolores Lopez (Appendix IV-B) seems to have led him to make at least one straw-covered cross, signed by him. Otherwise it remained for the Federal Arts Projects, nearly a century later, to revive straw working in New Mexico. Today only one or two Indians of Santa Ana Pueblo have continued with the work, but their sense of design makes it most attractive.

Use of local material for love of decorative glitter is found in objects sprinkled or encrusted with pulverized mica called *talco*. Its use on painted walls was noted in the 18th century (Sec. I-B) and continued on portable objects much later. ". . . the high altar (at Trampas Church). Its furnishing consists of a board niche painted and spattered with what they call talco here (it is like tinsel, but very flexible)." At Taos mission "there is a leather lamp, but very well made and spattered with so much mica that it has a silver sheen. . ." (Dominguez, p. 100 and 104). Other mica-trimmed things were missal stands, crosses, bulto bases, and some late 19th century picture frames.

---

[5] Wallrich, W. J., "The Santero Tradition in the San Luis Valley," in *Western Folklore,* V.X/2, 1951, Berkeley, California.

APPENDIX
Wills, Inventories and Invoices

An inventory of the effects of the late Conde de San Bartolomé de Xala, one of the wealthiest men in New Spain, was made in 1780. The family rooms in his Mexico City home numbered thirteen not including halls, kitchens and service rooms or business offices. Many pages are filled by lists of luxury items with their cash valuations of the time, including jewels, silver, religious paintings and statuary with silver or gilded frames, canopies or shrines, crystal chandeliers, damask wall hangings, ornamental folding screens, Chinese porcelains and ivories, gilded or hardwood and marble tables, commodes, buffets, decorative brackets and portable writing desks, French and English clocks and watches, pistols, gilded coaches lined with velvet, fancy saddles and horse trappings. No mention is made of a bedstead; as persons of such quality would have had them, it is apparent that they were rough frames covered with fabric which had no intrinsic value without the velvet or satin hangings.

Under the heading of *Camapes* (Archaic form of canapé which had then recently been taken from the French word for an upholstered sofa with back and arms), eleven were listed, large and small. The next classification of seating was that of *Taburetes* or stools. Of these there were:

Stools	42
Stools for men	16
Small stools for women	22
Large stools	4
Scissors (folding) stools	2
Small side chair	1
Night chairs for the bed	4
	91

All but the last three entries were described as covered with velvet or damask and galloon. This view of the status of beds and chairs in the most luxurious private home of Mexico City in 1780 throws a light upon their relative scarcity on the New Mexican frontier.[1]

Excerpt from disposition of the estate of the deceased husband of Maria Mestas.

---

[1] "Una Casa del Siglo XVIII En Mexico," edited by Manuel Romero de Terreros, University of Mexico Press, 1957.

"On the fifth day of November, 1784 I . . . Alcalde Mayor Don José Garcia de la Mora came at the petition of Maria Mestas for the distribution of the few goods given to her by her late husband. Those that are taxable and to be appraised are the following: first, all of the carpentering tools that are worth forty pesos, and those for the forge, another forty pesos which are eighty pesos. Four hundred and ninetyfour varas of land that come to two thousand one hundred and ninety-four reales from which must be taken ninety varas of land for the funeral." . . . "The share that Maria Mestas received from the whole, the iron tools for the forge, forty pesos, a shaving knife at one peso, an ax at six pesos and two hundred varas of land, which are worth two hundred fortyseven pesos . . ."

"The share of Don Juan del Prado . . . first a blacksmith's iron, a compass, a bellows, a molding iron, at fifteen pesos, and thirty-one and a half varas of land worth fortysix and a half pesos . . ."

"More, that which was given to Señora Maria Mestas was three portions of land consisting of more than fifteen hundred varas, and fifteen goats and an ass with which to fetch wood that she gave to her husband when they were married . . ."

"Signed in the said day, month and year,
Jose Garcia de la Mora
Esmerejildo Sisneros
Francisco Garcia."[2]

Those cited are typical of many more in that the persons making disposition were all amply provided with lands and livestock. The specific mention of certain articles in the wills indicates their importance in the eyes of their owners and prospective heirs.

Excerpts from the Will of Josefa Martin,[3] of San Antonio del Embudo (now Dixon), 21st August, 1786:

Testator had ten children by two marriages; to the four of her second marriage she left nothing but "algunos mueblesitos" (some little pieces of furniture), to be equally divided among them, and "una holla de cobre" (a copper pot), to her granddaughter Rosa, and "el comal de hierro" (the iron griddle), to her daughter Gertrude. The rest of the three pages disposed of land and livestock.

Excerpts from the Will of Juan Antonio Suaso, 26th April, 1818, at San Antonio del Embudo: He was the eldest son of Josefa Martin and left eight children among whom he divided lands at Rio Chiquito of Chimayo, at Truchas, at Embudo, Rinconada, and "Las Jollas," some with irrigation rights and some without access to water, and three houses and two torreons consisting altogether of eleven rooms. Further:

---

[2] Renehan Papers, New Mexico State Records Center.
[3] Josefa was the great granddaughter of Luis Martín Serrano, son of Hernan Martin Serrano, a first settler at Yunque in 1598. She married Luis Suazo of El Paso in 1734, her first husband.

"Three troughs for making syrup, a press board and a barrel, a serviceable loom with three combs — and a spinning wheel with spindle and shaft, an ax, a chisel, an iron griddle, an iron spoon, a chest with lock, two chests without locks, a half fanega measure, two adzs, a set of bedding, an old chocolate pot, two corrals, a hayrack without roof, two burros (sawhorses), one colcha, five cow hides, one buffalo hide, one sarape, three awls, one bridle bit, one iron whip, one branding iron, two saddle bags, one barrel, four hand sickles, one ramillete, one catechism, twenty-six novenas, one crucifix "de bulto," in the round, one image of St. Anthony and Our Lady of St. John, also in the round, and six more retablos, sixteen apple trees, an old cart, a metate without grinding stone."

Of these Suaso made equal division among the eight children as they might later decide. Specific directions were given as to "My two pistols and lance, which it is my will to have given to the Holy St. Anthony for the protection of his chapel that shall go to whomsoever of the living defend his holy temple." Also specific was the matter of the apple trees, one of which was to be given to St. Anthony and the other to the "Most Holy"; the remaining fourteen to be divided "equally" among the children. Furthermore, the sons were ordered to "maintain the fence around the trees forever for protection of the said trees so that no one whomsoever shall touch nor cut them. By this (I) command that the fence be forever kept up for the benefit of all." In a postscript Suaso added, after arrangements for novenas for the repose of his soul: "I declare that I own three more fire arms than those cited; these arms are ordered to be divided amongst my heirs."

More worldly goods of the same prominent New Mexican family are represented in the will of Don Severino Martinez, 8th June, 1827. Don Severino was the father of the controversial Padre Martinez and five other children; he also left a widow. The extensive lands he owned were scattered around Abiquiu, El Rito and principally in and around Taos, most of which tracts had houses on them. In addition to those and herds of various domestic animals, large quantities of different textiles, "ready cash" or silver of 800 pesos plus more than 800 pesos owed to him by others, he noted that: "I declare to have all the household furnishings, without taking time to enumerate what they may be . . .," but he did specify that he had "ten pairs of scissors" in his commercial storerooms. He also declared as personal belongings "four plates, four spoons with their respective forks and a middle-sized cup, all of silver." It is the importance attached to such items as scissors in such a household that brings to our minds the way of life in those days. Large shears or scissors had been brought from New Spain in the past but were scarce. The Chihuahua fairs and recent Santa Fe Trail traders had made these conveniences more generally available by 1827.

The Martinez family and, one suspects, particularly Padre Martinez, who was one of the executors, kept an unusually detailed record of the disposition of properties to the heirs, dividing lands, houses, animals, cloth yardage, hides, colchas, pounds of sugar and so on equally among them, and compensating one heir for some indivisible article by other goods of equivalent monetary value. The widow received two sofas and four stools. All heirs, including women, each received pairs of the scissors, an ax, a hoe, hand sickles, and "pieces" or "one pound" of iron, valued at one real each and carefully mentioned in addition to more luxurious items. It is interesting to note that the son of Juan Antonio Suaso of Embudo, quoted above, was one of the witnesses to the will of Severino Martinez in 1827.[4] As his grandmother was Josefa Martín, and the Abiquiu branch of the Martinez family had gone by the name of Martín until only a few years before, they were all members of the same 1598 Martín Serrano family.

Figure 189: The *vara* or official measuring stick 32.3 to 33.3 inches, used in New Mexico until 1846 for all land surveys.

A receipt for goods from J. Roubidoux to Manuel Gregoire*

40 lances @ 1.75	$70.00
2 gros boutons	4.00
5 yd. cottoneu croisé	5.62
2 yd. cotton	2.00
2 mouchoirs bleu	4.00
Payé a son fils	12.00
Payé a A.B.B. et son fils	1.50
	$99.12

Certifie b.c/e Juste
et veritable, 6 Mai, 1827
   J. Roubidoux

(AASF, L.D., 1827, #7)

(40 lances @ 1.75	$70.00
2 large buttons	4.00
5 yds. plaid cotton	5.62
2 yds. cotton	2.00
2 blue handkerchiefs	4.00
Paid to his son	12.00
Paid to A.B.B. and his son	1.50
	$99.12

Certified [that this is] fair
and true, 6th of May 1827
   J. Roubidoux)

(Fray Angelico Chavez reads the name as "Gregoin" while I read it Gregoire. New Mexicans converted the English name Samuel to Manuel, which would make this trader's name Samuel Gregory. For more on the names Gregoin, Gregoire, Gregan, cf. "New Names in New Mexico" in *El Palacio,* V. 64/9, Sept. 1957, p. 308.)

Manifest which W. H. Anderson presents of the goods which he introduced to the National Custom House of Santa Fe, New Mexico with the following measure and amounts:

---

[4]"The Last Will and Testament of Don Severino Martinez," translated by Ward Alan Minge in New Mexico Quarterly," V.XXXIII/1, 1963.

Chest		Ps.	Rs.	Grs.
18 pieces calico 446¾ yards — 481 varas @ 10 granos		050.	0.	10.

Chest				
2 dozen cotton handkerchiefs @ 4 reales, 7 granos		001.	1.	4.
3 pieces coco cloth 36 yards @ 6 reales, 8 granos		002.	4.	0
6 cotton shawls		002.	2.	0
2 packages of pins		001.	7.	4.
2 dozen threaded glass beads		000.	6.	0
1 piece water-proof cloth 18 yards = 19 varas @ 10 granos		001.	7.	10

Mule load				
10 pieces coarse cotton cloth 306¾ yards — 330 varas @ 1 real		061.	5.	0

		Ps.	Rs.	Grs.
total		122.	2.	4.
excise tax		020	5.	9.

Santa Fe, August 14, 1835
W. H. Anderson

sum of both taxes	143.	0.	1.

Deduction

Amount of import tax including the money reserved by the law of April 6, 1830	122.	2.	4.
Reduction of the said tax as reserved	065.	6.	10.
Remaining subject to the import tax	56.	3.	6.

Santa Fe, August 15, 1835

Acting Administrator
Vicente S. Vergara   Sarracino governor
    rubric   rubric

(From: Mexican Archives of New Mexico State Records Center and Archives, Santa Fe, New Mexico.)

Langham and Boggs, 1835.

"Manifest presented by Langham and Boggs of the goods that they have bought in the caravan from the United States and have introduced into the Territorial Customhouse of Santa Fe on New Mexico.

		Ps.	Rs.	Grs.
Bundle	13 reams of half flowered wall paper	013.	3.	4.
121	4 pounds in white for their use	000	00	00
Barrel	30 doz. dishes of white flint (ironstone) ware	036.	0	0
1	4 & 9/12 doz. shovels, free of duty	000	00	00
	1 mattock, free of duty	000	00	00
Box	33 pieces of calicoes, 924 yds.			
5	2 pieces of water proof cloth, 58 yds.	110.	3.	4.
	2 pieces of gauze veiling, 48 yds.	006.	3.	0.
	1 piece of black neck cloths	005.	1.	8.
	2 doz. tinted papers for their use	000.	0.	0.
Keg	10 lbs. of special nails @ 4 rs, 2 gs.	005.	1.	8.
Box	5 doz. spigots P	006.	0.	0.
13	10 umbrellas	014.	4.	8.
Barrel	Sugar and Coffee for their use	000.	0.	0.
Small Box	1 doz. axes, free of duty	000.	0.	0.

Same	8/12 doz. axes, free of duty	000.	0.	0.
Box	10 doz. scissors, various kinds	001.	4.	6.
	6 gross common buttons	002.	4.	0.
	6 doz. knives with wooden handles	001.	2.	0.
	3 doz. clasp knives with horn handles	000.	3.	9.
	1 doz. tooth brushes	000.	1.	8.
	2 thousand caps	000.	4.	7.
	3 thousand brass headed tacks	001.	7.	0.
	½ doz. tinned flasks	001.	1.	8.
	1 doz. composition pencils	000.	1.	7.
	1 gross of augurs	001.	7.	0.
	7 doz. iron spoons	002.	0.	0.
	11 small chisels for their use	000.	0.	0.
	2 lancets (surgical) for their use	000.	0.	0.
Sack	60 pounds of pepper	003.	0.	0.
Box 7	4 doz. kerchiefs of silk	020.	6.	8.
	5 doz. ornamental rosettes	002.	0.	0.
	3 lengths of printed cloth, 32 yds.	010.	7.	6.
	2 doz. madras kerchiefs	001.	7.	0.
	80 pieces of ribbon no. 75	021.	2.	0.
	6 gross of shirt buttons	005.	0.	0.
	18 doz. of false pearls	005.	5.	0.
	1 doz. necklaces	001.	5.	6.
	10/12 doz. pear shaped pendants	000.	4.	2.
	1 piece black neck cloths	002.	1.	8.
	1 doz. cologne water	000.	2.	0.
	11 pieces of ordinary kerchiefs	006.	2.	5.
	2 silk kerchiefs	000.	4.	2.
	8 spigots	003.	2.	8.
	1 length of bombazine	001.	5.	4.
Box 24	20 pieces of canvas, 597 yds.	230.	3.	6.
Bundle 551	18 pieces of manta, 541 yds.			
No. 1	6 pieces of heavy cotton cloth, 178 yds.	024.	0.	0.
Box	12 doz. spigots	005.	0.	0.
		361.	3.	0.

Santa Fe September 25, 1835.
Langham and Boggs

Consumers tax	095.	3.	0.
sum of both taxes	657.	0.	0.

Deduction
Amount of import tax including

the money reserved	561.	3.	0.
The reserved money is deducted	230	3.	6.
Balance remaining subject to			
import tax	331.	1.	6.

Santa Fe September 25, 1835

S. Vergara	Sarracino "
rubric	rubric

(Courtesy of the New Mexico State Archives and Records Center.)

II-D

M. O. Yrisarri, 1853
"Invoice of the following goods bought in St. Louis"
M.O.Y.

H. & K. B. Whittemore

1 box of 6 doz. Sombreros, of black wool	@ 7.50	45.00
1 box of 3 doz. Sombreros, of black wool	8.50	25.50
1 doz. Sombreros, of black wool		10.50
1 doz. Sombreros, of black wool		15.00
½ doz. Sombreros, white	36.00	18.00
1 doz. Sombreros, assorted		9.00
1 doz. Sombreros, black		6.00
2 doz. Sombreros, white	9.00	18.00
2 doz. Sombreros, white and coffee color	18.00	36.00
6 Young ladies' Caps	2.25	13.50
3 Young ladies' Caps	.25	.75
1 doz. White Sombreros		22.50
½ doz. black Sombreros	20.00	10.00
1½ doz. assorted Sombreros	7.50	11.25
1 doz. white Sombreros		9.00
1 doz. black Sombreros		9.00
½ doz. little Sombreros	12.00	6.00
½ doz. little Sombreros	10.50	5.25
1 doz. little baby caps		3.00
4 doz. small black Sombreros	5.00	20.00
2 doz. coffee colored Sombreros	4.50	9.00
1 doz. Panama hats		30.00
1 doz. Panama hats		35.00
1 doz. Panama hats		24.00
1 doz. Panama hats		27.00
1 doz. Panama hats, small		15.00
1 doz. Sombreros of straw		10.50
1 doz. Sombreros of straw		13.50
1 doz. Sombreros of straw		8.00
1 doz. Sombreros of straw, small		7.50
2 doz. Sombreros of palm leaf, small		4.00
2 doz. Sombreros of palm leaf, small	1.00	2.00
2 doz. Sombreros of palm leaf, large	2.00	4.00
2 doz. Sombreros of palm leaf, small	1.50	3.00
½ doz. Sombreros for little girls	10.00	5.00
		490.75
2-doz. caps for little boys	5.50	11.00
1 doz. caps for little boys, finer grade		8.50
5 doz. caps	3.00	15.00
Packing, boxes and handling		5.00
		530.25

Eddy Jamison & Co.

25 pieces of cotton yardage, 886 yds	@ .09	79.74
26 pieces of cotton yardage, 839 yds	.09	75.50
25 pieces of cotton yardage, 883 yds	.09	79.47
20 pieces of cotton yardage, 655 yds	.09	58.95
5 pieces of cotton yardage, 181⅓ yds	.12	16.36
20 pieces of cotton yardage, 682 yds	.09	61.38
18 pieces of cotton yardage, 629 yds	.09	56.61
5 pieces of cotton yardage, 179 yds	.09	16.13

2 pieces of cotton yardage, 67 3/yds	.09	6.10
6 pieces of cotton yardage, 189 2/yds	.09	17.06
10 pieces of cotton yardage, 321 yds	.09	28.89
1 pieces of cotton yardage, 34 2/yds	.09	3.10
2 pieces of the kind for curtains, 95 yds	12½	11.88
2 pieces of coarse blue cotton cloth, 52 3/yds	.09	4.75
5 pieces of cashmere*, 134 2/ yds	.75	100.88
1 piece of cashmere, 30 yds	.75	22.50
4 pieces of cashmere, blue, 151 2/ yds	.50	75.75
9 pieces of blue cotton cloth, 292 yds	.09	26.28
*(Inferior grade of cashmere)		
9 pieces of blue cotton cloth, 281 yds	.09	25.31
9 pieces of blue cambric linen no. 10, 144 yds	.12½	18.00
11 pieces of cambric linen no. 2, 132 yds	.12½	16.50
20 pieces of cambric linen no. 3, 240 yds	.15	36.00
7 pieces of cambric linen no. 4, 112 yds	.14	15.68
18 pieces of cambric linen no. 5, 360 yds	.14	50.40
10 pieces of cambric linen no. 6, 160 yds	.19	30.40
20 pieces of canvas, white, 739 yds	.07½	55.43
20 pieces of canvas, white, 736 2/ yds	.07½	55.24
6 pieces of canvas, white, 217 2/ yds	.07½	16.31
20 pieces of canvas, white, 521 2/ yds	.07½	39.09
Carried forward		1121.60

(follows a total of)		
305 pieces of canvas, 10,583 yds	.07½	794.18
44 pieces of canvas, 2,215 yds	.08½	188.32
manta (cotton cloth), 10,408 yds	.07¾	806.62
3 pieces packing tarpaulins, 9x14		13.44
box		.75
		2,924.90
discount, 6%		175.49
		2,749.71
packing		32.00
handling		3.75
		2,785.16

Martin & Bro.

1 trunk with 1 doz. black flannel pantaloons			24.00
Trunk			2.50
1 trunk with 1 doz. linen coats			10.50
½ doz. blue coats	@	10.50	5.25
Trunk			2.50
1 trunk with 1 doz. flannel pants			24.00
½ doz. blue coats		10.50	5.25
Trunk			2.50
Handling			.25
			76.75

Pittman & Tennent

The following goods are packed in trunks numbers 1 & 2
of the house of Martin & Bro.

38 pieces of ribbon	@	.30	11.40
1 piece of ribbon			.90
3 pieces of ribbon		1.50	4.50

7 pieces of ribbon	2.75	19.25
3 pieces of neck cloths (bandannas?)	5.50	16.50
1 piece of neck cloths		6.00
8 doz. white stockings	2.25	18.00
90 doz. white thread	.12½	11.25
		87.80
discount, 5%		4.39
		83.41

T. W. Hoit

40 doz. kerchiefs	1.50	60.00
11 pieces of bandannas	2.75	30.25
3 pieces of bandannas	2.25	6.75
3 pieces of bandannas	6.00	18.00
Box		.25
		115.25

R. C. Shackleford

5 doz. men's shoes	@	15.00	75.00
5 doz. men's shoes		16.00	80.00
5 doz. women's shoes		7.50	37.50
2 doz. women's shoes		11.50	23.00
Handling			.25
			215.75
Carried forward			3,806.57

E. C. Yoste & Co.

5 doz. women's shoes	9.00	45.00
50 pairs of boys' shoes	6.00	25.00
2 doz. women's buttoned shoes	9.00	18.00
2 doz. women's buttoned shoes	10.50	21.00
3 doz. little shoes for girls	2.75	8.25
2 doz. little shoes	4.00	8.00
2 doz. women's shoes	13.50	27.00
1 doz. women's shoes		7.50
1 doz. women's shoes		12.00
Boxes & cartons		1.25
Handling		.25
		173.25

Young Brothers

4 doz. pantaloons	15.00	60.00
1 doz. pantaloons		15.00
1 doz. coats		12.00
1 doz. coats		12.00
1¼ doz. coats	12.00	15.00
1 doz. coats		24.00
1 doz. coats		24.00
2 doz. coats	12.00	24.00
2 doz. coats	14.00	28.00
1 raincoat		5.50
1 doz. pantaloons		18.00
½ doz. pantaloons	15.00	7.50
1 doz. pantaloons		13.50
3 doz. pantaloons	12.00	36.00

1 doz. pantaloons		17.00
6 doz. pantaloons	12.00	72.00
Boxes & handling		1.75
		385.25

Weil & Brother

20 pieces of striped canvas, 979½ yds.	.09	88.16
3 doz. wool shawls	18.00	54.00
36 pieces wool shawls	1.75	63.00
5 doz shawls	12.00	60.00
1 piece of the kind for pantaloons, 46½ yds.	.26½	12.32
1 piece of the kind for pantaloons, 45 yds.	.16½	7.42
13 pieces of the kind for pantaloons, 523 yds.	.12½	65.38
3 doz. shawls	18.00	54.00
2 doz. shawls	12.00	24.00
5 doz. pantaloons	4.50	22.50
20 doz. shirts of present style	4.00	80.00
10 doz. drawers	4.00	40.00
2 pieces of the kind for towels, 30 yds.	.15	4.50
2 pieces of Irish linen, 26½ yds.	.33	8.74
2 pieces of Irish linen, 28 yds.	.43	12.04
3 pieces of Irish linen, 82 yds.	.35	28.70
10 doz. vests	9.00	90.00
10 doz. vests of silk	12.00	120.00
3 doz. merino coats	21.00	63.00
3 doz. coats	15.00	45.00
2 doz. coats	12.00	24.00
1 8/12 doz.	30.00	50.00
½ doz.	18.00	9.00
½ doz.	60.00	30.00
8 doz. pantaloons	7.50	60.00
5 doz. pantaloons	10.50	52.50
3 doz. pantaloons	9.00	27.00
7 doz. pantaloons	15.00	105.00
2 doz. pantaloons	12.00	24.00
2 doz. pantaloons	18.00	36.00
3 doz. pantaloons	15.00	45.00
24 yds. black lace	.08	1.92
36 yds. black lace	.06¼	2.25
36 yds. black lace	.02	.72
24 yds. black lace	.05	1.20
24 yds. black lace	.02½	.60
48 yds black lace	.03½	1.68
24 yds. black lace	.03	.72
48 yds. black lace	.04	1.92
84 yds. lace	.01½	1.26
48 yds. lace	.06¼	3.00
24 yds. lace	.05	1.20
24 yds. lace	.03	.72
36 yds lace	.01½	.54
96 yds. lace	.00¾	.72
36 yds. lace	.01	.36
48 yds. lace	.00¾	.36
24 yds. of linen lace	.05	1.20
Boxes and handling		8.25
		1,433.88

A.J. McCreery & Co.

1 piece of rubber, 12 yds.	.50	6.00
6 cotton umbrellas	.18¾	1.13
18 cotton umbrellas	.25	4.50
6 silk umbrellas	.87½	5.25
1 silk umbrella		2.00
1 feather duster		.50
2 doz. carriage whips	2.50	5.00
½ doz. carriage whips	4.50	2.25
30 pieces of paper for the walls	.12½	3.75
1 piece of paper for borders		.75
4 lbs. of hemp thread	.80	3.20
2 lbs. of blue silk	6.00	12.00
5 doz. fine toothed combs	1.00	5.00
150 spools of silk		2.25
24 doz. spools of silk	.30	7.20
4 big metal buttons	1.00	4.00
4 big metal buttons	.75	3.00
4 big metal buttons for a vest	.75	3.00
4 doz. thick strings for violins	.25	1.00
3 bundles of strings for violins	1.00	3.00
3 bundles of strings for violins	1.50	4.50
3 bundles of strings for violins	1.25	3.75
10 doz. small colored plates	.25	2.50
9 pieces of cotton handkerchiefs	1.00	9.00
7 pieces of red handkerchiefs	1.00	7.00
1 piece of the kind for veils, 16¼ yds.	.30	4.87
1 piece of the kind for veils, 15 yds.	.40	6.00
2 pieces of black neck cloths	5.00	10.00
10 doz. white stockings	1.25	12.50
1 doz. silk stockings		9.00
1 doz. silk stockings		12.00
3 doz. little stockings of cotton	1.25	3.75
3 doz. shawls	6.00	18.00
5 doz. cravats	2.50	12.50
4 doz. white gloves	.75	3.00
3 doz. colored gloves	.75	2.25
4 doz. white gloves	1.00	4.00
2 doz. small gloves	.50	1.00
4 doz. mittens, black	1.50	6.00
1 doz. mittens, black		3.00
4 pieces of merino, 147½ yds.	.22½	33.18
1 doz. wool belts		2.00
1 doz. wool belts		3.00
11/12 doz. wool belts	4.50	4.13
7 pieces of muslin, 70 yds.	.22	15.40
10 pieces of muslin, 100 yds.	.20	20.00
4 pieces of lace, 8 doz.	.37½	3.00
3½ doz. cravats	2.50	7.71
3 doz. mittens	1.00	3.00
4 doz. mittens, small	1.00	4.00
3 doz. women's gloves	1.50	4.50
3 doz. kerchiefs	1.00	3.00
2 doz. wool stockings	1.25	2.50
2½ doz. fancy stockings	1.50	3.75
5 doz. colored stockings	1.25	6.25

4 doz. white stockings	2.25	9.00
4 doz. stockings	2.00	8.00
Boxes and handling		2.00
		343.82
5% discount		17.19
		326.63
Carried Forward		$6,125.58

Hanford Thayer & Co.

2 doz. pants	9.00	18.00
1 doz. pants		33.00
2 10/12 doz. pants	7.50	12.00
6/12 doz. pants	24.00	12.00
1 doz. pants		25.50
5/12 doz. pants	24.00	10.00
2 doz. pants	6.00	12.00
1 doz. vests	9.35	18.00
2 doz. vests	8.00	16.00
3 doz. vests	5.00	15.00
1 doz. coats, cashmere		36.00
8 pairs of damaged pants (seconds)	.44	3.52
5 pairs of pants	.52	2.60
18 pairs of pants	.44	7.92
Box		1.50
10 doz. white shirts	6.00	60.00
2 doz. flannel shirts	7.50	15.00
4 doz. shirts	7.50	30.00
3 doz. colored flannel shirts	10.00	30.00
4 pieces of neck cloths	4.00	16.00
1 doz. coats		36.00
2 pairs damaged pants (seconds)	.48	.96
4 pairs damaged pants	.48	1.92
4 pairs damaged pants	.44	1.76
1 pair damaged pants		.70
2 pairs damaged pants	1.00	2.00
1 pair damaged pants		.85
1 pair damaged pants		.75
2 pairs damaged pants	.52	1.04
1 pair of pants, seconds		1.10
3 pairs of pants, seconds	.87	2.61
1 pair of pants, seconds		.32
1 pair of pants, seconds		.48
1 pair of pants, seconds		.70
1 pair of pants, seconds		.48
1 pair of pants, seconds		1.00
1 pair of pants, seconds		.75
1 pair of pants, seconds		1.15
1 pair of pants, seconds		.60
3 pairs of pants, seconds	.85	2.55
3 pairs of pants, seconds	.65	1.95
1 pair of pants, seconds		.90
3 pairs of pants, seconds	.55	1.65

3 pairs of pants, seconds	.55	1.65
Box		1.50
		448.66
Less 5%		22.43
		426.23

Noonan Tooly & Co.

16 doz. cups	.60	9.60
11 doz. cups	.60	6.60
6 doz. cups	.70	4.20
15 doz. plates	.55	8.25
8 doz. plates	.50	4.00
6 doz. mugs	.65	3.90
6 doz. plates	.90	5.40
4 doz. plates	.90	3.60
4 doz. plates	1.25	5.00
4 doz. plates	1.00	4.00
8 doz. small goblets	1.25	10.00
1 coffee pot		6.75
6 doz. glasses	1.00	6.00
6 doz. glasses	.65	3.90
6 doz. glasses	.90	5.40
6 doz. glasses	.65	3.90
6 doz. glasses	.50	3.00
6 doz. glasses	.50	3.00
6 doz. glasses	.50	3.00
6 doz. glasses	.50	3.00
1 hamper, 9 boxes, handling		3.50
		106.00

Wilcox & McDowell

19 yards of carpet	.90	17.10
(A folio is lost here) Carry forward		$6,674.91
Wolff & Hoppe Carry forward		7,415.56
1 11/12 cartons of scissors @	1.50	2.88
1 doz. large spoons		3.00
½ doz. forks	1.50	.75
½ doz. spoons	1.10	.55
1 gross of iron spoons		3.25
1 doz. large scissors		3.00
1 doz. saucer scales		2.00
½ doz. knives and forks		4.50
1,000 needles		1.00
1,000 needles for bead work		4.00
4 doz. fine toothed combs	.80	3.20
100 fish hooks, each one @ .45, .40 & .35		1.20
2 doz. floats	.75	1.50
1 doz. boys' belts		2.00
2 doz. pomades	.60	1.20
4 doz. pomades	1.25	5.00
½ doz. pomades	3.00	1.50
4 doz. bottles of ink	.40	1.60
3 doz. bottles of eau de cologne	.75	2.25
5 small boxes of pendants	1.00	5.00
1 small box of pendants		.75

1 doz. brooches		.75
1 doz. brooches		5.00
9 doz. small points	.40	3.60
Packing		.77
		78.70

O. S. Filley & Co.

6 doz. platters	1.00	6.00
6 doz. platters	.50	3.00
3 doz. platters	.33	1.00
6 measuring gadgets	.90	2.70
1 doz. funnels		.60
¼ doz. large spoons		1.37
½ doz. sieves	4.00	2.00
½ doz. lanterns	4.00	2.00
1 doz. tin pails		2.25
3 doz. platters, each one $3.00	2.00	15.00
2 doz. platters	1.70	3.40
Box and handling		.55
		39.87
Discount of 10%		3.98
		35.89
Two tin boxes	12.00	24.00
		59.89
		$7,554.15

McCreery & Co.

½ doz. mirrors	24.00	12.00
Box		.50
		12.50

Eddy Jamison & Co.

9 pieces of Indiana (cotton yardage), 294½ yds.	.09½	27.98
7 pieces of Indiana, blue, 262½ yds.	.09½	24.94
Packing and Handling		1.67
		54.59

Dean King & Co.

10 dress lengths	@ 2.25	22.50
2 pieces of printed muslin, 50½ yds.	.15	7.54
13 doz. kerchiefs	2.00	26.00
2 pieces of black muslin, 50½ yds.	.20	10.10
1 piece of black muslin, 33 yds.	.15	4.95
12 doz. stockings	1.00	12.00
5 doz. stockings	2.00	10.00
1 doz. belts		18.00
2 pieces black cravats	5.00	10.00
1 piece silk lace, 36 yds.	.11	3.96
1 pieces silk lace, 36 yds.	.08	2.88
1 piece of the kind for curtains, 46⅜ yds.	.37½	17.34
3 pieces of cotton yardage, 107¾ yds.	.10	10.77
25 pieces of blue cotton yardage, 720¼ yds.	.10	72.02
25 pieces of cotton yardage, 840 yds.	.10	84.00
30 pieces of cotton yardage, 1020¼ yds.	.09½	96.92
Trunk		3.00

Packing and handling		4.50
		8,037.72

Commission on 8,037
@ 2½ % 200.93

$8,238.65

Glasgow & Brother

Invoice of Groceries from the House of Glasgow & Brother.

(A folio is lost here)

8 barrels of powder	5.00	40.00
@.50, 1 box of pipes		1.25
1 box with 6 percussion rifles, and	5.00	30.50
14 flintlock rifles	4.00	56.00
1 box @.25, 3 doz. sardines	3.50	10.75
1 keg of alcohol, 41 gals.	.42	17.22
Iron bands for keg		1.00
1 half box of chewing tobacco, 69 lbs.	.12½	8.63
3 half boxes window glass, 8x10 @ 3.50 a box		5.25
3 half boxes window glass, 10x12 @ 3.75 box		5.62
8 boxes of tobacco in small packages	2.75	22.00
3 bundles of candle wicks, 45½ lbs.	.22	9.26
8 boxes of candle wicks, 45½ lbs.	.22	9.26
1 box @.40, 3 reams of paper	2.00	6.40
2 boxes of chocolate, 24 lbs.	.22	5.28
2 boxes of puro cigars	1.50	3.00
2 bundles of cinnamon sticks, 8 lbs.	.43	3.44
8 lbs. of cloves	.30	2.40
10 thousand caps (percussion)	.50	5.00
1 half gross of playing cards	20.00	10.00
1 lb. nutmeg		1.40
30 boxes @.25 each of soap, 1950 lbs.	.05	105.00
15 kegs @.50 each of sugar cones, 1990 lbs.	.08¼	171.67
17 double sacks @.33 ea. of sugar, 2034 lbs.	.04½	97.14
20 double sacks @.33 ea. of sugar, 2000 lbs. (white)	.06	126.60
5 double sacks @.33 ea. of rice, 533 lbs.	.05½	30.96
1 keg of tar		4.50
1 sack @.16 of almonds, 70 lbs.	.13	9.26
1 box @.40 of indigo 54/6, 48 lbs.	1.10	53.20
15 boxes @.25 ea. of tallow candles, 686 lbs.	.13	92.93
20 boxes @.25 ea. of hard candles (sperm whale oil), 800 lbs.	.21	173.00
8 sacks of coffee, 1302 lbs.	.10	130.20
1 sack of fine coffee, 156 lbs.	.16	24.96
1 barrel of assorted nails		5.25
4 doz. buckets	2.50	10.00
4 boxes of sweets	3.00	12.00
1 box of preserved fruit, 2 doz.	5.00	10.00
1 box @.50 with 20 gross of matches	1.00	20.50
1 keg of biscuits		4.25
1 barrel@ 1.50 of cognac, 10 gals.	1.50	16.50
3 kegs of brandy, 126 gals.	.33	41.58
Iron bands for kegs		3.00
1 box lemonade (or, lemon squash) ½		2.75
8 kegs of whiskey, 325 gals.	.19	61.84
Iron bands for kegs		8.00
1 keg of whiskey, grain, 44 gals.	.37½	16.50
Iron bands for keg		1.00

4 hampers of champagne	11.00	44.00
2 barrels of honey, 20 gals.	.60	12.00
1 doz. ropes		2.25
1 bundle of ropes for cordage, 63 lbs.	.14	8.82
2 sacks of munitions (paper cartridges)	1.90	3.80
2 sacks of large munitions	2.37	4.75
6 bundles of "papantes" (?), 600 lbs.	.08	48.00
Handling		5.25
		1,605.86
1 demijohn @.75 of brandy, 2 gals.	1.50	3.75
1 sack of frijoles, 194 lbs., 3¼ bushels	.80	2.96
1 barrel of whiskey, 5 gals.	.37½	2.88
1 sack @.33 of brown sugar, 117 lbs.	.04	5.01
1 sack of sassafras		3.00
Handling		.25
		1,623.71

Glasgow and Brother

Señor Don Mariano O. Yrisarri*
His account with Glasgow & Brother

Due

For money paid to the College for the expenses, etc., of Manuel	$	285.00
— Credit —		
For money given by you in last May		200.00
Balance due against you from the old account		85.00
For the account for groceries according to the invoice		1,623.71
For the account for goods bought in other houses of business in St. Louis		8,238.65
For insurance paid as far as Kansas on $9,862 @ 1¼%		123.27
For cost of 4 dozen wooden sieves		17.00
		10,087.63

— Credit —

April 17 For the value of a note on L. C. Easton		
against D. H. Vinton	$9,189.75	
For the value of gold sold to the		
credit of your account	565.69	9,755.44
Balance due		332.19

St. Louis, April 27, of 1854.

Glasgow & Brother

*Pablo Yrisarri, a European, had married Maria Manuela Rael at Alameda before 1780. He died in 1782. His son, Pablo Yrisarre the second, married Antonia Teresa Romero in 1811. Their son, Mariano Yrisarri, was married to Juana Otero on March 26, 1836. They had two children, one of whom, Manuel, was sent to St. Louis to be educated. He died without heirs, before his father. Mariano Yrissarri was one of several Spanish New Mexicans who found it profitable to bring wagon trains of merchandise from Missouri for his store at Ranchos de Albuquerque. The quantities and kinds of goods found in this invoice of 1854 are strikingly different from those of the years prior to the annexation of New Mexico in 1846, both in variety and, in some instances, in being nonessential or luxury items.

(Addenda to New Mexico Families, Fray Angelico Chavez, in El Palacio, V. 64/7-8, 1957, p. 248.

The ledger containing the foregoing invoice of 1854, and an incomplete draft of the last will and testament of Mariano Yrisarri, written at Ranchos de Albuquerque. For permission to publish these documents I am indebted to Miss Eloisa D. Yrisarri.)

II-D

THE SANTERO

PEDRO ANTONIO FRESQUIS

For some twenty years santos, mostly retablos, of a peculiarly linear, distinctive style of drawing were called the works of the anonymous "Calligraphic Santero" in order to conveniently refer to the group. The name was suggested by W. S. Stallings, former curator of the Taylor Museum, Colorado Springs; it is appropriate in describing the personal mannerisms of this long-unidentified New Mexico santero. At the time, it was apparent that he had been prolific on the basis of the number of his panels already classified by style, and owned in New Mexico, Colorado and elsewhere, such as those in the small group of New Mexico retablos at the Hispanic Society in New York.

This personal style is best described as one of flowing, nervous lines, two dimensional treatment, distinctive space fillers of flying, flamelike forms, arabesques and cross-hatching. The santero made use of graffito ornamentation, incising through the paint into the still wet gesso ground, meanders, stars, scrolls and vines that add texture to his panels. His method of painting and incising on wet gesso indicates that the final drawing and painting of a retablo must have been rapid, as in painting true frescos, before the gesso had dried. His work was spontaneous, uncorrected and almost abstract. His figures are willowy, with broad cheekbones, almond eyes and long, slender noses. They suggest an effort to express visually the ascetic and mystic qualities of saintliness and not corporeal humanity.

The chance finding of a document among archdiocesan archives led to the identification of the santero of this calligraphic style and also to his relationship with a long line of historic New Mexico figures, reaching back to 1625 and forward to our own times. For convenience the first sources are given here in chronological order:

"It will be nine years since there came into [New Mexico] in search of mines, three Flemings, citizens of this city of Mexico, named Juan Fresco, Juan Descalzo and Rodrigo Lorenzo, very honest men of entire truth and good example. They found many ore-bodies, made many assays, got out silver — as we all saw — and came back to this New

Spain, where they bought tools and other necessary articles and got a miner and a refiner. They returned a second time. The day the news reached Santa Fe that these Flemings were returning to work mines, that same night the Spanish set fire to the workshops in which they were to treat the ore . . . By this is seen their depraved temper, and that it troubles them, since they are enemies of silver, that others should mine it."[1]

According to Fray Angelico Chavez, Juan Fresco first came to New Mexico in 1617 and returned with equipment with the wagon train of Benavides in 1625. His name seems to have been Jan Frishz, hispanicized to Fresco and later on to Fresquí, Fresquís and then to the modern form, Fresquez. In spite of the antimining episode, Fresco stayed in New Mexico. His son, Juan, who died in 1667, had sons who escaped to El Paso in 1680 and returned with the reconquest. They are mentioned in the accounts of the Conquistadora confraternity in 1686 as "Francisco Fresquez paid his dues for himself and for his wife with one sheep and one ewe a year old, each head worth one peso, they are two pesos; . . . Ambrosio Fresquez paid his dues with some small shoes valued at two pesos, for himself and his wife."[2] They were among the settlers at the new town of Santa Cruz by 1703. Ambrosio had a son, Joseph, who had two sons, Diego and Joseph, and a daughter, Gertrudis. Francisco, married to Maria Ortíz, had a son, Pedro, who had two wives, Micaela de Archuleta and Clara Granillo.

Because the early records of marriages and baptisms at Santa Cruz de la Cañada are missing, we lack a connecting link in Fresquís genealogy. Pedro Antonio Fresquís, the santero, was baptized at Santa Cruz on October 29, 1749. His parents were Christóbal Fresquís and Augustina Vigil; the godparents were Antonio Martín and Manuela Bargas and the priest was Father Manuel Sopeña. Unfortunately, the padre neglected to name the grandparents as so often happened in colonial records. Therefore it is not clear whether Christóbal was a grandson of the first Joseph Fresquís or of Pedro, or, indeed, a son of either of these men. In any case he was a fourth or fifth generation descendant of Jan Frishz — Juan Fresco — the Fleming. All persons named Fresquez in New Mexico today are from the same family. The name is so distinctive in being non-Spanish that it is easily noticed; it is not common in New Mexico. Manuela Bargas was a daughter of Sebastián de Vargas who was recorded as a "maestro" in the rebuilding of San Miguel chapel at Santa Fe in 1710 when he forged iron spikes for its woodwork. The Fresquís family was connected by marriage with the Martín Serranos, the Garcia de Noriegas, the Miera y Pachecos, the

[1]Zarate de Salmerón, Fray Geronimo. "Relación de Todas las Cosas en el Nuevo Mexico, 1538–1626," quoted in Benavides Memorial of 1634, fn. 12, p. 227.
[2]Fray Angelico Chavez, *Our Lady of the Conquest,* Santa Fe, 1948, p. 69.

Ortízes, Tenorio de Albas and Beitias (now spelled Abeyta), all prominent New Mexicans of the 17th and 18th centuries.[3]

The document which led to identification of Fresquís with the Calligraphic Santero is an obscure note, as follows:

I received a note from R. P. Fray Teodoro Alcina; he said that D. Pedro Fresques, a neighbor of las Truchas in the jurisdiction of la Cañada, has worked as an act of devotion on various material projects of the said church and in the chapels of Las Truchas and of the Lord of Esquipulas without having received any material recompense whatsoever. Furthermore, he had been much praised for his zeal by the Lord Visitors who came here previously. Being at present aged and infirm he prays for the privilege of burial, for himself and also his family, in the burial grounds adjacent to the said chapel. Depending upon the decision of the Parroco, if he would concede another favor, that of making outside cemeteries, and exhort the faithful on the matter of their maintenance . . .

Ortega
March 20, 1831,
Santa Fe[4]

Fray Alcina had been in New Mexico since 1793 and was then stationed at Santa Cruz. He had seen local opposition to burial in outside graveyards and was passing on a request for this then-unpopular custom as well as a request for gratuitous interment of the Fresquís family (Ref. Sec. IV-A). There is nothing in this memorandum that refers to locally made santos, which were dimly viewed by the seculars from Durango. Fresquís, however, may well have worked on construction or woodcarving for the church fabrics, or even, like the rest of the men of his community, helped to repair roofs.

Association of residence at las Truchas and the calligraphic altar screens at the old las Truchas church prompted a re-examination of retablos by the Calligraphic Santero. Not one was signed but three panels bore the initials, P F, in the form of an old Spanish brand mark. Two were appropriately placed on the rumps of a horse and a donkey as a brand mark would logically be. A third, inverted P F is hidden in the painted, shaggy mane of a harpy on a panel depicting St. Ignatius Loyola, lettered by the santero *"San Inacio de Nollola,"* and on the back of another small retablo the same brand mark is carved into the wood. These ciphers had been remarked earlier, but, without a clue to the meaning, had been thought to represent the private mark of the patron or customer for whom the santo was made rather than the initials of the santero. To restrict one's monogram to areas of painting depicting beasts or monsters was a sign of humility in the long existing

---

[3] AASF, Baptisms, Book 34, Box 48, Santa Cruz de la Cañada, 1730–67, and ONMF, Chavez, 1954. (See Appendix, III-A, Fresquís family.)
[4] AASF, Patentes, Book LXX, Box 4, Official Acts of Vicar Rascón, 1829–33. Melquiades Antonio Ortega was a secretary.

tradition that it was blasphemous to place the artist's name on, or with, images of holy persons. As is often the case with an accidental discovery, after the first appearance of undocumented examples, others emerge from obscurity. It is to be hoped that other initialled examples by Pedro Fresquís will be reported by owners of his work.

With the date of March 20, 1831, when Fresquís' request for burial was forwarded to Santa Fe, search in the burial records of Santa Cruz de la Cañada produced the following entry:

> Pedro Fresquís, adulto, vecino de las Truchas. En el Santuario del S^{or} d'Esquipulas, en 4 de Noviembre de 1831, por licencia del Sor Vicario General de este Territorio, Don Juan Rafael Rascón, dedio sepultura Ecclesiástica al cuerpo de Pedro Fresquís difunto, Recibio los S^{mos} Sacramentos queda su cuerpo sepultado en el sementario de dicho Santuario. . . .

Fray Teodoro Alcina.[5]

So Pedro Fresquís was laid to rest in the churchyard of el Santuario de Esquipulas at el Potrero at the age of eighty-two on November 4, 1831. It is true that nothing from his hand remains today in el Santuario nor in the church of Santa Cruz de la Cañada, but this is a negative factor as the latter has been modernized and its former contents disposed of or overpainted. El Santuario at Chimayo has also had considerable renovation and removal of its earlier ornaments, a process that has continued into very recent years. Many of Fresquís' retablos are in poor condition or have been overpainted. The few figures in the round by him have only been recognized as his after the removal of both secondary tempera and oil painting, when his original painted surfaces were exposed. As gesso and water soluble paints are fragile, it is not surprising that Fresquís' santos have suffered more damage than those by later santeros of the 19th century. His have had more years in which to be affected by time, weather and the "improvements" of men.

The Rosario chapel at Santa Fe was licensed by the Bishop of Durango in 1806, "el Ilustrisimo Señor Obispo Dn. Francisco Grabiel d'Olivares y Benito." Before extensive alterations to the chapel in 1915, it was small with the main door facing south and the sanctuary on the north of the building, supposedly completed in the winter of 1708–09. The chapel and its surrounding cemetery stand on the site where de Vargas encamped the returned settlers in 1693 while he and his soldiers fought the Indians entrenched in the Governor's Palace on the Santa Fe plaza. After stiff resistance the Indians were dislodged. Their surrender allowed the Spanish to occupy the defensible Palace while they undertook the rebuilding of Santa Fe. The statue of Our Lady of the Rosary, or la Conquistadora, which is thought to have been brought to Santa Fe by Benavides, carried to El Paso by the refugee Spaniards in 1680 and returned with de Vargas and the re-

---

[5] AASF, Burials, 34, Box 25, Santa Cruz, 1795–1833, p. 198, verso.

settlers in 1693, had awaited the outcome of the battle for possession of Santa Fe with women and children at the camp. The statue was lodged in the Palace until the north chapel of the rebuilt parroquia was completed soon after 1714. It is still in this chapel. It is claimed that the statue has been taken on a yearly pilgrimage to de Vargas' campsite since 1712 with due ceremonial observances.

Unfortunately for this popular legend there is no evidence that there was any chapel at Rosario cemetery, the old campsite, before 1806. There is also the historical record that, after the prominent citizen, Nicolas Ortíz III, was killed by Comanches at San Antonio Mountain in 1769, Governor Pedro de Mendinueta paid a visit of condolence to the widow. During the conversation she said that such calamities occurred because every other Christian country had a patron to protect it but that New Mexico had none. Upon reflection the Governor decided to hold a function in honor of Our Lady of the Rosary in 1770 and did so at his own expense. In the next year relatives of the Ortíz family and other citizens subscribed to a similar function.

By collection of public alms and election of officers of the confraternity, the fiesta continued for some years. When Dominguez saw it in 1776 it was held in October. He said that the statue went in procession with the Governor, clergy, garrison and citizens "through the streets" with no mention of the de Vargas campsite, nor of the statue remaining away from the parroquia for a nine day novena (Dominguez, p. 240). In time the observance in honor of la Conquistadora was moved to the first Sunday after Corpus Christi without relationship to the date of de Vargas' final recapturing of Santa Fe in December 1693. The other Santa Fe function supposedly in commemoration of the Spanish reconquest, the modern Fiesta, is held on Labor Day weekend and also has no connection with the reconquest date but recalls the day of August 31, 1769, when Comanches killed Nicolas Ortíz III. The antiquity of the Santa Fe Fiesta, although claimed to stem from 1712, is more obviously from 1770 with many years of lapse in the observance.[6] During the lifetime of Antonio José Ortíz and his children, devotions to la Conquistadora prospered; he paid part of the cost of Rosario chapel when he died in 1806.

---

[6] *El Palacio,* Vol. VII No. 3, Aug. 15, 1919, p. 54: a preamble on the history of the Santa Fe Fiesta, noting that the novena in honor of la Conquistadora took place on the first Sunday after Corpus Christi but: "It is this year, for the first time in more than a century, that the great patriotic Fiesta proclaimed by the Marquis de la Peñuela in 1712, will be revived and will be made an occasion of transcendent historic interest. A three day's Fiesta has been planned, Thursday–Saturday, September 11–13th. All of Santa Fe's civic, patriotic and fraternal organizations, as well as state, county and city authorities, will participate." An account of the Fiesta in *El Palacio,* V. VII Nos. 5/6, Sept. 30, 1919, noted that "there had been others" naming the summer of 1883 when a "Tertio Millenial" celebration was held, and again in 1913 and 1914.

Against the north wall of Rosario chapel's sanctuary a wooden collateral was built above the altar with a niche at the center. The height and width of this niche were adequate to contain the statue of la Conquistadora before recent alterations of the pedestal. The altar screen was planned as a frame for the statue, without images on it. The panels were painted in sage green and flame pink with daisies and feathers. Naive marbleized pillars divided the panels; on the tabernacle door was a finely stylized crucifix as characteristic of the work of Pedro Fresquís as a signature. Two cartouches were painted at the sides of the tabernacle like those on the stone retable of la Castrense.

In later years the love of novelty inspired putting several layers of wallpaper over the painted gesso panels. Removal of some of these exposed fragments of the date, 1809, in the lower right panel.

While the works of New Mexico santeros have been despised by most of the people and clergy of New Mexico for some generations, and it has been claimed by certain historical writers on the region that the rustic folk artist was never accepted by the upper class group of the capital city of Santa Fe, it is quite evident that the native santero, in his day, was as much admired and employed by Santa Fe *ricos* as by the rural villagers.

Santero altar screens have partly survived in spite of modern vandalism in the Santa Fe chapels of San Miguel and Rosario, and were described at length in the parroquia by Dominguez, although without a clue to the style or name of the santero. It is interesting to know that the wealthy Ortíz family commissioned an altar screen by Pedro Fresquís of las Truchas for the Rosario chapel in 1809; whatever later generations may think of his composition it was evidently admired by the donors.

Fresquís had been assumed to be an early 19th century santero from his own dated works (1809 and 1827) and from tree-ring dated panels which gave a bark date of 1814 (the year that the tree was cut down) and from other, plus-X, readings falling between 1809 and 1818. In the case of boards that dated in the 1770s, it had been suspected that Fresquís, like others of his time, had reused an old piece of prepared wood. It is now established that Fresquís was working in the later 18th century.

Don Juan Ladrón de Guevara, from the diocese of Durango, visited the hill town of Truchas in 1818 and inspected another Rosario chapel there. He found a painted wooden retable with a bulto of the Patroness. Although this 18th century church had the catastrophe of having its eastern facade and tower collapse early in this century, and was then fitted with sheet iron roofing, it still exists. The church is no longer in use for Masses since a new one was built. The painted altar screen, with a boldly brushed inscription above the panels, "Abe Maxia Puxísima," is clearly the work of Pedro Fresquís. On the south wall is a small side altar, also by Fresquís, one of whose four panels depicts the Mass of St. Gregory and which is lettered "Sʳ Sⁿ Gregorio." The subject was never painted by other New Mexican santeros. The panel shows

Figure 190: The Martyrdom of Santa Apolonia, Pedro Antonio Fresquís.

St. Gregory in profile before an altar on which is a crucifix with a larger crucifix floating above.

Fresquís also painted two exquisite panels for the chapel that represent his style at its peak of perfection; they were gifts of one Dolores de Oliva (Appendix III-A, Inventories, 1818 and 1826).

Oldtimers say that two more side altars were destroyed when the walls fell in, but how they looked they cannot say. The hazards of structural neglect, severe winter weather, vandalism and the innocent fondness for cheap, modern decoration all make the ultimate fate of Rosario church at las Truchas and the remaining works of Fresquís therein a sad uncertainty.

In the little chapel of San Pedro y San Pablo at Chamita there is another small retable by Fresquís. Although it is in fair condition it has been "improved" by some local volunteer who overpainted the delicately brushed outlines of Fresquís in heavy black. The original crest at the top of the Trinity as the traditional three identical persons, a favorite subject of the santero, was deliberately removed by a priest in 1958 and is now in private hands.

There is good reason to suspect that Pedro Fresquís may have painted the heavy, hand-hewn altar screens in the church of San José de Gracia at las Trampas before the existing paintings were done. This probably can not be proven or disproven without removal of at least part of the present images. The inventory of San José de Gracia in 1776 says of the interior, "The only altar in this chapel is the high altar. Its furnishing consists of a board niche painted and spattered with what they call talco here (it is like tinsel, but very flexible). In this niche there is a middle-sized image in the round of Lord St. Joseph."[7]

By 1818, however, the inventory described the high altar as surmounted by an image of "Nuestra Señora de la Purisima" and six images. In the transepts were altars with screens on which were painted San Lorenzo, San Felipe de Jesus, San Antonio de Padua, Our Lady of Sorrows and "Señor Santiago." In the nave were other altar screens painted with the Holy Trinity, Our Lady of Carmel and the souls, and San Juan Nepomuceno.[8] All of those subjects are in the same places today, but painted by a later santero. The only existing altar and screen not mentioned in 1818 is that of St. Francis of Assisi, with the Franciscan shield and several bultos, which backs the Penitente morada built on the outside of the church (Ref. Sec. IV-B). Apparently, the Third Order did not then have an altar at las Trampas.

Although the former adobe main altar has been replaced by a wooden one, it is possible to examine the rear wall of the sanctuary behind the present painted retable. On the wall are the remains of

---

[7]Dominguez, p. 100. The statue was made by Bernardo Miera y Pacheco, still in the church at las Trampas.

[8]AASF, Accounts, Book LXII, Box 5, II, June 8, 1818.

painting, a dark red background surrounding a blank space, probably where the "board niche" mentioned by Dominguez was placed. Small designs and flowers are scattered over the red areas, and the glitter of micaceous earth (talco) is visible in places in spite of extensive damages from old leaks in the roof. Painting on adobe plaster will of necessity be coarser than painting on smooth gesso on wood panels; the sanctuary may have been the work of Fresquís. By inference, he may also have painted the pre-1818 wooden altar screens. Given the erosions of water damage of sixty years or more in the church, it is logical that the retables were ready for repainting after our Civil War. The existing paintings in San José de Gracia were done by an emigrant from Sonora named José Gonzales soon after 1862, and are characteristic of popular Mexican painting of the period (Appendix III-A, José Gonzales).

Fresquís must have referred to prints and the illustrations in Hispanic missals for some of his renderings. He was prolific, and represented the favorite images of his period such as Anthony, Barbara, Gertrude, Joseph, Raymond Nonnatus, Rita and Santiago, the Archangels, the Crucifix, Veronica's image and the identical Trinity, as well as the Virgin of Guadalupe, and also uncommon subjects such as St. Athenogenes. St. Apollonia, St. Colette, Sts. Processus and Martiniano, St. Agnes, the Mass of St. Gregory, Christ entering Jerusalem on Palm Sunday astride a donkey, and several allegorical compositions.

Pedro Antonio Fresquís was a true folk artist as well as a truly New Mexican figure whose family had come to the colony 124 years before he was born. They figured in the prosperity as well as the hardships of the New Mexicans, surviving the Pueblo rebellion, and were among the founders of two officially authorized new villages, Santa Cruz and las Truchas. Fresquís disproves the statements of some historians that New Mexico santeros were poor, ignorant, illiterate nobodies. Perhaps some of them were, but some, as recorded, were Franciscans, or newcomers from Spain or New Spain, and still others native-born colonials, well known and respected in their time.

In spite of his limited materials and technical knowledge, Fresquís found a personal way of presenting Christian mysteries and symbols in an original style which does not seem to have been imitated by later santeros.

Figure 191: Christ Entering Jerusalem on Palm Sunday, Pedro Fresquís. (Private owner)

Figure 192: The Crucifixion, with incised designs on black field, Pedro Fresquís. (Courtesy Museum of History and Technology, Smithsonian Institution)

APPENDIX

The first Joseph Fresquís had two known sons, Diego, and Joseph who married Polonia Vigil in 1730. For the lack of the earlier record books, and the omissions of later records, it is uncertain if Christóbal, the father of Pedro Antonio Fresquís, the santero, was also a son of the first Joseph, or of Pedro, the other great-grandson of Jan Frishz, whose descendants, if any, have not as yet been found in Santa Cruz books. On the other hand, Christóbal might have been a son of Diego Fresquís or even of the second Joseph. Youths married young in that time, and old widowers took young wives.

Juan de Avila Fresquís is another man probably contemporary with Christóbal, but whether they were brothers is a matter of speculation. In a lengthy series of documents concerning a dispute over title to Santa Cruz property in 1801 there are references to the Fresquís family and to some of their relatives by marriage, but, unfortunately, neither Christóbal nor Pedro Antonio is mentioned. Josef Truxillo and Mariano Truxillo appeared before Alcalde Manuel García de la Mora on June 25, 1801, at Santa Cruz de la Cañada, claiming title to a house on the plaza and a ranch on the Santa Cruz river, by virtue of the gift of these by their grandmother, Maria Tapia, to Josef's father, Francisco Truxillo. They stated that Adauto Isidro Fresquís now occupied said properties, and demanded to see the will or other papers by which Adauto could prove his claims to possession.

Adauto then appeared before the Alcalde stating that the Truxillos were misinformed by something that they had read or heard, and that he had the correct and necessary documents. His proof of title, he said, was the royal letter of gift, which the Truxillos mistakenly called a will, from Diego Romero to his stepson, Mateo Truxillo, which the litigants were hunting for.

Alcalde García de la Mora noted that he saw the eight documents brought by Adauto Fresquís, "all in good order" on July 11, 1801. Josef Truxillo insisted that a will by Maria Tapia existed, that one Juan Vigil had seen it two years before, with original titles to the ranch and house, also itemizing such things as iron griddles, plough points, ox goads, etc. He insisted on having it produced to learn if it was indeed by Maria Tapia or by Josef Fresquís, father of Adauto. Witnesses to the claims of the Truxillos were Juan Vigil, Domingo Martín, Damian Archuleta, Pedro Chacón, Nicolas Archuleta, etc. Most of these were relatives of the Fresquís by marriage.

Having received a copy of Josef Fresquís' will in favor of Adauto, his son, the Truxillos filed a complaint that it was faulty, that the house was described as on the plaza of la Cañada, but that the ranch was without location. Therefore Adauto was without proper proof of claim

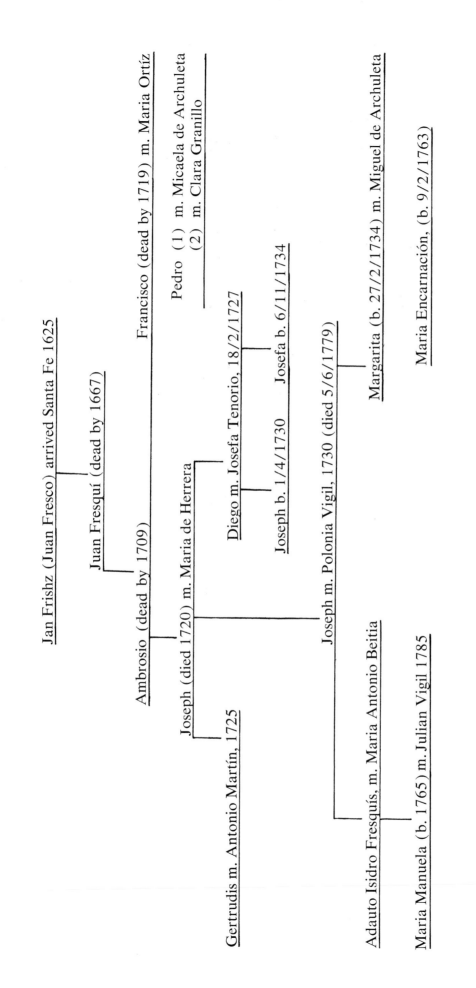

Jan Frishz (Juan Fresco) arrived Santa Fe 1625

Juan Fresquí (dead by 1667)

Francisco (dead by 1719) m. Maria Ortíz

Pedro (1) m. Micaela de Archuleta
(2) m. Clara Granillo

Ambrosio (dead by 1709)

Diego m. Josefa Tenorio, 18/2/1727

Josefa b. 6/11/1734

Joseph (died 1720) m. Maria de Herrera

Joseph b. 1/4/1730

Joseph m. Polonia Vigil, 1730 (died 5/6/1779)

Margarita (b. 27/2/1734) m. Miguel de Archuleta

Maria Encarnación, (b. 9/2/1763)

Gertrudis m. Antonio Martín, 1725

Adauto Isidro Fresquís, m. Maria Antonio Beitia

Maria Manuela (b. 1765) m. Julian Vigil 1785

338

III-A

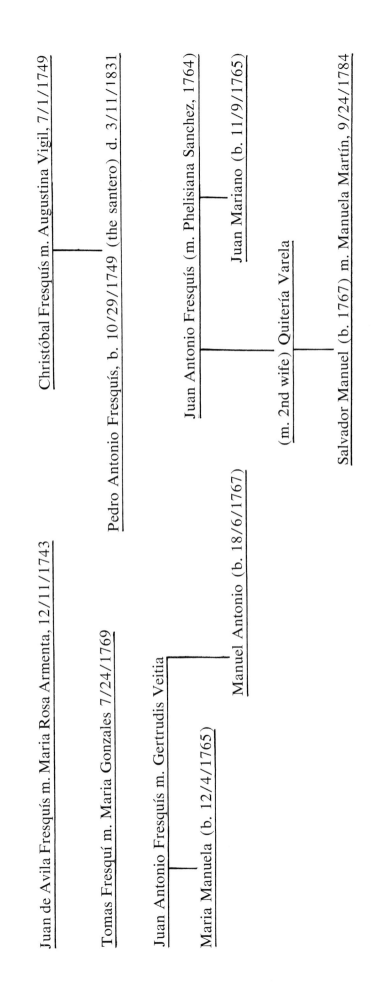

Christóbal Fresquís m. Augustina Vigil, 7/1/1749

Pedro Antonio Fresquís, b. 10/29/1749 (the santero) d. 3/11/1831

Juan Antonio Fresquís (m. Phelisiana Sanchez, 1764)

Juan Mariano (b. 11/9/1765)

(m. 2nd wife) Quitería Varela

Salvador Manuel (b. 1767) m. Manuela Martín, 9/24/1784

Juan de Avila Fresquís m. Maria Rosa Armenta, 12/11/1743

Tomas Fresquí m. Maria Gonzales 7/24/1769

Juan Antonio Fresquís m. Gertrudis Veitia

Manuel Antonio (b. 18/6/1767)

Maria Manuela (b. 12/4/1765)

to it. (Adauto died in 1830, "aged more than ninety years." His burial entry, dated April 14, gives place of burial as Quarteles, in the cemetery. This placita is about halfway between Santa Cruz plaza and Chimayo and was probably his residence and location of the disputed ranch.)

In a later appearance Adauto stated that he knew nothing of the alleged will of Maria Tapia nor had he ever seen it, but that his papers, in his possession, proved original title to the ranch; as for the house, first in documents of Juan de Dios Sandobal Martines, and secondly in the document of Miguel Sandobal Martines, deceased, which sold the lands to Mateo Truxillo. Then Francisco, Manuela and Alonso Truxillo and other heirs had all sold their shares to Josef Fresquís, father of Adauto. Other documents confirming letters of royal donation owned by Adauto were given by Captain General Gerbasio Cruzat y Gongora, "sixty eight years ago. Our deceased father had them for forty six years." Cruzat y Gongora was governor from 1731 to 1736. Adauto's reference to this governor makes it clear that his father was the son of the first Joseph and Maria de Herrera and not the Joseph born to Diego Fresquís and Josefa Tenorio in 1730. Adauto's mention of "Our deceased father" indicates the existence of brothers or sisters, but whether these were only his sister, Margarita, or included one or more brothers is left unsolved. Adauto himself must have been born in the 1730s. By the time of his death, in 1830, and that of Pedro Antonio Fresquís in 1831, marriage and baptismal books for the Santa Cruz region were filled with entries of later Fresquís people, all descended from old Jan Frishz, and to some degree related to Pedro the santero.

INVENTORIES

Dominguez noted the village of las Truchas, but made no mention of a chapel there. The visitor representing the Bishop of Durango in 1818, Don Juan Francisco de Castañiza, was Don Juan Bautista Ladrón del Niño de Guevara. He noted that the chapel of Our Lady of the Rosary of las Truchas, an auxiliary of Santa Cruz de la Cañada, was nine leagues distant from la Cañada. License for it had first been granted by Bishop Tamarón on June 17, 1760, renewed on August 31, 1787 by Bishop Esteban Lorenzo de Tristán, and on September 6, 1796 by Bishop Francisco Grabiel de Olivares y Benito, and again by the same, "in virtue of having all necessary furnishings" on February 23, 1805.

De Guevara said that the chapel was twenty-two by seven varas with an altar of painted wood, a bulto of Our Lady of Rosario and ten retablos. In addition there were the following:

Item   A curtain of white gauze given by Gertrudis Cordova
Item   2 silver cruets paid by Señor Zubiare Lopez for the making
Item   2 bultos and two retablos given by Dolores de Oliva
Item   1 bulto of San Antonio given by a devotee
Item   1 image of N.S. de Guadalupe, retablo
Item   1 crucifix
Item   1 manual given by a devotee and a little table

The interim priest of Santa Cruz, Cura Correa, told the visitor, Don Ladrón de Guevara, that there was one Mass yearly at las Truchas, "with enough grief to him," and that out of the "150 Moradores" (residents) Don Gregorio Sandoval and other men over 80 years old would leave the chapel while he (Correa) was explaining the word of God to them, and revert to their ferocious insubordination by which means they expressed their contradiction of the commands of their priest in the same way that they had failed to obey the orders of Bishop Tristán.[1]

More than seven leagues of bad road lie between las Truchas and

---

[1] Bishop Esteban Lorenzo de Tristán of Durango, around 1790–91, never visited New Mexico.

Santa Cruz. It is not only the aged, pregnant women, and children who do not come [to Santa Cruz], but in good weather hardly two or four, of the well and strong come to hear Mass at Santa Cruz, and in the winter, the snows being so thick and deep in this province, there is no doubt that none present themselves on feast days in compliance with precepts of the church.

In order to save such miserable poor folk the Lord Visitor gave his attention with all the fullness of his commiseration and piety, before going on to other serious matters, the more to emphasize the fact that all of the foregoing was criminal indolence, undermining the spiritual structure of the Church that was planted in this territory... the incumbent Cura Correa should, together with his superiors, exert all of their zeal for the best service, honor and glory of God and the spiritual betterment of his Faithful.[2]

In 1826 the same main altar and screen, the bulto of the Patroness, and the few furnishings and vestments at las Truchas church were noted, including a bell which then had a clapper. Additions were:

Item 1 Santo Niño medal
Item 1 altar screen and five images
Item 1 new missal
Item 1 censer of iron
Item 6 metal candlesticks
Item 1 "arco"[3]
Item 2 small altar bells
Item 1 door, with key, to chapel[4]
Item 1 lock and key
Item 1 "sabana labrada"[5]
Item 2 rosaries of silver
Item 1 rosary of crystal
Item 1 pearl necklace
Item 2 dresses of the Virgin
Item 1 blue cloak of the same
Item 1 altar frontal of "Indiana"[6]
Item 2 varas of lace
Item ½ ounce of gold galoon
        (Ref. AASF Accounts, Book LXIV, July, 1826)

The 1818 inventory at las Trampas makes these additions to that of 1776 (Dominguez'):

Item 26 mirrors which serve as candle sconces

---

[2] AASF. Accounts, Book LXII, Box 5, II, 1818.
[3] *Arco,* arch-shaped framework which was covered with cloth, flowers, paper, etc., as a movable canopy for one or more images.
[4] Locks and keys in New Mexico were more often remarked for their absence.
[5] Another example of embroidered cottons, appearing in the region as the 19th century grew older.
[6] Notation of printed cotton or calico coming into use.

Item   1 lamp of wood with metal vase [7]
Item   1 silver spoon
Item   1 regular copper censer
Item   2 benches
Item   1 table
Item   1 table with two drawers, one with iron lock and key,
         the other without
Item   1 custodia and cup of silver gilt, new
Item   1 good missal
Item   1 chair

(Ref. AASF, Accounts, Book LXII, Box 5, II, 1818)

JOSÉ GONZALES

According to W. S. Stallings, Jr., Gregorio Leyba of las Trampas told him that he could remember that a man from Sonora came and painted the retablos in the church when Leyba was 19 or 20 years old and not yet married. Leyba died during the winter of 1949–50 and was said to have been 100 years old. He said that the Sonoran married a local girl and lived there until he moved to Trinidad, Colorado, to work on the new railroad then under construction.[1] If Gregorio Leyba was 100 at his death this would have placed the painted altar screens about 1869. The railroad was being laid about 1878, allowing nearly ten years for the Sonoran to live at las Trampas.

Another resident, Ely Leyba, said that two santeros, José Manuel Montolla and Juan Montolla, "left Mexico in 1587 and returned there in 1590," having painted the wooden retables at las Trampas after earlier works of art painted on the adobe walls had been spoiled by the leaking roof.[2]

These dates of course are historically absurd in view of the well-documented origins of las Trampas, but even today the people there like to claim that their church is 300 years old. The name of Manuel Montolla, however, may still be seen carved on the beam that supports the choir loft, and is probably that of a donor to the chapel. It is also

---

[7]This lantern of wooden slabs, covered with gesso and painted in tempera with santero style flowers, still has one of the original selenite panes; the "vase of metal" is of heavy, cast bronze engraved with bands of small hunting figures, animals, and trees, of 17th century style. It was never intended as an oil reservoir but is the container for a set of graduated weights, which was simply used as a lamp after its weights, as well as its lid, hinge, and hasp, had been lost. The lantern and "vase" are now in the collections of the Museum of New Mexico.

[1]Unpublished mss. by W. S. Stallings, Jr., at the Taylor Museum, Colorado Springs.

[2]*New Mexico Magazine,* V. 11, June, 1933, p. 19.

true that there were painted walls, at least in the sanctuary, in the early decades of San José de Gracia's existence.

In 1961 the custodian of the church, Telesfor Lopez, said that he was born in 1889, and that he had been told many times by his grandfather that the painted retables were done by a santero, José Gonzales, from Guaymas, Sonora, about 1883. Sr. Lopez repeated that he, of course, was not yet born, but that he had heard of Gonzales so often that he could not forget the name. He also said that Gonzales had moved away to work on the new railroad and did not go back to las Trampas. Lopez added that his grandfather had often impressed upon him the fact that the white horse ridden by Santiago on a panel in the west transept was painted from a very fine white horse owned by his grandfather. The latter also had presented the church with the set of rustic, wooden framed French lithographs of the Stations of the Cross, still in place, which he had brought from Santa Fe by wagon. The style of these prints and frames suggests the 1880s. The costume of the painted Santiago suggests the fancy Mexican uniforms of the period of Maximilian, 1864.

What marks the las Trampas panels as the work of someone from the outside world rather than that of a native-born santero of the time is not one but several strikingly foreign elements: use of oil paints at that date, and the extensive use of stencils on all of the brightly colored borders. Only freehand painting was done in New Mexico then while Gonzales' freehand work was limited to his figures and marbleized backgrounds. His personal coloring of hair and eyes in reddish brown and attempts at three dimensional realism by gray shading were also atypical of the period in New Mexico.

Thus local memory and the internal evidence of the paintings pointed to a foreign santero named José Gonzales and a post-1860 date for the present las Trampas retables. It remained for decisions of the Ecumenical Councils at Rome to expose positive evidence of the existence of José Gonzales and the years in which he lived and worked in the region of las Trampas.

In the parish of Picuris, the expanding population had moved far up the Santa Barbara river by 1831. The people of the high upland farms requested permission to build a new chapel dedicated to San Juan Nepomuceno (St. John Nepomuk), at Llano Largo, nine miles from Picuris. License was granted on February 13, 1832. The chapel was small and simple with few windows. Until recent years it contained a few old bultos and a single altar screen of thick, hand-hewn slabs painted in oils, with borders of flowers, crude, marbleized backgrounds and images similar in style to those at las Trampas, although smaller and more delicate in drawing. A wooden altar table with the usual altar coverings stood against the retable until the new placement of altars was decreed, facing the congregation. This reversal of old custom in small New Mexico chapels has placed the altar table against the sanctuary rail, or the rail has been removed, while the celebrant priest stands behind the altar with his back to the rear sanctuary wall, or whatever may be painted or hanging on it. After the Ecumenical revisions of the Mass, an inscription was exposed across the bottom of the retable and just above the floor. It is lettered in black on dark red paint as follows:

Este corateral lo pinto José de Gracia Gonzales/ a costa de Dñ. José Dolores Duran, Dicha pintura/ se concluida hoy 20 de Julio año de 1864." (José de Gracia Gonzales painted this altar screen at the expense of Don José Dolores Duran; the said painting was completed today, July 20, in the year of 1864.)

The inscription is in excellent condition because it was protected from brooms and cleaning mops by the altar table until 1965. Whether or not it remains so in the future is doubtful since the space from the retable to the altar is barely two feet. The visible part of the painted altar screen has, unfortunately, been spoiled by a layer of shiny white enamel paint applied around the figures by a well-intentioned amateur, possibly to brighten up the panels. The images and uncovered decorative borders are still visible and identifiable with those at las Trampas. The inscription proves that José Gonzales was working in the Picuris parish area in 1864. Whether he did the las Trampas retables in the same year or close to it remains to be discovered.

The dedication of two chapels in northern New Mexico to San Juan Nepomuceno in 1832, at Llano de San Juan and El Rito Colorado, may be explained by the introduction of special indulgences to congregations who celebrated his feast day "in a special manner." These indulgences had been granted from Rome in 1828, had reached Durango in 1829 and Santa Fe in the same year. Such news was read aloud from the pulpit and evidently inspired dedication of chapels to this non-Franciscan saint in the two new communities.[3]

The oldest of the present churches at Arroyo Seco, Taos County, also contains a retable by José Gonzales in his coarse folk style. It is probable that he made another for a now-vanished chapel at Llano de Santa Barbara, also east of Peñasco, since it was built at the end of the Civil War by José Dolores Duran, who is recorded as having paid for the San Juan Nepomuceno chapel altar screen in 1864. The Duran chapel is said to have been furnished at the expense of the owner-builder, and contained altar cloths and other vestments, some of which are now in the collections of the Museum of New Mexico. However, the building and its possible painted screen have disappeared (Personal communication from Mrs. Laura Martinez Mullins, granddaughter of José Dolores Duran).

As might be expected Gonzales did not travel from Sonora to remote las Trampas without stopping in Santa Fe. A now dim photograph of the interior of the chapel of Guadalupe shows two pedestals before the altar, recognizably painted with figures by Gonzales. This was undoubt-

---

[3] AASF Patentes, 1829, LXIX, LXXXXII, XI.

Plate 17: *Nra. Señora del Carmen, Madre de Pecadores,* Our Lady of Carmel, Mother of Sinners, as lettered by the santero Pedro Fresquís. Vatican collections. (Plates 11 through 17, Photographs by Eliot Porter)

III-A

Plate 18: Our Lady of Immaculate Conception by Pedro Fresquís.

Figure 194: Overall view of altar screen by Gonzales, recently partly overpainted.

edly done after the arrival of Bishop Lamy, to judge by other gimcrack ornaments, and before the remodeling of the chapel by Father de Fouri after 1881. Two fragments of a now dismantled altar screen from the region of Las Vegas, San Miguel County, also by Gonzales, have recently come to the Museum of New Mexico. He may have done them in his later years as they are crudely put together with commercial cotton cloth and cut nails.

Gonzales' legible script shows that he had learned to write if not to paint academically. His transition from santero to railroad construction laborer is typical of the impacts of progress and cash wages on the old patterns of living in New Mexico.

THE SANTERO MOLLENO

The rejection of the three-dimensional plane and of realism by folk artists of New Mexico was, perhaps, carried to the ultimate limit by a santero whose name was, according to an inscription on the reverse of one of his panels, Molleno. Before this inscription was recorded local collectors had dubbed the santero "the chile painter" because many of his panels contain red spacefillers that suggest ripe chile peppers. On the other hand some of the same santero's panels have the same forms colored brown, blue or green and still others have no such forms in them. Local folk painters used leaves and flowers as ornaments but not edible vegetables. The "chile" forms were simply naive simplifications of the architectural acanthus leaves found on many 18th century prints from Mexico that were often the source of santero compositions.

Local folksay also has it that the santero was named Molino, or Monero, or Manilla or Monillo, and it has been argued that there is no such Spanish patronym as Molleno. This is true, but one has only to review the corruption of other proper names and words during the New Mexican colonial period and later to realize that the Spanish name, Moreno, might easily have been converted into Molleno. Both citizens and Franciscans named Moreno were in New Mexico in the 18th century, and might have served as godparents to a boy born "de padre no conocido" and given him their name, as often happened. Except for the inscription mentioned above, no documentary evidence in the form of vital statistics or of business transactions has been found; the person of the santero Molleno remains a shadow, but it is suggestive that recent folksay has offered names so closely akin to that of the inscription of 1845.

If Molleno the man is still indefinite, his prolific works indicate a long career and considerable popularity in northern New Mexico. From his few dated panels, from others dated by their tree-rings and from inventories, we know that he was working between 1804 and 1845. His earlier panels were competent if more reflective of canvases from New

Plate 19: San José by Molleno
in his early style.

Spain than are his later, original examples. At first Molleno, like the 18th century Novice painter, employed colored backgrounds but in time took to using the white gesso surface of his panels to set off his figures, which he drew with increasing brevity and assurance. They became literally shorthand symbols of images, often with triangular heads. As time went on, Molleno seems to have acquired the optical ailment suffered by some other painters, of whom Renoir is a prominent example: the inability to register cool colors. The palette is weighted by the red and yellow range, as were Molleno's later panels. His middle period was marked by a refreshing use of floral spacefillers, with balanced areas of warm and cool color.

With one Franciscan, Father José Benito Pereyro, Molleno must have had contacts while he was working in the Taos region. The first license for the auxiliary chapel of "Nuestro Padre San Francisco en el puesto de las Trampas" was given September 20, 1803. This was present-day Ranchos de Taos, three leagues from Taos Pueblo, and not to be confused with San José de las Trampas, south of Picuris. At Ranchos de Taos fields had been cultivated in the 18th century, but Indian raids had discouraged settlement until the turn of the century when settlers requested a chapel for their new plaza. There is little record of construction of the chapel or of its completion (in spite of claims that it was built in 1710 or 1778) until 1815 when one Ignacio Duran petitioned the provincial *Custos,* Fray Isidoro Barcenilla, on behalf of himself and his neighbors, to receive the ministrations of Fray Benito Pereyro in the plazas of San Francisco de las Trampas and of San Francisco de Paula. For this service the residents bound themselves to pay in grains as had been commanded by the King, Carlos IV.[1] Fray Pereyro had served at other missions and as *Custos* before he was assigned to San Gerónimo de Taos in 1810. The petition of Ignacio Duran makes it clear that Pereyro was not previously in charge of the Ranchos chapel but received permission to add it to his parish soon after, for in 1816 he was given license to bury parishioners there.

In 1818 our first known inventory of San Francisco de los Ranchos de Taos was made for the visitor Guevara. The ornaments were few and briefly noted:

"One altar screen with an image of the Lord of Esquipulas,
"The high altar with two figures in the round,
"One altar screen dedicated to the Patriarch St. Joseph,
 and an image of the Holy Patriarch."

The high altar screen with its canvases from New Spain is still in place, and so is that of Esquipulas in the east transept with the crucifix and two large statues, all of the latter in the style of Molleno. This altar screen is the largest left in New Mexico with about 425 square feet of surface. It has eight panels in three tiers; at the top are the Franciscan

Plate 20: Our Lady of Sorrows by Molleno in his middle style. (Plates 19, 20, photographs by Eliot Porter)

---

[1] AASF, L. D. 1815, No. 21.

emblem, Christ at the Column and Christ Bearing the Cross; in the center are Our Lady of Talpa, St. Lawrence and St. Polycarpius. Below, St. Francis, the patron, and St. Anthony of Padua flank the niche containing the three statues. Small, twisted versions of Salomonic pillars, so handsomely carved only a few years before at Acoma, Laguna and at San Miguel chapel in Santa Fe, divide the panels. Their skimpiness suggests that they were made by someone unacquainted with the already out-of-date, architectural Baroque form.

Molleno was evidently still working in his early period when he used colored backgrounds and was plainly puzzled by the problems of filling such a large space. This he did with neo-Classic swags and moldings but without the decorative floral forms of his later, middle period.

The crucifix of Esquipulas has been partly overpainted, but is much like four others that bear the stamp of Molleno's style of carving and brushwork. These are, respectively, in the Santuario del Señor de Esquipulas at the Potrero de Chimayó, in the church of Cristo Rey in Santa Fe, in the mission at Santa Clara Pueblo and a fourth in the new church at San Ildefonso Pueblo. Three of these retain the original crosses with stylized wooden leaves along their sides. The cult of the Christ of Esquipulas from Guatemala was not then limited to the shrine at the healing mud springs at Chimayó.

The two large statues now with the Ranchos crucifix may have been those of the 1818 inventory noted as at the high altar. They are of the Virgin of Sorrows and of the Blessed Lydwina of Holland, an uncommon subject among local santeros.[2] Like later 19th century santeros, Molleno seems to have deliberately chosen a two-dimensional style in flat painting although he well understood carving in the round. Also, like his successors and contemporaries, he elongated his statues to give a superhuman effect. His heads are small in proportion with animated expressions and often with opened mouths, while his hands, when they have survived, have long, curving fingers. In the last quarter of the 19th century, the altar screen in the east transept was whitewashed over except for the niche and the three large figures in it. In 1953 the incumbent priest had various repairs done in the church. He inquired what might be done to clean the Molleno retable. I made tests with various solvents and found that naphtha would remove the whitewash without damage to the water-soluble paints beneath. The whitewash was removed in five days. The lower panels had been somewhat eroded by well-intentioned cleaning with wet rags. Above the level that could be reached from the floor, the paint was in good condition, as was the gesso ground. This was evenly applied in a thinner layer than was the case at San Miguel or San José at Laguna Pueblo.

When the retable had been cleaned as much as it could be, no

---

[2] "Little Dutch Girl Far From Home," José E. Espinosa in *El Palacio,* V. 61/3, March 1954.

Plate 22: Virgin of the Immaculate Conception, hollow frame construction, by Molleno.

retouching of paint and no patching were necessary. Working from the top downwards a layer of hot liquid wax was applied to the panels, cornices and pillars.

Molleno's painting of garments on statues was rich in color and detail, suggesting jeweled brocaded silks.

The altar and screen of the Patriarch St. Joseph have vanished from the west transept. In 1953 a former sacristan said that it had been bought "maybe thirty years ago by a rich American." Possibly it too was the work of Molleno, and perchance was composed of the eight unassembled panels now in the collections of the Denver Art Museum. Although smaller than those of the east transept, they are also by Molleno and include a panel of San José.

A little more speculation on Molleno's activities in the Taos region is apropos at this point. The auxiliary chapel of Our Lady of Guadalupe in Spanish Taos was first licensed from Durango in 1796–97 and by the King in 1801. As usual it was requested by the people of Spanish Taos to save them from the perils of walking three miles to the Pueblo for Mass with the attendant risk of attacks by Comanches. The 1818 inventory described an altar screen of wood painted with seven images of the Guadalupe and a statue of the same, seated on a throne. These too have vanished long ago, like the church itself, and one is free to wonder if such an extravagant imagery of the patroness was also Molleno's. Perhaps he, or whoever the santero may have been, had seen the large canvas by José de Alcibar (Mexico, 1725–1810), with its multiple scenes of the apparition which had been recently installed over the high altar in the Guadalupe Chapel in Santa Fe.

That Fray Pereyro had a long record of undertaking ornamentation of his various missions and churches is illustrated by an *aumento* or postscript to the inventory of San Geronimo church in Taos Pueblo which he made in 1815.

The Minister Father Fray José Benito Pereyro had paid for a baptismal font and blue satin dress for the Holy Virgin." . . . [Of the convent, he wrote:] Father Pereyro added to the building a porters lodge, kitchen, four doors, two windows, a balcony, he built the cloister but the Indians made the roof, he made a reception room of the old office and a storage room of the old outhouse. . . On the eighth of December I ordered the Justices of the Pueblo to break the wall of the church to place in it a niche for the (image of) Jesus of Nazareth, in the presence of the entire neighboring people who were come to hear Mass, telling them that for my part I would pay whoever did the work and would give an ax and hoe to the boy who helped. The Indians did not want to do this and the chief Indian assistant to the church told me that they did not want to. I did this at my own expense; witnesses Francisco Esteban Dominguez and Christóbal Barela will verify that I paid two pesos for the carpenter's work and four pesos for him who broke the wall.[3]

---

[3] AASF, Patentes, Book XV, Box 6, Taos, 1826–50, p. 31–33.

For all of his efforts, Father Pereyro was scathingly criticized by de Guevara during his visits of 1818, not only for his artistic improvements but for his methods of administering the sacraments, of keeping church records, for the filthy condition of his mission and his personal life. Guevara strongly recommended that Pereyro and other Franciscans be returned to their provincial headquarters; Taos was Pereyro's last post in New Mexico.[4]

In an effort to identify the santero, it was suggested that he was the Ignacio Duran of the petition of 1815 (Stallings, unpublished Mss., the Taylor Museum, Colorado Springs). The inference was drawn from an account by Pereyro of the ornamentation of the Ranchos church in which he stated that the retablos were painted from scaffolds at the expense of the incumbent Padre, of Don Ignacio Duran and other neighbors. All wooden altar screens made in New Mexico were mortised and dowelled together and keyed into the retaining wall behind them. They were then smoothed where chinks between the rough-hewn boards existed by placing strips of hide or cloth over the cracks. The whole surface was then covered with gesso and, finally, painted. Of necessity, painting was always done from scaffolds or ladders. The literal wording "these were made by" must be interpreted as meaning "these were paid for by" and not that the painting or construction was done by those named.

An inventory of 1831, quoted by Stallings (supra), gives the clue to identification of the formerly mysterious subject of the right-hand center panel; it stated that the citizens Policarpio and Lorenzo Cordova had been donors of the retablo on the Epistle side of the church.[5] At the center the panel of St. Lawrence is easily recognized by the gridiron in it, the symbol of his martyrdom. At the right is a figure in white tunic and tights studded with metal discs and holding what look like skewers. St. Polycarpius is alleged to have been a disciple of St. John the Evangelist and a bishop of the Asiatic church. During the persecutions of Marcus Aurelius, when flames failed to consume the bishop he was stabbed to death. Molleno's presentation of the martyr is original and hence unidentifiable if it were not for the recorded names of the donors. Although Policarpio is not an uncommon masculine name in New Mexico, there is a conspicuous absence of santero images of this saint.

The public chapel of Our Lady of St. John of the Lakes at present-day Talpa, a village south of Ranchos de Taos, also is closely connected with the working period of Molleno. In 1823 a citizen of Taos gave

---

[4] AASF, Patentes, Book IX, Box 9, 1816–33.
[5] There is a folk tradition in Ranchos de Taos that the chapel was originally built by the burgeoning brotherhood of penitents. See Sec. IV , request of 60 brothers of the Third Order at Santa Cruz to observe Lent at Taos, represented by Policarpio Cordova and Dionicio Vigil, in 1831, page 449.

Plate 23: Head from a crucifix
by Molleno. (Photograph by
Eliot Porter)

Plate 24: San Acacio by José Aragon.

land for the "new settlement of Rio Chiquito" which was then the name of Talpa.[6] Population in the Taos region was growing, and many families were moving in from the south where recurrent outbreaks connected with the establishment of the Mexican Republic had made life unsettled. With them came at least one devotion new to New Mexico, that of Our Lady of St. John of the Lakes. The original of this advocation of the Virgin was a small statue of Our Lady of the Immaculate Conception, thought to have been made by Tarascan Indians and given to the church at San Juan de los Lagos in Jalisco. In time the fame of the figure's miraculous favors led to the building of a larger church dedicated to it and completed in 1769. As so often occurred, the statue took the name of the place where it was displayed: St. John of the Lakes. By the time devotees of this statue had moved to Rio Chiquito near Taos, they had forgotten or left off the last part of the name, "of the Lakes," and the advocation was called "Our Lady of St. John."

In 1827 Bernardo Duran, representing thirty families of Rio Chiquito, petitioned Father Antonio José Martinez for permission to celebrate the Mass of Our Lady of St. John as their patroness[7] (See Appendix III-B).

In 1833 Bernardo Duran, Faustin Vigil and forty-odd citizens petitioned Bishop Zubiría for permission to have regular Masses said in the Chapel of Nuestra Señora de San Juan del Rio Chiquito, which the citizens had built at their own expense. This license was granted on July 7, 1833.[8]

The altar screen in the Talpa chapel is the work of Molleno and is plainly dated, 1828. He had acquired full command of his colors, composition and decorative elements. The proportions of the cornice, valances, shell pediment, and panels harmonize perfectly with the exuberantly painted floral scrolls and figures. The brushwork has a masterly sweep which Molleno had not learned when he was working at the Ranchos church. It is also remarkable that at Talpa he placed figures on the left-hand panels facing inward, or to our right and toward the tabernacle and bulto of the patroness. For reasons thus far unknown, New Mexican santeros faced most of their painted figures looking to the left of the panel, even on an altar screen requiring balanced placement for esthetic reasons. The figures of the retables of Ranchos de Taos, as in so many others, all face to the left of the viewer, but at Talpa Molleno had been struck by the idea of facing the images toward the center.

The bulto of the patroness in the upper niche may have been carved by Molleno, to judge by the small size of the head in proportion to the

---

[6] AASF, L. D. 1823, No. 7.
[7] AASF, L. D. 1827, No. 10.
[8] AASF, L. D. 1833, Nos. 6 and 26.

body, but it has been overpainted and, swathed in veils and gowns, it is difficult to identify the original style.

The panels are interesting from the viewpoint of iconography; the upper left one contains a crowned figure in flowing robes who holds a crucifix and sceptre. This panel is lettered "San Brnrdo," probably the abbreviation of San Bernardino de Siena who was most likely to have been the patron saint of the donor, because he was a Franciscan while the other Saint Bernards were Cistercians or Dominicans. At the sides are pairs of tapers in sockets like those that Molleno painted on his panels of Our Lady of St. John. At the lower right is St. Anthony with this inscription:

> Se yso y se /pinto en ese / el año de 1828 / a debosyon / de Bexnaxdo / Duxan este o / xatoxio de Mi Sxª / de San Juan / (In this, the year of 1828, was built and painted, through the devotion of Bernardo Duran, this oratory of My Lady of St. John).[9]

The formation of the script letter *r* like a lower case *x* was common in Spanish and Mexican documents, but Molleno's spelling, abbreviations and spacing were below the level of contemporary manuscripts. The survival of this inscription is fortunate as it gives a positive date for the santero's finest middle style and identifies the patronage and donor of the little chapel.

At the upper right is Santiago, very similar to others of the Apostle painted by Molleno and particularly a large one on buffalo hide in the Museum of New Mexico. At the lower left is an image of the Virgin standing by a tower and holding a swaddled infant; it is inscribed, "Mi Sñora de Talpa." The original Our Lady of Talpa was a statue of Our Lady of the Rosary located in Jalisco, Mexico. Beyond the small region of Taos the cult of Our Lady of Talpa does not seem to have extended in New Mexico. Today the village of Rio Chiquito bears the name Talpa, instead of the name of the original patroness.

In 1856 efforts were being made to raise funds for the repair of the chapel of "San Juan de Rio Chiquito."[10] By whatever means and under whatever titles, the people of Talpa have cared for the chapel and the exquisite retablo of Molleno and Bernardo Duran for more than a century. The altar screen is one of the finest of all New Mexican santero compositions.

The chapel of the Lord of Esquipulas at el Potrero de Chimayo is well documented in its early years and thus gives dates for two of Molleno's surviving altar screens. When Bernardo Abeitia received permission to build the chapel from Durango in 1814, it is said that he made a trip to New Spain to purchase ornaments for it (Sec. I-B, Page

---

[9]Charles D. Carroll, "The Talpa Altar Screen," in *El Palacio,* V. 68/4, 1961, p. 220: I do not read an abbreviation for feliz in the inscription, but simply: "en ese el año de 1828."

[10]AASF, L. D. 1856, No. 1.

68). In the inventory made for Visitor de Guevara in 1818 is noted an altar screen of wood, painted in tempera, with a niche framed with gilded wood containing the image of Our Lord of Esquipulas, of one and three-quarter varas, more or less. The carved and gilded frame, like the ivory Christ Child (Page 75), were obviously among the ornaments that Abeitia brought from the south. Given the limits of the altar screen, the niche and its gilded frame, Molleno devised panels containing the Franciscan shield, the Cross of Jerusalem, the Five Wounds and symbols of the Sacraments, a sheaf of wheat and a bunch of grapes. Minor spaces were filled with geometric forms; the whole was worked out in soft reds, blues, pinks and yellows interwoven to direct the eye to the central crucifix. The sanctuary itself controlled the somewhat low, squat proportions of the retable within which Molleno arranged his panels. He must have made it at some time between 1816, when the chapel was completed, and 1818, probably very soon before or after he had painted the great altar screen at Ranchos de Taos. The donor, Abeitia, was willing to pay for the best available in his day, and that he had Molleno make his main altar screen indicates that the santero had some local prestige at the time.

In 1818 the only retables in the Santuario were the main one and one other:

"Opening out of the sacristy is an oratory, which is the original, 3 and ¾ varas by 2 and ½ varas and 3 varas high, with its altarpiece and eight images in the round, painted in tempera." While there is here no reference to miraculous earth, it is clear that this "oratory" was the first structure to enclose the healing mud, which is still reached by a small door on the north side of the sacristy. Like so much else, the probably tiny altar screen and its eight images vanished long ago. Whether Molleno or someone else made these is unknown. The inventory of 1826 listed few minor additions and no new retables. Therefore the four now in the nave must have been made after 1826.[11] That on the right-hand side nearest to the entrance is also by Molleno but done in a far more bold style of brushwork and simplified coloring than his earlier, main altar screen. The later retable at the Santuario has a central panel of the cross, suggesting wrought ironwork. Of the four images around it only those of the Dolores and San Felipe of Neri are identifiable; the two bearded males in black robes are examples of Molleno's cryptic iconography. The whole retable smoulders with muted reds like glowing coals; the cool gamut of blues in the 1828 screen at Talpa is absent. Whether this retable was damaged when the former choir loft collapsed early in this century, or by the inevitable leaking roof, or some other hazard, it had grown dim and suffered paint losses. In the mid-1960s it was retouched by a contemporary maker of repro-

---

[11] AASF, Accounts, LXIV, Book I, 1826.

duced santos, Andrew Johnston. In the process he found a fragment of gilded wood originally placed as a moulding over the central niche. This, presumably, was a part of the gilded woodwork imported by Bernardo Abeitia, perhaps left over from the main retable.

Molleno seems to have been versatile in making altar screens, carved figures, portable panels, painting on tanned hides (Sec. I-E) and, it has been surmised, working with gesso in relief. Details of surface painting on some gesso reliefs markedly resemble others on Molleno's statues and retablos (Sec. I-F). So also do the unnaturally long fingers and thumbs of the reliefs and Molleno's panels. On the other hand, such treatments may have been conventions of folk artists without training or interest in anatomy. Gesso relief details are present on several of Molleno's bultos, used as garment trimming or on the wounds of a crucified corpus and its crown of thorns as well as to ornament the cross. Of portable-size images, literally hundreds still exist; before they were scattered, the majority seems to have come from the Taos area and as far south as San Juan and Chimayó. His popularity among his contemporaries is a commentary on New Mexican taste which had learned to admire the works of their more gifted neighbors over several generations.

To the eyes of a visitor like Guevara, accustomed to formal Baroque and Neo-Classicism so familiar in Mexican architecture and art, a retable by Molleno must have seemed ugly and childish. It is possible that such works were responsible for Bishop Zubiría's criticism during his visit in 1833 of "ugly images" which he saw everywhere in the territory. These men could no more be expected to admire folk art than the local development of the Third Order of St. Francis which they so strongly denounced. Today, 150 years later, the popular taste has been conditioned to commercial plaster images, and also rejects regional santos. The more sophisticated observer, brought up on symbolism, primitive arts and abstraction, recognizes Molleno's originality, rich coloring and facile brushwork. He seems to have been uninhibited from improvising images for which he had no prototypes, unlike other contemporary santeros.

Authorization of annual function
in honor of Our Lady of San Juan

[The orthography is as written in the document.]
"En este Pueblo de San Geronimo de Taos hoy, ocho de Mayo de 1827, se prèsente ante mi Dñ. Varnardo Duran, ciudadano del rio chiquito, departmento del Varrio de San Fran^{co} de las Trampas y en la actualidad territorial del dcho. departamento, solicitanes el que diera un documento por escrito como por tal le doy este, para que reconoscan los habitantes de esta plasa del rio chiquito y sus correspondientes ranchos por especial Patrona la Virgen Maria en el titulo de la Señora de San Juan. A la que se prometen acerle su función de Yglesia todos los años una ves y de que por principio le

Another panel is worded:

"SANTA ROSALIA Se Pinto/ a 22 Julio deste Año de 1830/ en el/ Chamisal/ José Aragon."[2]

A third panel is inscribed:

"N.S. DE LOS DOLORES se pin/ to A 22 de Julio des/ te Año de 1830   José Aragon, Chamisal[3]

A fourth small panel, unsigned but lettered, is of the Crucifixion:

"MATER DOLOROSA/ SAN JUAQUIN/ se pinto el año/ de 1830 el dia/ 21 de Julio."[4]

Still another of this series is in the hands of José Aragon's descendants. It is lettered:

N.S. DE LOS DOLORES se pin/ to A 22 de Julio deste Año de 1830   José Aragon, Chamisal[5]

A sixth, that I have not seen, is worded:

"SANTA LIBRADA, se pinto en (el?) Chamisal A 22 de Julio deste año de 1830."[6]

Were these delicate little panels all done in two days? Or were they already painted with only the inscriptions left off, to be filled in when they were completed or sold? If the latter were the case, it might explain why Aragon's inscriptions are often of fugitive pigments while the rest of his colors are not. Much of the lettering on his panels has been lost or partly worn away. One of his inscriptions suggests that Don José held exhibitions or, perhaps, gave demonstrations of his skills. This approach to potential customers was not traditional among New Mexican santeros, according to recorded accounts, and would appear to reflect his Spanish background. Aragon's neat lettering and fine line-work suggest that he used engravings as models, frequently copying their framing ornaments and even the prayers on them. The same flowering tree, which certainly came from an engraving, appears on at least four of his panels of the Archangel Gabriel, St. Ignatius Loyola and N.S. del Camino. The rococo influence that pervades José Aragon's more painstaking works suggests 18th century popular prints rather than those of his own times. When he did not have a print at hand he tended to make confused, or asymmetrical, compositions, but his finest panels obviously were based on graphic sources like those of archangels dated 1825 and 1835. The first of these is inscribed:

ORACION AL ANGEL S. GABRIEL. O glorioso S. Gabriel yamado por fortaleza de Dios y embajador del Padre celestial tu q^e meresiste trair la nueva, dichosa para la genera humana; de la

---

[2] Private owner.
[3] Private owner.
[4] Private owner.
[5] Private owner.
[6] Collected by the late Colonel Charles H. Woodard now in the Adams State College Museum, Alamosa, Colorado.

Figure 196: The Archangel San Gabriel signed and dated, José Aragon, 1825.

encarnación del Hijo de Dios en las entrañas de la Virgen. Ven por bien de rogar al mismo Señor por un ... pecador para que me aprobeche del fruta copiosa de su Redención y meresca gozar de aventuranza. Amen. Se pinto el 18 Febrero de 1825 y firme en este qᵉ yse a mano de D. José Aragon. [rubric][7]

(Prayer to the Angel St. Gabriel. Oh glorious St. Gabriel, called by the power of God as ambassador of the heavenly Father, thou who was worthy to bring the glad news to mankind of the incarnation of the Son of God in the womb of the Virgin; be good enough to pray the same Lord for a ... sinner that I may be granted the copious fruit of His redemption and deserve to taste blessedness. Amen.

(Painted the 18th of February of 1825 and signed in this [day], by the hand of don José Aragon. [rubric])

Two panels of the Guardian Angel by Aragon seem to be from the same original print, but there are minor differences. Both have tiny parallel lines in halos and swags, scalpel-like drawing of features and costume detail as if copied with care from a fine engraving. One, however, was dated in 1825, and its drawing and color are more vigorous than the second panel which is dated ten years later. The angel wears a cuirass and tunic, jeweled belt, brooches, and fancy buskins in both, and holds up the same symbols — a sword, large crown and veil — and stands on clouds, similarities which certainly indicate one prototype. However, the prayers at the bottom are not exactly the same. The 1825 panel reads:

ORACION AL ANGEL DE NUESTRA/ GUARDA. Dios que con su divina Providencia Proveistes al linage/ humano del socoro ... de nuestros deleitos la luz de los Angeles dadme grasia/ con que asi honore al Angel de mi Guarda Que meresca ser en todo tiempo defendido por el, por Jesu Christo/ Nuestro Señor, Amen./ Se pinto el dia 18 de Febrero de 1825/ en este ... muestrario ... del pinturería en la escultería de/D.ⁿ José Aragon. [rubric][8]

(Prayer to Our Guardian Angel. God who in his divine Providence provides to mankind the aid ... for our delight the light of the angels, give me grace with which, thus, to honor my Guardian Angel, that I may at all times deserve to be defended by him, for Jesus Christ, Our Lord. Amen. Painted the 18th day of February of 1825 in this exhibition of painting in the sculpture studio of Don José Aragon.)

From the two inscriptions just quoted, one notes that the panels of the Archangel Gabriel and Guardian Angel were dated on the *same day*

---

[7] (Ellipses stand for loss of words.) Museum of New Mexico collection No. A.21.-58-1. Reproduced in Bulletin of California Palace of the Legion of Honor, Vol. 17, No. 11.
[8] Taylor Museum Collection, No. 1556.

Figure 197: Santa Rosalia signed and dated, José Aragon, 1830.

SANTA ROSALIA. se pint
a 22 de julio de ese Año de 1830.
en el   Jose araon i
Chamisal

Figure 198: Lettered cross: "To John, I Jesus, give this woman for thy Mother." (Private owner)

as well as the same year, just as the first six were dated on two consecutive days of July of the same year.

The time required for preparation of wood panels, gesso surfaces, and the making of pigments and brushes was considerable, but the time consumed in the actual painting of a retablo is at present unknown. What is nearly consistent in New Mexico santero painting is that no visible corrections of line or color areas appear; perhaps it took very little time to complete a retablo.

The words pinturería and escultería are more pretentious than the wording of inscriptions found on other santeros' works, and imply that José Aragon had a studio or workshop. Did he also give lessons to others wanting to learn to make santos, or merely have a relative or apprentice to help him and, incidentally, learn to do the same work? While New Mexicans spoke of a santero, a man who made or mended holy images, they do not seem to have used the noun, santería, the place or room where the images were made, much less such imposing terms as muestrario (exhibition or demonstration of), or a painting or sculpture studio.

Perhaps José Aragon brought with him from the Spain that had just been overrun by Napoleonic armies a vocabulary slightly different from that of isolated New Mexico of the same time. Although his panels are essentially naive, and his use of prints as models was traditional among folk artists, his fine, neat lettering and fondness for inscriptions as well as for signing his name and dates, set him somewhat apart from New Mexicans of his time.

His panel of the Guardian Angel dated 1835 is eleven centimeters smaller in size than the earlier one and is a paler rendering of the prototype. Its inscription runs:

ORACION AL AN/gel de nuestra guarda. Dios que con Divina providencia proviera por lux del camino del pecador de los Angeles: dadme gracia con que así del Santo Angel de mi Guarda, que pudiera ser en todo tiempo de mi vida con el por Jesus Christo nuestro Señor Amen. Se pinto el dia 18 de Marzo 1835 en la esculturía de José Aragon.[9]

(Prayer to Our Guardian Angel. God who with Divine wisdom provides the light of the Angels on the road of the sinner, give me grace that, thus, I may be with the holy Angel of my ward at all times of my life, for Jesus Christ our Lord Amen. Painted the 18th day of March 1835 in the sculpture shop of José Aragon.)

Here there is a scrambled sense of wording as well as a finer, if less forceful, rendering of the image. Had José Aragon lost and forgotten his engraving, or was he working from another slightly different one? The date is also of interest; March 18 is now the annual feast day of the Archangel Gabriel, but Aragon's panel of Gabriel was dated

---

[9]Museum of New Mexico collection, No. A.9.54-140-R.

February 18. The symbols of imperial crown and veil (of virginity) obviously refer to the Virgin Mary, and so, in spite of the caption to the Guardian Angel, José Aragon had in mind the Archangel Gabriel in his role of heavenly messenger to Mary so often painted under the title of the Annunciation.

Iconographically, a Guardian Angel is assigned to every mortal at birth to guide him along the road of his lifespan, and these hosts of angels were not the archangels of the upper hierarchy of heaven but the guardians of humanity. The cult of the Guardian Angel, to whom each man, woman and child could appeal in time of need, was of Medieval origin, but seems to have had a great popularity in Mexico and New Mexico during the santero, or 19th century, period.

It is also possible that the day of devotion to the Archangel Gabriel was observed a month earlier than now in José Aragon's time. In any case, his work points to a strong interest in the Angel Gabriel. In addition to these titled panels he painted this archangel with Moses and Zacharias, who holds a chalice as symbol of the future comings of St. John the Baptist and Christ. In this panel Zacharias seems to be blind — possibly an effort to depict the loss of his speech when he doubted the message delivered by Gabriel that a son would be born to him and his wife in their old age. Among New Mexico santeros such involved symbolism and the depiction of Old Testament figures such as Moses are rare, but in this panel the reference to the apparition of Gabriel to the temple priest and to Moses is clear.

Unlike other santeros of his day, José Aragon seldom portrayed the Archangel Raphael, whose popularity was then universal in New Mexico, and he seems to have paid little attention to the Archangel Michael. This last fact suggests that Don José had no military connections and that his customers were not deeply involved with soldiering. It is a family tradition that Aragon lived north of Santa Fe during his years in New Mexico so his patrons would have been ranchers and villagers. In Santa Fe the aristocratic military chapel, la Castrense, soon lost its congregation after the new Republic of Mexico abolished stipends for military chaplains, with the consequent decay of the building itself.

Some of Aragon's subjects suggest his Spanish background, such as a panel of N.S. del Camino, an image of Our Lady that is venerated at Pamplona, capital of Navarre and on the old pilgrim route from France to Compostela. The cult of Our Lady of Valvanera also originated in Navarre. Except for the panel of this advocation on Governor Marín del Valle's stone altar piece made in Santa Fe in 1761, and a retablo by Aragon, New Mexican santeros ignored the subject. Certainly his choice of allegorical and Old Testament subjects, as well as of the apostles Bartholomew and Matthew, were not locally popular.

He may very well have introduced, or at least advanced, a devotion that was already flourishing in Mexico and California, that of Our Lady of Refuge of Sinners. The original painting was of the Roman school of ca. 1700; a copy of it was sent from Italy to Jesuit missionaries at

Zacatecas, Mexico, about 1720. Analysis of the composition suggests that it was painted in the prevailing saccharine style of the day, after the well-known, earlier Madonna della Sedia by Raphael Sanzio, even to the striped Roman scarf around the neck of the Virgin. At Zacatecas it became an object of devotion and pilgrimage. A charmingly rococo polychromed wooden statue of Refugio, of typically mid-18th century Mexican style, is now owned by a Santa Barbara, California, family, and is said to have traveled with Fr. Junípero Serra as he founded the Alta California mission chain.

Numerous other "copies" of the Refugio were painted — of all degrees of competence, primitivism and variation — and José Aragon made at least one carved bulto of it as well as several retablos. The bulto is lacking in the professional poise and sophistication found in the Roman original and Mexican carving, but has a rustic charm of its own. The modest looking Virgin sits on a most ambitious, if slightly confused, architectural pedestal of the same wood, gesso and tempera as the figure. The painting on the bulto is similar to that of retablos by Don José, and the lettered plaque on the pedestal is also like his panel inscriptions. It says simply:

"REFVGIO DE PECADORES Año de 1820."[10]

The dating of a bulto is not known to have been done by any other New Mexican santero, nor even by Don José himself. It is possible that this statue was made as a celebration of the birth or baptism of José Aragon's daughter, whose name was Refugio, and who may very well have been born in that year. Of five small retablos by him of the same Virgin of Refuge the inscription on one is partly legible and reads:

"N.S. DEL REFUGIO Se Pinto en el Escultería
. . . año [de] 1827, José Aragon."

This may have been a gift to the same little daughter on her saint's name day, July 4. A multiple-compartmented panel of the size used in family oratories shows the Holy Family in its center and the Virgin of Refuge in the place of honor above the other saints. Although without inscription, it is possible that this was used for the devotions of the José Aragon family. In any case, it is an outstanding example of the creative invention of Don José, with little or no suggestion of a prototype.

A living descendant of José Aragon possesses a crucifix attributed to his hand. The corpus, insofar as the dissimilarities of the subject allow, resembles the little Virgin of Refuge in characteristics of treatment in carving and painting. The wooden cross of the crucifix is also of interest, for into its painted gesso surface there was scratched or incised the following:

"Juanᵃ yo Jᵉ da la Mujer por Vuestra Madre."

---

[10] Reproduced in *Santos, Religious Folk Art of New Mexico* by Wilder & Breitenbach, Pl. 43.

As interpreted by Father Angelico Chavez, the outstanding scholar of colonial New Mexico, this is a colloquial rendering of the words of Christ to His Mother and the disciple John: "Woman, behold thy son!" and to John: "Behold thy mother!" (St. John, XIX, 26, 27) "To John I Jesus give this woman for thy Mother."

A family tradition has it that Don José did not wish to become a citizen of the United States, and for this reason moved down the Rio Grande to Senecu, near El Paso. He probably left the Rio Arriba long before 1846 as the last recorded dated panel by him is 1835. Aragon must have had some experience and education. His artistic efforts give an overall impression of real piety, of one who envisioned heaven and its population as beautiful, merciful and calm. No suggestions of bodily violence or pain appear in his work, although his New Mexican years coincided with the expansion of the regional defection of the brotherhood of penitents from the old Third Order of St. Francis (Sec. IV-A). Whether he had an apprentice, or several, the body of his work is consistent in its conservatism, coloring and mannerisms. A smaller group that is hardly distinguishable from the rest, except for negative features such as less inventiveness in composition, color and lack of delicacy, has been hypothetically regarded as the work of a pupil or associate, and is discussed in the following pages.

A great granddaughter of José Aragon's, Teresita Garcia, married Albert J. Fountain, Jr., the eldest son of the famous Colonel Albert J. Fountain of la Mesilla, whose mysterious disappearance while on a journey across the White Sands was for long New Mexico's most famous unsolved murder case. Colonel Fountain was a distinguished military figure and active in the difficult pacification of the southern Apaches. He was respected by his army colleagues and also by the Indians. I am indebted to Mrs. Elizabeth Fountain Armendariz, José Aragon's great-great granddaughter, for information on the santero (Appendix, III-D, Aragon-Fountain family).

* * *

The name "Dot and Dash" may seem a peculiar way to identify a santero, but it is appropriate to the series of retablos discussed here due to the frequency with which the panels are framed or decorated with rows of dots or spots and short brush strokes, often bordered by a line. Figures are drawn with outlines of monotonous quality, lacking accent or variety of width, like the drawings of a conscientious copyist. The pupils of their eyes are round and black, the noses too long and aquiline, and chins recede. Color is often limited to the dark outlines (mixed indigo and brown), and an earthy red. Only a few panels have the full palette of available colors.

Uneven in their sizes, and in success or failure of performance, there is a set of twelve large panels in the Taylor Museum. The rough-hewn panels are bevelled, and are from one meter seven centimeters to one meter eighteen centimeters in height and sixty-three to eighty-two centimeters wide. They are alike in having been prepared with patches of cotton cloth to cover knotholes and other defects in the wood before gesso was laid over the fronts. They are painted in dark outlines and earth red; space fillers are curlicues and dots and dashes. The heads are larger, more myopic and more hooknosed than those on smaller panels by the Dot and Dash painter.

In his study of New Mexico retablos, W. S. Stallings, Jr., classed these perfunctory panels as the work of José Aragon or as that of his school.[11] It is true that traits of drawing do remind us of José Aragon's mannerisms, but in a coarse and casual way. When Aragon worked after an engraving he was more finicky and painstaking than in some of his original compositions, but his delicacy of drawing and sweetness of color was consistent. The Dot and Dash series could hardly have been the work of José Aragon of Chamisal but may have been done by an apprentice, or even an admirer, of his.

Stallings tested twenty-two panels which he assigned to "José Aragon and School," and from these he estimated a mean average cutting date for fifteen panels of 1827–31 (See Appendix I-G). Since the sampling included work by José Aragon and the Dot and Dash santero, it may be inferred that the latter worked at the same time as Aragon whose panels, dated by his own hand, run between 1823 and 1835.

Like other santeros, the Dot and Dash painter executed some subjects seldom met with in New Mexico in his period, such as Sts. Augustine, Bartholomew, Margaret of Cortona and Thomas Aquinas. He lettered the names of a few saints on his panels in fairly clear block letters. This also suggests experience with José Aragon of Chamisal, who seems to have been a conspicuously literate santero.

José Aragon — Fountain Family

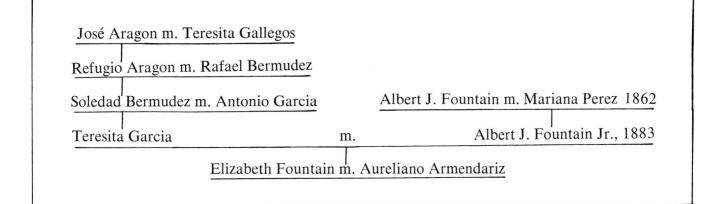

José Aragon m. Teresita Gallegos
Refugio Aragon m. Rafael Bermudez
Soledad Bermudez m. Antonio Garcia   Albert J. Fountain m. Mariana Perez 1862
Teresita Garcia   m.   Albert J. Fountain Jr., 1883
Elizabeth Fountain m. Aureliano Armendariz

[11]Unpublished MS by W. S. Stallings, Jr., in Taylor Museum.

THE ANONYMOUS "SANTO NINO" SANTERO

There is as yet no clue to the identity of the most appealing maker of images (to some tastes) of New Mexico. One panel by this man gave a tree-ring date of 1828 plus X years. This santero made relatively few panels and, so far as we know, no large altar screens. The first published note on this series gave him the tentative name of the "Santo Niño Perdido" santero: (E. Boyd, *El Palacio,* V. 57/1, 1950), but as the santero made a number of images of the Christ Child under different titles, it has been abbreviated to the "Santo Niño" santero. The retablos all show a proficiency of line, pure, simple colors and uncluttered compositions. They are, as a rule, of a single figure on a white or pastel ground; drapery is drawn in angular, flat folds, and there is a minimum of decorative spacefillers. Heads have close-set, sometimes dissipated looking eyes and oddly convoluted ears. The well-prepared gesso grounds, pigments and the control of drawing suggest experience in spite of the few recorded panels by this folk artist.

His experience was gained while making bultos, of which many more exist. The association of panels and bultos as one man's work was noted in cleaning overpaint from several bultos on which similar design elements appeared as ornaments of painted clothing or bases that also appear on the retablos. Further comparisons of the qualities of gesso and pigments, traits of human features and pose, when translated into three dimensions, definitely linked the bultos and panels.[1]

Like other New Mexico santeros this one deliberately discarded three dimensional form when painting in a picture plane but understood it well when carving a figure. His bultos are gracefully proportioned with exquisitely carved hands, where they have not been damaged, and lean, Hamitic profiles. The figures have peculiarly formed ears and, sometimes, an enigmatic smile as if they feel sympathy for their devotees.

The santero was adept in making hollow frame statues of the Virgin, not only from a mechanical point of view but from that of attractiveness.

One of his hollow frame images has had a romantic history. During a temporary defection to a Protestant sect by a part of the people of Laguna Pueblo in the latter part of the 19th century, the Mission of San José was closed for a few years. Tradition says that portable contents of the mission were removed for safekeeping during that time. In the 1930s an elderly couple in the pueblo asked Father Agnellus Lammert, a well-beloved Franciscan, who was stationed at Laguna for twenty years, to come to their home and exorcise a demon. The couple complained that they were awakened every night by the wailing of a woman and could not find a source for the sounds. Father Lammert, being of a practical turn of mind, told the Indians to clear away the debris in an old, abandoned room next to their house. Then, if they still heard the wailing at night, they might come and tell him about it; he suspected that it was only a cat living in the ruins which would be driven away by clearing out the rubbish. In digging through the accumulated fill of the old room, part of a bulto of Our Lady was found, the head, arms, torso, scraps of frame and a base. The paint and most of the gesso were lost, but the delicacy of the wood carving was recognized by Father Lammert. By a fortunate accident a man named Stanley Crittenden was staying at Laguna. He had previously been a dealer in antiques at Santa Fe and handled and repaired santos as well as other things. Crittenden made a new hollow frame for the figure, covered it with cloth and gesso and painted the whole in the traditional santero method. Whether for lack of other colors or to suggest an Indian maiden, he gave the face a tawny complexion.

The wailing of demon (or cat) was heard no more, and the devout among the pueblo believed that it was the Lady crying for release from her underground prison. The bulto has been in San José Mission for some thirty years, and has recently been arrayed in garments unlike any seen on other images of the Virgin. It is a true Virgin of Laguna Pueblo, clad in a handwoven, dark robe like those worn by the women in ceremonials, nylon lingerie and apron, a challis shawl, rosary,

---

[1]Alan C. Vedder, "Establishing a Retablo-Bulto Connection," in *El Palacio,* V. 68/2, 1961.

Plate 26: Santa Librada by José Aragon.

Figure 199: Virgin with hollow frame construction by the anonymous Santo Niño Santero.

Figure 200: The Virgin of Mission San José, Laguna Pueblo, after her discovery underground and repairs. (Photograph by G. F. Crabtree, Jr.)

Plate 27: Santa Librada by the anonymous "Santo Niño" santero.

III-E

turquoise and coral jewelry. All are in perfect scale and set off the basic statue made by the Santo Niño santero. For this story I am indebted to the late Father Lammert from whom I had the pleasure of hearing it.

It is worth considering that the santero may have been José Manuel Benabides, who is referred to in an unsigned memorandum dated in 1842 as a sculptor then working on altar screen images and a crucifix. The location, Santa Cruz de la Cañada, at the bottom of the page, however, has been crossed out. There is no positive evidence available to connect the name and the works of the Santo Niño santero, and nothing now in the church of Santa Cruz de la Cañada is by him. In the 1930s there were two bultos of different advocations of the Virgin that were typical of his style but they, like so much else once in the church, have long ago disappeared.

APPENDIX
Santa Cruz Accounts, 1842

(Page 1)

A punta de lo nueba resibiendo el escultor José Manuel Benabides de cuenta de las imagenes coraterales que esta trabajando contando con lo q^e tiene ya resibio con esta fecha de 11 Abril de 1842.

Tres cabras de las que tiene D^n Diego	Ps	3
Una fanega y tales cuartillas de maís que		
resibió en el año pasado		1.3
un buelle y una borrica nuebos y en lección		
cada uno en el presio de doce pesos fuertes		24
Una fanega de maís que resibió en el presente año		3
Se le abona un peso q^e le debia a D^{on} Juan		
Domingo p^{or} debe mi lo el tal Juan Domingo		1

(Page 2)
11 Abril, 1842

Se le abonan al escultor José Manuel Benabides
    por la Sangre de Cristo quince pˢ en moneda   15

Por la echura de cada corateral se le abonan   48
    cincuenta pˢ de la tierra.
Villa de Sta Cruz de la Cañada [crossed out][1]

(Translation)

Apropos of the new the sculptor José Manuel Benabides
    has received on account for the altar screen images on
    which he is working, including those that I have received, on
    this date of the 11th of April, 1842.

Three she goats of those that Don Diego has   Pesos 3
One and some fractions of a fanega of corn
    that I received last year   1.3
One ox and one she burro, young and in training,
    each one at the price of twelve hard pesos   24
One fanega of corn that I received in the present year   3
He was credited with one peso that he owed to Don
    Juan Domingo because the said Juan Domingo owed it to me   1

11 April, 1842
The sculptor José Manuel Benabides was credited with
    fifteen pesos in money for the Sangre de Cristo   15

For the making of each altar screen he was credited   48
    with fifty pesos of the country.
Village of Santa Cruz de la Cañada [crossed out].

    The rewards of the santero were varied, not only in kind, but in the kind of pesos he earned. Typically, the live ox and burro were valued at the hard peso while the cash he was to receive for the construction as well as the painting of the altar screen was the country peso — or about one-quarter of the value of the other. (Moorhead, 1958, page 50). Perhaps because of the reverence attached to the "Sangre de Cristo," he received 15 hard pesos for it in cash.

---

[1] AASF, L. D., 1840, No. 7, fgmt. of accounts, but MSS dated as above, April 11, 1842.

Plate 29: El Santo Niño de
Atocha by the Santo Niño santero.

Plate 30: Nuestra Señora de San Juan de los Lagos by the Santo Niño santero. (Plates 28, 29, photographs by Eliot Porter)

THE ANONYMOUS "QUILL PEN" SANTERO

This simple name was chosen to describe the painter of a series of panels whose creator seems to have used a sharp-ended quill or other fine-pointed implement for making delicate outlines. The indentation of his quill is clearly visible on the gesso surfaces of many of his panels, a feature not found in the work of other santeros. The rest of his painted areas is covered with rather thin, sloppy swipes of acid coloring, some of which is fugitive. His peculiarly personal mannerisms of drawing shoe-button eyes with elliptical lids and pothook brows, razor sharp noses, and long Iberian jaws (perhaps we should say Hapsburg jaws) are consistent. So also are his indifference to and lack of control over composition, symmetry and proportions.

So far as is known, altar screens of public chapel size by the Quill Pen santero are now unassembled or lost except for single panels, but two of the kind made for private chapels or family oratorios are now in the collections of the Denver Art Museum[1] and the Oklahoma Historical Society.[2] Both feature the Virgin of Guadalupe of Mexico with eight surrounding panels containing some images not connected with the story of the apparitions. Both are fifty-seven centimeters high. There are also two panels containing two subjects each by the same anonymous folk artist in the Taylor Museum.[3]

The santero, or perhaps his customers, knew of the image of the "Pieta" and of St. Isabel of Portugal which had not previously been among New Mexico subjects. On the other hand, Mexican "laminas" painted in oils on tin by folk painters to the south were beginning to arrive in the internal provinces of the north, along with printed woodblocks and lithographs which introduced new devotions and such novelties as republican emblems and tailored garments for men. These reached New Mexico during a period of friction between newly arrived secular priests and the adherents of former Franciscan missionaries, together with the autonomous offspring of the Franciscans, the Penitentes. Devotion persisted and flourished, but at the time private enterprise expended funds on home chapels rather than on those for the clergy to supervise. In this environment the Quill Pen santero seems to have been engaged. Certainly his work is uneven and lacking in competence in some instances, although other examples have a quaint charm of their own. The chief interest of the corpus of this santero's painting is that it serves as a reflection, somewhat distorted, as in an old mirror, of his time. Only two panels were tested for tree-ring dating by Stallings, and these gave tree-cutting dates of 1830 plus X and 1835 plus X.

---

[1] Denver Art Museum "Santos of the Southwest," 1970, No. DAM-142.

[2] See *El Palacio,* Vol. 64/7, Stephen Borhegyi, 1957.

[3] T.M.3897, 3898. Identified as by the "Arroyo Hondo" santero, *in* Shalkop, Robert L. — "The Folk Art of a New Mexican Village," Taylor Museum, Colorado Springs, 1969, pl.17.

Figure 201: Nuestra Señora de
la Piedad by the anonymous
"Quill Pen" santero.

Figure 202: St. Vincent Ferrer
by the Quill Pen santero.

Plate 31: Bultos by the Santo Niño santero. (Photograph by Laura Gilpin)

Plate 32: El Santo Niño de Atocha by Rafael Aragon.

A somewhat scarred retablo of San Roque is of unusual interest for its painted record of a majolica bowl decorated with a small bird. The panel was published in 1929,[4] reproduced as it was restored. In the process of history, the panel was presented to the Museum of New Mexico, and was found to have been rather heavily restored and still in deteriorating condition. Removal of overpainting and putty fills where gesso had been lost showed that the original figure had held the bowl in the right hand above the dog's head. The restorer had painted this out, had folded the Saint's arm over his chest, and had the dog in begging pose instead of on all fours. The depiction of a majolica dish on a santo is somewhat unprecedented in New Mexico, and the more interesting because such vessels were sent to the province and today are known only through excavated fragments.

If the Quill Pen santero made bultos they have not yet been recognized.

JOSE RAFAEL ARAGON

There was no relationship between this santero and José Aragon who signed and dated many of his works and moved to the El Paso region about 1835 (Sec. III-D). José Rafael Aragon lived for much of his life at Pueblo Quemado, now Cordova, New Mexico, and is hereafter referred to as Rafael Aragon. He was a prolific santero; his work was much in demand, as it is today. His gracefully elongated figures, their large, pensive eyes and fresh, clear coloring are elegant yet spiritual. Like other santeros Rafael treated panels in two dimensions but carved in the round with a fine sense of volume.

In the literature Aragon's work has been referred to as the "Santa Cruz school" or of the Cordova style because many santos and altar screens by him were found in those places.[1] However, they were also located in several other villages and valleys and in number around Taos. Rafael Aragon's santos were identified as having been made by Miguel Aragon by Frank Applegate who had collected the name in Cordova.[2] The name of Miguel has been repeated in print ever since but what or how many santos Miguel Aragon made is today unknown. A Miguel Aragon and his wife Maria Juana Trujillo, had their daughter Marcelina baptized on February 24, 1871. Twenty years later Marcelina had married José del Carmen Lopez, a brother of José Dolores Lopez (App.

---

[4]*International Studio,* Vol. 94, No. 388, p. 35, by Odd S. Halseth, 1929.
[1]Wilder and Breitenbach, 1943.
[2]Unpub. Mss., Applegate and Mary Austin, and Charles D. Carroll, 1943 and E. Boyd, 1946.

Figure 203: St. Martin of Tours shares his cloak with the beggar, by J. Rafael Aragon. (Courtesy of the Amerind Foundation)

III-G

394   III-G

IV , the Lopez family), and the couple acted as godparents on November 22.[3] According to information from the Lopez family today, Marcelina was a granddaughter of Rafael Aragon; hence her father, Miguel, was his son. He may well have helped his father and learned from him but as nothing signed by him has been found (nor are there any documentary references) this is still a matter of conjecture.

Four examples with more or less complete signatures of Rafael Aragon are known. One is a small and sharply drawn panel of San Calletano collected by the late Dr. Herbert J. Spinden about 1910 and now in the Museum of New Mexico. It is lettered *"Aragon, Jose Rafel."*

The other known inscriptions are on the altar screen of the Cordova church, on an altar screen in the Taylor Museum and on the roof boards of the now ruinous Duran chapel at Talpa, New Mexico. In 1832 the residents of the then new village of Pueblo Quemado requested episcopal license for a public chapel dedicated to San Antonio de Padua, to be administered from Santa Cruz de la Cañada. Don Bernardo Beitia would be responsible for the funds to construct and build the chapel and would provide holy vessels and ornaments for it. This was the same Bernardo Abeitia who built the Santuario at el Potrero in 1814–16 but the plan and decoration at Cordova were more rustic than his earlier chapel.[4] The remains of the inscription on Rafael Aragon's main altar screen at Cordova read:

"Con . . . hizo esa . . . se pintado . . . Raiefal Jose . . . Estando de Guardia el Sr Cura Don Fernando Ortis"

(With . . . was made this . . . was painted   Rafael José . . . the Guardian [of the chapel] being the Señor Curate Don Fernando Ortíz"

Although the date, if any, is lost, Fernando Ortíz was a secular priest in charge of the Santa Cruz church between June 1834 and January 1838,[5] which gives a four-year period in which Rafael Aragon may have worked in the Cordova chapel.

A tall, narrow retable in the Taylor Museum where it is only documented as "from the Santa Cruz valley" may have been for a side altar on account of its proportions. The figures in its panels are lettered: (upper left to right)

"Señor San Lorenso, Biba la Santicima Txinidad, San atenoxenes ovispo," lower left *"Nxta Sxa del Rosaxio, Año de 1800 a 24 de Enero."* Lower right *"Patriaxca San José, Este coaxteral se pinto por mano de m . . stro Rafel Ara . . . se aca . o de . . ."*

This may be interpreted as: "This altar screen was painted by the hand of the master Rafael Aragon, it was finished . . ."when the date

---

[3] Baptisms, Villa de Santa Cruz, Book 2, begun May 1869.
[4] AASF, Patentes, Book LXX, Box 4, 1828–33, Log of Vicar Rascon; and AASF, L.D. 1832, Nos. 4 and 8.
[5] AASF, Baptisms, B-39, Santa Cruz, 1834–43.

should have followed. Although the writing of all the inscriptions is by the same hand the date of 24 January, 1800, beside the image of Our Lady of the Rosary, would not be likely to be that of Aragon's retable, but probably referred to the date when the chapel was built, or to the founding of a local cofradía of the Rosario. The retable itself was a later work of Rafael Aragon's because of the square cut nails and flimsy muslin used in its construction, both imports of the Trail traders. Ten boards of this altar screen gave a mean age estimated dating of 1865-plus, according to the dendrochronologist W. S. Stallings.

The Duran family chapel at Talpa was in good repair when scaled drawings and measurements were made in the early 1930s by the Historic American Buildings Survey (HABS 36 N.M. 10). The contents of the chapel were also well cared for but by 1950 heirs of the former Duran owner had sold the contents, altar screen and santos to the Taylor Museum at Colorado Springs. Since this transaction the empty chapel has crumbled into ruins. Tree-ring tests of beams in the chapel's narthex gave cutting dates of 1830–38. On the interior ceiling of the chapel there is, or was, a black inscription stating that the chapel was dedicated to the use of the priest Don Antonio José Martinez, today, July 21, 1851. Another red lettered inscription consisted of a prayer ending with:

"se techo éste oratorio el dia 2 de Julio, 1851." (This oratory was roofed on July 2, 1851.)

A third inscription in red paint read:

en el nombre de Dios todo poderoso y de la siempre Virgen Maria de Talpa, desde el año de 1838 se fabrica. Jesus, Maria y José. A debocción del esclabo (. . .) colas Sandoval por mano del es (. . .) Rafael Aragon, aprovado por el (. . .) ini^{mo} Don Jose Ant^c de Subiría. Viva Jesus Maria y José.

(In the name of God Almighty and the ever Virgin Mary of Talpa, (this) was built since 1838 by the devotion of the servant of Jesus, Mary and Joseph, Nicolas Sandoval, by the hand of the sculptor Rafael Aragon. Approved by the most worthy Don José Antonio de Zubiría. Hail Jesus, Mary and Joseph!)[6]

Stallings interpreted the tree-ring dates and inscriptions as indicating that the chapel was begun, or commissioned, in 1838 and finally dedicated in 1851. However the habit of saying that a church or chapel was new at a given date when it had, in fact, only been given a new roof or retable, was common in New Mexico church records. My interpretation of the data cited here is that the chapel was built in 1838 at the expense of one Nicolas Sandoval, and that *its design, woodcarving and painted decorations were by Rafael Aragon* the sculptor. By 1838 Aragon had completed several retablos, as we shall see. The later notations that the

---

[6]Material quoted here on the Duran chapel is from the unpublished Mss. by W. S. Stallings Jr., in the Taylor Museum.

roof was put on in 1851 were on the ceiling of the chapel itself; in thirteen years a new roof may have been required for the use of Father Martinez. Stallings' tests of beams were taken from the narthex or small portico in front of the chapel. The approval of Bishop Zubiría noted in the inscription must have been given during the bishop's second visit to New Mexico, in 1845. His first, in 1833, was too early and his last was in 1850. Zubiría was on his way home and at El Paso in December 1850 and if, as Stallings surmised, the entire chapel was only completed in 1851 the bishop would not have seen it roofed, let alone decorated.

What is definite is that the new diocese of Santa Fe had been created in 1850 and that on June 29, 1851, the new Bishop, Lamy, was in El Paso on his way to Santa Fe.[7] Hostility to the incoming French priests among Mexican seculars is now a matter of history. While private family chapels were customary in New Mexico the renovation of the Duran chapel, its frank dedication to Martinez and the coincidence in time seem to foreshadow the future differences between the two men and their factions. The greatest complaints by Zubiría of his New Mexico flock, from 1833 on, had been about those who were Penitentes, then a majority of the people. The Duran chapel, however, was only a few steps away from a morada or Penitente chapter house, so that its functions were clearly intended to be those of a place of worship away from diocesan supervision.

Comparison of the foregoing known signatures of Rafael Aragon shows that he was not particular as to the spelling of any name, including his own. On the other hand his lettering was as bold as his brush-strokes. In one case he reverted to a convention practiced by artists in the Middle Ages and abandoned at the advent of the Renaissance, that of reversing lettered inscriptions issuing from the mouth of a holy person pictured facing to the left. This was done in obedience to the iconographic prescription that the letters of each word must be shown in spoken order so that the lettering was done as if reversed in a mirror. Rafael Aragon was the only New Mexico santero who used, or misused, this forgotten mode. It is a matter of interest as to the source of his inspiration, and an intriguing solution is that it was contact between Aragon and Martinez. Martinez made his priestly studies in Durango where he may have seen illuminated manuscripts in this ancient style and then have told Aragon of them.

The earliest of Aragon's large retables now known was noted in the 1826 inventory of the mission of San Lorenzo at Picurís Pueblo.[8] The altar screen is still there and shows an already well defined personal style. A side retable in the Santuario del Potrero de Chimayó by Aragon was made after 1826 as it is not mentioned in the inventory of that

---

[7] AASF L.D.D. 1851, No. 8.
[8] AASF, Accounts, Book LXIV, Box 5, Fernandez de San Vicente Visitation, August 5, 1826.

year. Perhaps Bernardo Abeitia ordered it for el Santuario when Aragon was working at the Cordova chapel in the 1830s.

The church of San José de Chama received license to be built in 1844 and was completed and blessed by Bishop Zubiría in 1850.[9] Whatever was painted on the main altar screen was in poor condition and overpainted by an amateur in the 1920s. A tall retable made for one of the transepts where the ceiling was higher than in the nave was done by Rafael Aragon. The central figures of the Virgin of Refuge and archangels were boldly brushed and bright in color but the upper tier of the Guadalupe with Juan Diego and San Ysidro are sketchy in treatment. Perhaps they were done in haste because Aragon did not like the height of the scaffolding, or were done by a helper who lacked Aragon's skill with the brush.

The San José de Chama altar screen is now on long-term loan to the Museum of New Mexico and it is proper to give the record of its present condition here. At some past time the central niche for a statue of the patron (now, apparently, St. John Nepomuk but presumably it originally was St. Joseph), was boarded up and covered with wallpaper. Most of the Aragon painting was whitewashed, evidently after water from the leaking roof had destroyed parts of the panels. Where the cotton strips pasted over cracks between the hand-hewn boards had come loose they had been pulled off for the length of the retable, thus losing more painted areas. The whole retable was moved from the transept into the nave and the legs were cut down to fit into the lower ceiling of the nave. In 1958 the incumbent priest sent the sorry remains to the Museum for conservation, intending to return the retable to the chapel.

Alan Vedder and I spent weeks in removing the whitewash and dirt film, when it was found that most of the right side of the composition was lost. Like the signed retable in the Taylor Museum this one had eastern commercial muslin instead of the old hand-woven linen or twilled cotton over the cracks. In order to replace lost areas the remaining fragments were used as clues to the subjects, dress, ornamental painted pillars and cornices. What existed at the center and left was the basis for reconstruction of the right side. The Archangel Gabriel was completely lost except for spots of color but was replaced by using a small retablo of the same subject by Aragon as the model.

A record of the work before, during, and after conservation was made in slides. This series shows what was original and what was done by the conservators. The unfortunate modernization of the chapel of San José de Chama at the time led to a decision to leave the altar screen on loan to the Museum, which has probably protected it from further damages in the name of progress.

---

[9] Fray Angelico Chavez, "San José de Chama and Its Author" in *El Palacio* V. 60/4, 1953.

Although no record of the licensing of San Miguel del Valle has been found this chapel has a sand-cast bell, presumably by Francisco Lujan (Sec. II-C), dated 1851 or 1857. The small valley was settled by families from las Trampas when irrigated land at the latter was no longer available to younger people. The chapel was finely detailed with hand-hewn boards for the choirloft, squared vigas, delicately carved corbels and a small retable characteristically designed and colored by Rafael Aragon. In traditional fashion the bell and the altar screen were probably made when the church was completed or new. In view of the inscription of 1838 quoted above from the Duran chapel at Talpa and its statement that Rafael Aragon the sculptor had made it, he may also have designed or carved the woodwork at San Miguel del Valle as well as having painted the retable.

Although the people of the small valley have refrained from the urge to modernize and have done their best to preserve the chapel in original condition, the usual sheet metal roof was put on a few years ago. The misdirection of drainage from it and improper drainage from the road running behind the sanctuary of the chapel have combined to seriously damage the adobe walls of the building. If it is to be saved work must be done in the form of protective drainage, water-resistant plastering and a correctly designed roof. It is hoped that this can be done in 1973, for if it is not the chapel may well collapse, burying its contents. Too many of Rafael Aragon's major works have been overpainted or taken out of their original locations.

This is the case in the large church of Santa Cruz de la Cañada, completed by Fray Andres García in the mid-18th century and for a long time the church of the second villa, or town, in New Mexico, Santa Fe being the first in importance. While the Franciscan Andres García had made a pulpit, high altar screen, images and other things described by Dominguez, only his jointed figure of Christ in the Sepulchre remains in the church of Santa Cruz today. Nearly the same may be said for the works of Rafael Aragon there. When he did the large altar screen in the nave and the smaller one in the south chapel — formerly called that of the Third Order — is unrecorded. Certainly he could not have done the latter retable when the chapel was new in 1787. Aragon also painted two large half-length angels at the lower sides of García's retable and added painted shells to the two upper side panels as well as a crest containing the Holy Ghost at the top. Of these only the two angel heads remain untouched and they are hidden behind ugly pedestals for plaster statues. The large nave retable has been retouched twice by a heavy hand since 1930 as have the lower panels of the south chapel. The entire altar screen by García and additions by Aragon, except for the two angels just noted, and the 18th century style painting on the wooden arch above the sanctuary rail, were all overpainted with enamels in the outmoded, stenciled motifs of Viollet le Duc in 1947.

Instead of any record on the work of Rafael Aragon there is a lengthy accounting for images on altar screens made by José Manuel Benabides

Figure 206: San Fernando Rey d'España by Rafael Aragon.

and dated April 11, 1842 (AASF, L.D. 1840, No. 7, Sec. III-E). What was once the altar screen for the north or Carmen chapel was recorded by George Wharton James around 1905 in photographs taken at the Santa Cruz church and now in the Southwest Museum. The altar screen then had the same arched framing moldings that are still around the panels of the south chapel, but there were no images within the frames. In the center was a gilded tabernacle probably of Mexican origin which looked like the one described by Dominguez as being there in 1776 (page 77), as of painted, gilded wood lined with blue satin, with a small curtain to match. It had doors with a key. The chapel of Our Lady of Carmel was the center of a once wealthy confraternity and had many ornaments, now all gone including the choirloft, altar screen, tabernacle and statue of the Virgin sent from New Spain in the late 18th century by a returned Franciscan.

By 1852 Bishop Lamy was making unfavorable comments on the native clergy in his diocese and the friction between them increased in spite of written recommendations from Bishop Zubiría at Durango to obey their new bishop. Much of the antagonism, although not all of it, centered around Taos where Padre Martinez and his family lived. In 1856 several documents refer to Martinez' use of private chapels after his suspension by Lamy from parochial duties. This suspension was in the form of the bishop's acceptance of Martinez' resignation which the latter claimed had not been a formal resignation but a request for an assistant due to ill health. The Bishop sent for papers on private chapels in the area including those of Ranchos de Taos, Rio Chiquito (now Talpa), and the "Carmen Oratory" at Llano de Talpa.[10] This village is directly west of Talpa, divided from it by the valley of the Rio Chiquito. When the oratory was built is not known but its altar screen was by Rafael Aragon and much the same in size, manner and coloring as that of the Duran chapel, now in the Taylor Museum. With the record that the Duran chapel had been dedicated to the use of Padre Martinez in 1851 it is possible that others near Taos were made available as well.

The retable from the Carmen oratory was sold to the Spanish Colonial Arts Society in 1928 and was installed in the Museum of New Mexico in 1929 where it was on display until recently when it was stored to make way for a gift shop. The people of Llano had decided to sell the retable in order to pay for a metal roof and other improvements to the chapel. Frank Applegate in a memorandum on the transaction said that the lower tier of the altar screen was discarded due to its poor condition. Traditionally this would have been the level where inscriptions, if any, would have flanked the central receptacle for the Host, and which might have given a date, or clue to one, for the oratory and

---

[10]AASF, L.D.D., 1856, Nos. 20, 21, 22, 24, 25, 26, 27, 28, 29, 30, 31, 32, 33, 34, 36.

retable. The rest of the panels were in excellent condition until the storage of the retable. It is to be hoped that it will survive the stresses of being laid on its side for some years.

The only lettering now on the Llano retable is on the lunette at the top beside the dove representing the Holy Spirit: the capital letters A. and a reversed R. Here is another example of Aragon's reversed lettering; its meaning has led to speculations that it represents the sanrtero's initials. However, these would not have been accepted at the time in such a prominent position although he did sign his panel of San Calletano in that order, Aragon, José Rafel (supra). Another of Aragon's small panels contains the letters reversed — D, A beside a figure. Suggestions that these mean Agnus Dei, or Anno Domini, fail to relate these Latin phrases to the subject; there is no date to accompany A.D. nor any visible connection with the Lamb of God.

Aragon, as might be expected in view of his long working career and the popular subjects of his time, made many panels and statues of Our Lady of Guadalupe, St. Anthony, el Santo Niño de Atocha, St. Joseph, the Crucifix, the advocations of the Virgin Carmen, Dolores Refugio and Rosario. He was the only santero to represent San Estanislado Kostka on several panels. This Jesuit saint may have been introduced into New Mexico by means of the *laminas* or popular oil paintings on sheet metal that came from Mexico in the 19th century, or by prints brought from Mexico, from Currier and Ives of New York, or from the prolific print shops of the Rue St. Sulpice in Paris after 1851.

Another aberrant subject often repeated by Rafael Aragon was that of St. Ferdinand, King of Castille and León. Although this militant king, distinguished for his reconquest of Cordoba, Seville, Murcia and Jaén from the Moors, died in 1252, Aragon depicted him in a military cloak with a stiff, high collar such as was worn by Santa Ana of Mexico and Manuel Armijo of New Mexico in Aragon's lifetime. This military garment was probably Aragon's and many other contemporary New Mexicans' notion of royal dress. Some of Aragon's panels of San Fernando Rey had formerly been misidentified as of the Virgin but one in the Taylor Museum showing Fernando seated on a New Mexico-style chair is clearly lettered with his title. Others are iconographically quaint in showing the King apparently clapping the Virgin on the back or, in one example, Our Lady in a hoop skirt and crown is admiring a portrait of San Fernando that she holds in her hand. References to Ferdinand's battles against the heathen are Aragon's minor figures on these panels of the lion of León and of what appear to be crows devouring snakes but were probably intended to be eagles, destroying serpents that represented heretics.

Aragon's panels of San Gerónimo show his iconographic inventions as well; instead of the traditional lion that the saint befriended in the Alexandrian desert, Aragon provided another, crowlike bird which is interpreted as a partridge, the symbol of one of the seven deadly sins, luxury, that the hermit saint struggled to reject during his stay in the

Figure 208: Our Lady of Carmel, retablo by José Benito Ortega.

desert. Still another panel of Jerome has a burro at the bottom, instead of the lion, perhaps to symbolize willful ignorance. Subjects then popular in New Mexico such as the archangels, San Acacio, San Ramón Nonato and San Ysidro Labrador were repeatedly made by Aragon and, of course, the Trinity as three identical persons was also in demand.

Although others, beginning with Pedro Fresquís, had occasionally drawn a human face in profile, Rafael Aragon made more use of the profile. As a rule the early efforts of children to draw faces are more successful with profiles than with full faces; Aragon was quite the opposite. His full or three-quarter view faces are drawn with ease and conviction while the profiles are childish to an extreme; some even show corrected lines, a trait in painting that rarely occurred in New Mexico.

That Rafael Aragon was satisfying the wants of his patrons up to or after 1865, in the face of imported religious art styles, is apparent. His work combined refinement, color, innocence and conviction.

Chapel of St. Anthony, Pueblo Quemado, now Cordova

"En virtud de la horden que el Senor Alc^de de paz de la Villa de Santa Cruz de la Cañada nos pasa de palavra a mi, el C. Manuel Santistevan y al Ciudadano Diego Cordova, a que tasaranos unas hobras de la santa Capilla de S^n Antonio del Pueblo quemado, hemos pasado esactamente acumplier la dicha horden, y emos tasado primeramente el Cajón de hornamentos en 16 p^s de la tierra, 2° el pulpito en 26 p^s de la tierra, 3° el confecionario en dose p^s de la tierra, 4° las Barandillas de los grados y las del coro 12 p^s de la tierra, 5° la escalera del pulpito 2 p^s de la tierra, 6° la Bentanita de la sacristilla, un p. de la tierra. Dichas obra la hemos tasado como Cristianos enrreacto de conciencia.

"El taso de dichos obras me costa a mi, el Alc^de de este barrio, y lo precentie con dos testigos y doy fee.

Man.[1] Santistevan x	Pedro Ygnacio Tafolla x
Diego Cordova	tgo. Man.[1] Martín x
(rubric)	
Tasadores	tgo. Rafael Ant. Martín. x"

(By virtue of the order which the Señor Alcalde of the Peace of the town of Santa Cruz de la Cañada gave verbally to us, I, the citizen Manuel Santistevan, and the citizen Diego Cordova, that we should assess certain works of the holy chapel of St. Anthony of Pueblo Quemado; we have gone promptly to comply with the said order. We have first assessed the box of ornaments at 16 pesos of the country, secondly,

---

[1] AASF. L. D. 1821, No. 28.

the pulpit at 26 pesos of the country, thirdly the confessional at 12 pesos of the country, fourthly, the railings of the [sanctuary] steps and those of the choir at 12 pesos of the country, fifthly, the ladder for the pulpit at two pesos of the country, sixth the little window of the sacristy, one peso of the country. The said work we have assessed like Christians according to our understanding.

(The assessment of the said works was done at my expense, I, the Alcalde of this district, and I present them with two witnesses and I swear it to be true.

Manuel Santistevan x	Pedro Ygnacio Tafolla x
Diego Cordova	Tgo. Manuel Martín x
(rubric)	
Assessors	Tgo. Rafael Antonio Martín[1] x

The original document is undated and was classified by Fray Chavez with others of the year 1821. In view of the licensing of the chapel at Durango in 1832, it is probable that this report was made in that year or when the Quemado chapel was newly completed. The report and all of the signatures are written by one hand, presumably that of the citizen Diego Cordova who signed with a rubric, while other names are marked by crosses "because they could not sign." The features itemized are the basic ones of any old New Mexican chapel, requiring lumber and a carpenter's skill. Their valuations shed light on the relative degrees of costs between such things as a pulpit and a ladder or window frame. The latter could be made by any man who built himself a new house or room. The box of ornaments, for the essential religious furnishings such as a chalice and cruets for the altar, were presumably furnished by Bernardo Abeitia according to his promise to do so. The presumably later making of the wooden altar screen by Rafael Aragon, between 1834 and 1838, explains why its *hobra* was not included in the above assessment.

THE END OF A TRADITION

At the end of the past century, the itinerant santero was still in demand in rural areas that were far from town stores. While part of the santero's time was spent in the repair and renovation of old santos, there were enough families who wanted new statues of their preferred patron saints to keep several men busy in three widely separated districts of northern New Mexico. Rural villages loved their familiar forms of santos long after townspeople had discarded them in favor of zinc or plaster statuary, chromos, and mission cards. Town parishes had contributed the funds to buy the zinc figures, but as their prices ran as high as one hundred dollars, according to size, the country folk could more easily afford those made by a santero who lived with a family while he did his work, and who was paid in goods or livestock.

Another customer of the santero was the morada, especially at that time when villages boasted two or three moradas apiece. The specialized images they required could not be ordered from commercial supply houses at any price. Therefore, most of the work of the last santeros was made in sets for moradas. As a result, there was a certain repetition in subject matter, but the individual expression varied enough to make the work of three santeros easily identifiable.

The first of the three outstanding late imagemakers was Miguel Herrera of Arroyo Hondo in Taos County. He is mentioned as a musician as well as a maker of bultos,[1] and was working in the 1880s. Herrera's figures were simply modeled, colored in soft shades, and their heads were usually tilted. The elliptically shaped eyes, rosy cheeks, and ears like small clamshells set low down on the jaws, give his subjects an elfin expression. He is said to have used live models for his bultos, a practice which may be suspected of other santeros because of strong resemblances between certain images and living Spanish New Mexicans.

West of the Rio Grande the most important santero was Juan Ramon Velasquez, who died in 1902 when more than 80 years old.[2] After settling in New Mexico under the name of Velasco, this large family was later known as Belasquez, or Velasquez. They were pioneers, frontiersmen, soldiers, carpenters, and were sometimes involved in crime.[3] In the 1850s several of the men were fighting Indians with the New Mexico Territorial Militia. After the installation of Fort Massachusetts (later known as Fort Garland), in southern Colorado, Ute raids from the north were reduced and country was opened up which had not before been habitable along the Chama river in Rio Arriba County and westward across the mountains. Juan Ramon Velasquez had settled at Canjilón, a crossroad connecting scattered ranches now surrounded by national forests.

Mr. Elmer Shupe of Taos remembers when his father owned a store at Canjilón, and the old santero, tall, with untrimmed white hair and beard and a fierce expression, would come into the store. By then Velasquez was near the end of his life. Abelino Velasquez, a son of Juan Ramon, whom Mr. Shupe met in recent years, said his father used to make santos on order for all the villages west of the Rio Grande.[4] Contrary to the popular myth that the santero peddled ready-made images from town to town by the burro load, Juan Ramon packed his family, tools, materials and bedding in a wagon and went to the village that had sent him an order. While he made the figures more orders were given and the family might spend several winter months away from home.

---

[1] Cleofas M. Jaramillo, *Shadows of the Past,* Santa Fe, 1941, p. 61.
[2] "The Discovery of the Bulto Maker Ramon Velasquez," by José E. Espinosa, in *El Palacio,* Vol. 61, No· 6, p. 185.
[3] Fray Angelico Chavez, *Origins of New Mexico Families,* 1954, p. 309–11.
[4] "Addendum to Espinosa," *El Palacio,* Vol. 61, No. 6, pp. 190–191.

According to Abelino Velasquez, his father had no helper. This would account for the consistency of style throughout his work which is only divided by the use of hand-prepared tempera paints on earlier examples and of commercial house paints on later ones. Velasquez, however, learned to apply the oils as neatly as he had his own tempera colors.

Although not all of Velasquez' bultos were made for moradas, the majority was; he did many figures of the Crucifix, the Nazarene Christ, the Virgin of Sorrows, St. John Nepomuk and the Archangel Michael. One of these is of unusual interest because it records the dress of Spanish soldiers on the frontier: padded buckskin breeches with quilted rawhide vest and coat. The *cuero* or coat was the substitute for a metal cuirass in the New World where metals were scarce and animal hides were plentiful. As long as firearms were scarce or lacking the cuero was proof against arrows and lances so that it was still worn by Mexican militia in California and New Mexico in 1846. Velasquez could well have remembered the cuero from his youth. The bulto in its gaudy colored armor is now entitled St. Raphael, because it holds a fish, the emblem of the "Physician of God."[5] However, the cuero is more suitable to the militant Archangel Michael, patron of soldiers. The fish may have been added when a former owner required an image of the healing angel.

Velasquez solved a technical problem in the construction of the corpus of a crucifix that had not been attempted by earlier santeros. They had pegged together the head, torso, arms, legs and feet after carving them separately. The stresses of three point suspension and inevitable shrinkage of wood resulted in frequent breakage of the ankles and feet. Velasquez did make separate arms but he shaped the torso, legs and feet from a single block of wood. This required a larger piece of wood and far more labor but he had plenty of time, patience and enterprise, and he was surrounded by virgin pine forests. It is uncertain whether he used this design for its practical value, or because he liked the flat, angular planes it produced, but the result is interestingly stylized, and has proven to be durable.

Unlike his contemporaries who carved fists or paws, Velasquez modeled exquisitely posed hands with long, tapered fingers. He was most original in his treatment of the head, which he shaped of interesting arcs and convexities. Even the ears are peculiarly stylized, all shaped like an open bivalve in high relief, serving to accent the skull form like the handles of a pot. His painting emphasized these forms so that his figures have an expression of superintensity akin in spirit to Etruscan concepts of imagery. After thousands of years, Velasquez unknowingly recreated a form of stylized effigy that emanates force, vitality, mystery and indifference to human frailties. Uncontaminated by sweetly naturalistic, mass-produced religious "art," Velasquez seems to have satisfied the wants of his customers by making images as they existed in the minds

---

[5] Wilder and Breitenbach, 1943, pl. 15.

Plate 33: The Flight into Egypt
by Rafael Aragon. (Photograph
by Eliot Porter)

III-H

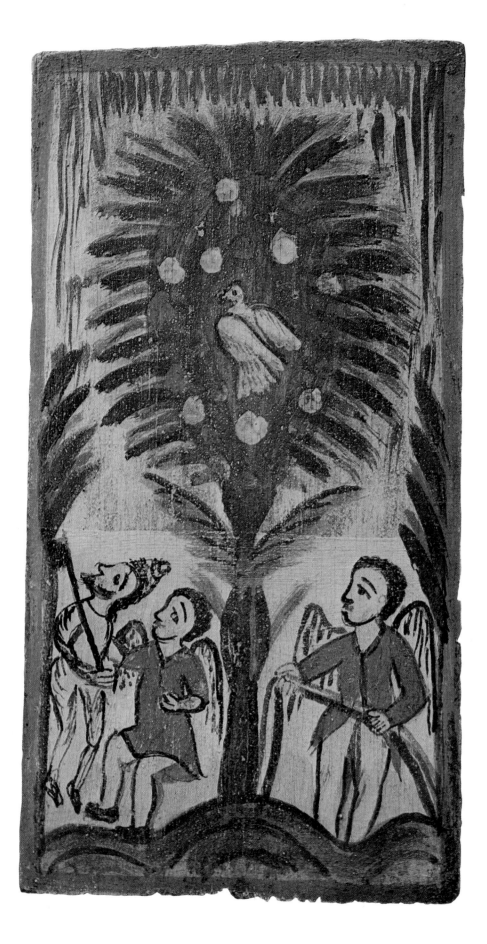

Plate 34: Abraham visited by three angels, by Rafael Aragon.

Figure 209: Our Lady of Refuge, retablo by José Benito Ortega.

Figure 210: Doña Sebastiana, *la Muerte* or Death, by José Benito Ortega. (Courtesy Museum of History and Technology, Smithsonian Institution)

Plate 35: San Calletano signed
"Aragon, José Rafel." (Photograph by Eliot Porter)

of himself and his neighbors, images representing all that they were not, but to whose likeness they aspired.

Figure 211: San Ysidro Labrador by José Benito Ortega.

Due to nomadic Indians who roamed the high plains east of the Rocky Mountains, the New Mexican colonists did not settle in this region until after the middle of the 19th century. Although Spain had claimed land all the way to the Mississippi, both royal and republican land grants had been left idle, for the open prairies were too dangerous to colonize. Instead of reducing Indian hostility, Anglo aggression from the eastern United States had aggravated it, and traders on the Santa Fe Trail frequently suffered from Indian attacks until Fort Union was established on the plains east of Mora, New Mexico, in 1851. This was the largest army post in the southwest, and, with a chain of smaller and more briefly occupied forts, made the plains safe for settlement. After the Civil War, villages and ranches scattered over eastern New Mexico, with a mixed population of land-hungry Spanish from the Rio Grande Valley, homesteaders released from military service, adventurers from the defeated Confederacy, and newly arrived immigrants from France, Germany and other countries.

The last of the notable santeros was born on March 20, 1858, on the banks of the Rio Mora. His name was José Benito Ortega, and he was baptized by the priest of St. Gertrude's parish of Mora, Father Munnecom, who recorded the infant's parents as José Guadalupe Ortega and Gabriela Maestas.[6] Another child of theirs, a daughter, married a retired soldier from Fort Union named Morris. She bore a son, José L. Morris, in 1886, and it is to him that I am indebted for information on his uncle, the santero José Benito Ortega.[7]

Ortega's methods were often makeshift, so that many of his figures have disintegrated faster than older santos. He sometimes used wood scrap from a sawmill, which he barely shaped with the knife, relying instead on excessively thick overlays of gesso to complete the modeling. The gesso was poorly prepared, full of air bubbles, and prone to peel away from the wood in chunks. When he made hollow-skirted or jointed figures, he reused cheap calico rags instead of the older leather or stronger twill.

His colors were few — indigo, light red, clear yellow, black, and spinach green — but these have proved fast against light, and he must have prepared the clear rosin varnish which now gilds his work with a warm aura. Before Ortega's name was known, his style of santo was described as a "Flat Figure" (Wilder and Breitenbach, 1943, page 29 and Pls. 7, 8, 9, 20, 39). However, his bultos are not consistently flat, especially those not made of sawmill lumber, and not in wide hoop skirts. The logical name, the Mora Santero, was also used in the past, since this seemed to be the region where he worked.

---

[6] Mora Parish, Bapt. Book I, page 91. (See Appendix III-H.)

[7] I am also indebted to Mr. Morris for sending me to Ortega's youngest daughter who gave me more information about her father.

Plate 37: Our Lady of Sorrows by Miguel Herrera. (Photograph by Eliot Porter)

Plate 38: San Antonio de Padua by José Benito Ortega.

Ortega certainly carved hands and bare feet like paws, but he introduced the new-style black pegged boot to the santos, bestowing them upon the Virgin, the Christ Child and male saints. These boots, newly arrived from St. Louis, first overland and then by rail, had replaced the homemade moccasins worn by nearly all New Mexicans, and so were none too good for the saints.

What saved Ortega's bultos from being merely inept was his treatment of the heads. These are long, narrow and slightly prognathous, with a retroussé nose. The eyes are carved with sharp definition of brow and lids, and accented by precise outlining, sometimes with fine rows of dots, while the pupils gaze fixedly forward, piercing into the thoughts of the supplicant.

In spite of Ortega's indifference to realism and his deliberate stylization of form and detail, many of his bultos resemble living people of Spanish descent in New Mexico, which suggests that he too may have used a relative or neighbor for a model. His versions of the Holy Family, the Santo Niño de Atocha, San Ysidro Labrador, and the apocryphal San Acacio, are as gay and appealing as possible, in sharp contrast to the agonized figures that he made for moradas. He revived an iconographic concept in painting once used by Italian primitive schools and discarded soon after Giotto, that of painting the corpus of the dead Christ a light blue.

Ortega's renderings of the death angel, or Muerte (Ref. Sec. IV), are quite distinctively different from those of the elder Lopez and the anonymous maker of the García Muerte. The lack of a lower jaw on Ortega's examples, and their semiskeletonized rather than skeletal bodies, have a certain shocking power.

The dual approach deliberately chosen by New Mexican santeros, work in the three-dimensional round or in two dimensions on a panel, has been remarked upon. Ortega was no exception, and in his few recorded panels, with no regard for form or depth, he turned out childish scrawls which sometimes look like old Spanish playing cards or modern comic strips, although the coloring is the same as on his bultos. A few examples of both with semiliterate inscriptions painted on them are lettered in the same hand.

Ortega's work is an excellent illustration of the paradox that the more primitive a New Mexican santo appears, the more recently it was made. Although it has been customary to attribute more professionally assembled images to later santeros "who had had more training," Ortega was actually farther removed from the older, urban prototypes. If he was not self-taught, he had seen some older santero at work, and had then launched upon his own career. His working years began at a time when new things and new standards of values had already reached New Mexico, and when the new clergy were engaged in discouraging just such "pagan" images as he was making in quantity. He seems to have been as totally unaffected by the example of new methods of iconography as were his customers. These, scattered over three counties in villages often isolated from the world by bad roads, were satisfied with Ortega's work

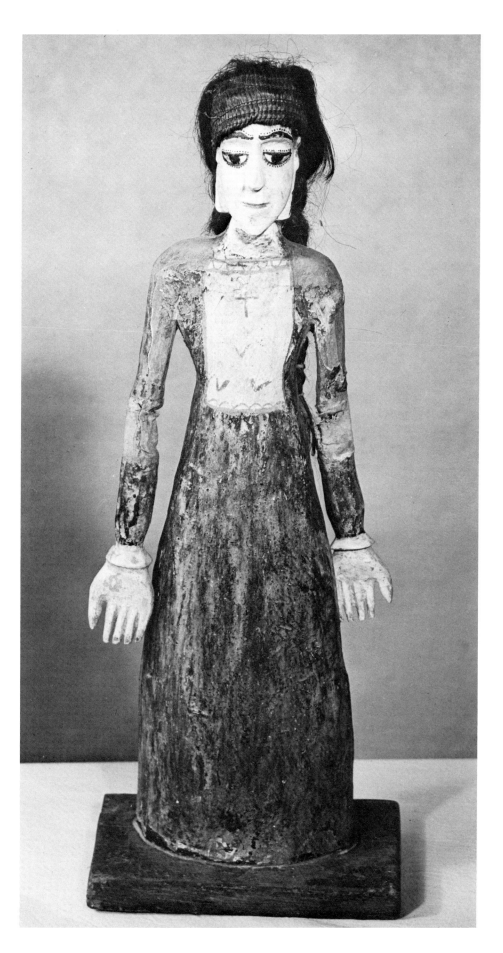

Plate 40: Our Lady of Carmel by José Benito Ortega.

Figure 213: José Dolores Lopez with some of his carvings, from a tintype. (Courtesy of Mr. and Mrs. Richard E. Ahlborn)

Figure 214: José Dolores Lopez in 1930. (Photograph by Ansel Adams)

III-H

and proud to own his santos. He worked for the devout and not for the curio dealer, and in every respect is a good example of the true popular artist.

José L. Morris could not remember when his uncle, José Ortega, had died, because he had moved to Raton in 1907 after the death of his wife. There, said Mr. Morris, Ortega had worked as a house plasterer for some years and no longer made santos. In 1967 I had the pleasure of visiting José Benito Ortega's youngest daughter, Refugio Sandoval, who lives in Raton. She is lively, gracious and witty with clear recollections of her father. Mrs. Sandoval had no santos made by him, because in 1908, a year after they went to Raton, the riverbanks overflowed and the whole eastern side of town, including their adobe house, was under water. Thus Ortega's santos were lost as well as their other belongings, and "Father never made any more." Mrs. Sandoval said that she was born in 1900; she thought that her father had died "during the last war." Through the kindness of Monsignor Sigmund Charewicz, then Pastor of St. Joseph's Church at Raton, the record of Ortega's death was found in the register. The date was September 2, 1941; burial was in Fairmount Cemetery, Raton (Appendix III-H, Ortega).

So the end of a tradition, a folk art and a popular school slipped by unnoted but not quite lost. The imagemaker who was not a religious, nor of the wealthier class, was recalled by his descendants as an ancestor or relative rather than as a santero. Although New Mexican saintmakers were for a long time dismissed as nameless, it is now evident that some of them were connected with important people and events of their time and that they were respected in their day. The remainder of the "anonymous" santeros may yet be identified through documents or other sources.

Figure 215: *Muerte* made to be carried by children, early 20th century.

APPENDIX
Ortega

EXCERPT:

March 28, 1858.

I, Pedro J. Munnecom, parish priest of Mora, solemnly baptized with holy oils an infant, born on March 20th of the same year, who received the name José Benito Ortega, legitimate son of José Guadalupe Ortega and Gabriela Maestas. The godparents were Rafael Cardenas and Juana Gertrudis Aragon, also of La Cueva, whom I instructed in their obligations and spiritual parenthood and to the foregoing I sign,

P. J. Munnecom

(Book of Baptisms of the Parish of St. Gertrudis of Lo de Mora, beginning on the 25th day of January, 1856, and having for the first parish priest Señor Don Pedro Juan Munnecom [page 91].)

AUTHOR'S NOTE:

In my conversation with Mr. José L. Morris, nephew of Ortega, in 1962 he stated that the boy's name was meant to be Juan Benito, but that some confusion during the baptismal ceremony had resulted in his being given the name of José Benito. In spite of this, it appears that in later life the santero was known as Juan Benito. In Book No. 5 of Mora parish baptismal records, we find Juan Benito and Maria de la Luz Ramirez Ortega, his wife, having their son baptized Macedonio, September 12, 1885. In 1876, the same couple had acted as sponsors to a boy named Maestas.

Juan Benito and Maria de la Luz had a daughter, Ana, in 1889, and another, Maria Delfina, in 1892. The earlier and later records give their home as La Cueva, while another says they lived at Coyote de Mora, a name no longer found on maps. Ortega's nephew, Morris, said Ortega had a son named Macedonio, Morris' cousin, and this confirms the identity of the santero as José (Juan) Benito Ortega. He is not to be confused with a contemporary named Juan Bautista Ortega, whose wife was Maria Casimira Martinez, and who had a son, Benjamín, in 1889. This man, like others of his day, seems to have been named in honor of Bishop Lamy as well as St. John Baptist.

Mr. Morris, a pious, visionary man who still lives with his family at Buenavista, across the river from La Cueva, described his uncle's habit of walking from village to ranch house under the wide skies with a small bundle of tools and materials. He would stay with the families who wanted santos until he had finished their orders. Before dealers had scattered the images from their owners' homes, chiefly since the 1920s, nearly all the santos in Mora, San Miguel and Colfax counties were works of Ortega. The few exceptions were older, and had been brought from the Rio Grande valley with settlers to northeastern New Mexico. For a long time Ortega lived at La Cueva, a drowsy village on the Mora river since the highway passed it by, with a handsome old stone mill and store. After his wife died, Ortega followed his children to Raton, New Mexico, where they had gone to find employment.

Mr. Morris was quite positive that his uncle had never had a helper, in spite of the astonishing number of figures he made. However, he said that as a boy of twelve, he was shown by Ortega how to make his first santo, a crucifix; after that Morris had made others which he sold. This would suggest that from time to time members of the family may have helped Ortega in roughing out work in the process of learning the trade. The crucifix made by the twelve-year-old Morris shows no trace of Ortega's style, but would be a creditable piece of work for any child of that age today.

Mora parish, in its beginnings, covered several modern counties, and the priests stationed there served Cimarron, Rayado, Wagon Mound, Ocaté, and Fort Union, as well as nearly two dozen nearby villages. The protection of the military forts on the plains led to rapid settlement to the east and north by settlers in various areas. In 1887, Reverend Father Fourchegui made a summary of his duties on the last day of December:

> During the year there were 294 baptisms. Illegitimate children are but a few in this parish . . . and it is not astonishing since bad women are very few . . . I have these chapels to visit — San Antonio of Agua Negra (Black Lake), San Isidro of Rio de Agua Negra, San Antonio of Santiago de Cebolla, San José Arriba de Cebolla, San Francisco de Cebolla, Carmen de Cebolla, San José de Cebolla, Santo Niño de Buena Vista, San Rafael of La Cueva, Santa Rita de Coyote, and Our Lady of Guadalupe. These are visited at least once each month and mass is celebrated each time.
>
> I have besides the chapels of Santiago de Mora, of Santo Niño in upper Cebolla, of the Sacred Heart of Jesus at Llano del Coyote, the little chapel of Cañada del Carro, the settlement of Ojo Felíz where mass is celebrated once in a while.

Names such as Nolan, Elliott, Roy, Gallagher, and Dougherty appear, together with those of Beaubien, Le Fevre, and St. Vrain, as husbands of Spanish girls. In this ambience of change and expansion, the santero Ortega roamed the plains, making his particular type of santos for all the little chapels, moradas and village homes for over thirty years.

DEATH CERTIFICATE OF ST. JOSEPH PARISH
RATON, NEW MEXICO

Juan Benito Ortega of Raton, New Mexico, died September 2, 1941, and was buried September 4, 1941, at Fairmount Cemetery. Age at time of death — 86 years. He was born in Mora, New Mexico. Cause of death is listed as old age.

Given at Raton, New Mexico, the Thirteenth of September, 1967.

Sigmund H. Charewicz

R. Rev. Msgr. Sigmund Charewicz, Pastor

In a covering note Monsignor Charewicz noted that the age of the deceased as given by relatives "is sometimes an approximate age," and that the name was recorded as Juan Benito and not José Benito. The discrepancy in names is an interesting example of individual self determination in the matter of a personal name in spite of the baptismal ritual and record.

THE LOOSE ENDS

As may be expected in any study of popular art, there are a good many loose ends of recorded or remembered names of artists with no associated specimens, and still more specimens with no connection to any maker's name.

Two 18th century Franciscans were named by Dominguez as having made ornaments for churches: Father Juan José Toledo and Father Rafael Benavides. In addition, the artistic efforts of Father Andres Garcia were well enough described by Dominguez to allow identification of those still in existence (Sec. I-D). Dominguez said that Father Toledo had made a small statue of the Virgin of the Immaculate Conception for Nambe mission. ". . . it is ugly enough, but very much adorned with little ribbon flowers and ordinary small medals" (Dominguez, 1776, p. 54). Father Toledo was at Nambe in 1753-55, and then went to Abiquiu. Father Benavides' altar screen in San Felipe de Neri church of Albuquerque was described as "very seemly," painted on canvas in two sections and in perspective. Below were painted three saints, and above a crucifix with Sts. Joseph and Augustín, and God the Father above all (Dominguez, p. 146). All of these were said to have been painted as if in architectural niches or alcoves, a fashion of persistent Baroque that was popular in Mexico. As usual we may wonder if Father Benavides merely had the retable painted or if he was really the artist. Dominguez, in speaking of unknown donors of furnishings to the church, said, "I specify what the King gave and the altar screen which Father Benavides made . . ." Benavides was in Albuquerque in 1774-75, but most of his northern service was in or near El Paso del Norte. In the course of time both of these artistic efforts have vanished, leaving no clues to the probable appearance of any other works of art which Benavides or Toledo might have done. As was his wont, Dominguez gave no suggestion as to who had made and painted the altars and retables of the old parroquia at Santa Fe, noting only the "seemly" pair of altars sent from Mexico City.

Local folksay has produced several names of 19th century santeros, sometimes pointing to a santo as an example of a particular man's work.

These, however, are usually in the style of an already identified santero, or else no concrete specimen is indicated to relate the name and type of work. José Manuel Benavides, who has not been named by living individuals but was recorded in an archive, is a case in point (page 384). The name of Miguel Aragon was collected from folksay by the late Frank Applegate as the author of santos now known to have been made by José Rafael Aragon.

In the baptismal records of Santa Cruz, there are the following entries:
31 August, 1868, a daughter, Maria Rosa, born to Miguel Aragon and Maria Juana Trujillo.
5 March, 1870, a daughter, Maria Casimira, born to Manuel Aragon and Juanita Trujillo.
24 February, 1871, a daughter, Marcelina, born to Miguel Aragon and Maria Juanita Trujillo.
30 October, 1883, a daughter, Maria Pilar, born to Manuel Aragon and Maria Josefa Montoya, of Quemado.
18 January, 1891, a son, Juan Benito Aragon, born to Manuel Aragon and Maria Josefa Montoyo, of Quemado.

Inaccuracy in writing Christian names and failure to record the names of grandparents of the baptized child as well as places of residence, make it difficult to decide whether these entries refer to one man who had two wives or two different individuals named Miguel and Manuel Aragon. The dates of these records make it unlikely that Miguel or Manuel were helpers of José Rafael Aragon, unless they had served him during childhood. Although the existence of a Miguel Aragon at Cordova is confirmed by these records, nothing else has been found to prove that he was a santero. Folk memory can be long, but is often unreliable in the matter of time.

Applegate, in the same incomplete manuscript by Mary Austin that is cited above, was quoted by her as follows:
Juan Flores, who, the last I knew of him, 1926, was living at Las Colonias, a little ranching village forty miles out of Santa Fe, is now past ninety years of age, and according to his account remembers when the American army under General Kearny invaded New Mexico and separated it permanently from Mexico. Juan formerly lived at San Miguel, fifty miles east of Santa Fe, where his father, whose name was also Juan, followed the art of the santero from about the year 1810 until about 1850, when the demand for handmade santos practically ceased. Juan Flores was a prolific santo maker and there were a great many santos in the territory about San Miguel made by him. In the little church of San Isidro, which stands in the tiny village of the same name, not far from San Miguel, there is a large carved figure of San Isidro, the patron saint of the village, which Flores made, and the oxen accompanying the group are as large as shepherd dogs. All of the santos of Juan Flores are quite distinct in character and technique from those of other santeros and can be readily distinguished from them.
How reliable this information was is uncertain; a son ought to have

430

III-I

Figure 216: Celso Gallegos of
Agua Fria. (Photograph by Ina
Sizer Cassidy)

Figure 217: Polychromed figure by great-great-grandfather
of Celso Gallegos.

been a good source about his own father's work and, with the lapse of time and nearly complete abandonment of San Miguel del Vado, no traditions about santeros there are left. It has already been noted that in rural areas the demand for regional santos did not cease as early as 1850 but this may have been due to the elder Flores' illness or death or a faulty memory on the part of his son in his old age.

Dr. Florence H. Ellis recorded village traditions in her "Santeros of Tomé" (*New Mexico Quarterly,* V. XXIV/3, 1954) about the bultos kept in the Tomé church and in private homes. The earliest name given her was that of Antonio Silva, said to have studied art in Spain or Portugal and to have come to Tomé about 1790. He was credited with having made the large crucifix and figure of "Nana Virgén" at Tomé, but beneath their heavy enamel overpainting the basic carving is typical of that of provincial 19th century Mexico. Tomé people also claimed that the large crucifix, taken from the nearby chapel at Valencia in 1938 and placed in the newly built church of Cristo Rey in Santa Fe, was also made by Silva. The two figures are completely different in treatment and detail. The Cristo Rey crucifix is closely related to a whole series of others assigned to the santero Molleno (Sec. III-B).

Another Silva's name is preserved on a yellowed scrap of paper attached to the fabric garments of a hollow-frame figure of the Virgin owned by Mrs. Elizabeth Fountain Armendariz of La Mesilla. This writing states that the bulto was made by the santero Rafael Silva in the 1840s. The date is plausible in relation to the rather sweetly carved head and mechanical construction of the statue. As yet no other santos have been noted that can be associated with Rafael Silva, nor is it known if he ever traveled to northern New Mexico. The identification of santero styles from the present border region between Mexico and the United States is complicated by several factors. Among these are the steady migration of Mexican nationals to the north, who brought their family saints with them, and the buying trips made by wagon to the Las Cruces-La Mesilla region early in this century by the Santa Fe trader, John Candelario (Personal communication from Mrs. Elizabeth Fountain Armendariz). Agents for the Fred Harvey Indian Company also collected in southern New Mexico, and in all cases little or no record was kept of the place of origin of the examples. Santos known to have come from the border region share pronounced characteristics with provincial Mexican folk images in the extensive use of glass eyes, cloth dipped in gesso and modeled to form drapery, feet composed of solid plaster built up on the base instead of being attached to the figure itself, more theatrical poses and presence of gold leaf or paint.

Robert Shalkop, former director of the Taylor Museum at the Colorado Springs Fine Arts Center, is a capable researcher and presented excellent exhibitions and catalogues for them during his stay there. He and I have agreed on most problems of identification of New Mexico santeros but I can not accept his attribution of a medley of styles to Miguel Herrera of Arroyo Hondo, on the basis of folk traditions. With the best of intentions local informants, relying on childhood memories

Figure 218: Plough horse by
Celso Gallegos. (Present owner
unknown)

and uncritical of style as well as materials, may be quite wrong. Shalkop attributed a nonhomogenous group to Herrera and included in this one of the bultos in the style that I assign to Miguel Herrera, that of pretty faces, small, clam-shell-like ears and strong consistency in treatment and technique, and named this latter type the work of the "anonymous Arroyo Hondo santero."[1] As these groups were so named on the basis of folklore rather than on stylistic characteristics it is another example of the hazards of reliance on folksay alone. I have had nondescript, 19th century bultos shown to me by their proud owners who firmly stated that one came from Spain before 1598, and another that was claimed to have been made by Miera y Pacheco (Sec. I-D). These claims were based on statements by parents or grandparents of the owners but the objects themselves disproved the traditions.

Taos and Arroyo Hondo folksay has spoken of a santero, José Miguel Rodriguez, again without association with works, and of his pupil, one Patricio Atencio. A bulto of the Guadalupe, alleged to have been made by Atencio, that was once shown to me was certainly of inept construction and of recent materials.

Alfonso Florence, a dealer-scout until his untimely death, told me in 1949 that he had been told by several older persons of a Spanish New Mexican schoolteacher who made crucifixes for his pupils' parents around 1875. This teacher, whose name was not recalled, was said to have taught at the one-room school at Chaperito on the Gallinas creek in San Miguel County. To judge by the crucifixes attributed to him that I have seen, he had a recognizable manner of carving: rather simplified bodies without emphasis on wounds, and a consistent habit of painting the loincloths blue.

At Fort Garland, among the exhibits arranged by the Colorado State Historical Society, there is a figure of San Ysidro with his oxen and plough which is credited to Diego Sandoval and assigned to a period around 1860. The label was made by a former curator, William J. Wallrich, but the bulto is identifiable as one of those made by Miguel Herrera of Arroyo Hondo, north of Taos (supra). Wallrich, in his excellent paper, "The Santero Tradition in the San Luis Valley" (*Western Folklore*, V.X/2, 1951) stressed the inability of his informants there to relate specific santos with the names of alleged santo makers. Wallrich collected several names, one being Antonio Herrera, who was said to have gone to San Luis from Taos in the 1850s. On the basis of a single bulto shown to Wallrich as a work by Antonio Herrera, he questioned the date; the bulto was like those made by several woodcarvers of the 20th century in New Mexico.

Wallrich was told of a Francisco Vigil who had made large figures with articulated limbs for Penitente chapters and who had died "only

---

[1] Shalkop, 1969.

Figure 219: Crucifix of wood and an apostle of stone, by Celso Gallegos.

a few years ago." Of this class there are certainly many examples, ranging from those competently carved, joined and painted to crudely assembled eyesores. Francisco Vigil may well have been the sculptor of many of these, but without some proof of association, it is presently impossible to say which were by him. Wallrich also quoted an elderly informant, Joe Sanchez, who told him that his father had been apprenticed as a youth to a santero at Ojo Caliente, a village of Rio Arriba County, New Mexico, until his father decided to move to the San Luis valley when he gave up santo making to become a farmer. Perhaps the santero of Ojo Caliente was Monico Villalpando whose name was given to Elmer Shupe in 1960 by an older resident of Ojo Caliente. This informant said that, as he recalled, Villalpando was at work about 1910. Allowing for his having been a santero earlier than 1910, he may have been the man to whom Joe Sanchez' father had been apprenticed. Villalpando may well have made some of the unidentified figures for any number of moradas in Rio Arriba County. As is usually the case, no example of Villalpando's work could be produced by the Ojo Caliente informants.

In my own experience, I have been unable to find residents of Ojo Caliente who could recall the existence of the painted altar screen that was once in the sanctuary of the old chapel of Santa Cruz at Ojo Caliente, let alone the name of the santero. From what can be seen of painted detail in one photograph, taken about 1880, it was done in the manner of the second half of the 19th century. The chapel of Santa Cruz del Ojo Caliente was licensed from Durango in 1811 and blessed in 1812. On his visitation of the eighth of July, 1818, de Guevara noted that there was an altar painted in oils. However, upon the next visitation of Vicar Fernandez de San Vicente, in 1826, the inventory described a retablo painted in tempera with seven images: St. Anthony and St. Francis, the Holy Trinity, St. John Nepomuk, Our Lady of Guadalupe, St. Raphael and "the Holy Cross which is the founder." It was noted that the people of Ojo Caliente were so poor that they did nothing to provide for the church, which was poorly furnished with "pulpit, confessional, an old metal censer, ten wooden candlesticks, one wooden chair and a baptismal font of copper." These were mostly supplied by Cura Antonio José Martinez, then at Abiquiu parish, of which Ojo Caliente was a visita.[1]

If there was a painted altar screen in the Ojo Caliente chapel by 1818, it is more than likely that the inevitable erosions of time and water would have led to repainting or at least retouching before 1880. In this photograph, five of the original subjects may be seen, although with discrepancies in the manner of painting among them. The Trinity

---

[1] AASF, Accounts, LXIV, Box 5-E, Visitation of Vicar Agustín Fernandez de San Vicente, 1826.

Figure 220: Crucifix with Mourning Figures by an unknown santero of the Pecos River.

was probably on the upper level which is hidden from view by the vigas of the nave ceiling; it may be assumed that the Holy Cross was depicted in the central panel of the retable, above that of the Guadalupe and concealed by a cloth in the photograph. The custom of reproducing the original subjects on an altar screen when it was repainted by a later santero has been noted here before. The fact that the entire Ojo Caliente retable has vanished is to be regretted.[2]

The makers of various morada figures, as already pointed out, must have been many or prolific in view of the existing number of more or less repetitious bultos of the Nazarene Christ, the Ecce Homo, the crucifix, Christ in the Sepulchre and of the sorrowing Virgin. The name of Francisco Vigil of San Luis, reported by Wallrich, was also collected from informants by Elmer Shupe, which suggests that his work was extensive enough to have impressed itself upon memories although no particular santo was produced as having been made by Vigil.

A few small groups of santos have been isolated on the basis of mannerisms, such as those bultos consistently carved in the half-round with flat backs, elongated bodies and small, pudgy-faced heads. Their traditional materials and usually battered condition suggest a fairly early, or pre-1850, date of making. A single crucifix with mourning figures, from Villanueva on the Pecos river, is strikingly Romanesque in character, and at present cannot be related to other New Mexican crucifixes. Villanueva was first settled before 1818 under the name of la Cuesta de Nuestra Señora de Guadalupe; its residents would have owned santos, but as in other places, the taste for modern images has led to disposal of older ones. In 1952 the only New Mexican bulto left in the church was one of the patroness, Our Lady of Guadalupe, a small figure swathed in nylon and veiling. It was relegated to the sacristy from which the resident nuns hoped soon to remove it.

With few exceptions the painters of several small series of retablos may be suspected of having been amateurs, or to have been working after the advent of commercial church art. The New Mexican habit of moving to new lands in the past century, taking belongings along, led to the equally active moving of santos. In the past forty years, the complete dispersal of old images by dealers has compounded the problem of lack of records, except in a few fortunate instances like those described in the preceding pages. While santos were basic symbols of devotion, it was taken for granted that there would always be a santero to replace or repair them. Thus, in spite of their religious import, santos were regarded as expendable; the santero would make another just as good, and he did. It was only when commercial religious "art" destroyed the profits of the regional imagemakers that their traditional skills and techniques were abandoned and lost.

---

[2] "Troubles at Ojo Caliente, A Frontier Post," E. Boyd, *El Palacio,* V. 64/11, 1957.

THE THIRD ORDER OF ST. FRANCIS AND THE PENITENTES OF NEW MEXICO

In order to understand the architectural unit known as a morada[1] in New Mexico, a review of certain historical events is necessary. Some of these are well known, others are obscure. Together they form the history of the Penitentes[2] in New Mexico. This internal evidence indicates that the Penitentes of New Mexico were not a native organization whose rules and practices were invented by the members overnight and fabricated from whole cloth, as has been suggested by one historian.[3]

Two great religious orders were founded at nearly the same time, one by St. Dominic of Guzman in 1206 and the other by St. Francis of Assisi in 1209. Each was composed of three groups, one for men, another for women, both of whom forsook the world and entered conventual life, and a third for lay men and women. These, under the direction of their spiritual guides, undertook to perform special religious duties and activities while pursuing a normal or worldly life. Designed to bridge the gap between the strict observance of the cloistered religious and the sometimes all too perfunctory devotions of the layman, the principle of a third, or lay, order was not first conceived by either St. Dominic or St. Francis. Of the existing Roman Catholic religious orders, eight have third orders for lay persons: the Augustinians,

---

[1] Morada: the Spanish noun for the home, "la casa de mi morada" the house of my residence, also used for a schoolhouse or building in which public meetings are held. In New Mexico it has come to refer to the private chapterhouses of members of the brotherhood of penitents.

[2] The regional name for the cult of the Brotherhood of Light and its members since their secession from the supervision of the Church early in the 19th century.

[3] "The Penitentes of New Mexico," Fray Angelico Chavez, O.F.M., *New Mexico Historical Review,* Vol. 29, 1954, p. 97.

Figure 222: Penitente procession, drawing by B. J. Nordfeldt.

Carmelites, Dominicans, Franciscans, Minims, Premonstratensians, Servites, and Trinitarians. Of these, the Dominicans' rules lay the most stress upon penance; the Franciscans are the most numerous today.

As the Franciscan Order grew and extended outside of Italy, new groups of the Third Order were organized. Since the first missionaries to Mexico were Franciscans, they founded many of the first churches and convents there, although other religious orders followed them soon after 1524. When Oñate founded the new kingdom of New Mexico in 1598, he brought Franciscans who were the spiritual pastors of the colonists for two hundred years. It was then usual for the aristocracy as well as plain people to belong to the Third Order in Catholic countries elsewhere, and not solely in New Mexico. Many old Spanish wills begin with the statement that the testator, being of sound mind, loyal to the King, believing in the doctrines of the Church, etc., desires to be buried in the habit of the Third Order. In New Mexico, however, after the two cults of Our Lady of Light, and Our Lady of Carmel were introduced in 1760, the prominent and well-to-do class transferred its interests and benefactions to these, leaving the Third Order composed mostly of the poorer people.

Because there was nothing unusual about the Third Order in New Mexico, there is hardly more than routine mention of it in records until the Dominguez report of 1776. In this he repeatedly criticized them for nonpayment of dues, for poorly kept altars in the churches (even in the Parroquia at Santa Fe), and for failure to keep records or have official licenses. At Santa Cruz, Dominguez noted the "poor wooden altar" of the Third Order, and that the images upon it belonged not to the group but to the church. He was told that members were so poor they could not pay, even in firewood, for altar ornaments and candles.

At Abiquiu Dominguez wrote:

> Fridays of Lent, Via Crucis by the father, and later, after dark, discipline attended by those who come voluntarily, because the father merely proposes it to them, and, following his good example, there is a crowd of Indians and citizens (Dominguez, p. 124).

The "father" was Fray Sebastian Fernandez, born in the province of Asturias, Spain, where he had undoubtedly been trained in the practice of various forms of physical self-discipline — especially on the Fridays of Lent — which were then in general usage not only by the most revered saints but by many humble members of the church. Voluntary physical penances have been traditional through many centuries of Christianity, and are still practiced unobtrusively today. It was only natural for laymen to emulate the example of their saints and spiritual mentors in devotional practices. Father Dominguez saw nothing untoward in his visit to Abiquiu; if he had he would have been quick to say so. It is apparent that the disciplines were familiar and unexceptionable.

IV

Abiquiu was a *genízaro*[4] settlement on the Chama river whose inhabitants were atypical of the nearby Pueblo Indians. The Chama and its tributary streams formed natural passes through the mountains for "Gentile" or un-Christianized Indian raiders; hence the Spanish planted genízaro families in buffer settlements between the wild tribes across the mountains and their towns and the peaceable pueblos in the fertile Rio Grande valley. While the Pueblo Indians had accepted Christianity, they had, since the earliest coming of the Spanish, ignored the Third Order and the Spanish practice of physical self-discipline, to which they pointed as a sign of Spanish dementia. Genízaros, however, uninfluenced by dual religions, adopted the complete teachings of their missionaries. This fact is one which in time made the Chama river and its principal village, Abiquiu, a Penitente stronghold.

Throughout his report of 1776, Dominguez did not once use the name *Penitente,* nor did he ever mention separate moradas, or houses used by the Third Order outside of the churches. This, obviously, was because neither the name nor the need for a morada existed in his time; the Third Order was conducted as usual by the Franciscan missionaries, and its members, whether Spanish or Indian, made whatever devotions or disciplines were "proposed" to them by the fathers.

As early as 1760 the recall of Franciscan missionaries from New Mexico had been started by Bishop Tamarón of the Diocese of Durango. With extraordinary enterprise he made a tour of his diocese which then included much of northern Mexico and the New Mexican frontier. Upon his return home he recommended that the Franciscans be withdrawn from the north and replaced by secular clergy. He argued that after 162 years the Indians should have been Christianized if they were ever to be, and that the increased Spanish population should not have to depend for spiritual ministrations upon missionaries inconveniently stationed at Indian pueblos. The bishop also advanced reasons of economy in administration, based upon theoretical statistics, urging that if the secular clergy were maintained by their parishioners instead of, as was then the case, by a far-distant mission headquarters (which was supported by royal or private grants), it would be more economical. His premise was to prove impractical for the next century.

As with other matters requiring the consideration and consent of the Crown and the Holy See, the recall of the Franciscans was eventually approved, and their withdrawal went on over several decades. As the Franciscans left New Mexico, secular replacements came in fewer numbers, and were met with the open opposition of the people. Although they were Spanish-speaking, the new priests had no mis-

---

[4] Genízaro: Spanish corruption of the Turkish name for mercenary soldiers; in New Mexico Spanish it is used to refer to Indians of mixed groups and breeds who had been ransomed from the nomadic tribes, or captured as infants by the Spanish from their Indian enemies. Since most of these were taken in childhood they had forgotten or never known their traditional Indian religions.

sionary experience and were unaccustomed to the rough ways of the frontier. Their criticisms of their charges' religious habits were as bitter as those of their lodgings and comforts — or lack of them. Cura Ortega, for example, was the first secular priest assigned to Santa Cruz which was, in 1798, a town second only to Santa Fe. His censures led the people to complain so vigorously of him to the vicar at Santa Fe that Ortega was transferred in six months. His successor, Father Lombíde, went to Santa Cruz in 1802, and in a few weeks was embroiled with the Franciscan at Picurís Indian mission over the jurisdiction of the Spanish village of las Trampas, which since 1751 had been assigned as a visita of Picurís because it was much nearer to the latter.

While waiting the arrival of the new seculars, the remaining Franciscan missionaries continued to hold their old posts in the Spanish villages as they did at the Indian missions. Apparently recall to Mexico was not total, for a few Franciscans remained in New Mexico until the last died, in 1840. Numerous documents exist which bear witness to the friction between the remaining Franciscans, the secular newcomers and the people of New Mexico. Various letters and directives were issued forbidding either religious group to complain to the governor, already a habit of long standing, or to influential citizens. The presence of a few Franciscans, unaware in their isolated situation of sweeping changes in religious as well as scientific thinking in the Old World, made them the moral and spiritual supporters of the local interpretations of religious observances. Thus they contributed unwittingly to friction and, ultimately, schism between members of the Third Order and the Church.

This is understandable when it is recalled that since 1598 the people of New Mexico had been exposed to no other interpretation of doctrine than that of the Franciscans. To alter, add to, or take away one iota of their accustomed teachings was unthinkable and unacceptable. This attitude was well summarized by Pedro Bautista Pino in his *Exposición Sucínta y Sencilla de la Provincia del Nuevo Mexico,* Cádiz, Spain, 1812, when, in urging that a diocese, schools and a college be established in Santa Fe, he wrote:

As the religion of St. Francis was that of the conquest and had remained the only one, New Mexicans were so accustomed to see their habit that they would hardly accept any other. Therefore the first religious and bishop would have to be Franciscans.[5]

Pino lived through the nascent period of the Penitentes although as a landed townsman he may not have been concerned with their activities. It is, however, plain to be seen that he, like other New Mexicans, favored the return of Franciscan religious administration.

---

[5] "Three New Mexico Chronicles," Tr. and Ed. by H. Bailey Carroll and J. Villasana Haggard. *Quivira Society,* Albuquerque, 1942, p. 236–37.

A description of the Santa Fe parish church in 1814 by Ignacio Sanchez Vergara includes this matter-of-fact statement:

> In the center of the front of the same church there is built a little chapel that serves the third order whose small fabric is, although adjacent to, independent of the said Church since, to enter it, a part of the principal cemetery is divided, as may be seen, from that which belongs exclusively to it.[6]

In the last will and testament of Rosa Bustamante, July 9, 1814, after provisions for her funeral she specified in Item 3a:

> I declare that it is my wish to give three minted pesos to each one of the benevolent orders[7] including that of Our Lady of Guadalupe and twelve to the one newly organized.[8]

Sanchez Vergara's description of the Santa Fe parish church was dated March 12, 1814, and Rosa Bustamante's will July 9 of the same year. In view of the lavish donations by Antonio José Ortíz and his widow, Rosa Bustamante, to religious buildings and their confraternities, and of the Ortíz family membership in the Third Order of St. Francis, it is likely that Rosa and her Ortíz children had paid for some part of the construction of this now forgotten "independent" chapel of Santa Fe, dividing the cemetery. Rosa's bequest of twelve minted pesos to the "newly organized" confraternity leads us to suspect that she referred to this chapel. No record of objection to it by any of the local New Mexico religious has been found in the archives of that period.

At least two burial entries mention interments in this chapel. The first, dated August 19, 1816, records the burial of Féliz Sanchez whose widow was Maria Gertrudis Martín, signed by Cura Juan Tomás Terrasas. The second reads:

> In this city of Santa Fe of New Mexico, on the sixth of September, 1816, I, Juan T. Terrasas, interim priest of this parish, gave ecclesiastical burial to José Rivera, adult son of Juan Rivera and Gertrudis Brito, in the Chapel of the Third Order.[9]

It is evident that the chapel was demolished soon afterwards, when Don Juan Bautista Ladron del Niño de Guevara made his visitation of New Mexico in the years 1817–20 as delegate of Bishop Castaníza of Durango. For slightly different reasons de Guevara was as critical of what he saw in New Mexico as his predecessor, Dominguez, had been, and he left almost as detailed accounts of what was, or was not, there at the time. After de Guevara's official inspection of the Parro-

---

[6] In Benjamin Read Papers, New Mexico State Records Center and Archives. See Appendix IV-A, Parroquia, 1814.

[7] In this case reference was made to the local confraternities and not to religious orders.

[8] Ortíz Family Papers, New Mexico State Records Center and Archives.

[9] AASF, Burials, 50, Box 27, Santa Fe Parroquia, 1800–1816.

quia, and among his other forcefully worded notations is the following drastic note:

The seven skulls that were exhumed in the next room [to the church] shall be immediately reburied; no one whomsoever shall any more, in the church or its auxiliary buildings, be permitted to do this in imitation of the Schools of Christ who, it is well known, make use of those of wood. It is ordered that all exhumations, partial or total, shall henceforth be made only with the express permission of the proper authorities instead of this intolerable abuse as it is now practiced (AASF, Accounts, Book LXII, A-II).

Burial in floors or crypts of Christian churches goes back as far as the first centuries when interment was no longer in catacombs. In colonial New Mexico it was usual, for those who could afford it, to pay the slightly higher fee for burial within the church rather than in the churchyard. A royal decree was sent from Spain to Mexico in 1798, reaching Santa Fe in 1799, forbidding burials in churches in the interest of public health. Another Cedula Real on the same subject was forwarded from Durango in 1819, but New Mexicans as usual clung to traditional behavior and interment inside the church. The republican government of Mexico issued more orders in 1822, 1826 and 1833 on outside burial and the removal of cemeteries from the churchyards to locations away from towns. Various documents record the objections of New Mexicans to these innovations, such as better protection inside churches from despoilment of graves by Indian raiders, as well as tradition and the difficulties of digging graves out of doors when the ground was frozen in winter. It is likely that prestige was also a factor, since the rich had until then the privilege of reposing in or close to the sanctuary.

Although ecclesiastical permission was refused after 1822, requests for burial within the churches of Alameda, Santa Cruz, Santa Fe, las Trampas and las Trampas de Taos, all Spanish congregations, continued to be made. From evidence of archeological excavations it has been demonstrated that from time to time burials in churches were done in secret. Folksay dates the last interment within San José de Gracia at las Trampas in the year 1905. When digging a new grave it was impossible not to disturb the bones of earlier burials; excavation of any 18th century mission in New Mexico turns up, like Hamlet's grave-digger, quantities of fragmentary remains. These are now supposed to be decently reburied. It is clear that de Guevara's inspection of the chapel of the Third Order was the occasion for his diatribe against "this intolerable abuse" of exposed human skulls. It is also to be inferred that de Guevara saw to it that the entire chapel in front of the parroquia was demolished; no more burials in it are recorded, nor has further mention of the building been found. As a rule, the later extension of the Third Order, the New Mexican brotherhoods of Penitentes, kept one or more yellowed human skulls in a wall niche in the morada, at least as late as the decade of the 1930s (personal observation).

With the innocence common to most of the 19th century diarists from the eastern United States, Lieutenant Simpson wrote with some amazement of the presence of human bones in the Jemez Pueblo church: "I noticed upon a projecting piece of the side pulpit a human skull and some bones ..."[10] If "side altar" is substituted for "side pulpit" it may be assumed that the skull and bones were adorning what was most probably the altar of the Third Order. No priest had been resident at Jemez since 1829; Indian attendance was poor and, as Simpson remarked, the church seemed to be "wasting away under the combined influence of neglect and moisture." With one or two visits a year from a religious, the church was left to the care of Spanish villagers from the area of San Ysidro, Vallecitos and Cañon de Jemez, and they, like other rural groups, were in process of crystallizing the rituals of the new brotherhoods, according to their own convictions.

Before sanitary regulations were invented the contemplation of a human skull by philosophers, religious, and even merely scholarly persons was an indication of profound thought. The skull was a graphic demonstration of mortal transience as opposed to pure truths, or supernatural forces, in order to point up heavenly eternity. Artists of the Renaissance and Baroque periods produced uncounted numbers of sculptures and paintings — many of which were later transferred to engravings — of saints, hermits, penitents and ascetics gazing upon a human skull held in the hand or placed upon a prie-Dieu. Among their subjects were St. Francis of Assisi, St. Louis King of France, St. Ferdinand King of Spain, St. Rita of Cascia, and St. Rosalie of Palermo, all particular patrons of the Franciscans and of their Third Order. From popular Mexican prints of these, New Mexican santeros made many santos with the same attribute of a human skull held in the hand or upon a small altar. The santeros were at work contemporaneously with the independent growth of the Third Order in northern New Mexico.

Although Dominguez had found the Third Order at Santa Cruz too poor to pay for candles in 1776, a new chapel connected with the south transept of the Santa Cruz church had been built and was described in an inventory of 1787. Dedicated to St. Francis at that time, it was used until recent years only as a catch-all storeroom and was left without modern lighting. It would appear that this chapel was used by members of the Third Order, and that by 1817 they had been conducting observances in it in ways not approved by the secular clergy. When de Guevara's visitation arrived at Santa Cruz he inspected the church and the inventory that was presented for his approval which stated:

---

[10] Journal of a Military Reconnaissance from Santa Fe, New Mexico, to the Navajo Country, made ... in 1849, by James H. Simpson, First Lieut. Corps of Topographical Engineers. Philadelphia, 1852, p. 20.

Figures 223, 224: *Descansos,* crosses marking where a funeral procession had rested a coffin on the way to the cemetery. These have been miscalled "Penitente crosses" in the past. (Photographs by William Maxwell Wyeth)

In the transept at the south side is a double door by which one enters into the Chapel of the Third Order and from there into the sacristy by a single door.

Vigorously underscoring his words, de Guevara wrote below the foregoing:

Neither the chapel nor anything in it do I recognize as belonging to the Third Order (AASF, Accounts, Book LXII, B).

The Third Order was still under the direction of the Church in 1817, at least in name, and still had the privilege of access to duly dedicated churches for its observances. Although de Guevara did not use the words penitente or morada in his accounts of his visitation of 1817–20, his lengthy stay in New Mexico and vigorous attempts at reform of existing practices were undoubtedly responsible for the beginnings of Penitente secession, or perhaps eviction, from their chapels and altars in authorized churches. Other clues to this gradual withdrawal are found, such as the request of sixty members of the Santa Cruz parish for permission to spend the whole period of Lent in Taos in 1831. Permission was granted by the vicar in Santa Fe, providing that no abuses should be tolerated (AASF, Patentes, Book 70, 1831). The wish to remove to Taos suggests that Lenten observances there at the time were differently conducted than those at Santa Cruz.

A controversial figure in this period was Cura Antonio José Martinez who was born at Abiquiu in 1793. He was of the historic Martín family, but during his youth his family had changed the name to the present one of Martinez. After having been ordained in Durango, Mexico, his first post was that of Franciscan missionary to Abiquiu in 1826. In the same year secularization of the Abiquiu mission was processed; Martinez entered his objections but remained there as secular priest until he was transferred to Taos as parish priest, a move undoubtedly negotiated by Martinez as his parents then lived there.

It is a moot point whether Father Martinez contributed to the strength of the Penitente organization up the Chama river, or whether in impressionable youth the environment of Abiquiu shaped his thinking on the duties and prerogatives of the Third Order. In any case, the Chama river region was solidly Penitente into recent years, as was the Taos Spanish area. After Father Martinez was stationed in Taos he became a forceful influence for education and progress, promoting education by establishing a school, and knowledge by acquiring and using a printing press. He served as a delegate on Mexican territorial legislative bodies in Santa Fe. At the same time he conducted a running war with ecclesiastical authorities in defense of the practices and privileges of the Third Order, culminating in 1856 when Bishop Lamy suspended his priestly license, and Martinez countered with a letter announcing his retirement.

Only in 1833 did the name Penitente first appear in writing, when Bishop Zubiría, on a visitation from Durango, attacked the group and said a better name for them would be that of *carnicería* (literally, meat market). His drastic orders for total suppression of the group had no practical effect, but may have been the final cause of the removal of the chapters from their allotted altars or chapels within churches and into private buildings of their own. The word Penitente evidently had been in common spoken usage before it was written down by a cleric.

In the minds of members of the cult, their adherence to traditional practices and to any additional routines devised by themselves, their forms of devotional penance were legitimate extensions of the old Franciscan Lenten observances. Graphic and verbal references to "Our Father St. Francis" were constantly preserved, although this fact has been overlooked in many surveys of Penitente ceremonies which have focused rather upon gory images of Our Father Jesus and the acts of members of the brotherhood.

Communal solidarity in resistance to official authority was an old colonial custom, summed up in the proverb, "We obey but nothing will be done." By such lip service and passive inaction Penitentes continued to attend Mass at church without visible proof of disobedience to church edicts. Enrollment of members was done by officials of the morada instead of, as before, by the priest, and thus membership in the Third Order became a secret. Certainly during this autonomous period of 1830 to 1950 or so, some brotherhoods went to excesses of self-mortification which seem incredible to us today. It is to be remembered that the Spanish ideal of a hero was very different from that of northern Europeans. Thousands of years of blending Near Eastern peoples with northern barbarians and of Moorish influences in the last centuries before New World colonization had produced standards of physical strength, indifference to suffering, resignation to the will of God and fanatical expressions of devotion, all to be combined in a single individual. Such a society accepted bodily laceration and voluntary risk of death during symbolic re-enactment of the Crucifixion as proof of spiritual virtue, even though the actor was a familiar neighbor or relative of the audience. Desire to personally experience the sufferings of the Passion led to closely realistic repetitions instead of, as had originally been intended, the enactment of a symbolic pageant in its commemoration. Even the Penitente hymns stress the physical sufferings of Christ more than the spiritual mysteries of His life.

By historical coincidence, the Penitentes banded together to practice their preferred devotional ceremonies just when they most needed a mutual protective organization on a year-round basis. The chapters of brotherhoods were better able to resist not only the effects of new religious laws but also the foreigners who now came with a new language and new business methods — the Santa Fe Trail traders, preceded by trappers from the east. By 1830 many of these had settled in New Mexico, and their commercial dealings materially changed the old economic system.

In 1845 Bishop Zubiría returned to New Mexico and found the Penitentes more numerous than ever. A second reading of his letter of 1833 from all pulpits, and a decree of suppression seem to have been as futile as before. When Bishop Lamy took stock of his new diocese of Santa Fe in 1851–52, he found the situation shocking. His reforms were first effective in towns: Albuquerque, Las Vegas and Santa Fe. There the people, proud to have their own bishop at last, accepted his suggestions and programs. Isolated villagers and ranchers, however, took refuge in their confraternities, which served as baffles against the foreigners, the new laws, the new language and, as it then seemed, new religious rulings and economic devices. The Penitentes formed a single society which by its unity and secrecy served the year through as a mutually beneficial union and clearing house for news, rumor and planned protective action. Although prejudice and ignorance did exist, these groups did a great deal of good in aiding the poor, sick and orphaned of local communities when no other agency existed for the purpose. As the new territorial government of Yanqui New Mexico came to be understood, membership in a Penitente chapter often served as a lever for political position or patronage.

A somewhat heated correspondence between Bishop Lamy and Father Martinez in Taos lasted for about five years and ended with the retirement of the latter. Not all their differences concerned the Penitentes, but these had a large share in the letters. After retirement Martinez wrote the bishop reminding him that he, Martinez, still held faculties to receive members into the Third Order, which had been given him by the last Franciscan custodian of the province with the approval of former Bishop Zubiría (Ref. AASF, L.D.D. 1856, No. 30). In the mind of Father Martinez, the Third Order and the Penitentes were one and the same, as they were in the minds of his Taos parishioners for whom he continued to say Mass in various private chapels in spite of his retirement. The clash between Bishop Lamy and Martinez was more fundamental than the liturgical points on which they differed. Martinez was spokesman for the Spanish New Mexican conservatives in defense of their entrenched social patterns, as against other patterns superimposed by newcomers.

Whatever excesses were developed by Penitentes in their rites after the Franciscans left New Mexico, they played a vital part in the delayed integration of rural Spanish New Mexicans. In view of the historical events unforeseen by official or ecclesiastical New Mexicans, this delay was a holding action against total loss of property, culture and identity to the more aggressive new culture, until the Spanish citizens could adjust to new concepts. The solidarity of the Penitentes, although based on religious beliefs, provided defense against exploitation which could hardly have been devised by any other means then known to rural New Mexico.

APPENDIX
Parroquia, 1814

"Demonstrative plan[1] of the Principal Church of the Capital of Santa Fe, its capacity, height, construction and the material of its buildings, the location in which it is and the property which surrounds it, commissioned to be done by Don Ignacio Sanchez Vergara by the Lord Governor of the Province in office, the twelfth of March of the year of 1814.

"Description of the Church

"This church is situated in the center of population of this Capital, whose lands are foothills of the mountain range known by the name of the said city. From east to west its length is 49 Castillian varas, its width is of eight and one-half varas and its height is ten varas, which measurements are divided by specific parts where it is possible.

"In the major length and width is formed the crossing of 14¾ varas in length, of eight and three quarters in width and of eleven in height, including the roof that serves as half vault to close the whole of the church, all put together of wood without any sort of finishing. Above the vestibule, on entering the principal door, there is a sort of corridor that serves as a choir, of the same width as the body, or nave, of the church with a crude enough railing of wood and without convenient access as it can only be reached by a movable ladder. This [choir] has one window that gives a view of the cemetery and gives light. The rest of the adornments of the church are five windows on the south side, all of similar construction.

"In the same crossing are built two chapels serving to adorn the said church on both sides; one with the advocation of Our Lady of the Rosary and the other with that of Lord St. Joseph whose extent and capacity are: the first, fourteen and a quarter varas long, six and a half in width and ten in height, adorned by four windows, two on each side, and a little choir. This, although it is wide enough, is somewhat cramped and its access is by a hand ladder. There is [a room] at the side of the same length although narrower in width that, although it retains the name of sacristy, is used to store pieces of temporary altars and other things of this nature. It is lighted by two windows that are the sole adornments to be seen. The second [chapel] is 15 varas long, 6 and ¾ in width and the same in height. Its adornments

---

[1] If there was a plan or map with this report it has not been found.

being windows like those of the first, with its own choir in the same circumstances but with more convenient access.

"The church is entered from the outside by the main door on the west and, on the inside, by one of the side chapels referred to in the crossing connecting it with the cloisters and dwellings reserved for the Religious that have served in the administration of this Capital.

"The cemetery is laid out around the main door without any order whatsoever in its proportions as on the south side it is 27 varas long and on the north 20½, its width being still another. This is entered by two gates, one in front and the other in one of the sides.

"The towers are formed in two masses of the material, without any rule, the total height of both being 16½ varas. These are squared and in the first part of one of them are placed two bells of regular size; one broken and useless and the other, in better condition, has a very confused tone. Access to these towers is by a movable wooden ladder on the outside of the Church.

"At the rear is a room that serves as sacristy, sufficient for the purpose, with another, smaller room on the inside, and very neglected, which only serves to store broken furniture. Light reaches both rooms by one window in each and a door to give thanks that connects with the sanctuary.[2]

"In the center of [the front of] the same Church there is built a little chapel that serves the Third Order, whose small fabric is, although adjacent to, independent of the said Church since, to enter it, a part of the principal cemetery is divided, as may be seen, from that which belongs exclusively to it.

"In the wall of the right side of the nave or body of the Principal Church there is a door that corresponds with a patio intended for a graveyard with its roof; it is 39½ varas long and 15 in width.

"Construction of the Convent

"Its material construction consists of twelve rooms, those that form the dwellings of the Religious, for which purpose they were built, and few of them are in a proper condition: It consists of two large rooms that could be more useful and four cells in similar condition. The rest of the rooms serve as offices or for domestic services. Its capacity and amplitude on the interior are three cloisters with six windows and, in their center, a small patio connects the said cloisters with a corral of little more extent with an opening to the outside. That exit leads to a tract of land that is, from north to south, 18½ Castilian varas and, from east to west is of 79 varas, the which is used for the cul-

---

[2] "puerta a dar gracias," a small door by which the fathers used to pass from their convent refectory to say grace after meals before the Blessed Sacrament on the high altar. Described by Dominguez, p. 18, and defined by the editors, *ibid.* fn. 44, p. 28.

tivation of corn and wheat. Along its side this has a little trickle of crystalline water and all of this is without any protection whatsoever.

"Attached to the same cloister, against the walls of the Church, is the porter's lodge that serves the said convent, reduced and small in comparison with the rest of the buildings and it is entirely consistent with the preceding account of the Church and convent in all respects.

"Note 1. The material of all of these buildings is of adobe and its construction [is] without the least rule of architecture, made by a few rude artisans. That they can not survive without constant repair because of the fragility of the material is plainly to be seen.

"Note 2. Its location is sufficiently damp, exposing it to damages in any protracted rains because it is surrounded by dry gulleys that run from the same nearby mountains, precipitously flooding all of the town. In addition there are some marshes next to all of this [church and convent] that on occasion act as aqueducts or drains for the great lake that is on the summit of the mountains.

"Note 3. To facilitate the residence of the Lord Bishops without the expense of having some houses of sufficient size in this Capital there are two, next to the principal Church that, combined, would be sufficient for the purpose. They may be used intermittently or permanently because they are not occupied by their legal owners.

"Note 4. In the same state of usefulness and with more ampleness is another that could serve as a collegiate seminary according to the proposal. There is no legal impediment because the owner offers it on the same terms as the previous ones.

"Note 5. The distance to the Parish Church from the houses that may be available as the residence of the Lord Bishop, according to note 3, is that of 25 varas, a little more or less. The same estimate of the distance of the house suitable for the seminary, according to note 4, is of 70 varas with the same regulation. The location of this house makes it less costly than the other to reduce the major danger, the expense in the current hard money."

APPENDIX
The Present Status of the Brotherhoods

In regard to the former role of the New Mexican Penitentes as a religious, charitable, and protective society, which came to include political activity, and its presently reformed position, the following extracts from an interview printed in the Santa Fe *New Mexican* on April 11, 1952, are of interest. The article is captioned "Holy Week Climaxed Penitente Lenten Rites," and was written by John B. Curtis, *Associated Press* staff writer, who quoted Miguel Archibeque, the head (or Hermano Supremo) of all chapters of La Fraternidad Piadosa de Jesus Nazareno existing within the state of New Mexico. Curtis began with the usual brief account of "strange rites . . . shrill piping of flutes . . ." and continued:

"The mysterious Catholic lay sect, believed to have originated in Europe in the 1300s, has been represented in New Mexico for more than a century.

"For most of that time the flagellations and other self-punishments practiced kept it in disrepute with the mother church.

"In 1947 Archbishop Edwin V. Byrne made the sect an official society of his church. But he extended his blessing only to those 'brethren who proceed with moderation and privately under our supervision' . . .

"Leader of the church-approved brotherhood is Miguel Archibeque of Santa Fe, governor of the Fraternidad de Jesus Nazareno. Now 67, he has 'been a Penitente longer than I can remember.' He told the Associated Press in an exclusive interview that he had never been able to verify oft-told reports that New Mexico Penitentes had been known to die upon the cross in the old days. And members under jurisdiction of the church-approved brotherhood, he said, have been ordered to refrain from flagellation or placing lifetime cruciform scars upon the backs of the initiates.

"'If there are any present-day extremes in self-punishment,' Archibeque said, 'they occur in those few moradas which have not come into the church-approved organization. Now,' he said, 'there are no fanatical procedures or excesses in our rites. Mass can even be said in our moradas.'

"He said he believed that stories of crucifixion deaths were 'not fact, but imaginative. It is true that in former years a Cristo was tied to a cross. But this was only for three minutes. That was long ago. I never saw it.'

.   .   .   .

". . . Archibeque said the Penitentes in New Mexico were founded by the Franciscan Fathers at Santa Cruz in 1835. The aim was to have members do penance throughout the year, not only during Lent. But excesses crept in, he said, when the priests were ordered out of New Mexico and the members were left without leadership. Then followed a period in which the Church frowned upon Penitente activities. This situation continued even after John B. Lamy, first bishop of Santa Fe, laid down certain rules to govern the sect in the 1850s.

"Archibeque, becoming active in Penitente leadership in 1934, said 'I wanted to limit the activities of the brotherhood to penance and prayer, and win the approval of the church. This we won in 1947.' He said he had no accurate estimate of the number of members. The church-recognized group, he said, has 45 moradas in Rio Arriba County, 32 in Taos, 30 in Mora, nine in Santa Fe, five in San Miguel, and others in Sandoval, Colfax, Harding, and Guadalupe Counties.

"The moradas not under jurisdiction of the supreme council, Archibeque said, include five in Rio Arriba County.

" 'I believe,' he said, 'that the Penitentes should limit their activities to penance and prayer. I thank the Lord I have been very successful in bringing that about. I fought to get the Penitentes completely out of politics and make them a purely religious organization. In that also I believe we have been successful.'

"He said members are told to exercise their rights as citizens by participating in politics as individuals; but they are not asked to take political action as a group under any political leader.

"Archibeque said his objections to most articles he has read are that 'for the most part these things happened 50 or 60 years ago and no longer exist. I say, give each period its proper place in time, and give each period its due. Most articles I have read lead to antagonism instead of to harmony.'"

Although the order had gotten under way some years earlier than 1835, the date given by Archibeque, his statements are otherwise valid and show his knowledge of the Franciscan source of the organization, as well as the later ramification of membership giving political power, a feature which, he made clear, was not consistent with the primary purposes of the order.

At Mr. Archibeque's death in 1970, the respect of all levels of New Mexico for his achievements was made evident by the statements given in the following account from the Santa Fe *New Mexican* of June 19, 1970.

Miguel Archibeque worked as a parking lot attendant in Santa Fe until old age retired him five years ago.

Today, the governor was going to his funeral mass, and the archbishop called Archibeque "a very reliable and positively motivated leader."

A writer-historian who knew him called him "one of the great spiritual leaders of our people."

Archibeque, born in 1883, was the leader — the hermano mayor — of New Mexico's "Penitentes" — La Cofradia de Nuestro Padre Jesus.

In the 1940's he was the leader in reorganizing the Penitente brotherhood and bringing it back within the good graces of the Roman Catholic church.

Ceremonies marking his passing were a combination of Roman Catholic liturgy and the mysteries of the two-centuries-old brotherhood.

The Penitentes conducted a public rosary for Archibeque Thursday evening, then took the body to a morada near the . . . village of San Miguel, where he was born; returning this morning for the funeral at Our Lady of Guadalupe Church in Santa Fe, and burial in Rosario Cemetery.

A standard with a painting of Christ bearing the cross and the words "Concilio Supremo (Supreme Council)" remained beside the coffin. The brotherhood sang the [hymns] that have been passed on [for generations].

The Penitente brotherhood in rural New Mexico is one of the world's last remnants of the religious tradition of penitente orders in late medieval Europe. Little is generally known about the New Mexico brotherhood or its rituals, although they were popularized by travelers [of the past] century who emphasized that the Penitentes at that time held "ceremonial Crucifixions."

[Archbishop] James Peter Davis remarked upon learning of Archibeque's death Tuesday in Santa Fe that he "was very instrumental in bringing some very good leadership into the Penitentes."

The archbishop noted that before Archibeque's leadership, "a number of excesses from time to time occurred with regard to their penitential disciplines."

[The Governor of New Mexico] said Archibeque "had a tremendous impact on New Mexico, particularly in the northern part of the state because of his activities among the Penitentes. Few people were aware of his influence." . . .

When Archibeque began his leadership in 1940, the Penitentes were divided, with organizations going their own ways in separate communities of northern New Mexico and southern Colorado.

Archibeque began traveling among the communities and by 1944 had succeeded in unifying all the factions under one supreme council. In 1947 the organization was approved by the late Archbishop Edwin V. Byrne.

The successor to Archibeque as the informal but clearly recognized leader is M. Santos Melendez of Albuquerque.

Through a mortuary spokesman Melendez said Friday the brotherhood would continue as the unified organization created by Archibeque. Melendez estimated there are about 1,700 active members of the brotherhood in dozens of moradas across New Mexico and southern Colorado.

An earlier news item appeared in the Santa Fe *New Mexican,* on September 16, 1948, reporting filing of a suit by an attorney in Rio Arriba County, New Mexico. The lawyer represented the "hermano mayor supremo" of the Pious Fraternity of Our Father Jesus of Nazareth Morada of Alcalde, which morada, it was claimed, had land belonging to it unlawfully appropriated by an individual named as defendant. The account ended thus:

"The plaintiff is a charitable association under the laws of the state, the complaint said."

Figure 226: A *pito* or flute.

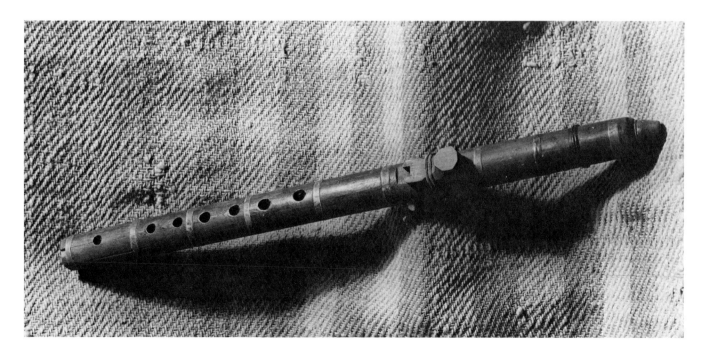

THE MORADA AND ITS CONTENTS

In this brief survey of tangibles it is not proposed to go into the psychiatric aspects of the Penitente cult which have been attributed to it by certain writers. Nor is it pertinent to cite a mass of irresponsible fiction, sometimes purporting to be news, which has been printed on the subject. For an honest description of Penitente ceremonies during Holy Week, Alice Corbin Henderson's *Brothers of Light* (Harcourt Brace, 1937) is recommended.

It is certain that the morada as an architectural feature of New Mexico came into existence after the first quarter of the 19th century, that it multiplied as pressure against the cult from Bishop Zubiría and his aides in Durango became stronger, and that it multiplied more rapidly after Bishop Lamy had established the diocese of Santa Fe in 1851. As long as the New Mexico members of the Third Order were tolerated in churches the morada was not required. An example of the removal from church to morada is pointed out by residents of the village of las Trampas in connection with the site of a now leveled torreon. Such towers had been built for community defense against Indian attack during colonial times. When the torreon stood idle and unwanted it was converted into the first morada to be built in las Trampas. The coincidence of timing between new military posts and Bishop Lamy's campaign against the Penitentes suggests that at isolated las Trampas there had been no need for a morada in earlier years when the torreon was still a necessary protection.[1]

Equally valid examples elsewhere indicate that the average New Mexico morada is scarcely one hundred years old. Many were built between the 1870s and the 1920s, according to their charters. As in domestic dwellings, locally found building materials were used; a

---

[1] The torreon-morada at las Trampas was torn down in recent years by the owners who used the adobes to add a new room to their house. It was north of the Rio de las Trampas and west of the plaza. The next morada at las Trampas had the distinction of being the only one known to be built directly against the exterior wall of a church. It adjoined the east end of the transept in which is the altar of St. Francis with the Franciscan shield on the retable. That morada faced to the south, like the church, and had a battened door of 1890 style with a cruciform panel in it as its chief distinction. Around the year 1960, the figure of La Muerte, or Death in her cart, which had been kept in the baptistry for generations, was moved into the morada where it has remained ever since. At the same time a bulto of Nuestro Padre Jesus Nazareno that had stood on the altar of St. Francis also went into the morada, and a crate containing four skulls. The latter had been unearthed during repairs to the church floor between the main altar and the sacristy about 1950, and had been exposed to the view of visitors in the nave of San José de Gracia, bedecked with nylon, for some ten years before they were taken from the church. Local folksay claimed that these skulls were those of priests martyred by Indians, although there is no record of any such incident having occurred at las Trampas. In the late 1960s the morada was physically separated from the church transept, and its long axis was changed to run from north to south. The remodeling produced an undistinguished building, and the crevice formed in the narrow, shaded space between morada and church has caused drainage problems during winter months that are eroding the church wall. The morada, however, remains within the cemetery wall.

morada was made of adobe, undressed stone, jacál, or logs, depending on its location. While some were placed in a village or at its edge, others were hidden in canyons. Older moradas were often partly below the surface level so that their flat roofs were only four or five feet above the ground.

Designed to accommodate members for forty days, there were rooms for prayer, singing, initiation, and rest. Larger chapter houses had a chapel, occasionally with angled walls where the altar stood. Windows, if there were any, were small and placed high in the walls with heavy wooden shutters or grilles. The maderos, or rough timber crosses twelve or more feet long, which were dragged in Holy Week processions, leaned against the outer walls during the rest of the year.

Inside there were packed earth floors, built-in benches of adobe, and one or two corner fireplaces for warmth and cooking. Walls were whitewashed or bordered with micaceous earth plaster in the log moradas of the north. In relatively recent years gory-hued Victorian wallpapers were sometimes brought from town stores.

Figure 227: Santiago Mata, a 20th century sculptor.

The images around which the Passion was enacted were kept in the chapel. The principal one was that of the Nazarene Christ which, if the chapter could afford it, was life-size. These had jointed arms to allow robing, and were clothed in long gowns, usually red, over ruffled and embroidered chemises. The head wore a flowing wig of human hair and a crown of plaited buckskin with real thorns. This figure represented the story of the Passion, and therefore the exercises of the Lenten season were addressed to it, as were the *alabados* or hymns, many of which stress the bodily pain of Christ and the sympathetic sufferings of the unworthy members of the brotherhood, whose minds and hearts dwell upon His tortures.

The corpus of the Crucifix was leather-jointed so that it might be removed from the Cross and laid in a sepulchre or bier on Good Friday. Realistic emphasis by folk sculptors on wounds upon the knees and back of these figures aroused condemnation by foreign ecclesiastical visitors. Many such figures had a hollowed ribcase whose openings, in chest and back, showed a pendant heart. Further realism was added by a wick, dripping with red oil, that hung from the open spear wound. A small Crucifix of this type was carried by the *resador* (the chapter member who read or recited prayers) as he walked backward in penitential processions so that the sight of the lacerated corpus might encourage flagellants.

Larger moradas had another life-sized image of the Christ in the Sepulchre in addition to one which could be taken from the Cross. These, called "El Santo Cristo Entierro," had formerly been in 18th century churches. A very long list of prototypes made in 17th century Spain might be cited to establish the fact that these images were traditional and not the invention of the poor frontiersmen. Some of these figures had been sent from Mexico, such as one which remained in the north chapel of the Cathedral of St. Francis in Santa Fe until recent years; others were made by Franciscans during their service in New

Mexico, such as the two made by Fray Andrés García for the church of Santa Cruz and the Taos Pueblo mission, where they may still be seen (Sec. I-D).

There were smaller figures of the Virgin of Sorrows and the Virgin of Solitude, often of hollow-frame construction under purple or black robes, and statues of Christ at the Pillar and of St. John Nepomuk. The cult of this saint reached New Mexico from Prague through Mexico, and his symbol of inviolable secrecy in regard to confession was in time adopted by the Penitentes as a symbol of secrecy per se.

A peculiarly specialized feature of the Penitente morada was the carved figure of the death angel, variously called "La Muerte" or "Doña Sebastiana." What is said to have been the earliest example of these now existing, if not the first in New Mexico, was made by Nazario Lopez, the father of the late José Dolores Lopez of Cordova, also a woodcarver, who died in 1938. This figure is now in the morada at las Trampas, New Mexico. According to the estimates of José Dolores Lopez' son George, the Muerte was made about the middle of the 19th century when Penitente secession was most active and ecclesiastical supervision in hill villages very scanty (See Appendix, Lopez Family, Sec. IV).

The reappearance of the death angel at this time is not as mysterious as it first appears, although no documentary references to such figures of death in 18th century New Mexico have yet been found. While the Third Order practiced penitential observances in churches, they had kept human skulls in plain view as excessive demonstration of devotion (Sec. IV p. 446). Upon removal or expulsion from churches, the human skull was sometimes retained as part of morada furnishings, but this was not universal, due either to difficulty in obtaining skulls or to a change of viewpoint as to the propriety of exposing human remains. Of the few older moradas I have seen, now torn down or renovated, those which owned a human skull did not have a figure of death. Thus it may be postulated that the death angel was a later substitute in Penitente imagery.

As with other New Mexican devotional expressions, the idea of the death angel was not invented by its local makers, but originated in Europe. While the Gothic age had devised crude images of animated skeletons during the great plagues and the subsequent popular frenzies known as the Dance of Death, this artistic form had no direct connection with New Mexico Muertes. Their source may be traced to the poem, *I Trionfi,* of the poet Petrarch (1304-74), in which his studies of what was then forgotten classical literature are interwoven with Christian symbolism and persons prominent in his lifetime. These included himself and the lady, Laura de Nova, to whom he dedicated many of his poems.[2]

---

[2] Each Triumph in the poems is an allegorical episode. That of Death over Chastity is said by scholars to refer to the death of his platonic love, Laura, during the plague of the Black Death. The following Triumph is that of Fame over Death, referring to Laura's fame surviving her death.

IV

As the Renaissance period matured, with its concentration upon a classical revival of the arts and scholarship, the themes of Petrarch's Triumphs and the many illustrations for them were dramatized at the courts of wealthy princes who staged real triumphal processions during the carnivals preceding Ash Wednesday, on feast days, and in private celebrations. While these were contemporary interpretations of ancient Roman triumphs, they contained many of Petrarch's basic allegorical subjects, and among them was that of the Death Angel.

The carved and painted images, borne on elaborately decorated processional cars, were accompanied by human actors in extravagant costumes. The connection between the Triumphs of the 15th century which spread over Europe and lasted into the reign of the Protestant Queen Elizabeth of England, and the 19th century Muerte of New Mexico was suggested by Wilder and Breitenbach in "Santos, Religious Folk Art of New Mexico," 1943 (Facing Pl. 30-32). The authors, however, failed to establish a sequence in time and space between the royal Triumphs of precolonial Europe and the humble New Mexican Muertes of the 19th century. They assumed that the death figure in its cart was brought to New Mexico by members of the Third Order of St. Francis, but there is as yet no written reference or fragment of material evidence to support this theory. It is true that the Triumphs survive today, embalmed in Holy Week processions in Spain and some of her former colonies, but in New Mexico religious processions were made on foot, and lack of wealth limited the elaboration of allegorical representations.

What was in fact the link between the Death Angel of Petrarch and of New Mexico was the common pack of Tarot cards. The antiquity of the game of Tarot is unknown. In packs now ascribed to the 15th century, trump cards bear the images of Fame, Death, and other subjects taken from *I Trionfi*.[3] During the Renaissance age, Tarot was played by the wealthy, and card packs were painted by artists; therefore they often varied in number, painted images and rules of the game. In time Tarot was adopted by the common people, and by the 18th century it became associated with fortune-telling. It is still claimed by occultists to be a key to divination and mystic wisdom.

The Tarot game was common in Spain and came to the New World with the Spanish, whose passion for gambling is well known. Modern, stereotyped, printed Tarot packs may still be bought in Mexico. It is reasonable to assume that they found their way to the northern frontier, and may even have been made there, as were Apache playing cards on rawhide after contact with the white man. The card numbered thirteen

---

[3] Earlier Tarot packs were larger than modern ones, having 60 to 70 odd cards. These had four suits with four court cards each, and 22 trump cards. Each card bore a figure from *I Trionfi,* or an adaptation of it. The word-root for trump and triumph are the same, from the Latin triumphus. The allusion to a winning card as a trump is easily seen. (Ref. "The Tarot Trumps and Petrarch's Trionfi," by Gertrude Moakley. *Bulletin of the New York Public Library,* Vol. V, 60, No. 2. Feb. 1956.)

among Tarot trumps is that of Death. Some old packs show either a skeleton or a mummified corpse holding a scythe or a bow. The two-handed scythe seems never to have reached New Mexico, which may be the reason that local Muerte figures held a bow, a weapon used into the 19th century for lack of firearms and gunpowder.

Like Petrarch's, the Penitente death angel was female and rode in a car or cart. Lopez made a car like the clumsy, wooden-axled carts used for hauling in New Mexico. The solid wooden wheels turned, although the axles did not, and were drawn by oxen. The car of Doña Sebastiana, or La Muerte, was loaded with rocks and dragged by a single, barefooted penitent. During Holy Week processions, she figured as a reminder of mortality. Later superstitions claimed that if her arrow slipped from the bow or even brushed a bystander, he who was struck would die within the year. Another legend was that he who was touched accidentally by her arrow was the next candidate for the symbolic crucifixion of Good Friday. During the rest of the year a man with guilt upon his conscience might ask for the privilege of dragging la Muerte in her loaded cart from the morada to the nearest Calvary on some rock-strewn hillside. The penitent, barefoot and stripped to the waist, scourged himself with his free hand while a member of the brotherhood walked by the cart to steady the Death figure, but did not help to pull it. So it was said to be by various members, in "the old days."

A survival of the original plan of the Third Order of St. Francis, to include women as well as men, are doll-sized figures of la Muerte to be carried by women and children who made a penitential pilgrimage, barefooted, to the local Calvary. As the Spanish people extended their settlements away from the Rio Grande valley, santeros working for new moradas modified the appearance of Doña Sebastiana. Surface detail was abandoned, and the head, hands and feet were often connected by rough sections of log, hidden by clothing. The symbol of an unearthly bearer of death was replaced by images suggesting partly decayed human corpses. The head shrank from a long mask to a bullet shape and lacked a lower jaw, exposing a red-smeared tongue and snags of upper teeth. Such recent Muertes from the north and east of New Mexico wield a wooden ax of modern shape. They wear black cotton hose, gowns, and bonnets, sometimes with a frill over the eyes. Even the name, Sebastiana, seems to have been another case of iconographic confusion in New Mexico, bestowed by association of the arrows of St. Sebastian's martyrdom with the arrow of the death angel.

The santero figures forming symbols of the Passion were made for the moradas, but by the time these had come into existence painted retablos were replaced by prints, litho or chromo, and mission cards, all framed in tin. Furnishings were few, a hanging shelf with wooden pegs for clothing, blankets or ropes, a few small benches, a tin trunk for storage of paraphernalia, wooden or tin candle sconces (or later, kerosene lamps), plain or straw-decorated small crosses, and bundles of *disciplinas*. These were loosely plaited yucca fibre whips which served as substitutes in New Mexico for the barbed link, iron whips of Spain and the iron-rich colonies. There was another form of small whip of finely knotted wool called *la cuerda,* the cord. Anciently used for personal discipline in Medieval Europe, the cuerda in New Mexico was reserved for lashes given by one member to another upon request, as an added form of devotion.

At the beginning of the days of self-flagellation a member assigned to the office of *sangrador,* or "blood-letter," scarified the candidates' backs to allow blood to flow freely from lashes and thus avoid gangrenous infections.

Sound accompaniment was provided by the *matraca* (from Arabic *mitraca,* a hammer) on Good Friday to suggest the hail during the hours of darkness of the Crucifixion, while a drum, chains, and modern washtubs supplied peals of thunder. The matraca was like the old English watchman's rattle with clapper and gear of wood. These were used for centuries in Spanish churches during the last three days of Holy Week as a substitute for bells, which were not rung on those days. Although no longer used in American churches, it is said that everyone carries a matraca on Good Friday in Haiti, where the mass noise is described as sounding like a field of crickets.

Also a survival of musical instruments brought from Spain is the Penitente *pito,* a wooden flute often bound with salvaged brass fittings from old flintlocks. The *pitero,* or flautist, fingers the stops, playing the theme of each verse of a hymn before the singers begin, rather than as an accompaniment to them. Much time was spent in teaching verses and in practice singing. If a few members could read from the book, most of them had to commit the whole repertoire to memory. Music was not written but was learned by ear (Appendix IV, Alabados).

Some of the traditional Penitente props underwent strange changes as new objects and materials came to New Mexico. For example, the flaked chert knives, like those of the Indians, that formerly served the sangrador were replaced by 1892, if not earlier, with flakes of broken bottles. Antlers, animal bones, and lengths of threaded plumbing pipes were fashioned into pitos with rather poor musical results. Even the matraca took a new form, and as hard usage wears these out quickly, new ones were frequently made. One from some fifty years ago stands thirty inches from the floor and was made to be stationary, the sound being produced by the operator who turned the wooden crank.[4]

After the Civil War, when the Indian question was fairly settled, land-poor Spaniards spread out over the eastern plains and the San Luis

---

[4] While this was not typical of New Mexico rattles, a similar one is shown in *Witmark's Amateur Minstrel Guide and Burnt Cork Encyclopedia* (Frank Dumont, New York, 1899) as "an offstage prop for the sound of someone falling." Many men went annually from northern New Mexico in those days to work in mines, smelters, and railroads as far away as Idaho and Chicago, where they saw all sorts of novelties. Some villager may well have seen such a matraca at a minstrel show, and on returning home copied it for his morada.

valley, building new towns and new moradas. However, as the incentive to work for wages instead of commodity barter became more general, men could no longer afford to spend forty days in the observance of Lent, so these moradas were smaller to accommodate the events of Holy Week.

At the end of World War II, many veterans who had enlisted as youths refused to join the Penitentes on their return home. However, during the war years, and at the end of a century of effort, the late Archbishop Byrne of Santa Fe arrived at an agreement with the Hermano Supremo of all New Mexico Penitentes which was mutually acceptable. Today the members may observe Lent with suitable devotions — fasting, keeping vigils in prayer and song, and making processions — but the old practices attributed to them are no longer performed. As a result of this entente cordial and the prestige connected with membership, there were, it was said in 1963, about one thousand members still active. Some moradas are newly built with windows that admit light, and have extensive attendance. The more sinister trappings of the past have disappeared, as have many of the old santos, now replaced by the usual plaster images of today. Folksay insists that a few renegade groups persist in their old ways, but these will end with the death of their present members.

As provincialism and language barriers fostered suspicion and secrecy, so have literacy and communications dispersed them. During the "underground" period many of the older works of regional folk art were saved from destruction when they were discarded from churches, beginning with the "unsuitable" holy images painted on animal hides that were so severely criticized by Mexican bishops. Respect for tradition and familiar objects led the Penitentes to give them refuge in their moradas until, in the recent past, they were recognized as a part of our regional historic and artistic heritage.

Figure 228: The expulsion from Eden.

Figure 229: The flight into Egypt. Both sculptures by José Dolores Lopez.

LOPEZ FAMILY

In Santa Cruz, New Mexico, José de la Cruz Lopez, legitimate son of Nazario Lopez and Maria Teresa Bustos, neighbors of San Antonio del Quemado, was baptized on May 4, 1856. On April 5, 1868, Cura Juan de Trujillo of Santa Cruz baptized José Dolores Lopez, who was born three days before and who was the legitimate son of the same couple, Nazario Lopez and Maria Teresa Bustos of Quemado (Baptisms, Santa Cruz, Books 1 and 2, 1851-69).

To trace the members of the Lopez family in the second half of the 19th century is a delicate problem, due to the almost universal habit of giving the name José to boys. Entries in Santa Cruz books include these names: José Miguel Lopez, José Teodoro Lopez, José Geronimo Lopez, José Desiderio Lopez, José Librado Lopez, José Manuel Lopez, José del Carmen Lopez and, to compound confusion, there were two other men named José Dolores Lopez who lived at las Truchas and la Puebla. One of these men acted as a godfather in 1867 and early 1868, before José Dolores Lopez the woodcarver was born to Nazario and Maria Teresa in the same year. The José Dolores Lopez of las Truchas had children by at least two wives in 1869, 1876, 1878 and 1879. The José Dolores Lopez of la Puebla also had two wives and they had children baptized in 1870, 1873 and 1876. In those years the José Dolores Lopez of Cordova was too young to be confused with the other men of the same name. The Lopez people had lived at las Truchas before moving down to Cordova.

José Dolores Lopez the woodcarver married Maria Candelaria Trujillo; their son Nicodemus was born in 1895, Rafael in 1897, George in 1900 and a daughter, Elidia, in later years. When Rafael Lopez was born his godparents were José del Carmen Lopez, a brother of José Dolores Lopez, and Maria Marcelina Aragon, José del Carmen's wife and granddaughter of Rafael Aragon (Sec. III-G and Santa Cruz Baptisms, book beginning March 1894).

According to information given by a grandson of José Dolores, and son of Elidia, José Dolores was a master carpenter who made doors, chests, roof beams and corbels, *repisas* and coffins among other utilitarian works during the earlier part of his life. The religious figures for which he became locally famous were not made until his son Nicodemus was called to the army in World War One. This event left José Dolores deeply disturbed; his daughter says that he walked each day to the Calvario that stood by the old highroad above Cordova to look at the hoof prints of the horse that had taken Nicodemus to the war. It was then that José Dolores began to carve santos and allegorical figures. His skill in woodworking was already well developed and his originality in graphic expression must have been inborn. His grandson Eluíd Martinez says that the fine chipcarving and lacy incised designs on José Dolores' pieces were the latter's adaptation of contemporary

Figure 230: San Pedro Apóstol.
Sculpture by José Dolores
Lopez.

filigree jewelry (Personal conversation with Eluíd Martinez, May 31, 1972).

This family information disproves the theory of religious image-makers passing on their skills in a family workshop. It has repeatedly been claimed that Nazario Lopez, father of José Dolores, made the first figure of la Muerte, or Doña Sebastiana, in northern New Mexico. If he did so he probably made other santos and Muertes but his son, evidently, did not follow his example until late in life when the possibility of personal tragedy led him to turn to imagemaking as propitiatory offerings. Nicodemus came safely home in due time but his father continued to make images of a nontraditional kind in that they were rarely painted. His subjects were more derived from Genesis than those of most earlier santeros: the Garden of Eden with the serpent tempting Eve and the expulsion therefrom. On the other hand Rafael Aragon made one atypical, horizontal panel in three sections showing Eve's creation from Adam's rib, the temptation and expulsion, in the traditional tempera colors over gesso, which José Dolores may well have seen in his youth. He was fond of carving the Flight Into Egypt, in which Mary and Joseph are shown, like Adam and Eve, attired in innocence alone. One of these groups has Joseph, a smooth shaven youth, with a chest of miniature carpenter's tools on his back as he leads the donkey. Other figures were of saints including the imposing San Pedro, a tour de force.

José Dolores was persuaded by sympathetic artists and writers of the later 1920s to make other kinds of carvings: fancy chests painted black and then incised, nichos, lazy Susans, hanging shelves, ornately decorated screen doors and his own versions of Swiss toys, the pecking rooster or hen, operated by strings. These, he said, represented the rooster of St. Peter but they had been based on foreign toys shown to him. Like other woodworkers he made grave markers including one for himself, a handsome, tall one with the filigree ornamentation. This he kept at home; his family says that everything was finished except the date of death which came in seven years. This cross stood by the door of the Cordova church for some ten years when it was broken by children and replaced with a cement marker.

In turn George Lopez, like many New Mexicans, went north to herd sheep and only began to carve santos when he returned home at his father's death, another example of nonapprenticeship within the family. At this point the pattern altered, possibly due to improved commercial outlets. George Lopez has worked along the lines of his father, somewhat less subtly, and has been prolific and achieved fame. His brother Nicodemus also did carvings for a few years, in the family style, until he joined a Protestant sect that holds it a sin to make idols.

Several of the younger generation carve today, some in the idiom of José Dolores and others make quantities of small boxes, spoons, trees, small animals and crosses. Inevitably others not of the extended family have picked up the basic concepts so that, today, this once distinctive type of twentieth century New Mexico carving is too often nondescript.

THE ALABADOS

In "The New Mexican Alabado" the author, Juan B. Rael,[1] gives extensive descriptions of the morada, the ceremonies of the members, and duties of their various officers. He also gives eighty-nine alabados or hymns which he collected on both sides of the New Mexico-Colorado border, quoting variations which occur from village to village in the same hymn, and comparable examples from other parts of Latin America. As Rael points out, many of the basic verses and musical themes came from Spain and were in time altered in different regions, either to suit local requirements or because they were largely preserved by memory in a nearly illiterate society. On the other hand, a broad difference in wording is apparent between hymns which were popular in Franciscan jurisdictions and those of areas where other orders were stationed, although the subject matter was inevitably the same. Musical themes as a rule are simplified versions of those from old missals, although the musical origins are not easily identified when, as is usually the case, the singers are untrained and unaccompanied by instruments.

While many alabados were sung during Lent and deal with the episodes of the Passion, they were not entirely limited to this theme. The devout were in the habit of observing every Friday of the year with a hymn on the Passion. As the principal, if not the only, lay organization in rural districts for generations, the Penitentes as a group attended the *velorio* or wake of the deceased where they sang hymns appropriate to the occasion, commending the soul of the departed to heaven. Other alabados were in honor of the Holy Cross, sung on May 3 as well as at vigils, or for the Holy Communion.

A first impression of the listener is the preoccupation with the physical sufferings of Christ and of the self-pity of the singers who beg forgiveness for their sins. Further reading, however, brings out practical precepts of charity to others — one of the responsibilities of the order — and a series of simple but effective verbal images which give dignity and color to the familiar themes. Alabados to the Virgin, the Infant Christ, and patron saints are sometimes Medieval in rhythm and wording. The repertoire ranges between lamentations, the sonority of revival hymns, madrigals, and lullabys. The range of musical forms is a reminder of the time when the Penitente Brothers performed a service to their communities as singers when the Church was too feebly present in New Mexico to do so.

A typical old handwritten songbook from the Chama river valley, an area not included by Rael, contains thirty alabados, fifteen of which are nearly the same as those found in Rael, with minor additions or missing stanzas, or in transposed order. At least four hymns and half of another have been lost from the Chama songbook. Written in three

---

[1]"The New Mexican Alabado," by Juan B. Rael, Stanford University Series, *Language and Literature*. Vol. IX, No. 3. 1951.

different hands and undoubtedly from memory, the spelling is often different for the same name or word, and usually phonetic. If the grammar seems rustic, the verses have a flavor distinctly reminiscent of the quality of Medieval Spanish. Sometimes an effect of arresting interest is made by a seemingly casual use of onomatopoeia.

A few of the Chama alabados which are not in Rael are given here. They are transcribed as they were written. It should be remembered that some of them change from stanza to stanza from narrative to dialogue, or from the first to the third person, without indication of the transition except in the sense of the words. A slight variation in the Chama version of "por el Rastro de la Sangre," which is otherwise the same as Rael's #3, "Santa Cruz version," is the substitution of the word *cantar,* to sing, for the words *rezar,* to pray, and *enseñar,* to teach.[2] This is a reflection of the strength of group singing when it was more active in daily life than private prayer or formal education.

The Chama songbook begins with the 17th stanza of the fourth alabado, the beginning being lost. It is given here, however, because of the precepts of active Christianity which it contains and which make it markedly different from other comparative examples.

Chama #4, stanza 17.   Cuando ya desfallesio
                 Sus alientos y sus fuersas
                 le dieron al serineo
                 el madero que moviera

        18.   Caminaba a paso tierno
             por que fuersa no tenia
             Sus ojos traiba en tinieblas
             en la clara lus del dia

        19.   Callendo diversas veses
             a las piedras que alli abia
             Sin poderse levantar
             el tormento le rendia

        20.   Con todos estos dolores
             Mi Jesus llego a espirar
             Clavado de pies y manos
             Colera de Varrabas

        21.   Las palabras que Jesus
             hablo al espirar amable
             Se dijo tengo en la cruz
             de que el pecador se salve

---

[2] Chama #11, stanza 10 — "El que esta pasión cantara"
   Rael #3,   — "El que esta pasión rezare"
   Chama #11, stanza 11 — "Si la sabe y no la canta"
   Rael #3,   — "Si la sabe y no la enseña"

22. Alli José y necudemos
    lo vagaron de la cruz
    y lo llevan a enterrar
    en una peña a Jesus

23. Este que resusito
    es mi Jesus ignosente
    aquello tribunal sea
    su cuerpo echo penitente

24. tiempla el cuerpo tiempla el alma
    al ber el cargo que as hase
    por esa sangre baliosa
     A tu corazon trespase

25. Y si no bes con pasencia
    A qui este grabe peñar
    Se a de llegar la ocasion
    En que te ande condenar

26. Si no saves la ocasion
    Me tengo de convenser
    De tus culpas el perdon
    A ora con biene saber

27. Ama a Dios con toda fe
    Guarda el presepto y su ley
    No te fies de personas
    Ni en la palavra del rrey

28. En el mundo caridad
    al pelegrino as de haser
    Socorro al nesesitado
    la rreconpensa as de ver

29. la esperanza en ti señor
    pensar que por mi murio
    y con una fe sin los a
    Conose a quien otro no

30. Al huerfano y a la viuda
    Al hambriento da le un pan
    Al sediento un baso de agua
    y al desnudo vestiras

31. Al cautivo rredimir
    Al infierno bisitar
    Al afligido consuelo
    Y a los muertos enterrar

32. Llora contrito tus culpas
Confiesa a tu rredentor
Como lloro Magdalena
Grasias allo en el señor

33. Mira es misericordioso
Y con poder absoluto
perdona de caridad
el gran pecado del mundo

34. Mira que es Dios de piedad
Y te promete el perdón
si amas a tu progimo hermano
A ti mismo en rrason

35. Llo soy la obra de tu mano
Hay mi Jesus nazareno
dame un corazon Cristiano
Con que siempre te abre bueno

36. El auto de mis potencias
Mis peñas inuminar
Por una piadosa senda
que siempre te ande agradar

37. En fin rresibe mes boses
Con lagrimas de mis ojos
Que puedan desagrabiar
Y que dar los enogos (enojos)
Amen.

Chama #19, stanza 1. Angustiado Aagonisante
Triste asta el ultimo estremo
Sercado de ancias mortales
Hora Jesus en el huerto

2. Le dice a su eterno Padre
Que la ora es llegada lla
E de vever este caliz
Que se haga su voluntad

3. Beve alli el amargo caliz
Que va preparando el cielo
ya apasado asta los seses
del suplicio mas orendo

4. Hay sovre su hermoso rostro
la vana un sudo sangriento
y este sangrino Señor
Corre hasta rregar el suelo

IV

475

5. De las miradas de un hombre
    inpio alevoso avariento
    Que con miradas de paz
    Consume su sacrificio

6. Encadenado despu(e)z
    Lla se miro el pricionero
    Ciendo de amor las cadenas
    Que trageron del cielo

7. Fatigado y Afligado
    afa lo precentaron prezo
    Ante el tribunal de anaz
    Que le exsamino severo

8. Gocence los Afligidos
    Pues que tienen el modelo
    De pacienca y de dolsura
    En este divino prezo

9. Hallase inprosivamente
    Herido su rrostro veo
    Con la mas cruel vofetada
    Que le da un hombre pequeña

10. Ynmediatamente fue
    Remetido el pricionero
    A Caifas que era aquel año
    El pontifice Severo

11. Jusgado de muerte fue
    Se alla alli el Salvador nuestro
    Y se le mando encerrar
    En el lugar mos orrendo.

Chama #20, stanza 1. Alma No Estes Tan Dormida
    Que en el Cielo tengo flores
    Ben con mi madre querida
    Refugio de pecadores

2. Ya hoygo La dulce voz
    Que al Santuario nos convida
    Ben con la madre de dios
    Alma no estes tan dormida

3. Ben Hijo de mis amores
    Ben oveja destrabiada
    Benio pronto ami morada
    Que en el cielo tengo flores

4. Este es el jardin de flores
   De la cruz y la alegrilla
   Esta es la virgin maria
   Refugio de pecadores

5. Escuchame Pecadora
   Si vienez arrepentida
   Olle que dice el Señor
   Alma no estes tan dormida

6. Bendita seas Maria
   Benditos sean tus favores
   Que dices con alegrilla
   En el cielo tengo flores

7. Alma de Dios Escojida
   Para su eterna manción
   Benid en este Ocacion
   Ben con mi madre querida

8. Soy echa de mil primores
   De la flor mas esquisita
   Porque eres virgen vendita
   Refugio de Pecadores

9. Pide ace Gran Señor
   El que te mude de vida
   Llora Llora pecador
   Alma no estes tan dormida

10. El que venga a Repentido
    De sus maldades y errores
    De dios sera vendecido
    Que en el cielo tengo flores

11. Avandona ya tus vicios
    No vez tu alma tan perdido
    A las casa de ejercicios
    Ben con mi madre querido

12. Que deveis tener hermanos
    Con nuestra madre de amores
    Entonces con dulce canto
    Refugio de pecadores

13. Virgen madre de mi vida
    Tu eres mi anparo y guilla
    Tu me dices madre mia
    Alma no estes tan dormida

IV

14. Acaso desprecias hoy
    Esos venditos favores
    y que mis culpas y errores
    Jamas los olvidaries

15. Beran la dulce mañana
    yo vengo amudar de vida
    yo vengo con alegrilla
    hoy con mi madre querida

16. Firme estandarte Sagrado
    Esta madre verdadera
    En los siglos y en la tierra
    Sea para ciempre alavada

17. Hermanos Ejercitantes
    hay esta el Santuario amado
    Pero es nececario que antes
    Abandonen el pecado

18. hoy a mi dulce Jesus
    hoy esta mi dios vendito
    Arrimate pecador
    Arrepentido y contrito

19. Repito ejercitante
    y de todo corazon
    Prometasen adelante
    hacer firme contrición

20. Si tienes Resulucion
    De tus culpas y pecados
    haya en la eterna manción
    De Dios seran perdonados

21. Quieres su Gloria Gosar
    . De nuestra Madre querida
    Ora es tiempo alma perdida
    Ben tus culpas allorar

22. hoy pecador desdichado
    Escuchame para verte
    Sella que venga la muerte
    Sella tu fin desgraciado

23. hoy con todo corazon
    Sigan a Jesus amado
    Nos peza el aver pecado
    Tu nos das la Salvación

Chama #21, stanza

1. Al Niño Recien Nasido
   Para luz de la Naciones
   Le anuncian Pececuciones
   y muerte cruda en pacion

2. A voz desdichada madre
   Tanto dolor y fatiga
   que cual espada enemiga
   Ostraspaza el corazon

3. Os dispierta en noche frilla
   En espera nuestra espozo
   Que por Sendero pragose
   Os aleja de velen

4. Pero siguen y estremecer
   Los clamores de soldados
   O de niños degollados
   y Jesus llora tambien

5. Tu Tesoro es aquel hijo
   ya perfecto en toda ciencia
   Gracias vondad y prudencia
   y hermosura angelical

6. Con que ancia le vuscavan
   Por las plallas y caminos
   el cumplilla los Festinos
   de su padre celestial

7. Boz la cruz y las espinas
   y el Rostro del que va prezo
   Rendido el enorme pezo
   Entre varvaro tropel

8. Es tu hijo y lo Golpellan
   y con insulto enefario
   le conducen al calvario
   Sigue madre en pos de el

9. Rudos golpes de martillo
   De sallones inumanos
   Enclavan de pies y manos
   A tu inosente Jesus

10. Su Desamparo y afrenta
    Sus lavios de ced ardidos
    Su muerte y su pecho cindidos
    Viendo estas junto a la cruz

IV

11. Besando el palido Rostro
    llamandole cielo millo
    Estrechando el cuerpo frio
    En tu regaso de amor

12. Cuvierta la Sacria tumba
    Se aullentan sus Guardias fellos
    y ollados vez los Requellos
    de la Sangre de tu Dios

13. Retiembla el monte y se hiende
    Espantado Rije el vruto
    Aun el cielo esta de luto
    Quien no a de llorar con voz.

Chama #27 — *Salve Santa Rita*[3]

1. Salve Santa Rita
    Salve vea aurora
    De los inposibles
    Eres vencedora

2. Todos los virtudes
    Tuvistes Señora
    Bien aventurado
    es el que te adora

3. O Rita querida
    Este un dios que te adora
    Eres un dios te crio
    Nuestra defensora

4. O Rita Preciosa
    O divina flora
    Dadme tus aucilios
    En la ultima ora

5. Asi el padre eterno
    le hizo gran Señora
    de los inposibles
    Fuistes vencedora

6. El Sol y la Luna
    El cielo te adora
    Pues y a dios te crio
    Para defensora

---

[3] Saint Rita of Cascia enjoyed great popularity in New Mexico. Of the old Franciscan list of the "Fourteen Holy Helpers," she and St. Achatius appear to have been the preferred patrons to whom New Mexicans addressed prayers to accomplish "the impossible."

7. De tu nasimiento
   Bendita sea la ora
   Entre los humildes
   Vos eres autora

8. Cumples la palavra
   Que te dio Señora
   El criador del cielo
   Vellisimo flora

9. El sol y la luna
   El cielo te adora
   Todo el universo
   Por tu ausencia

10. De todos los fieles
    Eres acredora (acreedora)
    Livranos del mal
    y de mala ora

11. Todos las criaturas
    del mundo Señora
    Dicen que vos eres
    La discuridora

12. Nos eres del arca
    de donde tesora
    Tu divino vervo
    Tu luz corrovora

13. Al mentor tu nombre
    Rita imperadora
    El infierno tiembla
    y lusifer llora

14. El fin solo el ver
    que eres vensedora
    el diablo se espanta
    y el infierno usora

15. Adios Santa Rita
    Adios vea Aurora
    Adios hasta el vernos
    yo y mi defensora

16. En fin Santa Rita
    En fin Gran Señora
    de los inposibles
    Eres vencedora

17. Adios Santa Rita
     Eres vencedora
     de los inposibles
     Vencelos desde ora

18. En fin Santa Rita
     Si alcansais victoria
     Alabar a dios
     Contigo en la Gloria
     Fin. Jesus. Amen.

The following version of an alabado celebrating the Nativity was apparently localized in reference to the shrine of the Santo Niño de Atocha, at el Potrero de Chimayo; it had five more stanzas, torn from the book; Stanza #7 in the Chama #29 hymn is not in Rael:

A tu santuario Vendito

Chama #29
Rael #45

1. A tu santuario vendito
    Gracias venimos darle
    Eternamente alavarte
    Niño de Atocha infinito

2. Entre escarchas y pajitas
    Nacio el masillas verdadero
    Todo el orve por entero
    cantemos en las mañanitas

3. Cuando nacio nuestro Bien
    O que prodigio se vio
    y por esto digo yo
    en el Portal de velen

4. Yo te saludo Niñito
    que canticos de alegrilla
    diciendole, "Ave Maria
    Niño lindo, Manuelito."

5. En el alto firmamente
    se ve un estrella brillar
    O que gracias, que portente
    de su reino celestial

6. y canten los pajaritos
    en sus colunas mas bonitas
    cantado con sus boquitas
    estas bellas mañanitas

7. los tres Relles al momento
    O que gusto que alegrilla
    al ver en su nacimiento
    el niñito de Maria

8. Todo lo que tengo ser
    las flores mas esquisitas
    alaben su gran poder
    estas bellas mañanitas

9. Adios Niñito de Atocha
    Adios, bello relicario
    que esta en ese retablo
    de tu divino santuario

10. la luna, el sol, las estrellas
    los flores mas esquisitas
    tambien las niñas doncellas
    te cantan las mañanitas

11. Los angeles en el cielo
    y las criaturas todites
    respetan son grande anhelo
    estas bellas mañanitas

12. El preso en el calabozo
    sospira con mucho anhelo
    Tu has de ser mi defensor
    Niño lindo milagroso

13. Adios Niñito de Atocha
    dueño de mi corazon
    Pidele a tu Eterno Padre
    que me eche su bendición.

BIBLIOGRAPHY

Abert, J. W.
  "Report of His Examination of New Mexico in the Years 1846–47" Senate Exec. Doc. No. 23, 30th Congress, 1st Session, V. IV, Washington, D.C., 1848 (Excellent descriptions of various domestic details of the time, as well as religious and architectural.)

Acuña, Luis Alberto
  "Diccionario Biografico de Artistas Que Trabajaron en el Nuevo Reino de Granada" Bogota, Colombia, 1964 (Illustrated)

Adair, John
  "The Navajo and Pueblo Silversmiths" Univ. of Oklahoma Press, Norman, 1958

Adams, Eleanor B. ed.
  "Bishop Tamaron's Visitation of New Mexico, 1760" in NMHR V. XXVII/2, 3 and 4, 1953 (General descriptions of the country and villages, mostly ecclesiastical, limited to New Mexico. Translation by Miss Adams from Tamaron y Romeral's "Demostración del Vastísimo Obispado de la Nueva Vizcaya, 1765," edited by Vito Alessio Robles, Mexico, 1937.)

Adrosko, Rita J.
  "Natural Dyes in the United States" Smithsonian Institution Press, Washington, D.C., 1968

Ahlborn, Richard E.
  "The Penitente Moradas of Abiquiu" Contributions from the Museum of History and Technology, Paper 63, Smithsonian Institution Press, Washington, D.C., 1968
  "The Ecclesiastical Silver of Colonial Mexico" and "Domestic Silver in Colonial Mexico" in 1968 Winterthur Conference Report, Henry Francis du Pont Winterthur Museum, Winterthur, Delaware, 1969
  "Spanish Colonial Woodcarving in New Mexico, 1598–1848" Unpublished thesis for M.A. degree, Univ. of Delaware, 1958 (Copy in Museum of New Mexico library)
  "The Spanish Churches of Central Luzón" in Philippine Studies, V. 8/4, Oct. 1960, Manila, P.I.
  "Spanish Churches of Central Luzón: the Provinces Near Manila" in Philippine Studies, V. 11/2, Apr. 1963

  "Two Colonial Variations in the Spanish Carved Chest" in El Palacio, V. 68/2, 1961 (Comparison of 18th century chests from Manila and New Mexico.)
  "Soldiers and Saints in Old Spain and New, and Latin American Art Today" Catalog of two exhibitions, Joslyn Art Museum, Omaha, Nebraska, 1962 (Well illustrated, includes note on a painting on hide of Santiago collected by Captain John W. Bourke in 1881, now among Joslyn Museum collections.)
  "American Beginnings, Prints in Sixteenth Century Mexico" in Winterthur Conference Report, 1970 Henry Francis duPont Winterthur Museum, Winterthur, Delaware.

Ainaud de la Sarte, Juan
  "Cerámica Popular y Vidrio" V. 10, Ars Hispaniae, Historia Universale del Arte Hispánico, Madrid, 1952

Aitken, Barbara
  "A Note on Pueblo Belt Weaving" (1913) in MAN, V. XLIX. 46–62, Apr. 1949 (Sta. Clara N.M., "no blankets had been woven at Santa Clara for many years past." Includes Sichomovi and Tewa Hano.)

Alegría, Ricardo E.
  "La Fiesta de Santiago Apóstol en Loiza Aldea," Madrid, Spain, 1954
  "The Fiesta of Santiago Apóstal (St. James the Apostle) in Loiza, Puerto Rico" Journal of American Folklore, V. 69/272, 1956

Allison, W. H. H.
  "Santa Fe As It Appeared During the Winter of the Years 1837 and 1838, as Narrated by the Late Colonel Francisco Perea" in Old Santa Fe, II, Oct. 1914

Almagro Basch, Martin, y Luis Maria Llubia Munné
  "C.E.R.A.M.I.C.A., V. 1, Aragon-Muel," Barcelona, 1952

Alvarado Lang, Carlos
  30 Estampas Populares (portfolio) Mexico, 1947

American Guide Series, Works Projects Administration
  "New Mexico: A Guide to the Colorful State" Hastings House, N.Y., 1940 (Now out of date but has good photographs of many buildings and scenes now gone or drastically altered.)

Anderson, Clinton P.
"The Adobe Palace" New Mexico Historical Review, V. 19/2 1944

Anderson, Lawrence
"The Art of the Silversmith in Mexico, 1519–1936" 2 vols., New York, 1941

Anonymous
"Altar Piece from Llano Quemado" in El Palacio, V. 28/5–9, 1930

Anonymous
"Art in Colonial Mexico" A catalog of an exhibition held at the John Herron Art Museum, the Columbus Gallery of Fine Arts, the Dayton Art Institute and Davenport Municipal Art Gallery, 1951–1952

Anonymous
"Catálogo de la Exposición de Artesanías Tradicionales Argentinas" and "Exposición de Artesanías Tradicionales Argentinas" (2nd V. illustrated) University of Buenos Aires, Buenos Aires, June 1967

Anonymous
"New Mexico Penitentes," in El Palacio, V. 8/31 Jan., 1920

Anonymous
"The Santa Fe Fiesta" in El Palacio, V. VII/3, Aug. 15, 1919 and El Palacio V. VII/5–6, Sept. 30, 1919 (Mentions absence of any "de Vargas" fiesta for many years.)

Anonymous
"Embudo, a Pilot Planning Project for the Embudo Watershed of New Mexico" Various authors, State Planning Office, Santa Fe, 1963

Applegate, Frank
"Spanish Colonial Arts" in Antiques Magazine, Feb. 1933 (On the revival of native crafts in Santa Fe, 1920s. Good survey in spite of historic misinformation.)

Archives of the Archdiocese of Santa Fe
L.D. 1712, 1
1758, 3
1798, 3
1802, 1, 2, 3
1821, 29
1827, 7, 10
1840, 7, (mss. dated 11 Apr., 1842.)
L.D.D. (post 1851)
1853, 17
1856, 6, 11,12, 26 through 34.

Accounts
Book XXIV,   Box 1, Santa Cruz, 1760
Book XXV,   Box 2, Santa Cruz, 1768–1831
Book XXXXVI, Box 1, Santa Cruz, 1782–95
Book LXII,   Box 5, "Acts of the de Guevara Visitation of New Mexico, 1817–20"
Book LXIV,   Box 5, "Acts of the Fernandez de San Vicente Visitation of New Mexico, 1826"
Book LXV,   Box 6, Fernandez Visitation, Cont.

Baptisms
Book 34, Box 48, Santa Cruz, 1730–67 (bapt. of Pedro Antonio Fresquís.)

Baptisms, Diocesan
Book beginning 25 Jan. 1856, Parish of St. Gertrudis of Lo de Mora (bapt. of Juan Benito Ortega.)
Book 3, Mora, 1867–69
Book 4, Mora, 1870–82 (references to Navajo slaves.)
Books 1 and 2, Parish of Santa Cruz de la Cañada, 1851–69 (bapt. of José Dolores Lopez.)

Burials
Book 52, Box 29, Santa Fe, 1816–34, (on royal decrees that burials must be in outside cemeteries and no longer in church floors, from 1798 to Republican period, 1821, and later, which New Mexicans continued to resist.)
Book 34, Box 25, Santa Cruz de la Cañada, 1795–1833 (burial of Pedro Antonio Fresquís.)

Patentes
Book LXX, Box 4, Official Acts of Vicar Juan Rafael Rascón, Santa Fe, 1828–33
Books XII, XI, LXXXXII, LXXIII, LXIX, XIX, LXXI Visitations of Bishop Zubiría of Durango, Mexico, 1833–1850, and official correspondence between 3 visitations.

Ariss, Robert M.
"A Mexican Standard Measuring Stick For the Vara" in Los Angeles County Museum Quarterly, V. 6/3, Fall, 1947

Attwater, Donald, ed.
"A Catholic Dictionary" 2d ed. rev., Macmillan, N.Y. 1956

Audsley, W. & G.
"Handbook of Christian Symbolism," London, 1865

Austin, Mary
"Spanish Colonial Furnishings in New Mexico" in Antiques Magazine, Feb. 1933 (Well illustrated, shows examples of good reproductions of 1930s but is historically misleading.)

Baer, Kurt
"Architecture of the California Missions," Univ. of Cal. Press, Berkeley, 1958
"California Indian Art" in The Americas, V. XVI/1, July 1959 (Deals with Indian art in missions.)

Baird, Joseph A.
"Style in 18th Century Mexico" *in* Journal of Inter-American Studies, V. 1/3, July 1953, Univ. of Florida, Gainesville.

Baird, Joseph Armstrong Jr., and Hugo Rudinger
"The Churches of Mexico, 1530–1810" Univ. of California Press, 1962

Bancroft, Hubert Howe
"History of the North Mexican States, V. 1, 1531–1800" V. XVI in the Works of H. H. Bancroft. A. L. Bancroft Publishing Co., San Francisco, Calif. 1884
"History of Arizona and New Mexico, 1530–1888" Vol. XVII of the Works of — San Francisco, 1889

Barber, Edwin Atlee
"Tin Enamelled Pottery" Doubleday Page Co., N.Y., 1907.
"Majolica of Mexico" Philadelphia Art Museum, 1908
"Catalogue of Mexican Majolica Belonging to Mrs. Robert W. DeForest" Hispanic Society of America, N.Y., 1911
"Hispano-Moresque Pottery in the Collection of the Hispanic Society of America" Hispanic Society of America, No. 91, N.Y., 1915
"Mexican Majolica in the Collection of the Hispanic Society of America" Hispanic Society of America, No. 92, New York, 1915

Barber, Ruth Kerns
"Indian Labor in the Spanish Colonies" Historical Society of New Mexico, Publications in History V. VI, 1932

Barker, Ruth Laughlin
"The Craft of Chimayó" *in* El Palacio, V. 28/26 (On the influence of 19th century sarapes from Chihuahua, San Luis Potosi and Oaxaca upon Rio Grande weaving, and notes European printed copies of the Mexican sarapes.)

Barreiro, Antonio
"Ojeada Sobre Nuevo-México, 1832" *in* Three New Mexico Chronicles, trans. & ed. by H. Bailey Carroll and J. Villasena Haggard, Quivira Society, Albuquerque, 1942

Bartlett, John Russell
"Personal Narrative of Explorations in Texas, New Mexico, California and Chihuahua Connected with the United States and Mexican Boundary Commission during the years 1850–53" 2 vols., Appleton, New York, 1856

Batllori, Munné, Andrés, y Luis Maria Llubia Munné
L.D. 1712,1
"Cerámica Catalana Decorada" Barcelona, 1949

Baudot, Dom, O. S. B.
Dictionnaire d'Hagiographie," Paris, 1925.

Bear, Donald
Introduction to "American Primitive Art" by Willard Hougland: a Catalog of the collection of santos owned by Jan Kleijkamp and Ellis Monroe, New York, 1946

(Bear's Introduction is an excellent esthetic evaluation of New Mexico santos.)

Beer, Alice Baldwin
"Trade Goods: a Study of Indian Chintz in the Collection of the Cooper-Hewitt Museum of Decorative Arts and Design" Smithsonian Institution, Washington D.C., 1970

Bello, José Luis, y Gustavo Ariza
"Pinturas Poblanas," Mexico, 1943

Benavides, Fray Alonso de
"Revised Memorial of 1634" edited by Frederick Webb Hodge, George P. Hammond and Agapito Rey. Univ. of New Mexico Press, 1945

Benrimo, Dorothy
"Camposantos" a Photographic Essay with a Commentary by Rebecca Salsbury James and Historical Notes by E. Boyd, Fort Worth, Texas, 1966

Berlin, Heinrich
"Historia de la Imaginería Colonial de Guatemala" Guatemala, 1952
"Artistas y Artesanos Coloniales de Guatemala" Cuadernos de Antropología, Univ. de San Carlos de Guatemala No. 5, Abr. – Sept., 1965 (Lists of painters, silversmiths, goldsmiths, masons, needleworkers, etc., collected from archives.)

Bernal, R. Custos Fray Cayetano José
"Report to Gov. Fernando Chacón, Oct. 1794" Doc. in Archivo General y Publico de la Nación, Mexico, Historia, V. 313, fo. 350, photo copy of this in Dorothy Woodward Collection, N.M. State Records Center. (On the Third Orders of Penitence at Santa Cruz and Santa Fe that have existed since the reconquest, 1693, and of Albuquerque whose beginning is unknown.)

Bloom, Lansing B.
"Early Weaving in New Mexico" *in* New Mexico Historical Review, V. 2/3, 1927 "A Trade Invoice of 1638" in NMHR V. 10/3, 1935

Bode, Wilhelm von
"Die Kunst der Fruhrenaissance in Italien" Propylaen Verlag, Berlin, 1923

Borhegyi, Stephan F.
"El Cristo de Esquipulas de Chimayó, Nuevo Mexico," *in* Antropología e Historia de Guatemala, V. 5/1, 1953
"The Miraculous Shrines of Our Lord of Esquipulas in Guatemala and Chimayó" *in* El Palacio, V. 60/3, 1953
"Culto a la Imagen del Señor de Esquipulas en Centro America y Nuevo Mexico" *in* Antropología e Historia de Guatemala, V. XI/I, Jan. 1959

Boyd, E.
"Antiques in New Mexico" *in* Antiques Magazine, V. 44, Aug. 1943
"Saints and Saintmakers" Santa Fe, 1946
"New Mexico Santos" *in* American Antiques Journal, IV, Apr. 1949

"A New Mexican Retablo and Its Mexican Prototype" *in* El Palacio, V. 56/12, 1949 (Note on Our Lady of Pueblito, patroness of Querétaro.)

"San Vicente Ferrer, a Rare Santero Subject" *in* El Palacio, V. 57/7, 1950

"Our Lady of Refuge, From Frascati to Northern New Mexico" *in* El Palacio V. 57/9, 1950

"The Literature of Santos" *in* The Southwest Review, Spring, 1950, Dallas, Texas. (Bibliography of early comments on New Mexico santos by English-speaking writers.)

"Penitentes in California" *in* El Palacio, V. 57/11, 1950 (Ref. from the Hugo Reid Letters of the 1840s on Penitentes at San Gabriel.)

"Retablos: The Alfred I. Barton Collection" Miami Beach, Florida, 1951

"New Mexican Bultos with Hollow Skirts: How They Were Made" *in* El Palacio, V. 58/5, 1951

"The Source of Certain Elements in Santero Paintings of the Crucifixion" *in* El Palacio, V. 58.8, 1951

"Mexican Milagros" *in* Los Angeles County Museum Quarterly, V. 10/2, Summer, 1953

"A Roman Missal From Santa Cruz Church" *in* El Palacio, V. 64/7–8, 1957 (On engravings in missals from the Plantin Press, Antwerp, as sources for santeros.)

"Arts of the Southwest" *in* The Concise Encyclopedia of American Antiques, V. 2, Hawthorn Books, 1958

"The Use of Tobacco in Spanish New Mexico" *in* El Palacio, V. 65/3 June 1958

"New Mexican Filigree Jewelry" *in* El Palacio, V. 65/4, Aug. 1958

"Fireplaces and Stoves in Colonial New Mexico" *in* El Palacio, V. 65/6, 1958

"Popular Arts of Colonial New Mexico" Museum of New Mexico, Santa Fe, 1959

"The Oldest Known Guadalupe Imprint" *in* El Palacio, V. 66/6, Dec. 1959 (On engraving by the Flemish Samuel Stradanus, done between 1613–1622.)

"A Bronze Medal of Sixteenth Century Style" *in* El Palacio, V. 68/2, 1961 (On a medal excavated at San Gabriel del Yunque, west of San Juan Pueblo, in 1960. The medal is of 16th century Spanish Renaissance style.)

"Ikat Dyeing in Southwestern Textiles" *in* El Palacio, V. 68/3, 1961

"Indigo" a catalog for an exhibition, Museum of International Folk Art, Santa Fe, 1962

"Rio Grande Blankets Containing Hand Spun Cotton Yarns" *in* El Palacio, V. 71/4, 1964

"The Conservation of New Mexico Santos and Other Painted and Gessoed Objects" *in* El Palacio, V. 74/4, 1967

"Two New Mexican Retablos from the M.S.U. Art Collection" *in* Kresge Art Center Bulletin, Vol. 1/8, Michigan State Univ., East Lansing, Mich., 1968

"The New Mexico Santero" *in* El Palacio, V. 76/1, 1969 (Stylistic and chronological identifications.)

"The First New Mexico Imprint" *in* The Princeton University Library Chronicle, V. XXXIII/I, 1971 (On a broadside listing citizens eligible as jurors in cases pertaining to freedom of the press in 1834, with some description of the territory at the time.)

"The Plaza of San Miguel del Vado" *in* El Palacio, V. 77/4, 1971

Boylan, Leona Mae Davis
"A Study of the Mary Lester Field Collection of Spanish Colonial Silver" unpub. mss. of thesis for M.A. degree, University of New Mexico, 1967

"The History of Spanish Colonial Silver in New Mexico" *in* Bulletin, Univ. of New Mexico Art Museum, No. 4, Spring, 1970

"Spanish Colonial Silver," Museum of New Mexico Press, Santa Fe, in press, 1974

Brenner, Anita
"Idols Behind Altars" Payson & Clark, 1929

Brewster, Mela Sedillo
"A Practical Study of the Use of the Natural Vegetable Dyes in New Mexico" Univ. of New Mexico Bulletin No. 306, May 1937

Bright, Robert
"The Life and Death of Little Jo" Doubleday Doran, 1944 (Fiction but a firsthand account of rural communities prior to 1942.)

Broun-Ronsdorf, M.
"Travel Clothes" *in* CIBA Review, 1962/3

Browne, J. Ross
"A Tour Through Arizona, 1864, or Adventures in the Apache Country" Arizona Silhouettes, Tucson, 1950

Buhler, A.
"The Ikat Technique,"
"Dyes and Dyeing Methods for Ikat Threads,"
"The Origin and Extent of Ikat Technique" CIBA Review, No. 44, August 1942

Bullock, Dillman S.
"Cruces y Figuras de Madera en Cementerios Mapuches" *in* Revista Universitaria, Univ. Catolica de Chile, Ano 49th, 1964 (Notes on cemetery figures of wood in recent years made by Mapuche, or Araucanians. Comparable to some grave markers in New Mexico Campo Santos.)

Bunting, Bainbridge
"Taos Adobes" Publication No. 2, Fort Burgwin Research Center & Museum of New Mexico Press, 1964

Byne, Arthur and Mildred Stapley
"Spanish Ironwork" Hispanic Society, N.Y., 1915

Byne, Mildred Stapley
"Popular Weaving and Embroidery in Spain" Helburn, N.Y., printed in Madrid, Spain, 1924

Cabrera, Luis G.
"Plantas Curativas de Mexico" Mexico, 1958

Cáceres Freyre, Julian
  "Navidad en la Rioja" *in* Cuadernos No. 3, Inst. Nacional de Investigaciones Folkloricas, Buenos Aires, 1963 (Songs with some musical notations, comparable to los Pastores of New Mexico.)
  "Biografia de Un Artesano Popular, el Santero Andrés J. Arancibia" Cuadernos del Instituto Nacional de Antropología No. 5, 1964–65 (Life of the last working *santero* of Argentina with reasons why he had no more patrons, pictures of his images, list of materials used, etc.)
  "La Celebración del Carnaval en la Provincia de la Rioja" *in* XXXVI Congreso Internacional de Americanistas, Vol. 2, Sevilla, 1966
  "El Encuentro o Tincunaco, Los Fiestas Religiosas Tradicionales de San Nicolas de Bari, y el Niño Alcalde en la Ciudad de la Rioja" Cuadernos del Instituto Nacional de Antropología No. 6, 1966–67 (Regional effigies of a light and dark St. Nicholas and of a regional image of the Christ Child.)
Calderon de la Barca, Fanny
  "Life in Mexico" Doubleday, N.Y. 1966 (Classic on mid-19th century in Mexico.)
Calkins, Hugh G., Editor
  "Proposals for the Santa Cruz Area" U.S. Dept. of Agriculture, Soil Conservation Service, Region 8, Albuquerque Reg. Bull. 28, July 1935 (Mimeographed)
  "Spanish American Villages" V. II, Parts I and II, Tewa Basin Studies, U.S. Dept. of Agriculture Soil Conservation Service, Region 8, Albuquerque, 1935 (Mimeographed) (Excellent picture of rural conditions at that time.)
  "Rural Rehabilitation in New Mexico" U. S. Dept. of Agriculture, Soil Conservation Service, Region 8, Regional Bull. 50 Albuquerque, 1935 (Mimeographed)
  "Village Dependence on Migratory Labor in the Upper Rio Grande Area" U.S. Dept. of Agriculture, Soil Conservation Services, Regional Bull. 47, Albuquerque, 1937 (Mimeographed)
  "Notes on Community Owned Land Grants in New Mexico" U.S. Dept. of Agriculture, Soil Conservation Service, Region 8, Regional Bull. No. 48, Albuquerque, 1937 (Mimeographed)
  "San Miguel County Villages — Villanueva" U.S. Dept. of Agriculture Soil Conservation Service, Region 8, Regional Bull. 51, Albuquerque 1938 (Mimeographed)
Callejo, Carlos
  "El Monasterio de Guadalupe" Madrid 1958 (On the Jeronymite monastery at Guadalupe de Estremadura.)
Calvo Berber, Laureano
  "Nociones de la Historia de Sonora" Porrua, Mexico, 1958
Campa, Arthur Leon
  "Spanish Folk Poetry in New Mexico" Univ. of New Mexico Press, Albuquerque, 1946
Carpenter, Edwin H. Jr.,
  "Copper Engraving in Mexico During the Late 18th Century" *in* Bull. New York Public Library, V. 57/6, June, 1953
Carrillo y Gariel, Abelardo
  "Imagineria Popular Novoespañola" Mexico, 1950 (Popular arts of the Colonial period, including references to those of New Mexico.)
  "Autografos de Pintores Coloniales" Mexico, 1951 (Facsimiles of signatures, dates and other data on painters who signed their works.)
  "Evolución del Mueble en Mexico" Mexico, D.F., 1957
  "El Traje en la Nueva España" Mexico, D.F., 1959
Carroll, Charles D.
  "Miguel Aragon, A Great Santero" *in* El Palacio, V. L/3, Mar. 1943
  "The Talpa Altar Screen" *in* El Palacio, V. 68/4, 1961
Castedo, Leopold
  "Art and Architecture of Latin America, Pre-Columbian to the Twentieth Century" Praeger, N.Y., 1969
Cervantes, Enrique A.
  "Loza Blanca y Azulejo de Puebla" (Two vols., text, photographs and drawings by the author) Mexico, 1939 (Excellent monograph)
Cervantes, Miguel de
  "Tres Novelas Ejemplares" in the original Spanish, Dell Pub. Co., 1964 (Refs. to Spanish Penitentes.)
Chapman, Katherine Muller
  "Adobe Notes or How to Keep the Weather Out With Just Plain Mud, Set Down in Prose and Linoleum by KATE & D.N.S. & Printed by SPUD" The Laughing Horse Press, Taos, N.M., and Willard Johnson, printer. Reprinted 1966
Charlot, Jean
  "Ex Votos" *in* Magazine of Art, V. 42/4, Apr. 1949
  "Mexican Art and the Academy of San Carlos, 1785–1915" Univ. of Texas Press, Austin, 1962.
Chase, Stuart
  "Mexico, a Study of Two Americas" Macmillan, N.Y., 1937
Chavez, Fray Angelico, O. F. M.
  "The Santa Fe Cathedral" Santa Fe, 1947 (Pamphlet with little-known details on earlier history of the Parroquia and Santa Fe plaza.)
  "El Vicario Don Santiago Roybal" *in* El Palacio, V. 55/8, 1948
  "Our Lady of the Conquest" Historical Society of New Mexico, Santa Fe, 1948. (On the statue of La Conquistadora, its documented history, and on the *Cofradía de la Conquistadora* in El Paso del Norte and Santa Fe.)
  "New Mexico Place Names From Spanish Proper Names" *in* El Palacio, V. 56/12, 1949

488

"How Old Is San Miguel?" *in* El Palacio, V. 60/4, 1953 (Overall survey of known history of the Santa Fe chapel but written prior to excavations by Stubbs and Ellis, 1955, which positively determined certain dates of construction.)

"The Penitentes of New Mexico: *in* New Mexico Historical Review, V. 29/2, Apr. 1954

"Origins of New Mexico Families" Santa Fe, 1954

"Addenda to New Mexico Families" *in* El Palacio, V. 62/11, Nov. 1955, V. 63/5–6, May–June, 1956, V. 63/7–8, July–Aug., 1956, V. 63/9–10, Sept.–Oct., 1956, 11–12, Nov.–Dec., 1956, V. 64/3–4, Mar.–Apr. 1957, 5–6, May–June, 1957

"New Names in New Mexico, 1820–50" *in* El Palacio, V. 64/9–10, Sept.–Oct., 1957 and 11–12, Nov.–Dec. 1957

"Archives of the Archdiocese of Santa Fe, 1678–1900" Academy of Franciscan History, Washington, D.C., 1957 (An index to the archives of the Archdiocese of Santa Fe.)

Chevallier, Dominique
"A Syrian Craft: the Ikat Weaves" *in* Middle East Forum, V. 39/8, 1963

Chinchilla Aguilar, Ernesto
"Ordenanzas de Escultura. Carpinteros, escultores, entalladores, ensambladores y violeros de la Ciudad de Mexico" *in* Antropología e Historia de Guatemala, V. V/1, Jan. 1953. (Guild regulations, 1568–1704 for woodworkers, with glossary of archaic terms.)

"Exposición del Nacimiento Guatemalteco" *in* Antropología e Historia de Guatemala, Vol. VII/2, June 1955

Christensen, Erwin O.
"Popular Art in the United States" King Penguin, 1948 (Illustrated with renderings from the Index of American Design.)

"The Index of American Design" Macmillan, N.Y. 1950 (Renderings from the Index of American Design.)

"Early American Woodcarving" World, Cleveland & New York, 1952 (Illustrations from Index of American Design.)

Christiansen, Paige W. and Frank E. Kottlowski, editors
"Mosaic of New Mexico's Scenery, Rocks and History" Various authors: State Bureau of Mines and Mineral Resources, Socorro, N.M., 1964

Clark, Merle, editor
"Historic Preservation, a Plan For New Mexico" New Mexico State Planning Office, Santa Fe, 1971 (Numerous authors, register of historic and cultural sites, proposed plans for preservation.)

Colton, Mary Russel Ferrell
"Hopi Dyes" Museum of Northern Arizona, Flagstaff, 1965

Cook, Walter William Spencer, and Jose Gudiol Ricart
"Pintura e Imaginería Románicas" Ars Hispaniae V.
6, Historia Universale del Arte Hispanico, Madrid, 1950

Cook, Walter W. S., and Juan Ainaud
"Spain – Romanesque Paintings" New York Graphic Society with UNESCO, 1957

Cordova, Lorenzo de (Lorin Brown)
"Echoes of the Flute" Ancient City Press, Santa Fe, 1972 (Excellent eyewitness account of Holy Week processions prior to 1941.)

Cortes, Antonio
"Hierros Forjados" Mexico, D.F., 1935

Cossio del Pomar, Felipe
"Arte del Peru Colonial" Fondo de Cultura Economica, Mexico, D.F., 1958

Crane, Leo
"Desert Drums" Little Brown, Boston, 1928 (Good account by an Indian agent of the early years of this century and the inextricably interlocking Indian and Spanish problems, mission architecture and customs now lost.)

Croissant, P. J., S. J.
"El Año Christiano o Ejercícios Devotos Para Todos los Dias de Año" 12 vols., Bouret, Paris and Mexico, 1878 (Detailed lives of the saints which have been discarded in later books of devotion as apocryphal, but which explain the iconography of many examples of popular religious art.)

—"Crosses in the Collections of the Museum" *in* The Museum, Vol. 12/2, Spring 1960, Bulletin of the Newark Museum, Newark, N. J. (Well illustrated.)

Cubilos Chaparro, Julio Cesar
"El Morro de Tulcan, Arqueología de Popayan, Cauca, Colombia" *in* Colombiana de Antropologia, V. VIII/, Bogota, 1959 (Ref. to Spanish olive jars.)

Cullimore, Clarence
"Santa Barbara Adobes" Santa Barbara Historical Society, Santa Barbara, Calif. 1948

Cumbreño, Caceres, Antonio C. Guadalupe
"Guia del Monasterio Estremadura." 1953

Cunninghame Graham, Robert B.
"The Horses of the Conquest" Heinemann, London, 1930 (Preferable to later edition printed in Texas.)

Darley, Alexander M.
"The Passionists of the Southwest" Pueblo, Colo. 1893 (The beginning of a long series of sensational and prejudiced stories on the Penitentes.)

Davis, Mary L. and Greta Pack
"Mexican Jewelry" Univ. of Texas Press, Austin, 1963

Davis, W. W. H.
"El Gringo, or New Mexico and Her People" 1856, reprinted Santa Fe, 1938

d'Harnoncourt, Rene
"Mexican Arts" Catalog of a traveling exhibition sponsored by the American Federation of Arts, 1930–31
"20 Centuries of Mexican Art" Museum of Modern

Art, N.Y., 1940

DeKorne, James B.
"Aspen Art in the New Mexico Highlands" Museum of New Mexico Press, Santa Fe, 1970 (Seventy carvings on aspen trees by sheepherders over a fifty-year period, shown in excellent photographs.)

de Lafuente Machain, R.
"La Asunción de Antaño" Buenos Aires, 1943 (Relative to colonial Paraguay.)

de la Maza, Francisco
"La Catedral de Chihuahua" in Anales de Instituto de Investigaciones Estéticas, No. 30, Mexico, 1961

DeLong, Scofield and Leffler B. Miller
"Architecture of the Sonora Missions, Sonora Expedition, Oct. 12–29, 1935" U.S. Dept. of the Interior, National Park Service, Berkeley, 1937

DeWar, John
"The China Poblana" in Los Angeles County Museum Quarterly, V. 2/2 Fall, 1963

Diaz del Castillo, Bernal
"Discovery and Conquest of Mexico" Grove Press, N.Y. 1958

Diccionario de la Lengua Española
Real Academia Española Madrid, 1925

Didron, Adolph Napoleon
"Christian Iconography" 2 Vols., Bell, London, 1886

Di Peso, Charles C. and Arthur Woodward
"The Sobaipuri Indians of Upper San Pedro River, Southeast Arizona" Amerind Foundation, Dragoon 1953
"The Upper Pima of San Cayetano del Tumacacori," Amerind Foundation, Dragoon, 1956

Dominguez, Francisco Atanasio
"The Missions of New Mexico, 1776" Tr. and ed. by Eleanor B. Adams and Fr. Angelico Chavez, O.F.M., Univ. of New Mexico Press, 1956

Duffield, Lathel F., and Edward B. Jelks
"The Pearson Site, a Historic Indian Site at Iron Bridge Reservoir, Rains County, Texas" Univ. of Texas, Austin, Archaeology Series No. 4, 1961

Dunton, Nellie
"The Spanish Colonial Ornament and the Motifs Depicted in the Textiles of the Period in the American Southwest" Part I, 40 plates, Part II, text. H. C. Perleberg, Philadelphia, 1935

Eckhart, George
"A Guide to the History of the Missions of Sonora 1614–1826 Tucson, 1960

Egenhoff, Elizabeth L.
"Fabricas. A Collection of Pictures and Statements on the Mineral Materials Used in Building in California Prior to 1850" Supplement to California Journal of Mines and Geology, April 1952

Eickemeyer, Carl and Lillian
"Among the Pueblo Indians" Merriam, New York 1895 (Notes santos in Pueblo homes and other details unfamiliar to Eastern tourists of the time.)

Ellis, Florence Hawley
"Santeros of Tomé" in The New Mexico Quarterly, V. XXIV/3, 1954 (A record of bultos in the church of Tomé with purely folklore or folksay notes on their history.)

Ellis, Havelock
"The Soul of Spain" Houghton Mifflin, 1931

Encyclopedia of World Art McGraw-Hill Co. 1959

Emery, Irene
"Wool Embroideries of New Mexico: Some Notes on the Stitch Employed" in El Palacio, V. 56/11, 1949
"Wool Embroideries of New Mexico: Notes on Some of the Spanish Terms" in El Palacio, V. 57/5, 1950
"Samplers Embroidered in String" in El Palacio, V. 60/2, 1953
"The Primary Structure of Fabrics: an Illustrated Classification" The Textile Museum, Washington, D.C., 1966 (Definitive identification of textile techniques.

Emory, Lt. Col. W. H.,and Lt. J. W. Abert
"Notes of a Military Reconnaissance from Fort Leavenworth, in Missouri, to San Diego, California . . ." Made in 1846–47, with the advanced guard of the Army of the West. Report of the Secretary of War, 30th Congress, Exec. Doc. 41, Washington, 1848

de Escudero, José Agustin
"Additions to the Exposición of Pedro B. Pino and the Ojeada of Antonio Barreiro, 1849" in Three New Mexico Chronicles," Quivira Society Albuquerque, 1942

Espinosa, Carmen
"Fashions in Filigree" in New Mexico Magazine, Vol. 17/9, Sept. 1939 (On 19th century New Mexico plateros.)

Espinosa, Gilberto
"New Mexican Santos" in New Mexico Quarterly V. VI/3, 1936

Espinosa, José E.
"Saints in the Valleys" Univ. of New Mexico Press, Albuquerque, 1960

Espinosa, J. Manuel
"Journal of the Vargas Expedition Into Colorado, 1694" in The Colorado Magazine, V. XVI/3, Denver, 1939

Espinosa, Reginaldo
"Cañute" in New Mexico Magazine, V. II, May, 1933 (The game and its pieces.)

Estrada, Genaro
"El Arte Mexicano en España" Mexico, 1937 (Objects sent to Spain after the conquest and still extant.)

Eustis, Edith Morton
"Eighteenth Century Catholic Stone Carvings in New Mexico" in Liturgical Arts, V. 1/3, Spring, 1932 (First good photographs to be published of the stone altar screen from the Castrense, Santa Fe, 1761.)

Fergusson, Harvey
"Blood of the Conquerors," Knopf, New York, 1926 (Fiction but based on personal observation.)
"Rio Grande" Knopf, New York, 1933
Fernandez, Justino
"El Grabado en lamina en la Academia de San Carlos de Mexico Durante el Siglo XIX" Universidad de la Habana, 1938
Fernandez Ledesma, Gabriel
"The Meaning of the Popular Retablos" *in* Mexican Art and Life, No. 6, Apr. 1939
"Los Retablos o el Arte Ingenuo de la Pintura Popular Religiosa" *in* Mexico en la Cultura, suplemento de Novedades, Mexico, D.F., 14 May 1972 (Good survey of the narrative-popular ex voto beginning with European prototypes and following the evolution to the present.)

Ferrandis, Pilar
"Nacimientos, Exposición Celebrada en el Museo Nacional de Artes Decorativas, 1951" Col. Artes Decorativas en España, V. IV, Madrid, 1951 (Covers history of nacimientos, styles, from St. Francis of Assisi to today.)
Ferrando Roig, Juan
"Iconografía de los Santos" Barcelona, 1950
Field, Matthew
"A Tourist in Santa Fe, 1840" *in* El Palacio, V. 66/1, 1959
Flandrau, Charles Macomb
"Viva Mexico" Appleton, N.Y. 1908 (A classic description of the pre-revolutionary rural life of Mexico.)
Flores Guerrero, P.
"Las Capillas Posas de Mexico" Mexico, D.F., 1951
Forrest, Earl Robert
"Missions and Pueblos of the Southwest" Arthur Clark, Cleveland, 1929 (Sometimes inaccurate but contains material on the Spanish around 1900 in text and photographs.)

The Franciscan Library, or what remains of it, which was kept in the Convento of the mission at Santo Domingo Pueblo during Spanish Franciscan period, is now in the Museum of New Mexico. Illustrations in several of the 33 volumes were obviously inspirations for New Mexican santeros, who did not make literal copies. The major illustrated missals were printed at the Plantin Press, Antwerp, for Spain and all Hispanic countries for nearly 400 years. The illustrations were frequently engraved by Flemish artists after paintings by great painters of Italy, Spain and Flanders.
1. Missale Romanum, Antwerp, 1711, with supplement of Hispanic Missal, 1711.
2. Missale Romanum, Antwerp, 1728, with Missal Propriae Sanctorum Trium Ordinum Fratrum Minorum S.P.N. Francisci, Antwerp 1731, and: Missae Romano, Mexici, 1772, with new feast days.
3. Missale Romanum, title p. lost but calendar of moveable feasts given for years 1677–1691. This volume contains notation of a Franciscan who retrieved it, damaged, from Indians after the rebellion of 1696. Bound with it is: Missae Propriae S. Philippi Neri, Mexici, 1691, and, all damaged, Missals for Hispanic Saints and the Three Orders of Franciscan Friars Minor.
7. Roman Breviary, Madrid, 1777, with Feast Days of Hispanic Saints, Madrid, 1776, title page copperplate of Santiago.
8. Roman Breviary, 1741, with Daily Hours for Hispanic Saints, Antwerp, 1741, and Offices of the Three Orders of St. Francis, Antwerp, 1737. Profusely illustrated, some engravings recognizable as direct prototypes of New Mexico santos.
29. "La Suma de Casos de Conciencia y Obras Morales," Valladolid, 1621, 3 vols. bound in one, in Spanish. Canon law then included cases on inheritance, simony, coinage, land sales, magisterial duties as well as those of morals and religion. V. II, p. 369, text on municipal support of wheat crops has written note on a mill run "by water of the rio de Sta. Fee, very convenient."
Fred Harvey Indian Company Ledgers containing records of Spanish or non-Indian textiles from 1902 to 1940. Gift of the company to E. Boyd.
Fred Harvey Indian Company Papers on New Mexico church bells which passed through their hands. In New Mexico State Records Center files.
Freyer, Mrs. Frank Barrows, Collection of Peruvian Art
"A Peruvian Art Collection (Freyer) in Washington," Bull. of Pan American Union, Aug. 1936
"The Frank Barrows Freyer Collection of Spanish-Peruvian Paintings," a catalog at the Joe and Emily Lowe Art Gallery, Coral Gables, Univ. of Miami, Florida, 1961.
"Treasures From Peru, Spanish Colonial Paintings From the School of Cuzco, the Frank Barrows Freyer Collection" a catalog by Mahonri Sharp Young, Columbus Gallery of Fine Arts, Columbus, Ohio, n.d.
Fountain, Teresita Garcia
Tape recordings of memoirs, transcribed by J. D. Robb, *in* New Mexico Folklore Record, V. 5/ 1950–51
Fox, Robert B.
"The Calatagan Excavations" *in* Philippine Studies, V. 7/3, Aug. 1959 (Ming porcelains traded to the Philippines in pre-Spanish era.)
Galter, J. S.
"El Arte Popular en España" Barcelona, 1948
Garcia Granados, Rafael, and Luis MacGregor
"Huejotzingo, la Ciudad y el Convento Franciscano" Mexico, 1934
Garcia Gutierrez, Jesús
"Ramillete de Flores Marianas, formado con el Calendario Mariano Universal y las Advocaciones de la

Virgen María en Méjico" Mexico, D.F., 1946

Garcilaso de la Vega, the Inca
"The Incas, The Royal Commentaries of the Inca, Garcilaso de la Vega, 1539–1616" Annotated by Alain Gheerbrant, Tr. by María Jolas, Orion Press, New York, 1961

Garrard, Lewis H.
"Wah-To-Yah and the Taos' Trail, 1847" Univ. of Oklahoma Press, Norman, 1955

Geo, Charles
"Art Baroque en Amerique Latine" Plon, Paris, 1954

Gerhard, Peter
"El Tinte de Caracol en Oaxaca" in Antropología e Historia de Guatemala Vol. XVI/I, 1964 (Native use of shellfish dye, Murex Purpura lapillus.)

Gettens, Rutherford J., and Evan H. Turner
"The Materials and Methods of Some Religious Paintings of Early Nineteenth-century New Mexico" in El Palacio, Vol. 58/1, Jan. 1951 (Identifies pigments on New Mexico retablos and painted walls of Laguna Pueblo mission.)

Gettens, Rutherford John
"A Visit to an Ancient Gypsum Quarry in Tuscany" in Studies in Conservation, V. 1, p. 190, 1954

Gibson, A. M.
"The Life and Death of Colonel Albert Jennings Fountain" Univ. of Oklahoma Press, Norman, 1965

Gilliam, Albert M.
"Travels in Mexico" Philadelphia, 1846 (Comments on popular arts, religious images and interiors of Mexican homes in usual superior style of Anglos at the time.)

Gissing, George
"By the Ionian Sea" London, 1921

Goggin, John M.
"Fort Pupo: a Spanish Frontier Outpost" in Florida Historical Quarterly, V. XXX/2, 1951
"The Spanish Olive Jar, an Introductory Study" in Yale Univ. Publications in Anthropology No. 62, 1960
"Spanish Majolica in the New World, Types of the Sixteenth to Eighteenth Centuries" Yale Univ., Dept. of Anthropology, New Haven, 1968

Gomez Moreno, María Elena
"Breve Historia de la Escultura Española" Madrid, 1951

Graham, María
"Journal of a Residence in Chile during the year 1822 and a Voyage from Chile to Brazil in 1823" Longmans, Hurst, Rees, Orme, Brown and Green and John Murray, London, 1824 (Her descriptions of domestic architecture, life, religious fiestas, etc., closely resemble those of New Mexico and Mexico at the same time.)

Gregg, Josiah
"Commerce of the Prairies" New York 1844

Gritzner, Charles Frederick
"Spanish Log Construction in New Mexico" unpub. doctoral dissertation, Louisiana State University, 1969
"Log Housing in New Mexico" in Journal of the Pioneer America Society V. III/2, July 1971

Halseth, Odd S.
"Saints of the New World" in International Studio, V. XCIV/388, Sept. 1929 (Survey of New Mexico santos with prediction that they will soon become rare.)

Halseth, Odd S. and E. Boyd
"The Laguna Santero" in El Palacio, V. 77/3, 1971 (Identification of a lost altar screen by the anonymous Laguna Santero, based on an unpublished photograph taken by Odd Halseth during his work of repairing the Zia Pueblo mission in 1923.)

Harper, Allan G., Andrew R. Cordova and Kalervo Oberg
"Man and Resources in the Middle Rio Grande Valley" U.N.M. Press, Albuquerque, 1943

Harrington, John Peabody
"The Ethnogeography of the Tewa Indians" 29th Report of the Bureau of American Ethnology Smithsonian Institute, 1907–08

Harrington, John Walker
"Spanish American Colonial Silver" in International Studio, V. 91/375, Aug. 1928

Harris, Louise A.
"The Art and Architecture of Trampas, New Mexico" Unpub. thesis for M.A. degree, Univ. of New Mexico, 1967

Harvey, Byron
"A Sidelight on Navajo Blankets" in The Masterkey, V. 39/1, 1965 (Notes on the volume of Indian blankets handled by the Fred Harvey Indian Company from 1902 to 1964. Of a total of 65,000 blankets, one percent was Spanish Colonial and non-Indian.)

Henderson, Alice Corbin
"Brothers of Light" Harcourt Brace, New York, 1937 (Good eyewitness account of Holy Week ceremonies in a New Mexico village.)

Herndon, William Lewis
"Exploration of the Valley of the Amazon Made Under the Direction of the Navy Dept." Part 1, Washington, D.C., 1853

Herndon, William Lewis and Gibbons, Lardner
"Exploration of the Valley of the Amazon" Washington, D.C. 1854

Hester, James J.
"Navajo Migrations and Acculturation" Museum of New Mexico Press, Santa Fe, 1962 (Includes non-Indian materials.)

Hibbard, Howard
"Bernini" Penguin-Pelican Books, 1965

Hodge, Frederick W.
"Coral Among Early Southwestern Indians" in The

Masterkey, V. 17/5, May 1943
Holweck, Rev. F. G.
"A Biographical Dictionary of the Saints" St. Louis and London, 1924
Howe, Jane
"Your Guide to the Spanish Mission Bells in New Mexico" Battenberg Press, Norman, Okla. 1956 (Old bells in ten pueblo missions with dated inscriptions:) Collection of photos with measurements of old bells of New Mexico, Arizona, California and northern Mexico, both in churches and private and public collections. Inscriptions recorded. Gift of Miss Howe, in files of the author.
Howlett, Rev. J. D.
"Life of the Right Reverend Joseph P. Machebeuf, D.D." Pueblo, Colorado 1908
Hume, Ivor Noel
"Here Lies Virginia" Knopf, New York, 1960
Huxley, Aldous
"Beyond the Mexique Bay" Harpers, 1934, Vintage Books, 1960
Ingersoll, Ernest
"The Crest of the Continent" R. R. Donnelly, Chicago, 1885 (A guide for the D. & R. G. Railroad, gives descriptions of northern New Mexico including the vanished contents of old church at Ojo Caliente.)
Iklé, Charles F.
"Ikat Technique and Dutch East Indian Ikats" in The Needle and Bobbin Club, V. 15, New York, 1931
Irwin, John
"Shawls, a Study in Indo-European Influences" Victoria and Albert Museum, London, 1955
Islas Garcia, Luis
"Las Pinturas al Fresco del Valle de Oaxaca" Mexico, D.F., 1946
Jaffe, Michael
"Rubens' Sketching in Paint" in Art News, V. 52/3, 1953 (References and illustrations of Rubens' sketches used in later prints which in turn were used by colonial imagemakers.)
James, Rebecca
"The Colcha Stitch: Embroideries by Rebecca James" Catalog of an exhibition, Museum of International Folk Art, Santa Fe, 1963, with a comment by Frieda Lawrence.
Jameson, Anna
"Legends of the Madonnas Represented in the Fine Arts" Longman, Brown, Green and Longmans, London, 1852
"Legends of the Monastic Orders as Represented in the Fine Arts" Houghton Mifflin and Co., Boston and New York, 1885
"Sacred and Legendary Art" 2 Vols., Houghton Mifflin & Co., Boston and New York, 1896
Jaramillo, Cleofas M.
"Shadows of the Past" Seton Press, Santa Fe, 1941

Ancient City Press, 1972 (Excellent descriptions of domestic and religious life in the last quarter of the 19th century.)
"Romance of a Little Village Girl" Naylor, San Antonio, Texas 1955
Jenkins, Myra Ellen
"The Baltasar Baca 'Grant': History of an Encroachment" in El Palacio V. 68/1, and V. 68/2, 1961
Jenyns, Soame
"Ming Pottery and Porcelain" Faber and Faber, London, 1953
Jimenez Benitez, José J.
"Atocha, Ensayos Historicos" Madrid, 1891
Jimenez Moreno, W., y A. Garcia Ruiz
"Historia de Mexico, una sintesis" Instituto Nacional de Antropología e Historia, Mexico, D.F. 1962
Johnson, Ada Marshall
"Hispanic Silverwork" Hispanic Society of America New York, 1944
Joseph Marie, Sister
"The Role of the Church and the Folk in the Development of the Early Drama in New Mexico" Doctoral Dissertation, University of Pennsylvania, 1948
Kelemen, Pál
"Baroque and Rococo in Latin America" Macmillan,. 1951, Dover, 1967, reprint, 2 vols.
"Art of the Americas Ancient and Hispanic" (with a comparative chapter on the Philippines) Crowell, 1969
"A Preliminary Study of Spanish Colonial Textiles" in Workshop Notes/ Paper 23, Mar., 1961, Textile Museum, Washington, D.C.
"El Greco Revisited, Candia, Venice, Toledo" Macmillan, New York, 1961 (A study of the Greek influences in the art of El Greco.)
"Lenten Curtains From Colonial Peru" Textile Museum Journal, Dec. 1970, Washington, D.C.
"Peruvian Colonial Painting" A Special Exhibition, Introduction and Catalog by Pál Kelemen. The Collection of the Stern Fund and Mr. and Mrs. Arthur Q. Davis and the Brooklyn Museum Meriden Gravure Co., 1971
Kendall, George Wilkins
"Narrative of the Texas Santa Fe Expedition, 1841" Harpers, N.Y., 1844 (Good descriptions of San Miguel del Vado as well as of Mexico, from a prisoner's viewpoint.)
Kent, Kate Peck
"The Cultivation and Weaving of Cotton in the Prehistoric Southwestern United States" Transactions of the American Philosophical Society, New Ser., V. 47/3, Philadelphia, 1957
"Archaeological Clues to Early Historic Navajo and Pueblo Weaving" in Plateau, Vol. 39/1, Summer 1966
Knaggs, Nelson S.
"Dyestuffs of the Ancients" in American Dyestuff Reporter, Aug. 27, 1956

Knee, Ernest
"Santa Fe" Hastings House, N.Y., 1942 (Good photographic record of architecture and landscapes before recent alterations.)

Kubler, George
"The Rebuilding of San Miguel Chapel at Santa Fe in 1710" Colorado Springs, 1939
"The Religious Architecture of New Mexico in the Colonial Period and Since the American Occupation" Colorado Springs, 1940, reprint, Rio Grande Press, 1962
"Mexican Architecture of the Sixteenth Century" 2 Vol., New Haven, 1948

Kubler, George and Martin Soria
"Art and Architecture in Spain, Portugal and Their American Dominions, 1500–1800" Penguin, 1959

LaFora, Nicolas De
"En Relación del Viaje que hizo a los Presidios Internos de la Frontera Septentrional, 1766" ed. by Vito Alessio Robles, Mexico, 1939 (Good descriptions of New Mexico at the time, specific and unprejudiced.)

Lee, Ruth
"Retablos, Paintings of Thanks" in Pemex Travel Club Bulletin, V. XIII, July 1953 (Mexico)

Lewittes, Esther
"A Mexican 18th Century Wool Rug" in Antiques, Vol. 67/4, Apr. 1955

Linati, Claudio
"Trajes Civiles, Militares y Religiosos de Mexico, 1828" Univ. of Mexico Press, Mexico, D.F., 1956

Livermore, Harold
"A History of Spain" Allen and Unwin, 1958

Llompart, C. R., Gabriel
"Desfile iconografico de penitentes españoles, (Siglos XVI al XX)" in Revista de Dialectología y Tradiciones Populares, V. XXV/1, 2 Madrid, 1969

Lockwood, Frank C.
"Story of the Spanish Missions of the Middle Southwest" Santa Ana, California, 1934

Locsin, Leandro and Cecilia
"Oriental Ceramics Discovered in the Philippines" Charles E. Tuttle, Rutland, Vt., Tokyo, 1967

Lowery, Woodbury
ed. by Philip Lee Phillips, Chief, Div. of Maps and Charts "The Lowery Collection, A Descriptive List of Maps of the Spanish Possessions Within the Present Limits of the United States, 1502–1820" Government Printing Office, Washington, 1912

Lozoya, Marques del and José Claret Rubira
"Muebles de Estilo Español" ed. Gili, Barcelona, 1962 (Includes Gothic into 19th century and peasant examples.)

Luhan, Mable Dodge
"The Santos of New Mexico" in Arts, V. VII/3, Mar. 1925
"Santos aus Neu Mexiko" in Das Kunstblatt, Berlin, Oct. 1927 (Illustrates different santos than those in Luhan's English paper in the Arts, 1925, but is the same text.)

MacMillan, James
"Fifteen New Mexico Santos" Santa Fe, 1941 (Portfolio of silkscreen prints with comments by MacMillan.)

Macomb, J. N. and John S. Newberry
"Report of the Exploring Expedition from Santa Fe, New Mexico, to the Junction of the Grand and Green Rivers of the Great Colorado of the West, in 1859, under the Command of Capt. J. N. Macomb . . . with Geological Report by J. S. Newberry." U.S. Army Engineering Dept., Washington, 1876 (Contains notes on minerals in the area and inspection of the Abiquiu copper mine, "El Cobre.")

Magoffin, Susan Shelby
"Down the Santa Fe Trail and Into Mexico, 1846–47" Yale Univ. Press, 1926 reprinted 1962 (Invaluable record of daily life and domestic details at the time.)

Mangravite-Peppino
"Saints and a Death Angel" in Magazine of Art, V/33/3, March, 1940 (Examples from the collection of the Taylor Museum photographed by Laura Gilpin.)

Marechal, Leopoldo
"Vida de Santa Rosa de Lima" Emecé, Buenos Aires, 1943

Marmaduke, M. M.
"Journal, 1844" Missouri Historical Review, Vol. VI

Marmon, Lee H., and George Clayton Pearl
"A Fortified Site Near Ojo del Padre: Big Bead Mesa Revisited" in El Palacio, V. 65/4 Aug. 1958 (On Spanish influences on architecture of a fortified, 18th century Navajo site.)

Marriott, Wharton B.
"Vestiarium Christianum. The Origin and Gradual Development of the Dress of the Holy Ministry in the Church" London, 1868

Martinez Family: mss., unpublished memoirs, courtesy of Mrs. Eusebio Vasquez, daughter of the author.

Martinez, Severino
"The Last Will and Testament of Severino Martinez" tr. and annotated by Ward Alan Minge in New Mexico Quarterly, V. 33/1, 1963 (Detailed account of execution of will by the eldest son, Padre Antonio J. Martinez.)

May, Florence Lewis
"Hispanic Lace and Lace Making" Hispanic Society of America, N.Y., 1939

McCall, George Archibald
"New Mexico in 1850: a Military View" ed. by Robert W. Frazer, Univ. of Oklahoma Press, Norman, 1968 (Gives good picture of the economy of the territory at the time but contains editorial inaccuracies.)

Meighan, Clement W.
"Excavations at Drake's Bay, Marin County" Univ. of California, Berkeley Archeological Survey, 1950

Mena, Ramón

"El Zarape" *in* Anales del Museo Nacional de Arqueología, Historia y Etnografía Epoca 5, Tomo 1, No. 4, Sept. 1925 Mexico (Early notes on Saltillo and other sarapes with some illustrations, and notes on beginnings of Aztecan gods and calendar stone in Mexican weaving, 19th century.)

Mendoza, Vicente T.

"Romance y Corrido" Universidad Nacional de Mexico, 1939

"La Décima en Mexico, Glosas y Valonas" Instituto Nacional de la Tradición Buenos Aires, 1947

"El Folklore y la Musicología" *in* Anales del Instituto de Investigaciones Estéticas No. 30, Mexico, 1961

Menendez Pidal, Ramón

"Onomástica Inspirada en el Culto Marianico" *in* Cuadernos del Idioma, V. 1/1, Buenos Aires, May 1965

Mera, Harry P.

"Style Trends of Pueblo Pottery in the Rio Grande and Little Colorado Cultural Areas From the Sixteenth to the Nineteenth Centuries" Memoirs, Laboratory of Anthropology, Santa Fe, 1939

"Population Changes in the Rio Grande Glaze Paint Area: Santa Fe, 1940 (Includes Rio Grande blankets and other Spanish New Mexican textiles.)

"Spanish Colonial Blanketry" unpub. mss. on Rio Grande blankets, courtesy of the School of American Research, Santa Fe.

Meyer, Theodosius, O.F.M.

"St. Francis and Franciscans in New Mexico" Historical Society of New Mexico, Santa Fe, 1926

Millan de Palavecino, Maria D., Cáceres Freyre, Julian, and six others

"Arte Popular y Artesania Tradicionales de la Argentina" Buenos Aires, 1964

Millan, de Palavecino, Maria D.

"Vestimenta Argentina" *in* Cuadernos del Instituto Nacional de Investigaciones Folkloricas, 2, Buenos Aires, 1961 (Hispanic influences on indigenous garments.)

Miller, John and Arthur Montgomery and Patrick Sutherland

"Geology of Part of the Southern Sangre de Cristo Mountains, New Mexico" State Bureau of Mines and Mining, Memoir II, Socorro, N.M. 1963

Mills, George

"The People of the Saints" Taylor Museum, Colorado Springs, 1967

Mills, George and Richard Grove

"Himmlische Zuflucht, Santos aus Neu-Mexiko" Munich, 1964 (This may be taken as a folktale or a spoof but for the plates of New Mexican Santos.)

Minsheu, John

"A Dictionarie in Spanish and English First Published into the English Tongue by Ric. Percivale, Gent., all done by John Minsheu" Bollifant, London, 1599 (Useful identification of words with Arabic roots.)

Miranda José

"San La Muerte" *in* Cuadernos del Inst. Nac. de Antropología, No. 4, Buenos Aires, 1963 (On the cult of la Muerte or image of death in western Argentina.

Montenegro, Roberto

"Pintura Mexicana, 1800–1860" Mexico, D.F. 1934

"Retablos de Mexico — Ex Votos" Ed. Mexicanas, Mexico, 1950

Montgomery, Ross, Watson Smith and John Otis Brew

"Franciscan Awatovi," Papers of the Peabody Museum, Harvard University, Vo. XXXVI, Report No. 3, Cambridge, Mass., 1949

Moorhead, Max L.

"New Mexico's Royal Road" Univ. of Oklahoma Press, Norman, 1958 (Trade and travel on the Chihuahua Trail.)

"The Apache Frontier; Jacobo Ugarte and Spanish-Indian Relations in Northern New Spain, 1769–1791" Univ. of Oklahoma Press, Norman, 1968

Mora, Jo

"Californios" Doubleday, N.Y., 1949 (Illustrated by the author. Deals with horse tack and vaqueros of the Spanish period.)

Nambe, Mission of San Francisco de Asís, Inventory, 1804–50 Mss. fo., in Archives Div., New Mexico State Records Center. (Supplies information not in archives of Archdiocese of Santa Fe for this period.)

Navarro y Noriega, Fernando

"Catálogo de los Curatos y Misiones que Tiene la Nueva España en cada una de sus diócesis o sea la Division Eclesiástica de este Reino, que has Sacado de las Constancias mas Auténticas y Modernas. 1813" Mexico, 1943 (Brief listing of census in northern provinces.)

Nebel, Carlos

"Viaje Pintoresco y Arqueológico Sobre la Parte mas interesante de la Republica Mexicana" Paris and Mexico, 1840; Porrua, 1963

Neumeyer, J. B.

"Indian Contribution to Latin American Colonial Decorative Art" *in* Art Bulletin, 1948

New Catholic Encyclopedia

McGraw-Hill Co. 1967

Newcomb, Rexford

"Spanish Colonial Architecture in the United States" Augustin, New York 1937

Newhall, Nancy

"Mission San Xavier del Bac" with photographs by Ansel Adams. Five Associates, San Francisco, Calif. 1954

Obregon-Gonzalo

"Influencia y Contrainfluencia del Arte Oriental en

Nueva España" *in* Historia Mexicana No. 54, V. XIV/2, 1964 (Surveys exchanges of art influences between New Spain and the Philippines.)

Och, Joseph, S. J. Sonora
"Missionary in Sonora — The Travel Reports of Joseph Och, S. J., 1755–1767" tr. & annot. by Theodore E. Treutlein, California Historical Society, San Francisco, 1965

O'Gorman, Edmundo
"An Early Mexican Xylograph Incunabula" *in* Mexican Art & Life, No. 7, July, 1939 (On the trial by the office of the Inquisition of Juan Ortiz, "ymaginario y impresor" in 1572–74. Ortiz had made the oldest existing woodcut in Mexico, dated 1571. O'Gorman's article included a colored facsimile of the print.)

Ortiz Garmendia, Juan
"Plantas Silvestres Chilenas de Frutos Comestibles Por el Hombre" Contribuciones Arqueológicas No. 8 Museo de la Serena, Chile, 1969

Parmenter, Ross
"Week in Yanhuitlan" with drawings by the author. University of New Mexico Press, 1964 (Survey of architecture of a 16th century church and of the life of the small village around it today.)

Pattie, James O.
"The Personal Narrative of James O. Pattie" ed. by Reuben Gold Thwaites, Vol. 18 of Early Western Travels, Arthur H. Clark, Cleveland, 1905 (To be taken with reservations as to veracity of the author.)

Pereyro, Fray Josef Benito
"Report on the Missions of the Custodia of the Conversion of St. Paul" with a Census of the population. 30 Dec. 1808. Listed in Twitchell, SANM, V. 1, Archive 1191, as "Religion, 1808. Census." Original now in the N.M. State Records Center, Santa Fe (1972). (Lengthy account of condition of missions and repairs recently made in 1808, also comments on status of weaving. Only Laguna, Acoma and Zuni pueblos were said to practice weaving at that time.)

Perez Salazar, Francisco
"El Grabado en la Ciudad de Puebla de los Angeles" Mexico, 1933

Perez de Villagra, Gaspar
"History of New Mexico" translated by Gilberto Espinosa, Quivira Society, Los Angeles, 1933 (Contemporary account of Oñate's years of settlement.)

Petersen, Harold L.
"Arms and Armor in Colonial America, 1526–1783" New York 1956
"Daggers and Fighting Knives of the Western World from the Stone Age till 1900" Bonanza Books, New York, 1970

Pfefferkorn, Ignatius
"A Description of the Province of Sonora" (1765) U.N.M. Press, 1949 Coronado Cuarto Centennial Pubs. 1540–1940

Phillips, John Goldsmith
"China Trade Porcelains" New York, 1956.

Picon-Salas, Mariano
"A Cultural History of Spanish America From Conquest to Independence" Univ. of California Press, 1963

Pierson, William H. Jr.,
"American Buildings and Their Architects — The Colonial and Neo-Classical Styles" Doubleday, 1970 (Good coverage of Spanish-Colonial buildings, Texas to California.)

Pike, Zebulon Montgomery
"The Expeditions of Zebulon Montgomery Pike, 1807" 2 Vols., ed. by Elliott Coues, New York, 1895

Pino, Pedro Bautista
"Exposición Sucinta y Sencilla de la Provincia de Nuevo Mexico" *in* Three New Mexico Chronicles," trans. & ed. by H. Bailey Carroll and J. Villasana Haggard, Quivira Society, Albuquerque, 1942

Pleasants, Frederick R.
"Museum Acquires Collection of Colonial Mexican Portraits" *in* Brooklyn Museum Bulletin, V. XIV/3, 1953

Plenderleith, Harold J.
"The Conservation of Antiquities and Works of Art" Oxford, London, 1956 (Reliable handbook on treatment, repair and restoration of many classes of materials.)

Plenderleith, H. J. and Stanley Cursiter
"The Problem of Lining Adhesives for Paintings: Wax Adhesives" *in* Technical Studies in the Field of the Fine Arts, V. 3/2, 1934

Plowden, W. W., Jr.
"Spanish and Mexican Majolica Found in New Mexico" *in* El Palacio, V. 65/6, 1958

Prince, L. Bradford
"Spanish Mission Churches of New Mexico" Cedar Rapids, Iowa, 1915

Puyol, Julio
"Platica de disciplinantes" *in* "Estudios eruditos in memoriam de Adolfo Bonilla y San Martín (1875–1926)" Madrid, 1927

Rael, Juan B.
"The New Mexican Alabado" Stanford Univ., 1951
"Origins and Diffusions of the Mexican Shepherds' Plays" Guadalajara, 1965
"Cuentos Españoles de Colorado y de Nuevo Méjico" 2 Vols., Stanford Univ. Palo Alto, n.d. (Rich collection of tales in phonetic spelling of regional Spanish, shows Hispano-Moresque roots of many. Brief English summaries in V. 2.)

Ralliére, Father J. B.
"Colección de Cánticos Espirituales" Las Vegas, N.M., 1892 Revised ed., El Paso, Texas, 1956

Ramsey, L. L. G., Editor
"The Complete Encyclopedia of Antiques" Hawthorn

Books, New York 1962

Read, Benjamin M.
"Illustrated History of New Mexico" Santa Fe, 1912 Benjamin Read Papers in N.M. State Records Center, Santa Fe. (Interviews with local residents who gave eyewitness accounts of church bells sand-cast in Santa Fe in the mid-19th century.)

Reed, Erik K.
"Aspects of Acculturation in the American Southwest" *in* the Acta Americana, V. II/1–2, 1944

Reed, John
"Insurgent Mexico" Appleton, N.Y. 1914

Reid, Hugo
"Penitentes in California" *in* The Los Angeles Star, March 20, 1852 reprinted with notes by E. Boyd *in* El Palacio, V. 7/11, Nov. 1950

Rhead, G. W., and Frederick A.
"Staffordshire Pots and Potters" London, 1906

Riaño, Juan F.
"The Industrial Arts in Spain" Chapman and Hall, London, 1890.

Ribera, Adolfo Luis, and Hector Schenone
"El Arte de la imaginería en el Rio de la Plata" Buenos Aires, 1948 (Mostly academic examples but gives some provincial ones and hollow framed statues.)

Ritch, W. G.
"New Mexico Blue Book, 1882" Santa Fe, N.M. 1882

Romero Flores, Jesus
"Iconografía Colonial" Mexico, D.F., 1940 (Useful series of colonial portraits shows costumes of the period.)

Romero de Terreros, Manuel
"Cosas Que Fueron" Mexico, 1937 (Sketches of colonial history.)
"Grabados y Grabadores en la Nueva España," Mexico 1948

Romero de Terreros, Manuel, editor
"Una Casa del Siglo XVII en Mexico, la del Conde de San Bartolomé de Xala" Univ. of Mexico Press, Mexico, D.F. 1957 (Extensive inventory of household goods in will of a well-to-do nobleman.)

Rosenthal, Ernest
"Pottery and Ceramics, from Common Brick to Fine China" Penguin Books, London, 1954

Rubio, Dario
"Refranes, Proverbios y Dichos y Dicharachos Mexicanos" 2 Vols., Mexico D.F. 1940

Rubio Sanchez, Manuel
"La Grana o Cochinilla" *in* Antropología e Historia de Guatemala, V. XIII/1, 1961 (Detailed history of the cochineal industry in Guatemala and of its decline after discovery of aniline dyes in 1856.)

Rudolph, Richard C.
"Chinese Armorial Porcelain in Mexico" *in* Archives of the Chinese Art Society of America, V. XV, 1961 (Discusses Chinese export porcelain, the lack of references on its influence in New Spain and Peru. Good, brief bibliography.)

Rusinow, Irving
"A Camera Report on El Cerrito" U.S. Dept. of Agriculture, Washington, D.C., 1942 (Documentary view of small village in San Miguel County as it was in 1942: architecture, life, religious images and people.

Ruxton, George F. A.
"Adventures in Mexico and the Rocky Mountains" Murray, London, 1847

Samayoa Chinchilla, Carlos
"Notas Sobre las Causas que mas Influyerón en las derrotas de los Ejércitos Indígenas Durante las guerras de la Conquesta" *in* Antropología e Historia de Guatemala, V. XII/1, Jan. 1960 (Covers ideological, tactical and material differences in offensive and defensive warfare between natives of the Americas and Europeans.)

Samayoa Guevara, Hector Humberto
"El Gremio de Plateros en la Ciudad de Guatemala y Sus Ordenanzas (1524–1821)" *in* Antropología e Historia de Guatemala, Col. IX/1, Jan. 1957 (Quotes original ordinances.)
"El Real Colegio de Nobles Americanas de Granada" *in* Antropología e Historia de Guatemala, Vol. XVII/2, 1965 (Prescribed dress of well-to-do young men of the late 18th century.)

Sanchez, George I.
"Forgotten People" Albuquerque, 1967

Santamaría, Francisco J., editor
"Diccionario General de Americanismos" 3 vols. Robredo, Méjico, 1942 (Invaluable for colonial vocabularies.)

Sanchez Perez, José Augusto
"El Culto Mariano en España" Madrid 1943. (This work supplies Marian iconography for colonial Hispanic countries.)

Saunders, Lyle, Compiler
"A Guide to Materials Bearing on Cultural Relations in New Mexico" Univ. of New Mexico Press, 1944 (Exhaustive bibliography up to 1944.)

Sawyer, Alan
"Catalogue List of Peruvian Spanish Colonial Textiles" — Exhibition, *in* Workshop Notes, Paper 23, Mar. 1961, Textile Museum, Washington, D.C.

Scholes, France V.
"Documents for the History of the New Mexico Missions in the Seventeenth Century" *in* N.M.H.R. Vol. IV/1929

Scholes, and Eleanor B. Adams
"Inventories of Church Furnishings in Some of the New Mexico Missions, 1672" Dargan Historical Essays, ed. William M. Dabney and Josiah C. Russell. Univ. of New Mexico Publications in History, No. 4, Albuquerque, 1952

Schoolcraft, Henry R.

"Information Respecting the History, Condition and Prospects of the Indian Tribes of the United States" Lippincott, Philadelphia, 1853–56

Schubring, Paul

"Die Kunst der Hochenrenaissance in Italien" Propylaen Verlag, Berlin, 1926

Schuetz, Mardith K.

"Historic Background of the Mission San Antonio de Valero" State Bldg. Comm. Archeological Program, Report No. 1, Austin, Texas, 1966 (Inventory of 1776: Silver in church.)

"The History and Archeology of Mission San Juan Capistrano, San Antonio, Texas" State Bldg. Commission Report No. 11, 1969.

Schurz, William Lytle

"The Manila Galleon" Dutton, N.Y. 1959 (Reprint paper)

Shalkop, Robert L.

"Wooden Saints; the Santos of New Mexico" The Taylor Museum, Colorado Springs, 1967

"Arroyo Hondo, the Folk Art of a New Mexican Village," catalog of an exhibition, the Taylor Museum, Colorado Springs, 1969

"Reflections of Spain II, a Comparative View of Spanish Colonial Painting" The Taylor Museum, Colorado Springs, 1970 (A catalog of an exhibition of paintings from Mexico, Andean countries and New Mexico.)

Sibley, George C.

"The Diary of, 1825–26" in "Southwest on the Turquoise Trail" ed. by Archer Butler Hurlbert; Stewart Commission of Colorado College and the Denver Public Library, 1933

Siguenza y Gongora

"Mercurio Volante" Quivira Society, Los Angeles, 1932

Simmons, Marc

"Governor Anza, the Lipan Apaches and Pecos Pueblo" in El Palacio, Vol. 77/1, 1970 (Translation of documents, 1786–88, on relations among Spanish, Navajos, Jicarillas and other Apaches and Comanches.)

Smiley, Terah L., Stanley A. Stubbs and
    Bryant Bannister

"A Foundation for the Dating of Some Late Archaeological Sites in the Rio Grande Area, New Mexico" Lab. of Tree-Ring Research Bull. No. 6, Univ. of Arizona, Tucson 1953

Smith, F. Hopkinson

"A White Umbrella in Mexico" Houghton Mifflin, 1917 (Reflects late 19th century life.)

Smith, Hale G.

"Archaeological Excavations at Santa Rosa, Pensacola" Notes in Anthropology V. 10, Florida State U. Tallahassee, 1965

Smith, Robert C., and Elizabeth Wilder

"A Guide to the Art of Latin America" Hispanic Foundation, Library of Congress, Washington, D.C., 1948

Smith, Watson

"Kiva Mural Decorations at Awatovi and Kawaika-a" Reports of the Awatovi Expedition No. 5, Papers of the Peabody Museum of American Archaeology, Harvard Univ., V. XXXVII, 1952

"Seventeenth Century Spanish Missions of the Western Pueblo Area" in The Smoke Signal, Tucson, Ariz. No. 21, 1970

Snow, David H.

"The Chronological Position of Mexican Majolica in the Southwest" in El Palacio, V. 72/1, 1965

Sola, Miguel

"Historia del Arte Hispano-Americano" Ed. Labor, Barcelona-Buenos Aires, 1935

Spiegelberg, A. F.

"Navajo Blankets" in Out West, V. XX/5, May, 1904

Spiess, Lincoln Bunce

"Benavides and Church Music in New Mexico in the Early 17th Century" in Journal of the American Musicological Society XVII, 1964

"Instruments in the Missions of New Mexico 1598–1680" in N.M.H.R. V. XL/1, 1965

"A Mercedarian Antiphonary" Museum of N. M. Press, Santa Fe 1965 (On an illuminated antiphonary from Guatemala with a hitherto unknown sequence: "Petrum Charitas," in Latin and English. Includes musical notations, original pages and notes on painted ornaments by E. Boyd.)

Spiess, Lincoln Bunce, and E. Thomas Stanford

"An Introduction to Certain Mexican Musical Archives" Detroit Studies in Music Bibliography No. 15 Information Coordinators Inc., Detroit, 1969 (Catalog of musical archives of Mexico, D.F., Tepotzotlan and Puebla listed by centuries and by composers; 16th through 19th centuries.)

Stallings, W. S. Jr.

"Dating Prehistoric Ruins by Tree Rings" Lab. of Anthropology, Santa Fe, N. M., 1939

Standish, Frank Hall

"Seville and Its Vicinity" London, 1840 (Detailed description of religious arts and incidental light on artistic tastes of the period.)

Stapley, Mildred

"Popular Weaving and Embroidery in Spain" Printed in Spain; William Helburn, New York, 1924

"Spanish Interiors and Furniture" with photographs and drawings by Arthur Byne, 2 vols. Helburn, N. Y., n.d.

Stark, Richard B.

"Music of the Spanish Folk Plays in New Mexico" Museum of New Mexico Press, Santa Fe, 1969

Steen, Charles R. and Rutherford J. Gettens

"Tumacacori Interior Decorations" in Arizoniana V. III/3, 1962

Steinmann, A.
"The Patterning of Ikats" *in* Ciba Review, No. 44, 1942

Stewart, Dorothy N.
"Hornacinas, Stories of Niches and Corners of Mexico City" Text and Illustrations by D.N.S. Ed. Cultura, Mexico, 1933

Stubbs, Stanley A. and Bruce T. Ellis
"Archaeological Investigations at the Chapel of San Miguel and the Site of La Castrense, Santa Fe, New Mexico" School of American Research Monograph No. 20, Santa Fe, 1955

Stubbs, Stanley A.
" 'New' Old Churches Found at Quarai and Tabira, (Pueblo Blanco)" *in* El Palacio, V. 66/5, Oct. 1959

Subias Galter, Juan
"El Arte Popular en España" Barcelona, 1948

Tamaron y Romeral, Obispo
"Demostración del Vastísimo Obispado de la Nueva Vizcaya, 1765. Durango Sinaloa, Sonora, Arizona, Nuevo Mexico, Chihuahua y Porciones de Texas Coahuila y Zacatecas" Con una introducción y bibliográfica y acotaciones por Vito Alessio Robles. Mexico, 1937

Taullard, A.
"Platería Sudamericana" Peuser, Buenos Aires, 1941

Terry, T. Philip
"Terry's Mexico, Handbook for Travellers" Mexico City and Houghton Miffin, Boston, 1909

Tewa Basin Studies U.S.D.A., S.C.S.
"Report on the Cuba Valley" S.C.S. Bull. 36, Conservation Economics Ser. 9, Mar. 1937 (Good survey of erosion and decline of Spanish settlements on the Rio Puerco, mimeographed.)

Thomas, Alfred B.
"Forgotten Frontiers" Univ. of Oklahoma Press, Norman, 1932 (Chiefly on administration of Governor de Anza.)

Thomas, Alfred B. Editor and translator
"After Coronado: Spanish Exploration of New Mexico, 1696–1726. Documents from Archives of Spain, Mexico and New Mexico" Univ. of Oklahoma Press, Norman, 1935

Thompson, George B.
"Spinning Wheels" Belfast Museum Bulletin, V. 1/5 1952 Belfast, North Ireland.

Toledo Palomo, Ricardo
"Aportaciones del Grabado Europeo al Arte de Guatemala" *in* Antropología e Historia de Guatemala, Vol. XIX/2, July-Dec. 1967 (Influence of imported prints on regional art, as prints also affected colonial arts of New Spain and New Mexico.)

Toro, Alfonso
"The Art of Engraving in Mexico" *in* Mexican Art & Life, No. 5, Jan. 1939 (Reproduces popular prints or *estampas* of previous centuries.)

Torre Revello, José
"El Gremio de Plateros en las Indias Occidentales" Univ. de Buenos Aires, 1932

Toulouse, Joseph H.
"Mission of San Gregorio de Abo" Santa Fe, 1949

Toussaint, Manuel
"Art Mudéjar en America" Mexico, D.F., 1946
"Arte Colonial en Mexico" Mexico, D.F., 1948
"La Pintura Mural en Nueva España" *in* Artes de Mexico No. 4, May 1954

Townshend, Richard Baxter
"The Tenderfoot in New Mexico" Dodd Mead, N. Y., 1924

Trens, Manuel
"Maria, Iconografía de la Virgen en el Arte Español" Barcelona, 1946 (Useful background for colonial Hispanic iconography.)

Trujillo, Josué
"La Penitencia a Través de la Civilización" Española, N. M., 1947 (Lists aims of brotherhoods and duties of officers.)

Tully, Marjorie F. and Juan B. Rael
"An Annotated Bibliography of Spanish Folklore in New Mexico and Southern Colorado" Univ. of New Mexico Press, 1950

Turmo, Isabel
"Bordados y Bordadores Sevillanos Siglos XVI a XVIII" Sevilla, 1955 (Good archival background for types of needlework and styles, mainly of church vestments, during this period in colonial areas as well as in Spain.)

Twitchell, Ralph Emerson
"Leading Facts of New Mexico History" Cedar Rapids, Iowa, 5 vols., 1912–17
"Old Santa Fe: The Story of New Mexico's Ancient Capital" Santa Fe, 1925

Uslar Pietri, Arturo and Carlos M. Moller
"La Imagen en su Nicho" *in* El Farol, No. 173, Nov. Dec. 1957, Creole Petroleum Corp., Caracas, Venezuela (Venezuelan santos illustrated in full color.)

Utley, Robert M. and Frank B. Sarles, William C. Everhart
"The National Survey of Historic Sites and Buildings" Theme IV, Spanish Exploration and Settlement" U.S. Dept. of the Interior, National Park Service, 1959 (Mimeographed.)

Valle-Arizpe, Artemio de
"Notas de Platería" Mexico, D.F., 1941
"Ladrones Sacrílegos y Plateros Inquisitoriados" *in* Arte y Plata, Mexico, Oct. 1945

Valle, Rafael Heliodoro
"Santiago en America" Mexico, D.F., 1946 (Covers images, fiestas and "authorized apparitions.")

Vazquez de Acuña G., Isidoro
"Costumbres Religiosas de Chile y Su Raigambre Hispaña" Univ. de Chile, Santiago de Chile, 1956

Vedder, Alan C.
"Establishing a Retablo-Bulto Connection" *in* El Palacio, V. 68/2, 1961 (On identification of style; panels and three-dimensional figures were found to have been made by the same anonymous New Mexican santero.)

Velásquez Chavez, Agustín
"Tres Siglos de pintura colonial Méxicana" Mexico, 1939

Verger, Pierre
"Fiestas y Danzas en el Cuzco y en los Andes" Buenos Aires, 1945
"Indians of Peru" New York, 1950 With text by Luis Valcárcel

Verissimo, Erico
"Mexico" Dolphin Book, Doubleday, 1962 (As Mexico is seen by a Brazilian writer.)

Villa, Agustín
"Breves Apuntes Sobre La Antigua Escuela de Pintura en México" Mexico, 1919 (First publication of the first known Mexican wood cut of 1571 by Juan Ortiz.)

Wagner, Henry R.
"The Spanish Southwest 1542–1794" 2 vol., Quivira Society, Albuquerque, 1938

Wagner, Kip
"Drowned Galleons Off Florida Yield Spanish Gold" *in* National Geographic V. 127/1, 1965 (Illustrates "K-ang-hsi" porcelains found in southwest U.S.)

Wallrich, William J.
"The Santero Tradition in the San Luis Valley" *in* Western Folklore, V. X/2, April 1951

Walton, James
"Carved Wooden Doors of the Bavenda" *in* Man, V. LIV/46–47, 1954 (On puncheon doors in the Transvaal, adapted from eastern Mediterranean.)

Weigle, Mary Marta
"The Penitentes of the Southwest, an Essay" Santa Fe, 1970
"Los Hermanos Penitentes: Historical and Ritual Aspects of Folk Religion in Northern New Mexico and Southern Colorado" Unpub. doctoral dissertation, Univ. of Pennsylvania, 1971 (754 pp. typescript, annotated bibl. of 988 titles.)

Weisbach, Werner
"Die Kunst des Barock in Italien, Frankreich, Deutschland und Spanien" Propylaen Verlag, Berlin, 1924

Wenham, Edward
"Spanish American Silver in New Mexico" *in* International Studio, V. 99/410, July 1931 (On the Mary Lester Field Collection, Albuquerque, N. M.)

Wescher, H.
"Rouen, French Textile Center" *in* Ciba Review, V. 12/135, 1959

Wethey, Harold E.
"Mexican Fortress Churches in the 16th Century" Art Bulletin, Dec. 1942

Whipple, A. W. and J. C. Ives
"Report of Exploration and Survey for a Railway Route From the Mississippi Valley to the Pacific Ocean" The War Dept., Washington, D.C. 1853–54

White, Leslie A.
"The Pueblo of Santa Ana, New Mexico" *in* American Anthropologist, XLIV/4, Part 2, Dec. 1942
"Punche: Tobacco in New Mexico History" N.M.H.R., V. 18/3, Oct. 1943

Wilder, Mitchell A. and Edgar Breitenbach
"Santos, the Religious Folk Art of New Mexico" Taylor Museum, Colorado Springs, 1943

Winship, George Parker
"The Coronado Expedition, 1540–42" *in* 14th An. Report, Bur. Am. Ethn. for 1892–93, Govt. Printing Office, Washington, 1896

Wislizenius, Adolph
"Memoir of a Tour to Northern Mexico Connected with Colonel Doniphan's Expedition, in 1846 and 1847" Washington, D.C., 1848

Woodward, Arthur
"A Brief History of Navajo Silversmithing" Bulletin, Museum of Northern Arizona No. 14, Flagstaff, 1938
"The Mission Trail" Los Angeles County Museum, 1940. Catalog of Spanish Mission Exhibition, Introduction by Arthur Woodward.
"Swords of California and Mexico in the Eighteenth and Nineteenth Centuries" *in* Antiques Magazine, V. 1, Aug. 1946
"California Costume of the Eighteen Thirties and Forties" *in* Los Angeles County Museum Quarterly, Vol. 6/3 and 6/4, 1947–48
"Church Saluting Mortars" *in* Los Angeles County Museum Quarterly, V. 8/2, Summer 1950
"California Leather Jackets," Los Angeles County Museum Leaflet Ser., No. 8
"The Evolution of the Cowboy's Chaps" *in* Los Angeles County Museum Quarterly, V. 8/3, 1951
"Saddles in the New World" *in* Los Angeles County Museum Quarterly, Vol. 10/2, Summer 1953
"Indian Trade Goods" Oregon Archaeological Society Publication No. 2, Portland, 1965

von Wuthenau, Alexander
"The Spanish Military Chapels in Santa Fe and the Reredos of Our Lady of Light" *in* New Mexico Historical Review, V. 10/3, 1935

Yrissari, Mariano
Mss. ledger "Factura Abarrotes de la Casa de Glasgow Brothers, folio 8." St. Louis, 1854 (Reference to 48 lbs. Indigo crystals shipped to Albuquerque at $1.10 per lb.)

Zobel de Ayala, Fernando
"Philippine Colonial Sculpture" *in* Philippine Studies, V. 6/3, 1958
"Philippine Religious Imagery" Ateneo de Manila, Manila, P.I., 1963

INDEX

506